C · O · N · C ·

ENCY CLO PEDIA

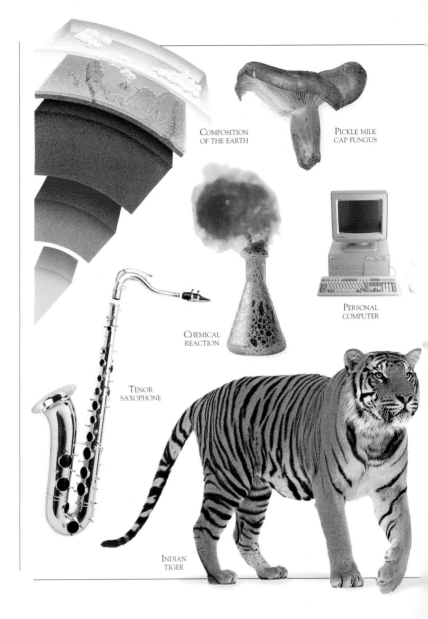

COMPOSITION
OF THE EARTH

PICKLE MILK
CAP FUNGUS

CHEMICAL
REACTION

PERSONAL
COMPUTER

TENOR
SAXOPHONE

INDIAN
TIGER

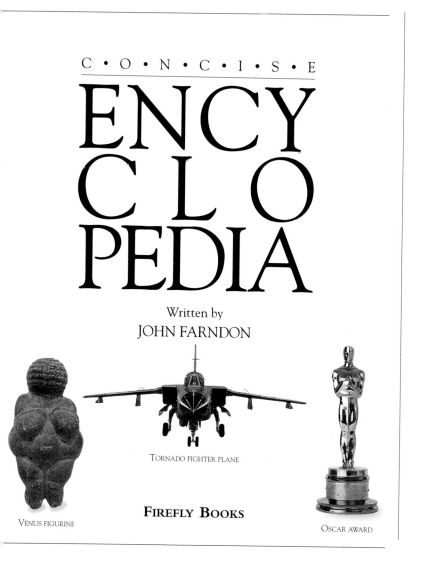

C · O · N · C · I · S · E
ENCY CLO PEDIA

Written by
JOHN FARNDON

TORNADO FIGHTER PLANE

FIREFLY BOOKS

VENUS FIGURINE

OSCAR AWARD

A DORLING KINDERSLEY BOOK

Published by Firefly Books Ltd., 1999

First Printing

First published in Canada in 1999 by
Firefly Books Ltd.
3680 Victoria Park Avenue
Willowdale, Ontario, M2H 3K1

Canadian Cataloguing in Publication Data

Farndon, John
Firefly concise encyclopedia
Includes index.
ISBN 1-55209-440-5

1. Children's encyclopedias and dictionaries. I. Title
AG5.F37 1999   j031   C99-931040-2

Produced for Dorling Kindersley by
PAGE*One*, Cairn House, Elgiva Lane, Chesham,
Buckinghamshire HP5 2JD

Project directors	Bob Gordon, Helen Parker
Editor	Neil Kelly
Designer	Matthew Cook
DTP Designer	Chris Clark
DK team	Anna Kruger, Peter Bailey, Alastair Dougall, Sarah Crouch Nomazwe Madonko, Darren Holt
Production	Ruth Cobb
Picture research	Cynthia Hole, Caroline Potts

Color reproduction by Colourscan, Singapore
Printed and bound in Italy by L.E.G.O.

CONTENTS

MANNED
MANOEUVRING
UNIT

FORMATION
OF AN
ICEBERG

HUMAN
HEART

BACTERIUM

CHEMICAL
SOLUTION

HOT-AIR
BALLOON AND
BASKET

PATAGONIAN PUDU

ICE-HOCKEY
PLAYER

CONTENTS

HOW TO USE THIS BOOK

These pages show you how to use the *DK Concise Encyclopedia*. The book is divided into nine sections of photographs, cutaway artworks, fact boxes, and illustrated timelines. At the beginning of each section there is a picture page with a list of contents.

INTRODUCTION
This provides a clear overview of the subject. After reading this, you should have an idea what the pages are about.

CORNER CODING
The corners of the pages in each section are color-coded to remind you which section you are in.

■ SPACE

■ PLANET EARTH

■ THE LIVING WORLD

■ THE HUMAN BODY

■ SCIENCE AND TECHNOLOGY

□ TRANSPORTATION

■ THE WORLD

□ PEOPLE AND SOCIETY

HISTORY

HEADING
This describes the subject of the page. This page is about crustaceans.

LABELS
For extra clarity, some pictures have labels. They may give extra information, or identify a picture when it is not obvious from the text what it is.

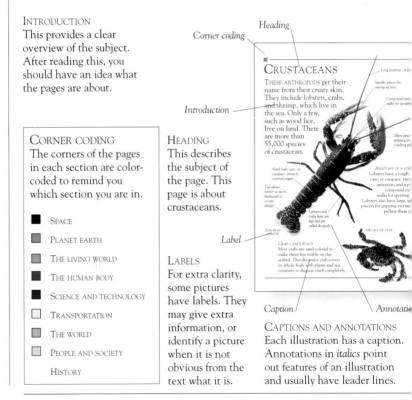

Heading

Corner coding

Introduction

CRUSTACEANS

THESE ARTHROPODS get their name from their crusty skin. They include lobsters, crabs, and shrimp, which live in the sea. Only a few, such as wood lice, live on land. There are more than 55,000 species of crustacean.

Long antenna, or feeler

Sawlike pincer for cutting up prey

Compound eyes on stalks for spotting

Blunt pincer for gripping and crushing prey

Hard body case, or carapace, protects external organs

Tail allows lobster to swim backward to escape danger

ANATOMY OF A LOBSTER
Lobsters have a tough case, or carapace, two antennae, and a pair of compound eyes. Lobsters also have large, strong pincers for gripping victims, pulling them apart.

Lobsters and crabs have ten legs and are called decapods.

EUROPEAN LOBSTER

DECORATOR CRAB

CRAB CAMOUFLAGE
Most crabs are sand-colored to make them less visible on the seabed. This decorator crab covers its whole body with plants and sea creatures to disguise itself completely.

Label

Caption

Annotation

CAPTIONS AND ANNOTATIONS
Each illustration has a caption. Annotations in *italics* point out features of an illustration and usually have leader lines.

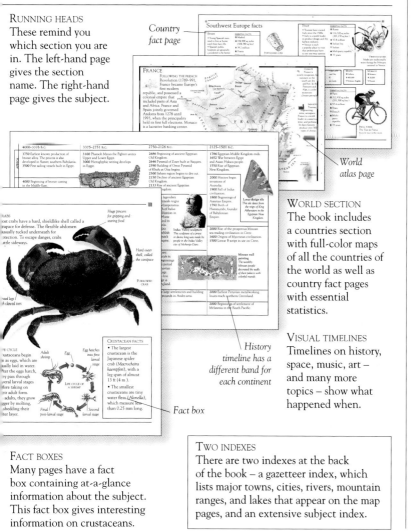

RUNNING HEADS
These remind you which section you are in. The left-hand page gives the section name. The right-hand page gives the subject.

Country fact page

World atlas page

WORLD SECTION
The book includes a countries section with full-color maps of all the countries of the world as well as country fact pages with essential statistics.

VISUAL TIMELINES
Timelines on history, space, music, art — and many more topics — show what happened when.

History timeline has a different band for each continent

Fact box

FACT BOXES
Many pages have a fact box containing at-a-glance information about the subject. This fact box gives interesting information on crustaceans.

TWO INDEXES
There are two indexes at the back of the book — a gazetteer index, which lists major towns, cities, rivers, mountain ranges, and lakes that appear on the map pages, and an extensive subject index.

SPACE

THE UNIVERSE

FROM THE EARTH under our feet to the farthest stars, everything that exists is part of the universe. The universe is so large that it contains countless billions of stars, and it is still expanding rapidly. However, most of it consists of nothing but empty space.

LIGHT FROM A STATIONARY STAR

LIGHT FROM A MOVING STAR

LIGHT AND MOTION
If a star is moving away from Earth, its light waves stretch out in comparison with those from other stars. The star's light becomes redder, moving toward the red end of the spectrum. This phenomenon is known as red shift.

UNIVERSE FACT

• There are an estimated 100 billion galaxies spread throughout the universe; each of these contains approximately 100 billion stars.

THE SCALE OF THE UNIVERSE
The universe is so vast that measurements such as miles and kilometers eventually become meaningless. A special unit called a light-year is used to calculate the distances between stars and galaxies. A light-year is equivalent to 5.9 trillion miles (9.4 trillion km), the distance that light travels in one year. The known universe spans more than 20 billion light-years.

| GROUND LEVEL | FLYING AT LOW ALTITUDE 0.6 MILES (1 KM) | ORBITING AT HIGH ALTITUDE 620 MILES (1,000 KM) | EARTH FROM SPACE 62,000 MILES (100,000 KM) | EARTH AND MOON 620,000 MILES (1 MILLION KM) |

The Milky Way galaxy took on its spiral shape about 5 billion years after the Big Bang

After 10 billion years, our solar system formed

Life appeared on Earth 11.5 billion years after the Big Bang

THE BIG BANG
All matter, energy, space, and time were created about 15 billion years ago in an explosion called the Big Bang. Atomic particles joined together to form hydrogen and helium atoms, and the universe expanded and cooled. Over several million years, galaxies, stars, planets, and organic life were produced.

Quasars were among the first objects to form

After 1.5 billion years, nebulae clumped together to form galaxies

Gases clustered into clouds called nebulae after 1 billion years

Within minutes, matter forms and the universe becomes 75% hydrogen and 25% helium gas

The initial temperature of the universe was about 10,000 million million million degrees

THE SOLAR SYSTEM 6.2 BILLION MILES (10 BILLION KM)	INTERSTELLAR SPACE 620 BILLION MILES (1,000 BILLION KM)	NEAREST STARS 100 LIGHT-YEARS	MILKY WAY GALAXY 100,000 LIGHT-YEARS	LOCAL GROUP OF GALAXIES 10 MILLION LIGHT-YEARS	EXTENT OF THE KNOWN UNIVERSE 20 BILLION LIGHT-YEARS

GALAXIES

STARS ARE clustered together in enormous groups called galaxies, which were created when stars forming from spinning clouds of condensing gas were pulled toward each other by gravity. Some galaxies still rotate rapidly, maintaining a spiral shape, while others slow down and form ellipses (ovals) or less regular shapes. Large galaxies may have 1 trillion stars, but even the smallest contains a few hundred thousand.

DISTANT NEIGHBOR
The Andromeda galaxy is one of the nearest to the Milky Way, but its light still takes 2.2 million years to reach Earth. We see the galaxy not as it is now, but as it was 2.2 million years ago.

FOUR TYPES OF GALAXIES

ELLIPTICAL
The most common type of galaxy, ellipticals contain mostly old stars and vary in shape from ball- to egg-like.

SPIRAL
These disk-shaped galaxies are flat, with a central nucleus of old stars. New stars form from clouds of gas in the spiral arms.

BARRED SPIRAL
One-third of spiral galaxies have a nucleus that is elongated into a bar. The vast spiral arms extend from the end of the bar.

THE MILKY WAY

The Sun is just one of 100 billion stars in our own galaxy, the Milky Way. Ours is a spiral galaxy, with a nucleus of old stars surrounded by a halo of even older stars. All the young stars are located in the spiral arms. The galaxy is called the Milky Way because it looks like a bright, creamy band of stars stretching through space when viewed from Earth.

MILKY WAY GALAXY:
EXTERNAL SIDE VIEW

Nucleus is the brightest region of the galaxy

Galactic halo contains the oldest stars

From the side the spiral arms look like a flattened disk

Crux–Centaurus arm

Galactic nucleus

MILKY WAY GALAXY:
EXTERNAL OVERHEAD VIEW

IRREGULAR

The rarest galaxies are those that do not fit any known pattern. Some have a hint of a spiral or elliptical structure.

Location of the solar system

Sagittarius arm

Orion arm (Local arm)

17

STARS

A STAR is an immense globe
of fiery hydrogen gas powered
by nuclear reactions at its core.
Stars range in size from massive
supergiants to small dwarf stars.
The Sun is one of billions of stars
scattered throughout the universe.
It is a yellow star, a typical star of
average size and temperature.

THE EVOLUTION OF A STAR

MAIN SEQUENCE STARS
The temperature, color,
brightness, and lifespan of
a star depend on its mass.

Brown dwarf
1,800°F
(1,000°C)

Red dwarf
5,040°F
(2,800°C)

Yellow star
9,900°F
(5,500°C)

THE
SUN

White star
18,000°F
(10,000°C)

Blue/White
star 28,800°F
(16,000°C)

Blue star
43,200°F
(24,000°C)

1 GAS CLOUD
A star begins life as
material within a nebula,
an enormous cloud of gas
and dust. Parts of the
cloud are pulled together
under their own gravity,
contracting into
spinning balls of gas
known as protostars.

2 STARBIRTH
The protostar shrinks,
and its core becomes
denser. Nuclear reactions
begin, creating heat and
light. As the star begins
to shine, the leftover dust
is blown away by stellar
wind or forms planets
around the star.

3 MAIN SEQUENCE
The major period of a
star's lifespan is called its
main sequence. During
this period, the star shines
steadily, radiating energy.
The bigger and brighter
the star, the quicker it
burns hydrogen, which
reduces its lifespan.

STAR FACTS

- The biggest stars collapse to form black holes, which are so dense and have such a powerful gravitational pull that even light cannot escape.

6 SUPERNOVA
Heat from the star's core leads to a massive explosion, called a supernova. The star is as bright as a billion suns as it blows apart. The core collapses in a single second.

5 RED SUPERGIANT
The star continues to swell, swallowing up its surrounding planets. Its core fuses carbon atoms into iron but lacks energy for further contraction.

INSIDE A STAR

A star shines because of the amount of light and heat produced by the nuclear reactions taking place within it. The fusion of hydrogen atoms, creating helium, produces so much energy that the core of a star reaches millions of degrees, making the surface glow.

Temperature and pressure increase toward core

Energy released at surface as light and heat

Nuclear reactions in core produce energy

4 GROWING OLD
When its supply of hydrogen is exhausted, the star's core contracts, fusing helium atoms to make carbon. The star's surface gases burn, and the outer layers swell and glow red. The star is now called a red giant.

THE NORTHERN SKY

PEOPLE LIVING IN the Northern Hemisphere see a completely different range of stars than do people in the Southern Hemisphere. The star pattern turns steadily through the sky as Earth rotates, so the stars visible on any given night depend on the latitude, time of year, and time of night.

ORION

CONSTELLATIONS
Stars viewed from Earth seem to form patterns in the sky. These patterns are known as constellations. Ancient astronomers divided Earth's skies into 88 different constellations, each of which, such as Orion, is supposed to represent a mythological person, creature, or object.

Arcturus

PROJECTED SPHERE
This sky map is a projection of the northern half of the celestial sphere onto a flat surface. Earth's North Pole is situated directly below the center of the map. The stars near the center of the sky map are called circumpolar and can be seen throughout the year. The North Star, also known as Polaris, appears to remain directly above the North Pole.

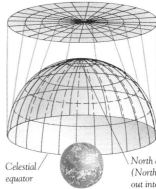

The Big Dipper

Celestial equator

North celestial pole (North Pole projected out into space)

The edge of the map marks the celestial equator – stars here can be seen by Southern Hemisphere observers

Polaris

The stars around the edge come into view month by month during the year.

Betelgeuse

21

THE SOUTHERN SKY

THE SOUTHERN HEMISPHERE presents a very different picture than the northern one, due to the rotation of Earth and the galaxies. The range of stars that people can see is dependent on factors such as climatic conditions, the latitude, the time of year, and the time of night.

THE CELESTIAL SPHERE

The stars viewed from Earth seem to be set on the inside of a giant sphere in the sky, called the celestial sphere. As Earth rotates on its axis and orbits around the Sun, different sections of the sphere are revealed. The motion of the planets can be plotted against the sphere.

PROJECTED SPHERE

This sky map is a projection of the southern half of the celestial sphere onto a flat surface. Earth's South Pole is situated directly below the center of the map. Alpha Centauri, one of the nearest stars to the Sun, is a Southern Hemisphere star. The celestial equator is a projection of Earth's equator out into space.

Alpha Centauri

Celestial equator

Antares

South celestial pole (South Pole projected out into space)

The edge of the map marks the celestial equator – stars here can also be see by Northern Hemisphere observers

Sirius

Canopus

The stars near the edge become visible month by month through the year.

THE SUN AND SOLAR SYSTEM

OUR SOLAR SYSTEM consists of the Sun and the many objects that orbit around it – nine planets, over 60 moons, and countless asteroids and comets. The system occupies a disk-shaped volume of space more than 7.45 billion miles (12 billion km) across. The Sun contains more than 99 percent of the system's mass.

PLUTO

Pluto has the most eccentric orbit

NEPTUNE   URANUS   SATURN

The inner system (Mercury, Venus, Earth, Mars) is separated from the rest by the asteroid belt

JUPITER

MARS   MERCURY
VENUS   EARTH

Enlargement of the inner solar system

SPINNING IN SPACE
The whole solar system moves through space. Within the system, individual planets orbit around the rotating Sun. The planets follow elliptical paths, all moving in the same direction but at different speeds. The time taken to complete one orbit varies greatly, depending on the planet's distance from the Sun. In addition, each planet also spins on its axis.

STRUCTURE OF THE SUN
The Sun is a vast, fiery ball of spinning hydrogen and helium gases. Heat produced by nuclear reactions at the Sun's core erupts from its surface as millions of upsurges of gas, called granules. Sunspots are dark surface patches of cooler gas caused by disturbances in the Sun's magnetic field.

Convective zone

Radiative zone

Supergranule – a convection cell

Chromosphere

Photosphere

Corona

Sunspot

THE SUN: INTERNAL AND EXTERNAL FEATURES

Core temperature 27 million°F (15 million°C)

Photosphere temperature about 9,900°F (5,500°C)

Orbits are elliptical (oval) rather than circular

The time taken for a planet to make one orbit of the Sun is called the orbital period

SOLAR PROMINENCES
Enormous jets of hot hydrogen gas shoot out from the Sun's surface at intervals, and can stretch for many thousands of miles. The largest jets, called solar prominences, may last for several months. Some prominences are held in loops by the Sun's magnetic field.

THE INNER PLANETS

THE FOUR PLANETS closest to the Sun – Mercury, Venus, Earth, and Mars – are known as the inner planets. Each planet has a core of hot iron and a rocky crust, but surface conditions vary greatly.

Iron core contains 80% of the planet's mass

Silicate rock mantle

NO MOONS

MERCURY DATA

- Distance from Sun: 36 million miles (57.9 million km)

- Time taken to orbit Sun: 88 Earth days

- Diameter at equator: 3,031 miles (4,878 km)

MERCURY

A small rock world with a large, dense core, Mercury is the planet closest to the Sun. It is marked with craters, has no real atmosphere, and experiences extreme variations in surface temperature.

Night temperature about −292°F (−180°C)

Semisolid iron-nickel core

Rocky mantle

Daytime temperature about 806°F (430°C)

Thin rocky crust

VENUS

The planet Venus is about the same size as Earth. Its surface is very different, however, with intense heat, crushing pressure, and unbreathable acid air. Overhead are thick clouds of sulfuric acid droplets.

VENUS DATA

- Distance from Sun: 67.2 million miles (108.2 million km)

- Time taken to orbit Sun: 224.7 Earth days

- Diameter at equator: 7,520 miles (12,102 km)

Silicate crust

NO MOONS

IMPACT CRATER FORMATION ON ROCK PLANETS

A meteorite impact blasts out a circular crater, ejecting debris.

Rock compressed by the impact forms a conical central peak.

Crater gradually filled as debris slips from walls and peak.

EARTH DATA

- Distance from Sun: 93 million miles (149.6 million km)
- Time taken to orbit Sun: 365 Earth days
- Diameter at equator: 7,926 miles (12,756 km)

2 MOONS

1 MOON

EARTH

The third planet from the Sun, Earth, is the only planet in the solar system with liquid water and an oxygen-rich atmosphere. These two factors make it the only known planet capable of supporting life.

Solid rock core

Mostly solid silicate mantle

Crust of silicate rock

MARS

A cold, barren planet with a thin atmosphere, Mars has polar ice caps, water-carved valleys, chasms, and giant volcanoes. Its red color is caused by iron oxide dust spread across its surface.

Silicate rock mantle

Rock crust with under ice permafrost

MARS DATA

- Distance from Sun: 141.6 million miles (227.9 million km)
- Time taken to orbit Sun: 687 Earth days
- Diameter at equator: 4,217 miles (6,786 km)

THE OUTER PLANETS

BEYOND THE ORBIT of Mars lie four giant
planets formed from liquefied
gas – Jupiter, Saturn, Uranus,
and Neptune. Farther out
still is Pluto, a small,
icy rock planet.

*Liquid hydrogen and
helium outer mantle*

*Rock core about
twice the size
of Earth*

JUPITER DATA

- Distance from Sun:
484 million miles
(778.3 million km)

- Time taken to orbit
Sun: 12 Earth years

- Diameter at
equator: 88,849
miles (142,984 km)

16
MOONS *Great
Red Spot*

*Metallic
hydrogen
inner mantle*

JUPITER
The largest, fastest-
spinning planet, Jupiter
could contain 1,300 Earths. Composed mainly
of swirling gases, its most prominent feature is the
Great Red Spot, a rotating storm bigger than the Earth.

*Metallic   18   Liquid
hydrogen   MOONS   hydrogen
inner mantle   outer mantle*

SATURN
The second largest planet
is Saturn, its famed ring
system made up of
tiny ice-coated rock
fragments and dust
particles. The
planet's mass is so
thinly spread that
on average it
is less dense
than
water.

*Rock
and ice
core*

SATURN DATA

- Distance from Sun:
887 million miles
(1,427 million km)

- Time taken to
orbit Sun:
29.5 Earth years

- Diameter at
equator:
74,900 miles
(20,536 km)

Rings of rock fragments about 39 in (1 m) across

15 MOONS

URANUS

The frozen methane atmosphere of Uranus gives it a blue-green appearance. The planet, and its rings and moons, are all tilted by more than 90°, traveling around the Sun on their side.

Mantle of water-ice, ammonia and methane

Solid rock core

URANUS DATA

- Distance from Sun: 1.8 billion miles (2.9 billion km)
- Time taken to orbit Sun: 84 Earth years
- Diameter at equator: 31,764 miles (51,118 km)

Silicate rock core

Methane, ammonia, and water-ice mantle

NEPTUNE DATA

- Distance from Sun: 2.8 billion miles (4.5 billion km)
- Time taken to orbit Sun: 165 Earth years
- Diameter at equator: 30,776 miles (49,528 km)

NEPTUNE

The outermost gas giant, Neptune's atmosphere is very similar to Uranus, but thinner methane in its outer layer gives it a deeper blue color. Huge, cyclonic storms form the planet's Great Dark Spot.

Great Dark Spot

8 MOONS

Dark, low clouds of hydrogen sulfide

Icy surface of water and methane

Thin atmosphere of methane and nitrogen

Ice mantle

1 MOON

PLUTO

The smallest and most distant of all the planets, Pluto is made of ice, rock, and frozen gases. Its orbit around the Sun is uniquely tilted at 17°, and for about ten percent of its journey it is closer to the Sun than Neptune is.

Large rock core

PLUTO DATA

- Distance from Sun: 3.7 billion miles (5.9 billion km)
- Time taken to orbit Sun: 248 Earth years
- Diameter at equator: 1,419 miles (2,284 km)

29

EARTH'S MOON

THE MOON, Earth's only natural satellite, is a ball of rock held in place by our planet's gravity. A quarter of the size of Earth, the Moon is dead, waterless, and airless. As Earth orbits the Sun, the Moon in turn rotates around Earth. Each rotation, or lunar cycle, takes about a month.

Waning

New Moon

SUNLIGHT

Full Moon

Waxing

PHASES OF THE MOON
The Moon shines when light from the Sun is reflected off the lunar surface. As it travels around Earth, the sunlit area we see changes. A monthly cycle of lunar phases is produced as it waxes (grows) from New Moon to Full Moon and wanes (shrinks) back to New Moon.

Asteroid collides with Earth

LUNAR ORIGINS
Most astronomers believe that a huge asteroid collided with Earth 4.6 billion years ago. Vast amounts of rock fragments thrown into space by the impact came together, forming the Moon.

MOON DATA

- Distance from Earth: 238,860 miles (384,400 km)

- Time to rotate on axis: 27.3 Earth days

- Diameter: 2,160 miles (3,476 km)

- Lunar temperature: −247°F to + 221°F (−155°C to +105°C)

BATTERED SURFACE

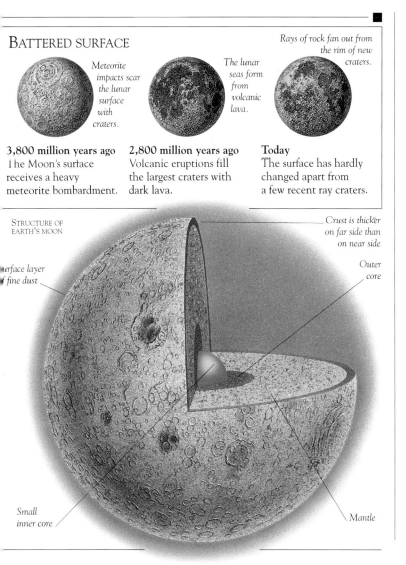

Meteorite impacts scar the lunar surface with craters.

The lunar seas form from volcanic lava.

Rays of rock fan out from the rim of new craters.

3,800 million years ago
The Moon's surface receives a heavy meteorite bombardment.

2,800 million years ago
Volcanic eruptions fill the largest craters with dark lava.

Today
The surface has hardly changed apart from a few recent ray craters.

STRUCTURE OF EARTH'S MOON

Crust is thicker on far side than on near side

Outer core

urface layer f fine dust

Small inner core

Mantle

ASTRONOMY

VISIBLE STARLIGHT magnified by
optical telescopes is only a small
part of the electromagnetic
spectrum, which includes all forms
of radiation. Astronomers learn
about the visible and invisible parts
of the universe by looking at other
types of radiation, such as radio
waves and X-rays. Space telescopes
provide the best view, collecting
information from wavelengths
usually absorbed by the atmosphere.

HIGH AND DR
The domes of the Cerr
Tololo Internationa
American Observatory a
sited in the Andes foothil
of Chile. A dry climat
with cloud-free nights an
a steady atmosphere make
this an ideal location fo
clear viewing through a
optical telescop

DIFFERENT IMAGES OF THE CRAB NEBULA

VISIBLE LIGHT
This visible light image
of the nebula has been
computer-enhanced to
show hydrogen (red)
and sulfur (blue) gas
filaments still streaming
out from the explosion.

X-RAY
The X-rays emitted
by the Crab Nebula
explosion show a
bright object at the
center of the nebula.
This pulsating star, or
pulsar, is the remains of
the presupernova star.

UV LIGHT
The Crab Nebula is the
remnant of a supernova
explosion. Viewing the
ultraviolet light (UV)
produced by the explosion
reveals glowing, energetic
particles interacting with
the surrounding space.

RADIO VISION

A radio telescope, like an ordinary radio, can be tuned to pick up a particular wavelength. After measuring the intensity of the radio energy, computers are used to produce a "radio map" of the sky. Radio astronomy was responsible for the discovery of quasar galaxies and pulsar stars.

Radio waves

The VLA dishes are arranged in a Y-shape

Radio signals from space collected by 27 linked dishes

Each dish is 82 ft (25 m) across

VERY LARGE ARRAY (VLA) RADIO TELESCOPE, NEW MEXICO

Large solar panels power the equipment aboard the HST

HUBBLE SPACE TELESCOPE

Operating outside the Earth's atmosphere, the orbiting Hubble Space Telescope (HST) can see much farther than Earth-based telescopes. Its large mirror detects very faint light, which is then directed by a secondary mirror into an onboard scientific instrument package or high-resolution camera.

Cameras and instruments located inside

Protective hinged cover

Antenna transmits information to Earth via a communication satellite

33

ROCKETS AND SPACECRAFT

THE FIRST ARTIFICIAL satellite, Sputnik 1, was launched into space in 1957. Since then, hundreds of spacecraft have been launched, including manned missions for exploration, orbiting space laboratories, and probes to other planets. Powerful rocket engines enable spacecraft to escape the pull of Earth's gravity.

STAGE FLIGHT
Rockets are designed in separate stages, so that when all the fuel from a stage has been used up, that stage drops away and the next takes over. The giant three-stage Saturn V rocket carried astronauts to the Moon.

Main engines on orbiter take fuel from external tank. Two solid-fuel rocket boosters fire for lift-off

SATURN
V

Solid fuel boosters jettisoned 2 mins 5 secs after lift-off, at an altitude of 28 miles (45 km). Shuttle now travelling at 4.5 times the speed of sound (Mach 4.5)

Solid fuel burns for two minutes. Each solid fuel rocket produces the thrust of 11 Boeing 747 airliners at take-off

External tank
Orbiter
Solid-fuel boosters

Shuttle reaches altitude of 81 miles (130 km) at Mach 15. External tank released, burning up in Earth's atmosphere

Shuttle engines put orbiter into circular orbit

THE SPACE SHUTTLE
The US space shuttle is the world's first reusable spacecraft. Typical shuttle missions include launching, retrieving, or repairing satellites, and performing scientific experiments. The shuttle is launched by reusable solid fuel rockets, and protected from the heat of reentry by 32,000 carbon or silica insulating tiles.

ORBITING LABORATORY

The *Mir* space station was launched by the former USSR in 1986, and has been visited by several crews of astronauts who have stayed aboard for weeks or months at a time. Scientific experiments that are impossible to perform on Earth can be carried out in the zero-gravity environment aboard the station.

Solar panels supply energy

MIR SPACE STATION

Docking port

Floor and ceiling painted different colors to help orientation in weightlessness of space

Main module for living and working

Orbiter remains in orbit for 5–30 days to carry out mission. Cargo bay doors open, venting excess heat

Cargo bay doors close. Engines rotate orbiter into reentry position

Orbiter maneuvers into precise angle for reentry, beginning 30-minute descent into atmosphere at Mach 22.4

Parts of nose and wings reach 2,660°F (1,460°C) during reentry

Orbiter glides in to land at a speed of 214 mph (345 km/h). It is towed, or flown on the back of a Boeing 747, to the next launch site

SPACE PROBES

Computer-controlled space probes are designed to gather data about planets in the solar system. The Galileo probe, launched in 1989, was sent to collect information about Jupiter.

Magnetic sensors mounted on long boom to minimize interference

Atmospheric descent probe

Instrument package for analyzing atmosphere samples

Double-dish antenna

Camera package

GALILEO PROBE

1926–1968

1926 US engineer Robert Goddard designs and launches first liquid fuel rocket.

1942 Wernher von Braun, later to play a major role in the postwar US space program, develops Nazi Germany's rocket-powered V2 flying bomb.

1957 Launch of USSR's *Sputnik 1*, the world's first artificial satellite.

1957 Russian dog Laika becomes first living creature in space aboard *Sputnik 2*.

1961 The first manned spacecraft, *Vostok 1*, carries Soviet cosmonaut Yuri Gagarin into Earth orbit.

Yuri Gagarin

1962 US probe *Mariner 2* flies past Venus, becoming first human-made object to "flyby" another planet.

1963 First woman in space is USSR's Valentina Tereshkova, orbiting Earth 48 times in two days in *Vostok 6*.

1965 Russian cosmonaut Alexei Leonov takes the first walk in space. US probe *Mariner 4* finds no sign of water or life on Mars.

1966 Unmanned Soviet probe *Lunar 9* lands on Moon.

1968 US astronauts enter lunar orbit in *Apollo 8*.

1969–1976

1969 US astronaut Neil Armstrong and Edwin M. Aldrin are the first humans to walk on the Moon.

Edwin M. Aldrin steps onto the lunar surface

1970 USSR's *Venera 7* lands on Venus. It is the first probe to touch down on another planet.

1970 Soviet robot *Lunokhods*, the first extraterrestrial land vehicles, are driven across the Moon's surface.

1971 The first orbiting space station, the USSR's *Salyut 1*, is launched.

1972 *Apollo 17* is sixth and last US manned mission to the moon.

1973 Launch of *Skylab*, the first US space station. Close-up images of Jupiter taken by US *Pioneer 10*.

1974 US *Mariner 10* transmits first pictures of Mercury.

1975 First images of the surface of Venus sent by USSR's *Venera 9*.

1976 Surface tests carried out by US probe *Viking 1* confirm no life on planet Mars.

Martian surface

1977 US *Voyagers 1* and *2* launched on their long journey to the outer planets and beyond.
1979 US *Pioneer 11* reaches Saturn after a six-year voyage, finding a new ring and new moons. *Voyagers 1* and *2* pass Jupiter, observing active volcanoes on the moon, Io, and discovering three new moons.
1980 *Voyager 1* takes the first detailed close-up photographs of Saturn's ring systems and discovers an additional six moons.

Saturn, photographed by Voyager 1

1981 Launch of US space shuttle *Columbia*, the world's first reusable spacecraft. *Voyager 2* finds four more moons around Saturn, bringing the total to 18.
1982 USSR's *Venera 13* probe approaches Venus, sending back color photographs of the planet's surface. US astronauts Mark Lee and Judy Davis become the first married couple in space aboard the shuttle *Endeavor*.

Bruce McCandless in MMU

1984 Manned Maneuvering Unit (MMU) used by US astronaut Bruce McCandless to maneuver independently alongside space shuttle *Challenger*.
1986 Shuttle program halted after *Challenger* explosion kills the crew of seven. *Voyager 2* reaches Uranus and finds a ring system and 15 moons.
1988 Launch of *Columbia* resumes the US space shuttle program.
1989 *Voyager 2* reaches Neptune and discovers six new moons.
1990 Hubble space telescope launched (with faulty mirror).
1992 US COBE (Cosmic Background Explorer) finds hotspots in "microwave background" radio energy, providing evidence for the Big Bang theory.

COBE image of microwave background

1994 Hubble telescope repaired.
1996 US scientists find fossil evidence in meteor fragments that microbes may once have existed on Mars.

PLANET EARTH

FORMATION OF EARTH

ABOUT 4.6 BILLION years ago, the planets of the solar system were just a vast cloud of gas swirling around the newly formed Sun. Earth and the other planets formed when parts of this cloud began to cluster together.

3 EARTH'S CRUST
About 4 billion years ago, Earth's crust began to form. Blocks of cooling, solid rock floated on a molten rock layer. The rock sometimes sank and remelted before rising again.

1 FORMING THE SUN
A spinning cloud of dust and gas contracted to form the Sun. Cooler matter from this dust cloud combined to shape the planets.

Dense cosmic gases surrounded Earth as it formed

Sea 70.8%

Land 29.2%
PROPORTION OF LAND AND SEA

2 FORMING EARTH
Radioactivity in Earth's rocks caused the planet's surface to melt. Lighter minerals floated to the surface, and heavier elements, such as iron and nickel, sank to form Earth's core.

4 MAKING THE ATMOSPHERE
Over millions of years Earth's crust thickened, while gases from erupting volcanoes began to form the atmosphere. Water vapor condensed to make oceans.

EARTH DATA

- Distance from Sun: 93 million miles (150 million km)

- Time to rotate on axis: 23 hours, 56 minutes

- Time to orbit Sun: 365 days, 6 hours

- Speed of Earth's orbits of Sun: 18.5 miles/sec (29.8 km/sec)

Crust composed of rocks similar to those on surface – 4–43 miles (6–70 km) deep

Mantle of mostly solid rock – 1,800 miles (2,900 km) deep

Atmosphere – about 400 miles (640 km) deep

COMPOSITION OF EARTH

Our planet is composed of several layers of rock around a core of iron and nickel. The deeper the layer, the higher the temperature.

Outer core of liquid iron, nickel, and oxygen – 1,240 miles (2,000 km) deep

Inner core of solid iron and nickel – 1,700 miles (2,740 km) deep

5 LAND FORMS
Large landmasses, or protocontinents, began to form on the planet's crust about 3,500 million years ago. Today's continents look very different.

6 EARTH TODAY
The planet is still changing – the huge tectonic plates (see pp. 42–43) that make up Earth's crust are constantly moving, pulling some continents nearer and pushing others apart.

CONTINENTS AND PLATES

THE SEVEN HUGE landmasses that make up most of Earth's surface are called continents. They are always slowly moving, shifted around by forces deep inside Earth. This movement is known as continental drift.

The crack or boundary between two plates sliding past each other is called a transform fault

TECTONIC PLATES
Earth's crust, or lithosphere, is made up of vast pieces of rock, called tectonic plates.

Earth's tectonic plates fit together like jigsaw puzzle pieces

PLATE BOUNDARIES
Where they meet, tectonic plates may be sliding past each other, pulling apart, or colliding. These different types of motion cause earthquakes and volcanoes, create steep-sided valleys, form deep-sea trenches, and build mountains.

CONTINENTAL DRIFT

N. America — Europe
PANGAEA
Asia
India
Africa
Australia
S. America — Antarctica

1 Some 220 million years ago (mya) the continents were joined together in the giant supercontinent of Pangaea (a Greek word meaning "all lands").

N. America — Asia
LAURASIA
Europe
Africa — GONDWANALAND — India
Australia
S. America — Antarctica

2 By 200 mya, Pangaea had split into two landmasses, Gondwanaland and Laurasia. Around 135 mya, these landmasses also began to divide.

Midocean ridge

Where two plates pull apart, molten rock bubbles up from the mantle and fills the gap, creating new crust

When two plates collide, one may ride over the other and force it down into the mantle – this is called a subduction zone

PUSH THEORY

PULL THEORY

PLATE MOVEMENT
In the "push" theory, heat makes the mantle rise and erupt, pushing the plates apart.
The "pull" theory says they are dragged down and apart under the weight of erupting magma (molten rock) as it cools near midocean ridges.

Magma forced down into mantle

N. America — Europe
Africa — Asia
India
Australia
S. America — Antarctica

3 Over the next 120 million years, the products of this division became the continents, drifting closer or farther apart to take up their current positions.

N. America — Europe
Africa
Asia
Australia
S. America — Antarctica

4 The continents are still moving at a slow but steady rate. This is how Earth may look in 150 million years.

43

VOLCANOES

A VOLCANIC ERUPTION takes place when hot, molten rock called magma rises up from deep inside Earth and forces its way to the surface. The magma may erupt as a flow of red-hot lava, or explode into clouds of ash, rock, and dust.

Ring of Fire continues through volcanic islands of Japan

The chain of volcanoes around the edge of the Pacific Ocean is known as the Ring of Fire

PACIFIC OCEAN

Crack in Earth's crust

Side vent

Lava

Vent

VOLCANO SITES
In general, volcanoes occur near plate boundaries or under the ocean at plate edges. Hotspot volcanoes, however, burst through the middle of a plate; they are not related to plate margins.

ERUPTION SIZES
The amount of ash thrown out during an eruption is a good indicator of the size of an eruption.

MT. ST. HELENS US 1980	MT. VESUVIUS ITALY A.D. 79	MT. KATMAI ALASKA 1912	MT. KRAKATOA INDONESIA 1883	MT. TAMBORA INDONESIA 1815

FISSURE VOLCANO
This type of volcano is a long crack in the crust. Liquid lava seeps out along its length and forms a plateau.

• The worst volcanic eruption was Mount Tambora, Indonesia, which killed 92,000 people in 1815.
• Kilauea, Hawaii, is the most frequently active volcano.

COMPOSITE VOLCANO
Cone-shaped volcanoes build up from hardening sticky lava. Inside are layers of thick lava and ash from previous eruptions. Gas builds up pressure inside the volcano until it erupts violently.

Clouds of ash, rock, and dust

Crater

Main pipe

Layers of ash and lava

Main vent

Lava flow

Side pipe

SHIELD VOLCANO
A shield volcano usually has several side vents. The lava is liquid and produces gently sloping sides.

Magma chamber

45

EARTHQUAKES

A MAJOR EARTHQUAKE occurs when the massive tectonic plates that make up Earth's crust suddenly move. A mild earthquake can feel like a truck passing; a severe one can destroy roads and buildings and cause huge tidal waves in the ocean.

The focus is usually deep inside Earth

The earthquake is strongest at its epicenter

Shock waves can travel right through Earth to the other side

FOCUS AND EPICENTER

The point at which an earthquake begins is the focus. The point on Earth's surface directly above the focus is the epicenter.

CLOSE-UP OF AN EARTHQUAKE

At transform faults, where two plates are moving in opposite directions, the jagged edges of the plates may lock together. Stress builds up within the plates, until suddenly they slip, making the ground shake violently as they jolt into a new position.

BEFORE AN EARTHQUAKE

AFTER AN EARTHQUAKE

The plates slip and lurch past each other, causing an earthquake.

This fault line marks the boundary of two plates

EARTHQUAKE FAULT ZONES

Most earthquakes occur on or near the edges of Earth's tectonic plates (see pp. 42–43) at cracks in the crust called faults. Deep earthquakes take place where one plate is sliding under another.

EARTHQUAKE-PROOF BUILDINGS

In earthquake-prone areas, specially designed buildings can lessen the effects of an earthquake.

Earthquake belts usually follow the edges of Earth's tectonic plates

Many earthquakes occur on the northeast coast of Asia. This is at the boundary of two of Earth's plates

Pyramid-shaped buildings are built to withstand stress

TRANSAMERICA BUILDING, SAN FRANCISCO

The central column of the pagoda absorbs the shaking

ANCIENT BUDDHIST PAGODA, JAPAN

EARTHQUAKE FACTS

• The strongest known earthquake occurred in Colombia in 1906, with a magnitude of 8.9 on the Richter scale.

• The highest recorded number of deaths from an earthquake is 830,000, occurring in Shansi, China, in 1556.

• The worst earthquake damage on record took place in Kwanto, Japan, in 1923, destroying 375,000 homes and killing 144,000 people.

47

ROCKS AND MINERALS

Earth's surface

THERE ARE MANY different types of rock, all of which are composed of one or more minerals. Rocks are the building blocks from which Earth's crust is formed.

Extrusive igneous rock   *Intrusive igneous rock*

TYPES OF ROCKS
The study of rocks is called geology. All types of rocks fall into one of three categories: igneous, sedimentary, or metamorphic.

EXTRUSIVE AND INTRUSIVE ROCKS
Igneous rock either settles within Earth's crust (intrusive igneous rock) or erupts from volcanoes onto the surface (extrusive igneous rock).

Basalt is an igneous rock.

METAMORPHIC ROCK
When igneous or sedimentary rock is changed by heat and/or pressure, it is called metamorphic rock.

Gneiss is a metamorphic rock.

IGNEOUS ROCK
When molten magma rising from deep within Earth begins to cool and solidify, it forms igneous rock.

Sandstone is a sedimentary rock.

SEDIMENTARY ROCK
Wind and rainwater deposit rock fragments as sediments in lakes, rivers, sand dunes, and on the sea floor. They are compressed over millions of years into layers of sedimentary rock.

MINERAL HARDNESS
The hardness of a mineral is graded on a scale of 1 to 10, devised by German mineralogist Friedrich Mohs (1773–1839).

MOHS' SCALE

1: TALC   2: GYPSUM   3: CALCITE   4: FLUORITE

MINERALS

A mineral is a non-living substance occurring naturally in Earth's crust. Most minerals are formed from silicates (compounds of oxygen and silicon).

Granite is composed of the minerals quartz, feldspar, and mica.

ROCK-FORMING MINERALS

Different combinations of minerals form different types of rock.

Chalcopyrite (copper ore); copper is a good conductor, widely used in the electricity industry.

ORE MINERALS

About 80 types of pure metal are extracted from ore minerals.

THE ROCK CYCLE

All rocks are constantly passing through a recycling process.

Mineral particles sink to the sea floor where they are compacted into sedimentary rock

Igneous rocks are weathered away and washed into the ocean

Rock may melt and rise to the surface where it cools to form igneous rock

Heat from molten rock changes surrounding sedimentary and igneous rock into metamorphic rock

5: APATITE

6: ORTHOCLASE

7: QUARTZ

8: TOPAZ

9: CORUNDUM

10: DIAMOND

CRYSTALS AND GEMSTONES

A CRYSTAL IS a solid material in which atoms are arranged in a regular pattern. Crystals form, or crystallize, either from molten minerals or from minerals that are dissolved in liquids.

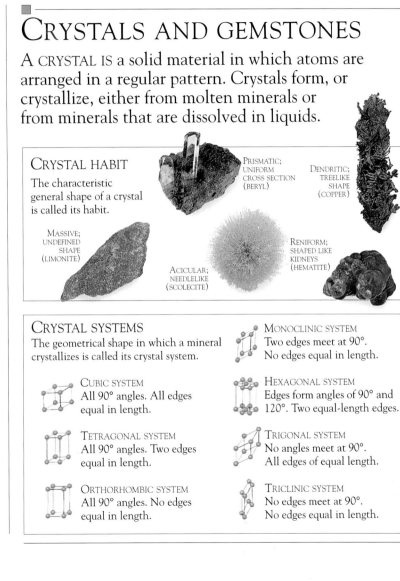

CRYSTAL HABIT

The characteristic general shape of a crystal is called its habit.

PRISMATIC; UNIFORM CROSS SECTION (BERYL)

DENDRITIC; TREELIKE SHAPE (COPPER)

MASSIVE; UNDEFINED SHAPE (LIMONITE)

RENIFORM; SHAPED LIKE KIDNEYS (HEMATITE)

ACICULAR; NEEDLELIKE (SCOLECITE)

CRYSTAL SYSTEMS

The geometrical shape in which a mineral crystallizes is called its crystal system.

CUBIC SYSTEM
All 90° angles. All edges equal in length.

TETRAGONAL SYSTEM
All 90° angles. Two edges equal in length.

ORTHORHOMBIC SYSTEM
All 90° angles. No edges equal in length.

MONOCLINIC SYSTEM
Two edges meet at 90°. No edges equal in length.

HEXAGONAL SYSTEM
Edges form angles of 90° and 120°. Two equal-length edges.

TRIGONAL SYSTEM
No angles meet at 90°. All edges of equal length.

TRICLINIC SYSTEM
No edges meet at 90°. No edges equal in length.

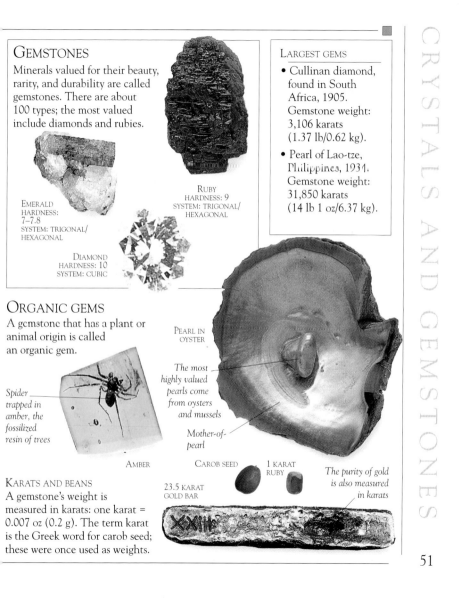

GEMSTONES

Minerals valued for their beauty, rarity, and durability are called gemstones. There are about 100 types; the most valued include diamonds and rubies.

EMERALD
HARDNESS:
7–7.8
SYSTEM: TRIGONAL/
HEXAGONAL

RUBY
HARDNESS: 9
SYSTEM: TRIGONAL/
HEXAGONAL

DIAMOND
HARDNESS: 10
SYSTEM: CUBIC

LARGEST GEMS

- Cullinan diamond, found in South Africa, 1905. Gemstone weight: 3,106 karats (1.37 lb/0.62 kg).

- Pearl of Lao-tze, Philippines, 1934. Gemstone weight: 31,850 karats (14 lb 1 oz/6.37 kg).

ORGANIC GEMS

A gemstone that has a plant or animal origin is called an organic gem.

Spider trapped in amber, the fossilized resin of trees

AMBER

PEARL IN OYSTER

The most highly valued pearls come from oysters and mussels

Mother-of-pearl

CAROB SEED

1 KARAT RUBY

23.5 KARAT GOLD BAR

The purity of gold is also measured in karats

KARATS AND BEANS

A gemstone's weight is measured in karats: one karat = 0.007 oz (0.2 g). The term karat is the Greek word for carob seed; these were once used as weights.

51

OCEANS

MORE THAN TWO-THIRDS of Earth's surface lies under its oceans. The water in these oceans is never still; it is constant motion from currents, tides, and waves.

Warm current (red arrow)

Cold current (blue arrow)

1 Volcanic gases form Earth's early atmosphere.

OCEAN CURRENTS
Major currents circulate the oceans in a clockwise direction in the northern hemisphere and counterclockwise in the southern hemisphere. Currents may be warm or cold, flowing across the surface of the ocean or deep beneath it.

2 Atmospheric water vapor falls as rain and collects in vast hollows.

3 Earth cools, eruptions reduce, and sea level stabilizes.

FEATURES OF THE OCEAN FLOOR

Island arc

Deep-sea trenches are about 60 miles (100 km) wide and may be thousands of miles long

Guyot (flat-topped seamount)

Escaping magma forms midocean ridge

ISLAND ARC
Molten rock from a melting, subducted oceanic plate rises through the upper plate, forming volcanic islands.

TRENCH
Where the ocean floor sinks into the mantle, long, deep trenches occur.

WAVES

Wind blowing over the surface of the ocean causes waves. The height and power of waves depend on the strength of the wind.

Particles near the surface turn over and over

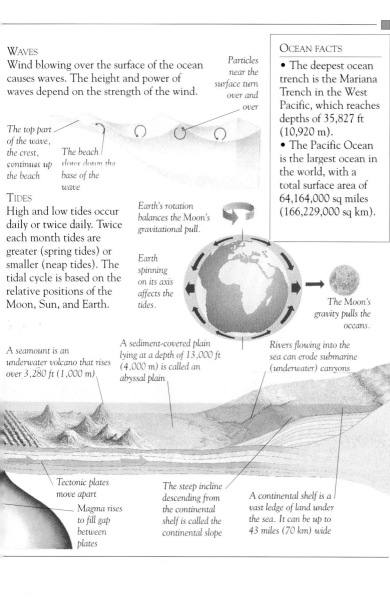

The top part of the wave, the crest, continues up the beach

The beach slows down the base of the wave

TIDES

High and low tides occur daily or twice daily. Twice each month tides are greater (spring tides) or smaller (neap tides). The tidal cycle is based on the relative positions of the Moon, Sun, and Earth.

Earth's rotation balances the Moon's gravitational pull.

Earth spinning on its axis affects the tides.

The Moon's gravity pulls the oceans.

OCEAN FACTS

• The deepest ocean trench is the Mariana Trench in the West Pacific, which reaches depths of 35,827 ft (10,920 m).
• The Pacific Ocean is the largest ocean in the world, with a total surface area of 64,164,000 sq miles (166,229,000 sq km).

A seamount is an underwater volcano that rises over 3,280 ft (1,000 m)

A sediment-covered plain lying at a depth of 13,000 ft (4,000 m) is called an abyssal plain

Rivers flowing into the sea can erode submarine (underwater) canyons

Tectonic plates move apart

Magma rises to fill gap between plates

The steep incline descending from the continental shelf is called the continental slope

A continental shelf is a vast ledge of land under the sea. It can be up to 43 miles (70 km) wide

OCEANS

MOUNTAINS AND VALLEYS

WHEN EARTH'S rocky tectonic plates collide, the crust may buckle and fold, forcing up lofty mountain peaks. Volcanoes also erupt at plate boundaries and sometimes build into mountains. All are slowly weathered away, as erosion wears down peaks, carves out valleys, and opens up underground caves.

LIFE OF A MOUNTAIN

1 YOUNG
High-peaked mountains that formed in the last few million years.

2 MATURE
Eroded mountains created several hundred million years ago.

3 ANCIENT
Mountains so old and worn down that only a few hills remain.

TYPES OF MOUNTAINS

FOLD MOUNTAIN
Where two of Earth's plates collide, the rock

layers buckle and bend, forcing the rocky crust up into a mountain range.

FAULT-BLOCK MOUNTAIN
When Earth's plates push

together, faults or cracks appear in the crust, forcing up huge blocks of rock.

VOLCANO
Layers of volcanic lava, ash, and rock

ejected from Earth's interior build up into a mountain.

DOME MOUNTAIN
Rising magma makes the rock above bulge upward, creating a dome-shaped mountain.

HOW A RIVER VALLEY FORMS

High up in the mountains, fast-flowing streams create steep-sided, V-shaped gullies. In the middle part of the valley, the water meanders (winds) across a broad valley. Near the sea, the river flows across a flat plain or fans out into a delta.

Rainfall runs down gullies

V-shape of a river valley's upper course

River curves back and forth in a series of meanders

Cut-off meander forms oxbow lake

Flat land slows water flow

MOUNTAIN FACTS

• The world's highest mountain is Mount Everest in the Himalayas, Nepal, reaching a height of 29,028 ft (8,848 m) at its peak.

Fan-shaped delta at river mouth

River sheds sediments on flat floodplain

Broad shape of valley at river mouth

HOW CAVES FORM

Limestone caves are formed when carbonic acid in rainwater seeps into cracks in limestone and dissolves the rock. Sea caves are created by the pressure of waves or the corrosive effect of salt on the foot of cliffs. Ice caves are carved out by a stream of meltwater running beneath a glacier (see pp. 56–57).

Stream plunging undergound at a sinkhole

Stalactites hang down from roof

Water seeps into cracks in rocks

Stalagmites grow upward from the cave floor

CROSS SECTION OF A LIMESTONE CAVE

Columns form where stalactites and stalagmites join

ICE AND GLACIERS

MORE THAN ONE-TENTH of Earth's surface is permanently covered with ice. At the Poles and in high mountain regions, vast areas are covered by ice sheets and rivers of ice called glaciers.

Ridge, or *arête*, between two glaciers

Cirque, or *corrie*, a hollow where glacier begins

Compacted "firn" ice

When ice moves over a sharp incline, it cracks to form crevasses

Snout or front of glacier

Melting ice flows from the snout

Pile of rocks and boulders called terminal moraine

FEATURES OF A GLACIER

Snow collects in a high mountain hollow called a cirque and compacts into "firn" ice. The firn flows slowly downhill, its hard ice and sediment scouring the surrounding rock along the way.

ICE MOVEMENT
Warm-based glaciers move mainly by basal slip, where the melting base causes the whole glacier to move. Cold-based glaciers move mainly by internal deformation, where a glacier slips and its surface flows faster than its base.

Warm base (about 32°F, 0°C)

Cold base (below 32°F, 0°C)

Direction of movement

Basal ice melts

Layers of ice slide over each other

BASAL SLIP

INTERNAL DEFORMATION

ICEBERGS

Fragments of ice that float out to sea after breaking off ice sheets, ice caps, and glaciers are called icebergs. This process is called calving. Only 12 percent of an iceberg is visible above the sea's surface.

FORMATION OF AN ICEBERG

Tidal movement and buffeting by waves breaks off iceberg

An iceberg's movement is controlled by ocean currents and the wind

PLEISTOCENE EPOCH – THE LAST ICE AGE

EXTENT OF ICE IN THE WORLD TODAY

ICE AGES

In Earth's history, there have been many ice ages interspersed with warmer periods called interglacials. During the most recent ice age, about 30,000 years ago, ice covered much of North America and Europe.

GLACIAL DEPOSITION

The ice in a glacier is choked with rocky debris. When the ice melts, it leaves behind piles of debris (moraine), which form small mounds or hummocks.

Horn peak

Cirque with tarn

Arête

Hanging valley

Striations

U-shaped valley

Lake chains jammed with moraine

ICE AND GLACIERS

57

LAKES AND RIVERS

WHEN RAINWATER falls on the land, it may seep into the ground, collect in lakes, or form rivers running down to the ocean. Rivers gradually mold the land, as they wear down material in some places, and re-deposit it in others.

Water vapor from plants released into atmosphere

Rain and snow fall on high ground

Wind

Water evaporates from oceans and lakes to form clouds of vapor

River flows into ocean

Water seeps underground and flows to sea

THE WATER CYCLE

The Sun's heat causes water to evaporate from oceans, lakes, and rivers. As it rises into the atmosphere, the water vapor cools and condenses into clouds. Eventually the droplets fall back to Earth as rain.

TYPES OF LAKES

Water fills depressions or hollows

Hollow eroded by glacier forms lake

Rainwater collects in crater

KETTLE LAKE
Melting ice blocks from glaciers fill depressions in rocky glacial debris to form kettle lakes.

TARN
Circular mountain lake that forms in hollows worn by glacial erosion or blocked by ice debris.

VOLCANIC LAKE
Ancient volcanic craters fill with water, producing lakes such as Crater Lake, Oregon.

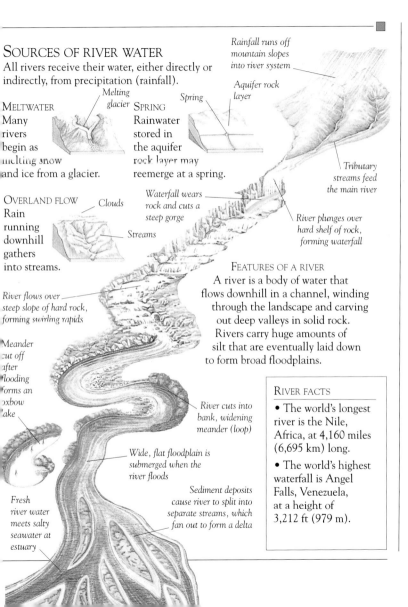

SOURCES OF RIVER WATER

All rivers receive their water, either directly or indirectly, from precipitation (rainfall).

Rainfall runs off mountain slopes into river system

MELTWATER
Many rivers begin as melting snow and ice from a glacier.

Melting glacier

Aquifer rock layer

SPRING
Rainwater stored in the aquifer rock layer may reemerge at a spring.

Spring

Tributary streams feed the main river

OVERLAND FLOW
Rain running downhill gathers into streams.

Clouds

Streams

Waterfall wears rock and cuts a steep gorge

River plunges over hard shelf of rock, forming waterfall

River flows over steep slope of hard rock, forming swirling rapids

FEATURES OF A RIVER

A river is a body of water that flows downhill in a channel, winding through the landscape and carving out deep valleys in solid rock. Rivers carry huge amounts of silt that are eventually laid down to form broad floodplains.

Meander cut off after flooding forms an oxbow lake

River cuts into bank, widening meander (loop)

Wide, flat floodplain is submerged when the river floods

Fresh river water meets salty seawater at estuary

Sediment deposits cause river to split into separate streams, which fan out to form a delta

---

RIVER FACTS

• The world's longest river is the Nile, Africa, at 4,160 miles (6,695 km) long.

• The world's highest waterfall is Angel Falls, Venezuela, at a height of 3,212 ft (979 m).

WEATHER

THE CONSTANT motion of the lower layers of the atmosphere means that air conditions are always changing, creating weather variations such as wind and rain, snow, frost, fog, and sunshine.

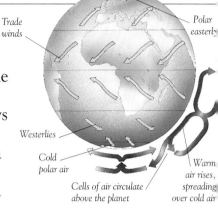

Trade winds

Polar easterly

Westerlies

Cold polar air

Warm air rises, spreading over cold air

Cells of air circulate above the planet

FORMATION OF CLOUDS
Clouds form when water vapor in warm air rises, cools, and condenses.

Warm air containing water vapor rises.

Water vapor cools and condenses, forming clouds.

Cloud continues to form as long as warm, moist air rises.

THE WORLD'S WINDS
Wind is simply air moving from areas of high pressure to areas of low pressure.
Three bands of prevailing (persistent) winds are found around the world – dry trade winds, warm westerlies, and cold polar easterlies.

AIR MASSES AND FRONTS
Huge bodies of air that form over continents and oceans are called air masses. They can be warm, cold, moist, or dry depending on where they form. A front is the boundary between two air masses.

Warm, moist air mass rises above cold air mass

Thin cloud

Thick rain clouds

Rain at base of front

WARM FRONT

Dense, high clouds

Cold air moves over warmer air along Earth's surface

Shallow gradient

Steep gradient

Heavy rain

COLD FRONT

TYPES OF CLOUDS

Clouds are classified according to their shape and their height above the ground.

Freezing level

Cumulonimbus – giant, dark, anvil-headed thundercloud – forms at 49,000 ft (15,000 m)

Stratocumulus – white or gray lumpy cloud at top of cumulus – forms at 0–6,500 ft (0–2,000 m)

Nimbostratus – thick, gray rain cloud – forms at 0–6,500 ft (0–2,000 m)

Stratus – low-level, flat, gray sheet of misty cloud – forms at 0–6,500 ft (0–2,000 m)

Cirrus – wisps of cloud made of ice crystals – forms at 16,000–42,000 ft (5,000–13,000 m)

Cirrocumulus – rippled ice crystal cloud like fish scales – forms at 16,000–42,000 ft (5,000–13,000 m)

Altocumulus – fluffy cloud – forms at 6,500–23,000 ft (2,000–7,000 m)

Altostratus – gray or white sheet of cloud – forms at 6,500–23,000 ft (2,000–7,000 m)

Cumulus – large, white, fluffy cloud – forms at 0–6,500 ft (0–2,000 m)

TYPES OF RAIN

Most of the world's rain comes from water droplets freezing into icy particles high in a cloud. The particles grow into snowflakes, turning to raindrops as they fall. In the tropics, small raindrops join up to make bigger drops heavy enough to fall as rain.

Drops smaller than 0.2 in (5 mm) fall as drizzle

Larger raindrops

Rising air

Water droplets freeze into ice crystals

Some rain falls without freezing

Snowflakes melt inside cloud or on their way to ground

Sleet

TROPICAL RAIN

MELTED SNOW

CLIMATES AND ECOSYSTEMS

THE TYPICAL LONG-TERM weather conditions of an area are referred to as its climate. A region's climate varies according to its distance from the Equator and the ocean, and its height above sea level. The interacting range of plants and animals within a climate is called an ecosystem.

MAP OF WORLD CLIMATE ZONES

TYPES OF CLIMATE
The world's climates are split into three broad zones: tropical, temperate, and polar. The farther from the Equator and above sea level a zone lies, the colder the climate. The greater distance from an ocean, the more extreme its winters and summers.

KEY TO CLIMATE ZONES
- Polar
- Taiga
- Mountain
- Temperate
- Tropical rain forest
- Hot desert

HOT DESERT
Few species can survive in desert climates. Temperatures can exceed 100°F (38°C) and it may not rain for several years.

TROPICAL RAIN FOREST
Heavy rain and high temperatures all year round make rain forests the world's richest plant and animal habitats.

POLAR AND TUNDRA

In the polar regions, temperatures rarely rise above freezing for more than a few months of the year. Fresh water is permanently frozen, and plants cannot grow. The cold, dry land bordering the ice caps is known as the tundra.

TAIGA (COLD TEMPERATE)

The vast coniferous forest called the Taiga stretches across Canada, Scandinavia, and the former Soviet Union. Four to six months of the year are dark, with the temperature falling well below 32°F (0°C).

TEMPERATE

Winters are cool and summers warm in temperate climates, with many plants and trees becoming dormant in winter.

MOUNTAIN REGIONS

Low temperatures prevent vegetation growing on mountain peaks; trees and plants thrive on the lower slopes.

ECOLOGY AND FOOD WEBS

THE LIVING WORLD is built on complex relationships between plants, animals, and the places they inhabit. Ecology is the study of these relationships and how communities of living things interact with their habitats.

Biosphere

All parts of Earth that are inhabited by living things

Succession stops, resultin in a woodland clima communit

Biome

Ecosystem

Community

Population

Individual

LIFE LAYERS
Individual plants and animals live together in communities, which are in turn part of an ecosystem. Groups of ecosystems make up biomes, which form Earth's living layer, or biosphere.

New species begin to establish themselves

SUCCESSION
The first species to colonize an area of land are gradually replaced or succeeded as different species establish themselves. Finally, succession stops and a stable habitat, called a climax community, develops.

Th first plan and animals mo into the habit

OOD WEBS

ome organisms within an ecosystem may feed off
ach other. In a salt marsh, for example, shrews feed
n snails and marsh hawks feed on shrews. This series
f feeding links is called a food chain. Each species is
nvolved in a number of chains, and these chains link
p to form interconnecting food webs.

FOOD WEBS LINKING ANIMALS
LIVING IN OPEN WOODLAND

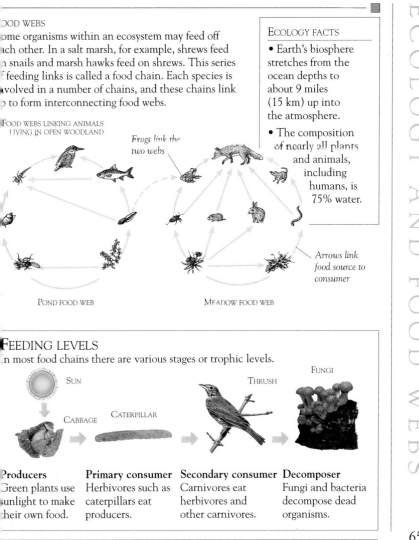

Frogs link the two webs

Arrows link food source to consumer

POND FOOD WEB   MEADOW FOOD WEB

FEEDING LEVELS

In most food chains there are various stages or trophic levels.

SUN   CABBAGE   CATERPILLAR   THRUSH   FUNGI

Producers
Green plants use
sunlight to make
their own food.

Primary consumer
Herbivores such as
caterpillars eat
producers.

Secondary consumer
Carnivores eat
herbivores and
other carnivores.

Decomposer
Fungi and bacteria
decompose dead
organisms.

ECOLOGY AND FOOD WEBS

THE LIVING WORLD

EVOLUTION

SINCE LIFE appeared 3.8 billion years ago, millions of different creatures have come and gone. As habitats changed, some species survived by adapting, while others died out quickly. This gradual turnover of species is called evolution.

PORPOISE
FRONT
FLIPPER

"Finger" bones form powerful flipper for swimming

Two sets of short "arm" bones

Two sets of long bones make up the arm

Five sets of finger bones make up hand

HUMAN
ARM

ADAPTATION
Evolution works by slowly adapting existing features to suit different purposes. Although they look very different, humans and porpoises both have two "arm" bones and five "finger" bones.

LIFE-FORMS
THROUGH THE AGES
By working out when certain rocks formed, and then studying the fossils found in them, paleontologists – who study the life-forms of the past – have built up a remarkable picture of the way species have changed since the dawn of the Cambrian period 590 million years ago. Little is known of Precambrian life forms because very few fossils remain.

PRECAMBRIAN	PALEOZOIC	
	Cambrian	Ordovician

4600–590 mya
Single-celled life-forms such as bacteria and algae appear, then soft multi-celled life-forms, like worms and jellyfish.

590–505 mya
No life on land. Invertebrates flourish in the seas. First mollusks and trilobites.

505–438 mya
First crustaceans and early jawless fish appear. Coral reefs form. Sahara glaciated

HOW EVOLUTION WORKS

According to Darwin's theory of evolution, animals and plants developed over millions of years, surviving according to their ability to adapt to a changing environment. Until the mid-19th-century, people believed that life-forms did not change since their creation by an omnipotent deity.

CHARLES DARWIN (1809–1882)

The theory of evolution was developed by English naturalist Charles Darwin after studying the animals of the Galápagos Islands. He published his findings in 1859 in his book *On the Origin of Species.*

EVOLUTION OF THE HORSE

Eohippus
This hare-sized creature browsed in woodlands.

Mesohippus
Over millions of years, Eohippus evolved into a larger grazing animal.

Merychippus
As early horses adapted to the grasslands, they developed longer limbs to escape from predators.

Modern horse
The horses of today are highly developed grazers; they have long legs for running and sharp senses.

Silurian	Devonian	Carboniferous	Permian
438–408 mya First jawed fish. Huge sea scorpions hunt in the sea. Small land plants colonize the shore.	408–355 mya Age of sharks and fish. Insects and amphibians appear on land. Giant ferns form forests.	355–290 mya Warm swampy forests leave remains that will turn to coal. First reptiles.	290–250 mya Reptiles diversify, conifers replace tree ferns. Mass extinction as Earth turns cold.

FOSSILS

THE REMAINS of living things
preserved naturally, often for many
millions of years, are called fossils.
Most fossils are formed in rocks;
however, remains can also be
preserved in ice, tar, peat, and
amber. Fossils tell us nearly all
we know about the history of
life on Earth.

Spider
trapped
inside resin

SPIDER IN AMBER
Amber is fossilized tree
resin that may also
preserve trapped insects

AMMONITES
BECAME
EXTINCT 65 MYA

KINDS OF FOSSILS

Most fossils form on the seabed, so shells and
sea creatures are the most common. Fossils of
land animals and plants are rarer. Footprints,
burrows, or droppings may also be preserved.

Fossilized
shell

MESOZOIC			CENOZOIC	
Triassic	Jurassic	Cretaceous	Tertiary	
			Palaeocene	Eocene
250–205 mya Mammals and dinosaurs appear. The climate warms and seed-bearing plants dominate.	205–135 mya The age of the dinosaurs. The first known bird, Archaeopteryx, appears.	135–66 mya First flowering plants. Period ends with a mass extinction that wipes out dinosaurs.	66–53 mya Warm, humid climate. Mammals, insects, and flowering plants flourish.	53–36 mya Mammals grow larger and diversify Primates evolve.

1 ANIMAL DIES
The body of a dead animal lies decaying on the surface of the land.

2 REMAINS SINK
Gradually, the body becomes covered with sand or mud.

FOSSILIZATION AT SEA
Dead organisms sink to the seabed and are buried. As the sediment turns to rock, their remains are either chemically altered or dissolve to leave a cavity, which may fill with minerals to form a cast.

3 BONES ALTER
Over time, the bones are altered, and the sand and mud turn to rock.

4 FOSSIL IS EXPOSED
Eventually, weather and erosion expose the fossil at the surface.

Oligocene	Miocene	Pliocene	Quaternary	
			Pleistocene	Holocene

| 36–23 mya First humanlike creatures appear. Hunting birds thrive. Some mammals die out. | 23–6.3 mya Climate cools, and forests shrink. Deerlike hoofed mammals flourish. First hominids. | 6.3–1.6 mya Cold and dry. Mammals reach maximum diversity. Many modern mammals appear. | 1.6m–10,000 ya Ice Ages. Homo sapiens evolves. Mammoths and saber-toothed tigers die out. | 10,000 ya to present Humans develop agriculture and technology. Human activity threatens many species. |

71

DINOSAURS

FOR 150 MILLION YEARS,
Earth was dominated by giant
reptiles called dinosaurs, including
Seismosaurus, the largest creature
ever to walk on land. Then,
65 million years ago, all the
dinosaurs mysteriously died out.

Light bones for flying *Wings of skin*

Furry body

PTEROSAUR
While dinosaurs ruled the
land, giant reptiles, like
Pterosaur, flew
in the air.

DINOSAUR GROUPS
Scientists divide dinosaurs into two orders according
to the arrangement of their hipbones. Saurischians
have lizardlike hips and include both plant and
meateaters. Ornithischians have
bird-like hips and are all plant
eaters. The two orders are
divided into five subgroups.

*Muscul
tail balanc
the front
the bo*

*Long neck
for browsing
in treetops* *Ruff*

SALTASAURUS

Horn

STYRACOSAURUS

*Sauropods (Saurischians) were huge,
long-necked four-legged planteaters.*

*Marginocephalians (Saurischians) had
a bony ruff and horns for self-defense.*

STEGOSAURUS

TYRANNOSAURUS

CORYTHOSAU

*Thyreophorans (Ornithischians)
were spiny-backed planteaters.*

*Theropods (Saurischians) were
two-legged meateaters.*

*Ornithopods (Ornithischians)
had a horny beak and birdlike f*

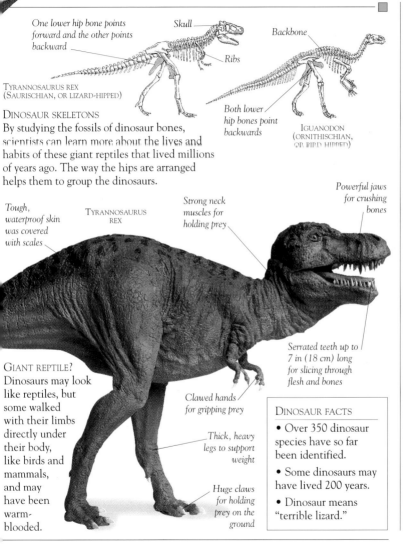

One lower hip bone points forward and the other points backward

Skull

Backbone

Ribs

TYRANNOSAURUS REX
(SAURISCHIAN, OR LIZARD-HIPPED)

Both lower hip bones point backwards

IGUANODON
(ORNITHISCHIAN, OR BIRD-HIPPED)

DINOSAUR SKELETONS

By studying the fossils of dinosaur bones, scientists can learn more about the lives and habits of these giant reptiles that lived millions of years ago. The way the hips are arranged helps them to group the dinosaurs.

Tough, waterproof skin was covered with scales

TYRANNOSAURUS REX

Strong neck muscles for holding prey

Powerful jaws for crushing bones

Serrated teeth up to 7 in (18 cm) long for slicing through flesh and bones

Clawed hands for gripping prey

GIANT REPTILE?

Dinosaurs may look like reptiles, but some walked with their limbs directly under their body, like birds and mammals, and may have been warm-blooded.

Thick, heavy legs to support weight

Huge claws for holding prey on the ground

DINOSAUR FACTS

• Over 350 dinosaur species have so far been identified.

• Some dinosaurs may have lived 200 years.

• Dinosaur means "terrible lizard."

73

CLASSIFICATION OF LIFE

THE NATURAL WORLD contains millions of living things, which can be classified according to the features they have in common. The largest groups are the five kingdoms: animals, plants, fungi, protists, and monerans.

ALGAE

PROTOZOA

MONERANS
These simple single-celled organisms, such as bacteria, are visible only under a microscope. They were the first life forms and there are now around 4,000 species.

BACTERIA

PROTISTS
Complex single-celled organisms, such as protozoa and amoebas, are called protists. Protozoa are like animals. Algae are like plants. There are over 50,000 protist species.

THE PANTHER

COMMON OYSTER MUSHROOM

MEADOW CORAL FUNGUS

CURLY-HAIRED ELF CUP

FUNGI
Fungi often look like plants but have no leaves and absorb food from other living or dead matter. There are about 100,000 species.

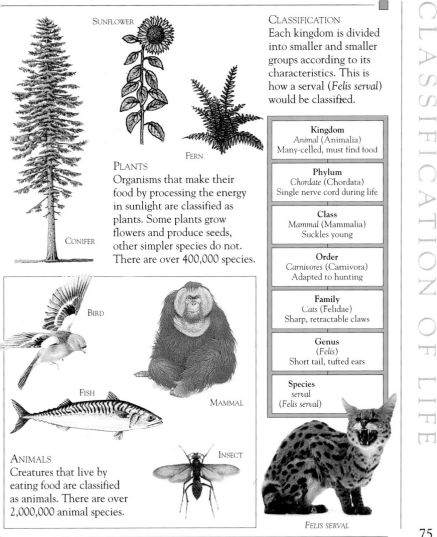

SUNFLOWER

FERN

PLANTS

Organisms that make their food by processing the energy in sunlight are classified as plants. Some plants grow flowers and produce seeds, other simpler species do not. There are over 400,000 species.

CONIFER

BIRD

FISH

MAMMAL

INSECT

ANIMALS

Creatures that live by eating food are classified as animals. There are over 2,000,000 animal species.

CLASSIFICATION

Each kingdom is divided into smaller and smaller groups according to its characteristics. This is how a serval (*Felis serval*) would be classified.

Kingdom
Animal (Animalia)
Many-celled, must find food

Phylum
Chordate (Chordata)
Single nerve cord during life

Class
Mammal (Mammalia)
Suckles young

Order
Carnivores (Carnivora)
Adapted to hunting

Family
Cats (Felidae)
Sharp, retractable claws

Genus
(*Felis*)
Short tail, tufted ears

Species
serval
(*Felis serval*)

FELIS SERVAL

CELLS

ALL LIVING THINGS are made up of tiny, self-contained units called cells, usually so small that they are visible only under a microscope. A cell takes in energy and uses it to grow and reproduce. Some organisms consist of just a single cell, others have billions.

EGG CELL
Cells vary in size from minute fractions of an inch to eggs, which are the largest cells of all.

ANIMAL CELL
An animal cell is a tiny jelly-filled sac with a soft and flexible skin or membrane. Different kinds of cells, such as blood cells and skin cells, perform different tasks in the body. Inside each, there are organelles that control and run the cell.

Vacuoles are used to store fats

The nucleus is the control center of the cell, and contains the cell's instructions in the form of DNA

Endoplasmic reticulum is the cell's warehouse and factory, making and storing vital substances

Mitochondria are organelles that act like the cell's power stations, breaking down food to release energy

Ribosomes are tiny granules scattered through the cell that make proteins

The cytoplasm is the jellylike fluid that fills the cell

The Golgi body is the cell's distribution center, packaging and transporting chemicals made in the cell

Plasma membrane holds cell together and filters materials passing in and out

PLANT CELL

The features of a plant cell are very similar to those of an animal cell, but plant cells are enclosed in a rigid shell of cellulose. They also have organelles called chloroplasts, made bright green by a pigment called chlorophyll. Chloroplasts are like solar batteries, enabling plants to trap energy from the sun in a process called photosynthesis.

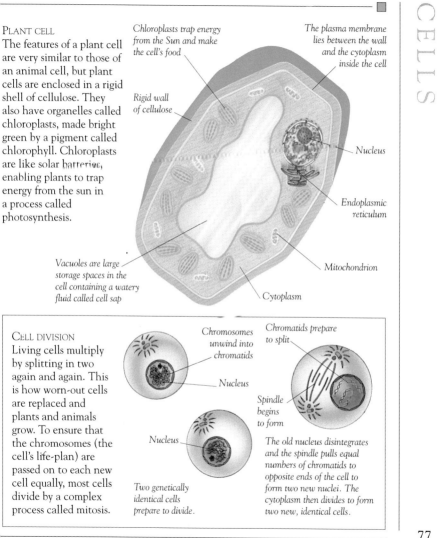

Chloroplasts trap energy from the Sun and make the cell's food

The plasma membrane lies between the wall and the cytoplasm inside the cell

Rigid wall of cellulose

Nucleus

Endoplasmic reticulum

Mitochondrion

Vacuoles are large storage spaces in the cell containing a watery fluid called cell sap

Cytoplasm

CELL DIVISION

Living cells multiply by splitting in two again and again. This is how worn-out cells are replaced and plants and animals grow. To ensure that the chromosomes (the cell's life-plan) are passed on to each new cell equally, most cells divide by a complex process called mitosis.

Chromosomes unwind into chromatids

Nucleus

Nucleus

Two genetically identical cells prepare to divide.

Chromatids prepare to split

Spindle begins to form

The old nucleus disintegrates and the spindle pulls equal numbers of chromatids to opposite ends of the cell to form two new nuclei. The cytoplasm then divides to form two new, identical cells.

MICROORGANISMS

THE MOST NUMEROUS living things
in the world are usually too small
to see except under a microscope.
These microorganisms, including
bacteria and protozoa, are
everywhere – there are 100 trillion
in your body alone. All are made
of just a single cell.

*A tough,
slimy capsule
protects the
cell wall*

*Long, hairlike
flagella on some
bacteria whip
from side to
side to move
the cell along*

Cell wall

BACTERIA
The most abundant
living things on Earth,
and among the most
ancient, bacteria live
everywhere from the
upper atmosphere
to the ocean depths.
Many feed on dead
matter and help to
recycle nutrients.
Others, called germs,
feed on living things and
cause disease. Bacteria
cells are prokaryotic,
which means they have
no nucleus.

*Ribosome
for making
protein*

*Tiny hairlike
pili attach the
cell to food or
other cells*

*Folded
plasma
membrane*

*A free-floating
nucleoid region
contains the
bacteria's instructions*

COCCUS

BACILLUS

SPIRILLUM

BACTERIA SHAPES
Bacteria may be classified
by shape – coccus (round),
bacillus (rod-shaped), or
spirillum (coiled).

PROTOZOA

Like bacteria, protozoa are single-celled organisms, but they have a nucleus and grow much bigger. They live in damp habitats, like soil, ponds, and oceans. Amoebas are protozoans with no fixed shape. They move by changing shape, and feed by engulfing food. Some live in water and soil. Others are parasites living inside plants and animals.

Nucleus

Cytoplasm

Pseudopods are lobes that flow out to move the amoeba along or engulf food

Food

AMOEBA

Food vacuole digests food

Contractile vacuole pumps out water

VIRUSES

A virus is a tiny package of chemicals coated with protein. It is not a living organism – it relies on invading living hosts to reproduce itself.

INFLUENZA VIRUSES
SEEN THROUGH AN
ELECTRON MICROSCOPE

USEFUL BACTERIA

Bacteria play a vital role in breaking down dead matter and recycling nutrients, helping us digest food. Bacteria are important in the production of many foods such as cheese, yogurt, vinegar, and beer.

YOGURT

CHEESE

VINEGAR

MICROORGANISM FACTS

• One gram of soil may contain 150,000 protozoa.

• There may be 2000 bacteria per square inch of human armpit.

• The largest protozoa (now extinct) grew to 7.9 in (20 cm) across.

• Viruses are visible only under an electron microscope.

FUNGI AND LICHENS

MUSHROOMS, toadstools, mildew, and mold are all kinds of fungi. Like plants, fungi often grow in soil, but they cannot make food from sunlight. Instead they absorb chemicals from living and dead plants and animals, manure, and other organic material.

FUNGUS VARIETY
There are fungi of all shapes and sizes. Some are good to eat, but many are so poisonous they can kill.

FUNGUS STRUCTURE
The stalk and head of the toadstool are the fungi's "fruiting body," which releases tiny, seed-like spores. Wherever these spores land, they send out new hyphae (threads).

Mature sporophore produces spores

Sporophore grows above ground

Cap releases spores

Spore germinates; mycelium develops

FUNGAL BONDING
Fungi begin to reproduce when one mass of underground threads meets another of the same species. They bond and produce a fruiting body (sporophore) that usually grows above ground and makes spores.

Sporophore forms

Cap

Stem ring

Spores form in gills

Stalk holds cap high enough for the spores to be released into the air

Hyphae form mycelium (main body), which absorbs nutrients and anchors sporophore (fruiting body)

FRUITING BODY AND MYCELIUM OF FLY AGARIC

BRACKET FUNGI
Instead of growing in soil,
some fungi grow in tiers
on dead or dying trees
and logs. Knowing
which types of wood
attract which types of
fungus makes it easier
to identify different
fungus species.

*Fruiting bodies
grow in tiers on
dead wood*

LICHENS

STRUCTURE

Lichens are a
partnership between
fungi and algae, a little
like a sandwich, with
fungal bread and algal
filling. The green algae
trap sunlight to make
food to feed the fungi,
which in turn
protect the algae
and retain water.

*Lichens attach
themselves to stones
or wood. They
eventually break
down rocks and help
to form soil.*

FOLIOSE
(*Hypogymnia physodes*)

*The many species
of lichens grow in five
distinct ways. Three
are shown here.*

FRUTICOSE (*Cladonia portentosa*)

SQUAMULOSE
(*Cladonia floerkeana*)

PLANTS

PLANTS make their own food out of water, air, and sunlight. This makes them the starting point of most food chains, and most other living organisms depend on them for food. Plants have adapted to the most extreme habitats, from hot desert to icy tundra.

Seeds ripen

Seed germinates — leaves and root grow

Seed

Ova is pollinated

Plant grows

SEXUAL REPRODUCTION
Many plants reproduce by ova being fertilized by pollen, whether from the same flower or plant or a different one. This is sexual reproduction.

ASEXUAL REPRODUCTION
Many plants can reproduce without pollination or fertilization taking place. This is called asexual reproduction.

Parent plant

Runner

New plant develop from tip of underground runner

STRAWBERRY PLANT

TYPES OF PLANTS
The earliest plants on Earth did not have flowers or produce seeds. Simple plants like this still exist, but now they share Earth with their flowering relatives. Plants come in all shapes and sizes, from tiny algae to grasses and giant trees.

NON-FLOWERING PLANTS

ALGAE   SEAWEED   MOSSES AND LIVERWORTS   FERNS

FLOWERING PLANTS

GRASSES   SHRUBS   HERBS   TREES

CO₂ enters via tiny holes called stomata

Sunlight is absorbed

Water enters leaf via stalk

Oxygen is given off

Flowers carry reproductive parts

Flower bud

Sepal

Leaf

Petal

PHOTOSYNTHESIS

A green pigment in the leaves called chlorophyll uses energy from the Sun to combine carbon dioxide (CO_2) from the air with water from the soil. This produces food in the form of sugars and starches, and oxygen is released.

New leaves growing from axil

PLANT STRUCTURE

During its life, a typical flowering plant, such as this hibiscus, grows a stem, roots, shoots, leaves, flowers, and fruits containing seeds.

AMARYLLIS BULB CROSS SECTION

New plant grows from tip

Fleshy scales store food

Midrib

Vein

TUBERS, RHIZOMES, AND BULBS

During the growing season, many plants produce swollen underground tubers, rhizomes, and bulbs to store food in the form of starch for the following growing season.

Roots anchor plant in soil

Stem supports plant and carries water and minerals from roots to leaves

Root hairs absorb water and minerals from soil

83

FLOWERS AND FRUITS

FLOWERS help ensure that a plant is pollinated so that it can produce seeds and fruit. A fruit is anything that contains a seed or seeds, from a coconut to a tomato.

Tough, bumpy surface

POLLEN GRAIN
Microscopic pollen grains, which look like orange dust, are produced by a flower's anthers. A plant is fertilized when a single grain lands on the stigma of the same type of flower.

FLOWER PARTS
The reproductive organs of a flowering plant are found within the flower. The flower heads of some plants have a stamen (male parts) and a pistil (female), while in others they are separate.

Filament

Anther – pollen is made in pollen sacs inside anther, which split open when ripe to release the pollen

Stigma – sticky head for trapping pollen

Style carries pollen from the stigma to the ovary

Stamens – the male parts of the flower that consist of an anther and a filament

Pistil – female parts of the flower consisting of an ovary, stigma, and style

Ovary – where the ova (eggs) are made. Once the ova are fertilized, the ovary swells to become a fruit

Sepal – protects flower when it is in bud

Petal – guides insects to anthers and stigma

Pollen sticks to bee's back as insect looks for nectar

Bright, scented petals attract pollinating insects

Stigma

Style

Ovary

Embryo

Micropyle

Pollen grain

Pollen tube

Ovule

Male nucleus

FERTILIZATION OF THE OVA BY POLLEN

POLLINATION AND FERTILIZATION

When pollen lands on a stigma, probably carried there on the back of an insect, it grows a tube that probes into the style and penetrates the ovule (the egg container) via a hole called the micropyle. Two male sex cells from the pollen ease their way through the tube to fertilize the egg.

FRUIT

Once fertilized, the ovary forms seeds then swells to become fruit. If the seeds are spread by animals, the fruit is soft and juicy. If they are spread by the wind, they are hard and dry.

Each segment forms from a single ovary

Seed

Prickly case protects nuts

Nut is seed

A pea pod is a legume – formed from a single ovary.

Fruit wall

A pea is a seed

PEA POD

Oranges are compound fruits – developed from several ovaries.

Horse chestnuts are nuts – single seeds in a hard, dry case.

Pits are seeds

Core is true fruit

Apples are false fruits – the apple is the swollen base of the flower.

Hard pit is seed

Nectarines are drupes – fleshy fruits containing a hard seed.

85

TREES

TREES ARE WOODY PLANTS, which means they have hard stems and grow for years – often to immense sizes. Leaves can be broad, like oaks and beeches, or narrow, such as pine needles, or palm fronds.

TALLEST TREE
The tallest living tree is a coast redwood in Redwood National Park, California. It soars 365 ft (111.25 m) high, as tall as an Apollo space rocket.

Leaves range from long "needles" like these to short, flat scales.

CONIFERS
Most conifers are evergreen with leaves that last three to four years and often have a dark, waxy skin to help save water.

Most conifers bear their seeds under the scales of hard cones.

Palm trees get their name because leaves are sometimes shaped like a hand

Palm trees are flowering plants

PALM TREES
Palm trees grow mainly in the tropics. They have no branches instead giant multiple leaves grow from a single point, called the apical bud

BROAD-LEAVED TREES

Most broad-leaved trees are deciduous, which means they shed their leaves seasonally to save water.

Many broad-leaved trees can be identified by the shape of their leaves.

Heartwood

Sapwood

One year's growth

Cambium

Waterproof bark

THE TRUNK

The series of rings that can be seen on a sawn log mark each year's growth. The dark center of the tree is dead "heartwood." Around this is paler, living, sapwood with a thin rim, or "cambium," where it grows. Protecting the sapwood is a layer of bark.

Crown

Leaves absorb sunlight and convert it to food

Oak trees produce nuts called "acorns" in autumn

COMMON OAK

All broad-leaved trees are flowering plants and bear flowers and fruits.

Single trunk carries nutrients from roots to leaves

TREE FACTS

• Mangroves are the only trees that can grow in salty water.

• The oldest living trees on Earth are 5,000-year-old bristlecone pines of Arizona.

Intestine

Body shape maintained by fluid

Dorsal blood vessel

Gizzard (part of stomach)

Ovary

Spermatheca (reproductive organ)

Ventral nerve cord

Mouth

EARTHWORM CROSS-SECTION

INVERTEBRATES

NINE-TENTHS of all animals are invertebrates, which means they have no backbone. They include jellyfish, sponges, starfish, coral, worms, crabs, spiders, and insects.

Hard shell to protect soft body

Soft body

Eyes on stalks

MOLLUSKS
These soft-bodied invertebrates are often protected by a hard shell. Most mollusks, such as squid and octopuses, clams, mussels, and scallops, live in water, but some, like snails and slugs, live on land.

WORMS
A worm is an animal with a long soft body and no legs. There are many different kinds, including flatworms, tapeworms, earthworms, roundworms, and leeches.

Echinoderms have a five-part body plan.

Arm

Ossicles ar hard plates ju under the ski that keep th body rig

STARFISH AND URCHINS
Starfish, sea urchins, and sea cucumbers are all echinoderms. All are predators, and most have sucker-tipped "tube feet" through which they pump water to move along and feed. The five broad arms of a starfish can wrench open a shellfish to suck out the contents.

Arm

Underside arm is covere with fluid-fille tube feet fo moving ar feedir

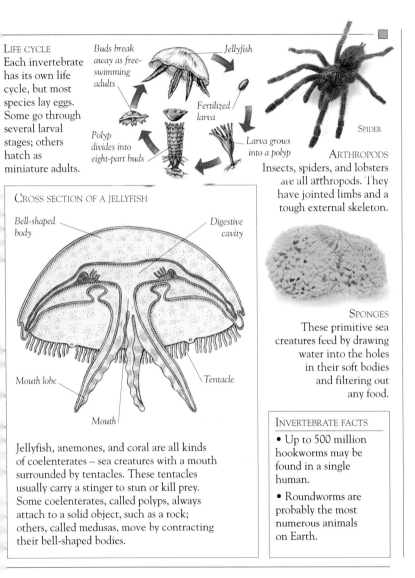

LIFE CYCLE
Each invertebrate has its own life cycle, but most species lay eggs. Some go through several larval stages; others hatch as miniature adults.

Buds break away as free-swimming adults

Jellyfish

Fertilized larva

Polyp divides into eight-part buds

Larva grows into a polyp

SPIDER

ARTHROPODS
Insects, spiders, and lobsters are all arthropods. They have jointed limbs and a tough external skeleton.

CROSS SECTION OF A JELLYFISH

Bell-shaped body

Digestive cavity

Mouth lobe

Tentacle

Mouth

SPONGES
These primitive sea creatures feed by drawing water into the holes in their soft bodies and filtering out any food.

Jellyfish, anemones, and coral are all kinds of coelenterates – sea creatures with a mouth surrounded by tentacles. These tentacles usually carry a stinger to stun or kill prey. Some coelenterates, called polyps, always attach to a solid object, such as a rock; others, called medusas, move by contracting their bell-shaped bodies.

INVERTEBRATE FACTS
• Up to 500 million hookworms may be found in a single human.

• Roundworms are probably the most numerous animals on Earth.

MOLLUSKS

AFTER ARTHROPODS, mollusks are the largest group of animals on Earth. There are over 50,000 species, ranging from tiny snails to giant squid as big as sperm whales. Most mollusks, except slugs, squid, cuttlefish, and octopuses, have soft, moist bodies protected by hard shells.

WHELK

MOLLUSK SHELLS
The shells produced by mollusks are made of layers of calcium carbonate, and form in many shapes, sizes, patterns, and colors.

ROYAL CLOAK SCALLOP

COCKLE SHELLS

PACIFIC THORNY OYSTER

TYPES OF MOLLUSK

GASTROPODS
There are 35,000 species of gastropods, including snails, slugs, and whelks.

CEPHALOPODS
There are 600 species of these complex mollusks including octopus, squid, and cuttlefish.

BIVALVES
There are 8,000 species of these double-shelled mollusks, such as oysters, clams, and cockles.

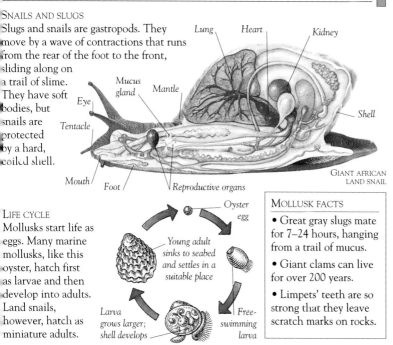

SNAILS AND SLUGS

Slugs and snails are gastropods. They move by a wave of contractions that runs from the rear of the foot to the front, sliding along on a trail of slime. They have soft bodies, but snails are protected by a hard, coiled shell.

Lung Heart Kidney

Mucus gland Mantle

Eye

Tentacle

Shell

Mouth Foot Reproductive organs

GIANT AFRICAN LAND SNAIL

LIFE CYCLE

Mollusks start life as eggs. Many marine mollusks, like this oyster, hatch first as larvae and then develop into adults. Land snails, however, hatch as miniature adults.

Oyster egg

Young adult sinks to seabed and settles in a suitable place

Larva grows larger; shell develops

Free-swimming larva

MOLLUSK FACTS

• Great gray slugs mate for 7–24 hours, hanging from a trail of mucus.

• Giant clams can live for over 200 years.

• Limpets' teeth are so strong that they leave scratch marks on rocks.

TUSK SHELLS
There are 350 species of these rare sea creatures with tusk-shaped shells.

SOLENOGASTERS
There are 5,540 species of these worm-like marine mollusks.

MONOPLACOPHORANS
There are only ten species of these limpets. They live in the depths of the ocean.

CHITONS
There are 500 species of these armor-plated shelled creatures.

MOLLUSKS

91

INSECTS

INSECTS MAY BE TINY, but there are more of them than all other animals put together. Over five million species, from tiny flies to giant beetles, are known, and there may be over 200 million insects for every human. They have existed for over 400 million years and are found everywhere from the Arctic to the Sahara.

WASP'S HEAD

Antenna

Compound eye

COMPOUND EYES
The compound eyes of most insects have six or more facets. Dragonflies have 30,000 facets in each eye, which help to spot movement.

DRAGONFLY

Compound eye

Head

Veins in wing keep it rigid   *Wing*

Thorax (middle section of the body), which bears the legs

Abdomen (rear part of the body)

FEELERS AND HAIRS
Insects use antennae to sense the world in different ways. Most work by smell or touch. Ants, bees, and wasps use their antennae for tasting.

BEETLE ANTENNAE

Branched antennae are supersensitive

INSECT BODY
An insect's body is divided into three parts – head, thorax, and abdomen – and it has six legs. The body is encased in a tough shell, or exoskeleton, made of a substance called chitin. Some insects have two or four wings.

COMPLETE METAMORPHOSIS

Insects such as butterflies, beetles, and flies start life as larvae, which hatch from eggs. The larvae then turn into pupae, from which an adult emerges. This process is known as complete metamorphosis. The larva bears no resemblance to the adult it becomes.

Egg

Caterpillar

Adult butterfly

Chrysalis

WASPS' NEST

Nest of chewed wood

INSECT NESTS

Some insects, such as bees, wasps, termites, and ants, live in ordered societies and build elaborate homes.

INCOMPLETE METAMORPHOSIS

Insects such as grasshoppers or damselflies hatch into wingless "nymphs" before molting and growing into adults. This is known as incomplete metamorphosis.

Winged adult emerges from final molt

Egg

Wingless nymph

Nymph grows and molts

Final nymph resembles adult

INSECT FACTS

• A queen termite lays 440 million eggs – one per second for 14 years.

• A bee must visit more than 4,000 flowers to make one tablespoon of honey.

MOLTING

A young insect's tough exoskeleton cannot stretch. Instead it is discarded and replaced with a new one several times. This sequence shows the final molt of a damselfly as it changes from nymph to adult.

Legs grip stem

Old skin

Wing buds

Nymph crawls out of water up a stem

Crinkled wings

Soft-bodied adult emerges

Blood pumps into wings

Adult rests before flying off

Abdomen turns blue

Types of insects

Insects range from fairyfly wasps only 0.2 mm long, to giant stick insects, up to 17.7 in (45 cm) long. They are divided into 32 orders, six of which are shown here. Other insects include flies, grasshoppers, earwigs, and fleas.

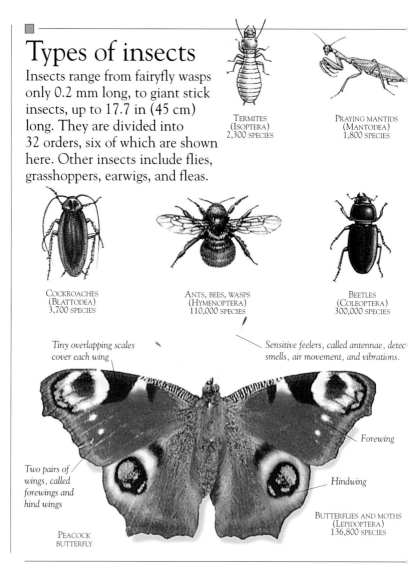

TERMITES
(ISOPTERA)
2,300 SPECIES

PRAYING MANTIDS
(MANTODEA)
1,800 SPECIES

COCKROACHES
(BLATTODEA)
3,700 SPECIES

ANTS, BEES, WASPS
(HYMENOPTERA)
110,000 SPECIES

BEETLES
(COLEOPTERA)
300,000 SPECIES

Tiny overlapping scales cover each wing

Sensitive feelers, called antennae, detec smells, air movement, and vibrations.

Forewing

Two pairs of wings, called forewings and hind wings

Hindwing

BUTTERFLIES AND MOTHS
(LEPIDOPTERA)
136,800 SPECIES

PEACOCK
BUTTERFLY

ARACHNIDS

Eight jointed legs

SPIDERS, SCORPIONS, ticks, and mites belong to a group of arthropods called arachnids. There are more than 73,000 species, living in almost every habitat.

CHILEAN RED-LEG SPIDER

Powerful jaws

SPIDERS
All spiders are meat-eaters. Some jump on prey; others trap prey in a web, paralyze it with venom, then eat it.

Poisonous sting in the tail for paralyzing prey

Waterproof, flexible outer covering, or exoskeleton

ARACHNID ANATOMY
Arachnids usually have eight legs and their body is divided into the cephalothorax (front and middle) and the abdomen (rear). Scorpions have six legs and two pincer-like pedipalps for gripping prey.

Legs are jointed in several places for flexibility

MITES AND TICKS
(ACARI)
30,000 SPECIES

SPIDERS
(ARANEAE)
40,000 SPECIES

ARACHNID FACTS

• The biggest arachnid is a bird-eating spider (*Theraphosa leblondi*), with a leg span of 11 in (28 cm).

• The largest web is spun by the tropical orb spider (*Nephila*), and measures up to 10 ft (3 m) across.

Powerful claws, called pedipalps, hold on to prey

SCORPION

CRUSTACEANS

THESE ARTHROPODS get their name from their crusty skin. They include lobsters, crabs, and shrimp, which live in the sea. Only a few, such as wood lice, live on land. There are more than 55,000 species of crustacean.

Long antenna, or feeler

Sawlike pincer for cutting up prey

Compound eyes on stalks for spotting prey

Blunt pincer for gripping and crushing prey

Hard body case, or carapace, protects internal organs

Tail allows lobster to swim backward to escape danger

Lobsters and crabs have ten legs and are called decapods

EUROPEAN LOBSTER

ANATOMY OF A LOBSTER
Lobsters have a tough body case, or carapace, two long antennae, and a pair of compound eyes on stalks for spotting prey. Lobsters also have large, strong pincers for gripping victims and pulling them apart.

DECORATOR CRAB

CRAB CAMOUFLAGE
Most crabs are sand-colored to make them less visible on the seabed. This decorator crab covers its whole body with plants and sea creatures to disguise itself completely.

CRABS

Most crabs have a hard, shieldlike shell called a carapace for defense. The flexible abdomen is usually tucked underneath for protection. Crabs move by scuttling sideways.

Huge pincers for gripping and tearing food

Hard outer shell, called the carapace

FURROWED CRAB

Jointed legs with clawed toes

LIFE CYCLE

Crustaceans begin life as eggs, which are usually laid in water. After the eggs hatch, they pass through several larval stages before taking on their adult form. As adults, they grow bigger by molting, or shedding their outer layer.

Adult shrimp

Egg

Egg hatches into first larval stage

LIFE CYCLE OF A SHRIMP

Final post-larval stage

Second larval stage

CRUSTACEAN FACTS

• The largest crustacean is the Japanese spider crab (*Macrocheira kaempferi*), with a leg span of almost 13 ft (4 m).

• The smallest crustaceans are tiny water fleas (*Alonella*), which measure less than 0.25 mm long.

97

VERTEBRATES

ONLY ABOUT three percent of all animals have backbones, and these are called vertebrates. There are more than 40,000 different species of vertebrates, divided into classes of mammals, birds, fish, reptiles, and amphibians. Their sense organs and nervous systems are well developed, and they have adapted to almost every habitat.

GORILLA
SKELETON

BACKBONE
Vertebrates have a skeleton of bone, with a backbone, two pairs of limbs, and a skull that protects the brain. Inside are the heart, lungs, and other organs.

REPTILES
Lizards, snakes, crocodiles, and geckos are reptiles. They all have a tough, scaly skin. Young reptiles hatch from eggs, and look like tiny versions of their parents. This chameleon is a type of lizard.

Spines along backbone give protection from attack

Scaly skin

Female frog lays eggs, called frogspawn

MADAGASCAN
CHAMELEON

Male fertilizes spawn

ANIMAL REPRODUCTION
In vertebrates, offspring are created when males and females come together and the male's sperm join the female's eggs. This is called sexual reproduction, and usually involves mating. A few animals are neither male nor female, and they reproduce asexually.

Prehensile tail for holding on to branches

SENSES

Mammals and other vertebrate animals have senses to help them find their way, locate food, and avoid enemies. For land animals, such as this caracal, sight, hearing, and smell are the most important senses. Sea creatures rely more on smell and taste to escape danger and find food.

Sharp eyesight for hunting, even at night

Long, sensitive ears pick up even the faintest sounds

Strong sense of smell

Sharp teeth

CARACAL

FISH

With streamlined bodies covered in slippery scales, these vertebrates are perfectly suited to life in the water.

TWINSPOT WRASSE

Scales covered in slimy mucus

BIRDS

The only animals that have feathers are birds, and most of them are powerful fliers. Birds have a beak, or bill, instead of teeth, and all reproduce by laying eggs.

COUNT RAGGI'S BIRD OF PARADISE

AMPHIBIANS

Frogs, toads, newts, and salamanders are amphibians. These vertebrates spend part of their lives in water and part on land. They all reproduce by laying eggs.

RED-EYED TREE FROG

Large eyes spot prey

Long legs for jumping

PORCUPINE

Spiny quills protect body

Fur helps keep body warm

MAMMAL

A mammal is usually covered by fur or hair. It gives birth to live young, which it feeds with milk.

AMPHIBIANS

THERE ARE more than 4,200 species of amphibians. They begin life in water as fish-like tadpoles, after hatching from clusters of eggs called spawn. Soon the tadpoles grow legs and lungs for life on land. Young amphibians breathe using gills, and the adults can breathe through their skin.

TIGER SALAMANDER

Damp sk[..] absor[..] oxyge[..]

Bright warning spots

NEWTS AND SALAMANDERS

Salamanders have long bodies, short, thin legs, and cylindrical tails. They usually spend their adult life on land and breathe by absorbing oxygen through their damp skin. The bright color of their skin is a warning to predators.

Large, bulging eyes for spotting prey

Round external eardrum called a tympanum

Thick, bumpy skin covered with warts

Squat body

FROGS AND TOAD[S]

Both frogs and toads hav[e] short, compact bodies, an[d] strong back legs for jumpin[g] long distances. As they gro[w] up from tadpole to adult, the[y] lose their tails. There is no clea[r] distinction between frogs and toad[s] but frogs tend to spend more o[f] their life in or near water, whil[e] toads can survive i[n] damp spots o[n] land, returning [..] water to bree[d]

Feet are webbed for swimming

EUROPEAN COMMON TOAD

Adult has no gills

Egg

Tadpole has gills

LIFE CYCLE OF A NEWT

Back legs appear

Front legs appear

LIFE CYCLE OF AN AMPHIBIAN

Amphibians lay their eggs in water; the eggs are not waterproof and would dry out on land. After a week or so, the eggs hatch into tadpoles, and these become strong swimmers. In newts, the front legs appear about three weeks after hatching. The back legs appear at seven to eight weeks. Finally, the gills disappear and the newt metamorphoses (changes) into an adult.

MIDWIFE TOAD

The female midwife toad lays about 0 eggs. After the male has fertilized he eggs, he carries them on his back or up to one-and-a-half months until hey are ready to hatch.

Male wraps eggs around back legs

MIDWIFE TOAD (MALE)

ivid colors act as arning signal to redators

DEADLY POISONS

Some amphibians produce powerful poisons from glands in their skin. These creatures are often brightly colored to warn predators of the danger. Poison-dart frogs are the most poisonous amphibians.

Patches of green complete the toad's disguise

YELLOW-BELLIED TOAD

OISON-DART FROG

AMPHIBIAN CAMOUFLAGE

Some amphibians manage to void predators by the unusual olors and patterns on their bodies. This yellow-bellied toad hardly hows up against tree bark.

EGGS
Most reptiles hatch from eggs with thick, leathery shells that stop them from drying out. Some reptiles are "viviparous," giving birth to live young.

REPTILES

SCALY-SKINNED crocodiles, lizards, and snakes are all reptiles. There are almost 6,000 species. Reptiles are found on land and in water, but they cannot live in cold places because they need the sun's warmth to give them energy.

IGUAN
These large America lizards often have crest on their back

Thick, scaly skin acts as a suit of armor

Crest

COMMON IGUANA

Long tail helps with balance

Sharp claws on each toe

LIZARDS
Iguanas, geckos, skinks, and chameleons are all lizards. Most lizards are swift-moving hunters, with sharp claws for catching prey and long tails to help with balance.

After eight months, the whole tail has grown back

Lizard has lost part of its tail

Tail begins to grow back after two months

GROWING A TAI
If a predator catches a lizard b its tail, the tail may break of which confuses the attacke The lizard grows a new ta within about eight month

TURTLES AND TORTOISES

Tortoises, turtles, and terrapins are called chelonians. They have a hard shell made of bony plates. By hiding inside the shell they can escape most predators, so they do not need to move quickly. Tortoises live on land and terrapins and turtles live in water.

Shell made of horn

STARRED TORTOISE SHELL

RED-EARED TERRAPIN

SNAKES

Cobra inflates hood to make itself appear bigger

MONOCLED COBRA

Long, thin body

Snakes are long, legless reptiles. They hunt prey by smelling the air with their forked tongue. Constrictors such as pythons coil around prey and suffocate them. Venomous snakes such as this cobra stun or kill their prey with poison from hollow teeth called fangs.

REPTILE FACTS

- A giant turtle found in Mauritius in 1766 survived for another 152 years.

- The venom glands of the Australian taipan snake hold enough poison to kill 200 people.

CROCODILES AND ALLIGATORS

Alligators, crocodiles, caimans, and gavials are called crocodilians. These hunters with huge jaws and sharp teeth live in tropical swamps and rivers.

Female carries young in her mouth and guards them until they can fend for themselves

Peglike teeth for tearing flesh apart

Crocodile swims by waving its flattened tail

Short, strong legs

ESTUARINE CROCODILE

103

FISH

THERE ARE more than 20,000 species of fish, all of which live in water from deep oceans to ponds, rivers, and lakes. Most fish have streamlined, scaly bodies, fins for swimming, and gills for breathing. They reproduce by laying eggs.

Water flows into mouth

Gill rakers stra... ... wat...

Water flows over gills

HOW FISH BREATH...
Fish are able to breathe underwate... using their gills. As water flow... over the gills, oxygen passes int... the bloodstream through specia... thin skins called membrane...

BONY FISH
The largest group of fish includes carp and other bony fish. These fish have bony skeletons and an internal air bag called the swim bladder that keeps them afloat in the water.

Dorsal fin

Scales

Eye

Mouth

Caudal fin

Gill cov...

CARP

Anal fin

Pelvic fin

Pectoral fin

HOW CARTILAGINOUS FISH SWIM
A cartilaginous fish, such as a dogfish, swims by swinging its tail in an "S" shape; it steers by waving its pectoral and pelvic fins. The dorsal fin helps keep the fish upright as it swims. Bony fish swim by moving their fins only.

Tail

Head

First dorsal fin

Pelvic fin

The fish swings its head to the right, and an S-shaped wave begins to travel along the body.

CARTILAGINOUS FISH

Sharks, skates, and rays are cartilaginous, as their skeletons are made of rubbery cartilage instead of bone. There are about 700 species, and most of them are hunters.

Single, large dorsal fin

Streamlined body shape for speeding through the water

Gills for breathing

Large, flexible tail for steering

GREAT WHITE SHARK

Pectoral fin on each side of body for swimming

Dozens of razor-sharp teeth

Eyes

FISH CAMOUFLAGE

Some fish, such as lionfish and porcupine fish, have spines to protect them. Others, like this flounder, are camouflaged by their color or shape, and escape from predators by blending in with their surroundings.

FLOUNDER ON SEABED

DOGFISH

Peak of wave

Peak of wave

Peak of wave

The peak of the wave reaches the area of pelvic and first dorsal fins.

The peak of the wave is now between the two dorsal fins, and the tail thrusts to the right.

The peak of the wave reaches the tail, and the fish's head swings for the next wave.

105

BIRDS

FROM THE TINY BEE hummingbird, which weighs only 0.056 oz (1.6 g), to the ostrich, which weighs up to 344 lb (156 kg) and grows up to 8.9 ft (2.7 m) tall, birds are the only animals with feathers. They also have wings and beaks, and most are expert fliers. Birds reproduce by laying eggs.

RED-TAILED MINLA

Wing size and shape depends on a bird's lifestyle

Wing feathers spread in flight to give lift

Beak made of bone covered by layer of horn

BIRDS IN FLIGHT

Birds fly by flapping their wings, or by gliding. Each bird has its own flight pattern. Small birds have a bouncing flight, and glide between flaps to save energy. Larger birds fly level and flap their wings all the time. Some birds take to the air for a few minutes at a time; others stay airborne for weeks or even months.

Tail helps bird to balance and change direction

Scaly, clawed feet for gripping branches

FROM EGG TO CHICK

As a chick develops inside an egg, the parent birds sit on the egg to keep it warm. This is called incubation. Small birds incubate their eggs for two weeks, eagles for seven weeks, and albatrosses for eleven weeks.

The chick hatches by pecking the shell with the "egg tooth" on its bill.

The chick pecks a circle around the top of the egg and pushes.

Flight feathers in wings and tail enable bird to fly

Body feathers overlap and keep bird waterproof

Down feathers trap warm air next to the skin

FEATHERS

A bird's feathers keep it warm and enable it to fly. Feathers are light yet strong because each strand is linked together with hooks called barbs and barbules.

Tail feathers are extra long for steering, balancing, and braking

NESTS AND YOUNG

Most birds build nests. A nest keeps the eggs warm and safe until they are ready to hatch, and provides a home for the newly hatched young. Each bird species has its own way of building a nest. Magpies build nests of twigs in trees; weaverbirds weave elaborate nests from grass.

NESTLINGS

CHICK EMERGING FROM EGG

The top of the shell breaks off and the chick struggles free. Its feathers are still wet.

The fluffy down soon dries out and will be replaced by feathers as the chick grows.

107

Types of birds

Birds have adapted to life in almost all parts of the world. Some, like birds of prey, are meateaters, while others eat only seeds and fruits. There are at least 9,000 species divided into 28 orders.

OSTRICH
(STRUTHIONIFORMES)
1 SPECIES

CRANES, RAILS,
AND BUSTARDS
(GRUIFORMES)
190 SPECIES

TINAMOUS
(TINAMIFORMES)
46 SPECIES

KIWIS
(APTERYGIFORMES)
3 SPECIES

ALBATROSSES, PETRELS
(PROCELLARIIFORMES)
110 SPECIES

EMUS, CASSOWARIES
(CASUARIIFORMES)
4 SPECIES

LOONS OR DIVERS
(GAVIIFORMES)
5 SPECIES

BIRDS OF PREY
(FALCONIFORMES)
290 SPECIES

OWLS
(STRIGIFORMES)
174 SPECIES

RHEAS
(RHEIFORMES)
2 SPECIES

WATERFOWL
(ANSERIFORMES)
150 SPECIES

GAME BIRDS
(GALLIFORMES)
274 SPECIES

SHOREBIRDS,
GULLS,
TERNS, AUKS
(CHARADRIIFORMES)
337 SPECIES

PELICANS, GANNETS,
CORMORANTS
(PELECANIFORMES)
55 SPECIES

PARROTS, LORIES, COCKATOOS
(PSITTACIFORMES)
342 SPECIES

MOUSEBIRDS
(COLIIFORMES)
6 SPECIES

HERONS,
STORKS, IBISES
(CICONIIFORMES)
117 SPECIES

NIGHTJARS, FROGMOUTHS
(CAPRIMULGIFORMES)
109 SPECIES

KINGFISHERS,
E-EATERS, HOOPOES
(CORACIIFORMES)
204 SPECIES

SANDGROUSE
(PTEROCLIDIFORMES)
16 SPECIES

PASSERINES
(PASSERIFORMES)
5,414 SPECIES

SWIFTS,
HUMMINGBIRDS
(APODIFORMES)
429 SPECIES

CUCKOOS,
TURACOS
(CUCULIFORMES)
159 SPECIES

PIGEONS
(COLUMBIFORMES)
300 SPECIES

GREBES
(PODICIPEDIFORMES)
21 SPECIES

WOODPECKERS,
TOUCANS, BARBETS
(PICIFORMES)
381 SPECIES

TROGONS
(TROGONIFORMES)
39 SPECIES

PENGUINS
(SPHENISCIFORMES)
18 SPECIES

MAMMALS

DOLPHIN

ALL MAMMALS are warm-blooded animals, so their blood is always at the correct temperature for their body processes to work well. To keep warm, mammals usually have thick fur or a layer of fat or blubber. Mammals are found all over the world, on land, in water, and even in the air.

CARNIVORES
Some mammals are carnivores (meat-eaters), and most carnivores are hunters. The deadliest hunters of the mammal world are the big cats, such as lions, tigers, cheetahs, and leopards. They have strong, agile bodies for chasing prey, and sharp claws and teeth for killing it.

SEA MAMMALS
Whales and dolphins spend their lives in the sea and come to the surface to breathe. They are called cetaceans.

Excellent hearing

Good senses of sight and smell

Striped pattern camouflages tiger in long grass

Body covered in fur for warmth

Powerful, low-slung body

Massive paws and sharp claws can strike a fatal blow

INDIAN TIGER

HERBIVORES

Mammals that eat only plants are called herbivores. Some herbivores, such as giraffes, browse on the buds of bushes and trees. Others, including zebras and cattle, graze on grass. Herbivores often have special teeth for grinding plant matter.

GUERNSEY COW

Tiny newborn kangaroo crawls into pouch

MARSUPIALS

Kangaroos, koalas, and other marsupial mammals have a pouch into which their newborn baby crawls. The young animal lives in its mother's pouch until it is fully developed and able to fend for itself.

GRAY KANGAROO

Young kangaroos are called joeys

MONOTREMES

Platypuses such as this Australian duck-billed platypus are the only mammals that lay eggs.

MOTHER'S MILK

Mammals are the only animals to feed their young on milk, produced in the mother's body. Milk is nourishing, and it contains substances that protect the young from disease.

Kittens feed on their mother's milk

MAMMAL FACTS

• Pygmy shrews lose body heat quickly because of their small size, so they must eat three times their body weight of food every day to survive.

• Elephants eat about 500 lb (228 kg) of vegetation every day.

Types of mammals

Mammals range from Kitti's long-nosed bat, which is the size of a bee, to the massive blue whale, which is the size of a jumbo jet. There are more than 4,600 species of mammals, found all over the world. Mammals are divided into 21 orders, shown here.

TREE SHREWS
(SCANDENTIA)
19 SPECIES

APES, MONKEYS, LEMURS
(PRIMATES)
233 SPECIES

ELEPHANT SHREWS
(MACROSCELIDIA)
15 SPECIES

PANGOLINS
(PHOLIDOTA)
7 SPECIES

MONOTREMES
(MONOTREMATA)
3 SPECIES

RODENTS
(RODENTIA)
2,021 SPECIES

MARSUPIALS
(MARSUPIALIA)
272 SPECIES

SEA COWS
(SIRENIA)
5 SPECIES

SEALS, SEA LIONS, WALRUSES
(PINNIPEDIA)
34 SPECIES

FLYING LEMURS
(DERMOPTERA)
2 SPECIES

ELEPHANTS
(PROBOSCIDEA)
2 SPECIES

EDENTATES
(EDENTATA)
29 SPECIES

EVEN-TOED HOOFED MAMMALS
(ARTIODACTYLA)
220 SPECIES

AARDVARK
(TUBULIDENTATA)
1 SPECIES

WHALES, DOLPHINS
(CETACEA)
78 SPECIES

BATS
(CHIROPTERA)
925 SPECIES

HYRAXES
(HYRACOIDEA)
6 SPECIES

HARES, RABBITS, PIKAS
(LAGOMORPHA)
80 SPECIES

INSECTIVORES
(INSECTIVORA)
428 SPECIES

ODD-TOED HOOFED MAMMALS
(PERISSODACTYLA)
18 SPECIES

CARNIVORES
(CARNIVORA)
237 SPECIES

113

THE HUMAN BODY

BODY SYSTEMS

THE HUMAN BODY is an amazingly complex organism made up of 50 trillion microscopic cells. There are more than 200 kinds of cell, all organized into a dozen or so body systems, each with its own function. Here are the major systems that are common to all humans

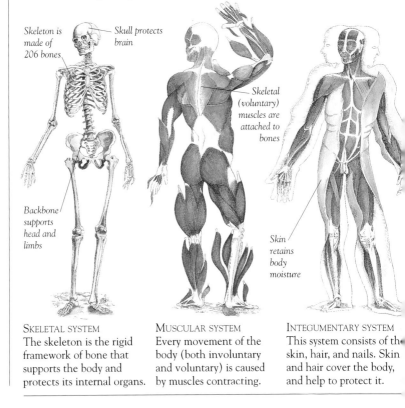

Skeleton is made of 206 bones

Skull protects brain

Backbone supports head and limbs

Skeletal (voluntary) muscles are attached to bones

Skin retains body moisture

SKELETAL SYSTEM
The skeleton is the rigid framework of bone that supports the body and protects its internal organs.

MUSCULAR SYSTEM
Every movement of the body (both involuntary and voluntary) is caused by muscles contracting.

INTEGUMENTARY SYSTEM
This system consists of the skin, hair, and nails. Skin and hair cover the body, and help to protect it.

RESPIRATORY SYSTEM
This takes oxygenated air into the lungs and pushes out waste gases.

DIGESTIVE SYSTEM
The digestive tract breaks down and absorbs food, and gets rid of solid waste.

URINARY SYSTEM
This filters soluble wastes from the blood for disposal as urine.

Nerves transmit signals to and from brain, the body's control center

Endocrine organs, such as the pancreas, produce hormones (chemical messengers)

Heart constantly pumps blood around body

Lymph nodes filter lymph and cleanse it of infection

Blood circulates through body in blood vessels

NERVES AND HORMONES
The nervous system and hormones coordinate all the body systems and direct our actions.

CARDIOVASCULAR SYSTEM
Blood pumped around the body by the heart supplies tissues with oxygen and removes waste products.

LYMPHATIC SYSTEM
Lymph, containing immune cells, is collected by a network of lymph vessels.

BONES AND TEETH

THE INNER FRAMEWORK of the human body consists of interconnecting bones that form the skeleton. Without a skeleton we could not stand or move.

Cranium (skull)

Clavicle (collarbone)

Scapula (shoulder blade)

Humerus (upper arm bone)

Rib

Vertebrae (spine)

Radius (forearm bone)

Ulna (forearm bone)

Carpals (wrist bones)

Coccyx (tailbone)

Phalanges (finger bones)

Femur (thigh bone)

Patella (kneecap)

Tibia (shinbone)

Tarsals (ankle bones)

Fibula (calf bone)

Metatarsals (foot bones)

Hard, compact, outer bone

Spongy bone

Fatty bone marrow

BONE STRUCTURE
The hardest part of a bone is the outer layer, containing calcium and phosphorus. Inside long bones there is a soft, living tissue called marrow. Yellow marrow stores fat, and red marrow forms blood cells.

SKELETON FACTS

- The femur is the longest, strongest bone.

- A woman's pelvic bones are shallower and wider than a man's to allow childbirth.

SKELETON

The skeleton supports and protects delicate internal organs such as the brain, lungs, and heart. It also provides strong, fixed points of attachment for the muscles.

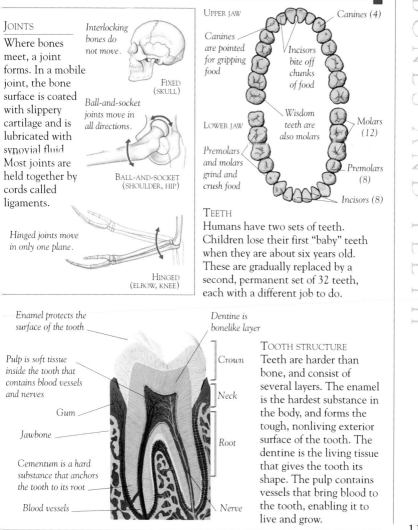

JOINTS

Where bones meet, a joint forms. In a mobile joint, the bone surface is coated with slippery cartilage and is lubricated with synovial fluid. Most joints are held together by cords called ligaments.

Interlocking bones do not move.

FIXED
(SKULL)

Ball-and-socket joints move in all directions.

BALL-AND-SOCKET
(SHOULDER, HIP)

Hinged joints move in only one plane.

HINGED
(ELBOW, KNEE)

UPPER JAW

Canines are pointed for gripping food

Incisors bite off chunks of food

Canines (4)

LOWER JAW

Wisdom teeth are also molars

Molars (12)

Premolars and molars grind and crush food

Premolars (8)

Incisors (8)

TEETH

Humans have two sets of teeth. Children lose their first "baby" teeth when they are about six years old. These are gradually replaced by a second, permanent set of 32 teeth, each with a different job to do.

Enamel protects the surface of the tooth

Pulp is soft tissue inside the tooth that contains blood vessels and nerves

Gum

Jawbone

Cementum is a hard substance that anchors the tooth to its root

Blood vessels

Dentine is bonelike layer

Crown

Neck

Root

Nerve

TOOTH STRUCTURE

Teeth are harder than bone, and consist of several layers. The enamel is the hardest substance in the body, and forms the tough, nonliving exterior surface of the tooth. The dentine is the living tissue that gives the tooth its shape. The pulp contains vessels that bring blood to the tooth, enabling it to live and grow.

MUSCLES

ALL THE body's functions are controlled by muscles, which convert chemical energy into movement. We consciously control voluntary muscles, but involuntary muscles work automatically.

MUSCLE USE

When muscles are used, they warm up, providing the body with about one-fifth of its heat. Regular exercise increases the flow of blood to the muscles. This keeps them toned and makes them grow in size.

TENDONS
Skeletal muscles are attached to bones at either end by tough cords called tendons.

Tendon of biceps femoris muscle at back of knee

Achilles tendon

Frontalis raises eyebrows

Serratus anterior pulls shoulder around

Deltoid raises and tilts upper arm

Biceps branchii bends lower arm and clenches fist

Rectus abdominis pulls in abdominal wall

Sartorius bends hip and knee and twists thigh

Quadriceps femoris bends hip and straightens knee

Gastrocnemius bends knee and lifts heel

Trapezius brac● shoulder

Pectoralis major rotates arm

Tibialis anterior raises foot

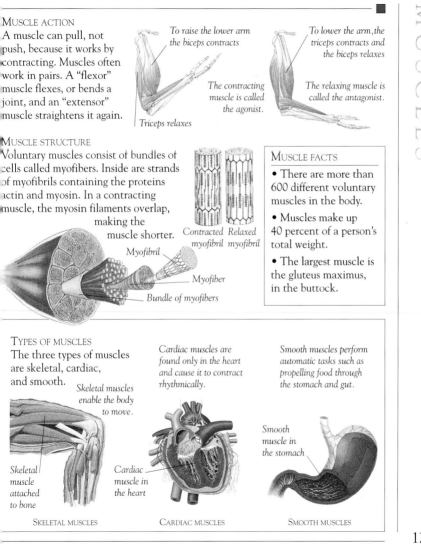

MUSCLE ACTION

A muscle can pull, not push, because it works by contracting. Muscles often work in pairs. A "flexor" muscle flexes, or bends a joint, and an "extensor" muscle straightens it again.

To raise the lower arm the biceps contracts

The contracting muscle is called the agonist.

Triceps relaxes

To lower the arm, the triceps contracts and the biceps relaxes

The relaxing muscle is called the antagonist.

MUSCLE STRUCTURE

Voluntary muscles consist of bundles of cells called myofibers. Inside are strands of myofibrils containing the proteins actin and myosin. In a contracting muscle, the myosin filaments overlap, making the muscle shorter.

Contracted   Relaxed myofibril   myofibril

Myofibril

Myofiber

Bundle of myofibers

MUSCLE FACTS

• There are more than 600 different voluntary muscles in the body.

• Muscles make up 40 percent of a person's total weight.

• The largest muscle is the gluteus maximus, in the buttock.

TYPES OF MUSCLES

The three types of muscles are skeletal, cardiac, and smooth.

Skeletal muscles enable the body to move.

Cardiac muscles are found only in the heart and cause it to contract rhythmically.

Smooth muscles perform automatic tasks such as propelling food through the stomach and gut.

Skeletal muscle attached to bone

Cardiac muscle in the heart

Smooth muscle in the stomach

SKELETAL MUSCLES   CARDIAC MUSCLES   SMOOTH MUSCLES

MUSCLES

121

SKIN, NAILS, AND HAIR

THE SKIN is the body's waterproof coat, protecting it from the outside world and preventing it from drying out. It is also a sense organ, sensitive to touch, pressure, warmth, and pain. The skin produces nails, which shield the tips of fingers and toes, and hair, to provide extra warmth and protection.

SKIN STRUCTURE

The skin has two main layers. The thin, tough, outer epidermis consists mostly of dead cells that are constantly shed and replaced by new skin cells. The thick, living inner dermis layer contains nerves, blood vessels, sense receptors, glands, and hair follicles.

Outer layers of epidermis consist of dead cells made of a hard protein called keratin

Each hair is coated with dead cells

Movement of hair gives sensation of touch

Hair erector muscle makes hair stand on end in the cold to help trap warmth

BLOOD CLOTTING

When skin is cut, the damaged blood vessels bleed. White blood cells fight infection. Fibrin threads bind small, sticky blood cells (platelets) together to form a clot. This clot dries as a scab.

Damaged blood vessel   *White blood cells attack germs*

Sebaceous glands make sebum (oil) to keep hair and skin supple

Hair follicle

Scab forms a protective layer over wound

Fibrin threads bind platelets together to stop blood flow

Sweat glands produce sweat to help keep the skin cool

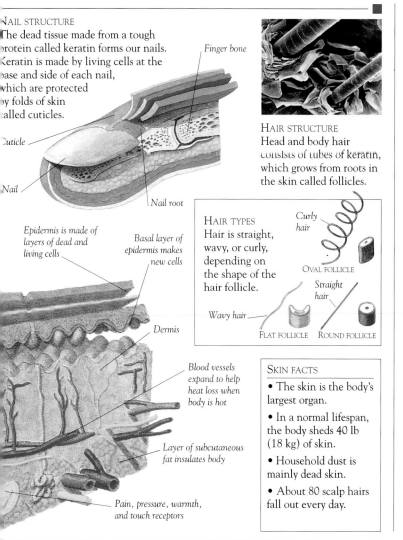

NAIL STRUCTURE

The dead tissue made from a tough protein called keratin forms our nails. Keratin is made by living cells at the base and side of each nail, which are protected by folds of skin called cuticles.

Cuticle

Nail

Finger bone

Nail root

HAIR STRUCTURE

Head and body hair consists of tubes of keratin, which grows from roots in the skin called follicles.

Epidermis is made of layers of dead and living cells

Basal layer of epidermis makes new cells

HAIR TYPES

Hair is straight, wavy, or curly, depending on the shape of the hair follicle.

Curly hair

OVAL FOLLICLE

Straight hair

Wavy hair

FLAT FOLLICLE   ROUND FOLLICLE

Dermis

Blood vessels expand to help heat loss when body is hot

Layer of subcutaneous fat insulates body

Pain, pressure, warmth, and touch receptors

SKIN FACTS

- The skin is the body's largest organ.

- In a normal lifespan, the body sheds 40 lb (18 kg) of skin.

- Household dust is mainly dead skin.

- About 80 scalp hairs fall out every day.

BRAIN AND NERVES

THE NERVOUS SYSTEM is a dense, branching network of nerve fibers. It coordinates the body's actions and sends a never-ending stream of sense data to the brain.

BRAIN STRUCTURE

The human brain is a complex network of nerve cells linked to the rest of the body via the cranial nerves and spinal cord. The brain has two halves, or hemispheres. Each controls the *opposite* side of the body.

Touch   *Vision*

Skilled movement

Behavior and emotion

Speech

Hearing

Taste

SENSORY AREAS

Parts of the brain are specialized. "Sensory" areas receive and interpret data from sense organs; "motor" areas control voluntary muscles.

Cerebrum is a folded mass of nerves where conscious activity takes place

Thalamus transmits nerve signals between brain and spinal cord

Hypothalamus controls hunger, thirst, body temperature, sleeping, and waking

Pituitary gland sends out hormones (chemical messengers) that stimulate other glands to release hormones

Brain stem, or medulla, controls basic bodily functions such as breathing and heart rate

Cerebellum works subconsciously to coordinate all of body movement

Spinal cord

NEURON

Dendrite
receives nerve
impulse

Axon
transmits
nerve
impulse

Cell body

NEURONS
Nerve cells, or
neurons, receive
chemical-electrical
signals, or nerve
impulses, via
branches called
dendrites, and pass
them on via a long
threadlike axon.

Nerve impulse

Chemical
neurotransmitters

Synaptic knob

SYNAPSE
When nerve impulses
pass from one nerve to
another, they cross a
tiny gap called a synapse.

Brain

Cranial nerves are the only
part of the peripheral
nervous system that
connect directly to brain

Sensory nerves such as the
optic nerve send data from
sense receptors to CNS
(central nervous system)

Spinal cord

Together, the brain
and spinal cord make
up the CNS.

Peripheral
nervous system
consists of all
sensory nerves
and nerves that
control
movement

BRAIN AND
NERVE FACTS

• There are 15 billion
nerve cells in the
brain, each connected
to 25,000 others.

• Nerve signals can
travel at more than
248 mph (400 km/h).

• The brain uses
25 percent of the
body's blood
supply.

SIGHT

AT THE FRONT of each eye is a lens system that projects an image onto the lining of the eye, called the retina. Millions of light-sensitive cells in the retina, called rods and cones, respond to the image and send signals to the brain.

Tear duct   *Tear gland*

TEARS
The tear glands above each eye continually produce tears. Tears keep the eyes moist and clean. Excess tears are drained down into the nose via the tear ducts.

Sclera

Muscle ring controls lens

Lens focuses image

Pupil lets light in

Cornea projects image

Aqueous humor is watery

Iris controls size of pupil

Retina contains light-sensitive rods and cones

Vitreous humor is jellylike

Optic nerve leads to brain

Choroid consists of blood vessels

EYES
The eyeball is divided into two chambers on either side of the lens. One chamber is filled with aqueous humor, the other with vitreous humor. The casing consists of three layers: the sclera (the white of the eye), the choroid, and the retina.

EYE FACTS

• Rods respond to light but not color.

• Cones respond to color but not without light.

• Most people blink about 15 times a minute.

126

HEARING

SOUND CONSISTS of tiny vibrations in the air. We hear sound because the ear amplifies the vibrations, channeling them toward sensitive hairs in the inner ear. These hairs are stimulated by the vibrations and send signals to the brain.

EAR FACTS

• The ear canal is about 1 in (2.5 cm) in length.

• Humans can detect 1,500 different tones.

• The sensation of ears "popping" is caused by air pressure equalized in the middle ear.

EARS

The ear consists of three parts – the outer ear (including the pinna and the ear canal), the middle ear (including the eardrum and ossicles), and the inner ear (including the cochlea).

Pinna (ear flap) directs sound waves (vibrations) to the ear canal.

Helix (outer rim of pinna)

Antihelix (inner rim of pinna)

The ear canal funnels sound waves toward the eardrum.

Earlobe

3 The vibrations shake the wall of skin called the eardrum, or tympanum.

4 The shaking of the eardrum rattles three tiny bones called ossicles, which amplify the vibration.

Eardrum

Middle ear

Ear canal

5 The ossicles pass the amplified vibrations onto another wall of skin, the oval window.

Oval window

Eustachian tube controls air pressure

Auditory nerve

Ossicles

6 As the oval window moves, it sends waves through a curly tube full of fluid, called the cochlea.

Cochlea

7 The waves in the cochlea waft tiny hairs back and forth.

8 The hairs send signals to the brain via the auditory nerve.

TASTE

THE SENSES OF taste and smell are closely related, and work together to help us identify flavors. The microscopic chemical receptor cells on the tongue, called taste buds, are the main organs of taste.

TONGUE SURFACE MAGNIFIED

TONGUE
This muscular structure is used in talking, eating, and tasting. It is covered with taste buds which can detect sweet, sour, bitter, and salty flavors.

Pore

Tongue tissue

Nerve fibers

Tas bud recepto

Bitterness is tasted at the back

Sourness is tasted along the edges at the back

Sweetness is tasted at the tip

Saltiness is tasted along the sides at the front

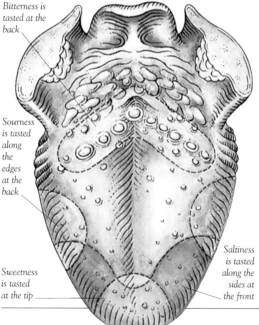

TASTE BUDS
There are about 10,000 taste buds on the tongue surface. Each taste bud contains 10–20 receptors Chemicals dissolved in saliva reach these taste receptors through pores.

TASTE FACTS
• Babies have taste buds all over the inside of their mouths.

• Taste bud cells last only a week before they are renewed.

SMELL

THE SENSE of smell detects chemicals in the air. These chemicals dissolve in the nasal mucus inside the nose and stimulate hairlike endings on the olfactory bulb. The fine hairs are so sensitive that they can detect even faint traces of chemicals.

Fine hairs, or cilia, on the olfactory bulb are sensitive to the chemicals in mucus

There are five million receptors in the olfactory area

15,000 fibers in the olfactory nerve send messages to the brain

NOSE
The septum divides the nose into two nostrils, each lined with hairs and membranes that secrete sticky mucus. Smell relies on the olfactory area at the top of the nose.

Nose warms and moistens air before it reaches the lungs

Nasal hairs filter out large particles as they are breathed in

Chemicals from the air dissolve in mucus before they reach smell receptors

SMELL CAPABILITY

Age 20
82%

Age 60
38%

Age 80
28%

LOSS OF SENSITIVITY
Babies are very sensitive to smells, which may help them to identify their mother. But as we grow older, our sensitivity to smell diminishes, as this chart shows.

SMELL FACTS

• Humans can identify about 3,000 different smells.

• Smell is processed by the part of the brain that also deals with taste, memory, and emotions.

LUNGS

LUNGS AND BREATHING

OXYGEN IS VITAL to every cell in the body. Without it, brain cells die in minutes. To keep up the supply of oxygen, we breathe air continuously into the lungs. From there the oxygen enters the bloodstream.

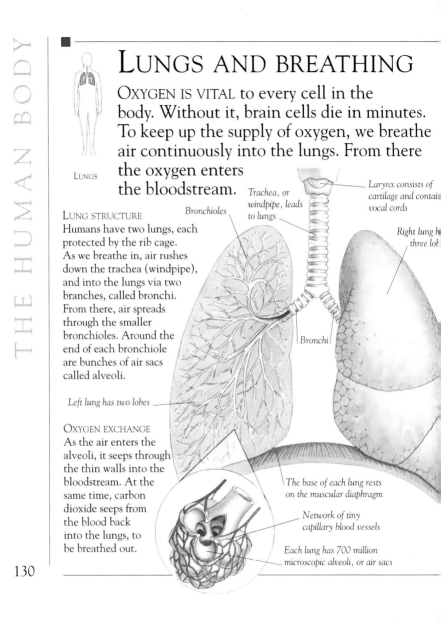

Trachea, or windpipe, leads to lungs

Bronchioles

Larynx consists of cartilage and contains vocal cords

Right lung has three lobes

Bronchi

Left lung has two lobes

The base of each lung rests on the muscular diaphragm

Network of tiny capillary blood vessels

Each lung has 700 million microscopic alveoli, or air sacs

LUNG STRUCTURE

Humans have two lungs, each protected by the rib cage. As we breathe in, air rushes down the trachea (windpipe), and into the lungs via two branches, called bronchi. From there, air spreads through the smaller bronchioles. Around the end of each bronchiole are bunches of air sacs called alveoli.

OXYGEN EXCHANGE

As the air enters the alveoli, it seeps through the thin walls into the bloodstream. At the same time, carbon dioxide seeps from the blood back into the lungs, to be breathed out.

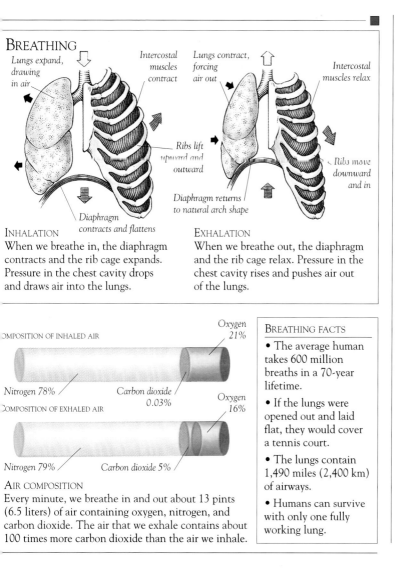

BREATHING

Lungs expand, drawing in air

Intercostal muscles contract

Lungs contract, forcing air out

Intercostal muscles relax

Ribs lift upward and outward

Ribs move downward and in

Diaphragm returns to natural arch shape

Diaphragm contracts and flattens

INHALATION
When we breathe in, the diaphragm contracts and the rib cage expands. Pressure in the chest cavity drops and draws air into the lungs.

EXHALATION
When we breathe out, the diaphragm and the rib cage relax. Pressure in the chest cavity rises and pushes air out of the lungs.

COMPOSITION OF INHALED AIR

Oxygen 21%

Nitrogen 78%

Carbon dioxide 0.03%

COMPOSITION OF EXHALED AIR

Oxygen 16%

Nitrogen 79%

Carbon dioxide 5%

AIR COMPOSITION
Every minute, we breathe in and out about 13 pints (6.5 liters) of air containing oxygen, nitrogen, and carbon dioxide. The air that we exhale contains about 100 times more carbon dioxide than the air we inhale.

BREATHING FACTS

• The average human takes 600 million breaths in a 70-year lifetime.

• If the lungs were opened out and laid flat, they would cover a tennis court.

• The lungs contain 1,490 miles (2,400 km) of airways.

• Humans can survive with only one fully working lung.

131

1 During diastole (resting), both atria fill with blood and some flows into the ventricles below.

2 During atrial systole (pumping), the atria contract, forcing blood into the ventricles.

3 During ventricular systole, the ventricles contract, forcing blood out into the arteries.

HEART AND BLOOD

THE BODY'S transportation network, the heart, blood, and blood vessels, is called the cardiovascular system. Blood carries oxygen to cells and also transports food, hormones, waste, and warmth.

Vena cava is main incoming blood vessel

Right atrium

Pulmonary artery is main blood vessel to lungs

Aorta is main outgoing blood vessel

Pulmonary valve

Left atriur

Right pulmonary vein

HEART STRUCTURE
The heart is a pump with two sides. Each side has two chambers – the atrium above and the ventricle below. These contract and relax every 0.8 seconds to pump blood around the body.

Right ventricle

Left ventric

Valves sto blood from flowing backward.

CIRCULATION

Blood flows out of the heart through arteries (shown in red) and back into the heart through veins (blue). Arteries branch into arterioles, which split into tiny capillaries. Their thin walls allow oxygen and nutrients to pass through.

Carotid artery

Jugular vein

Pulmonary arteries

Gastric artery

Iliac artery

Femoral artery

Tibial arteries

MAIN ARTERIES

Pulmonary vein

Iliac vein

Femoral vein

Great saphenous vein

Small saphenous vein

MAIN VEINS

HEART FACTS

• A human heart beats more than 30 million times a year.

• The heart rate increases with exercise to provide muscles with extra oxygen.

• With every heart beat, the heart pumps out about 2.8 fl oz (80 ml) of blood.

BLOOD

The liquid part of blood, called plasma, contains a rich mixture of blood cells, proteins, antibodies, hormones, and minerals. Red blood cells are button-shaped, and carry oxygen around the body. White cells, or leukocytes, fight infection. The tiny platelets help to plug leaks by forming blood clots.

133

DIGESTION

FOOD IS BROKEN down by a process called digestion. Once food has been swallowed, it slips into the alimentary canal, or gut, which runs from mouth to anus. As food passes through the gut, it is gradually digested and absorbed until all that emerges at the far end is waste.

ALIMENTARY CANAL
The digestive tract runs from the mouth to the anus and is about 30 ft (9 m) long. Food passes from the mouth, down the esophagus into the stomach. From here, it passses into the small intestine, made up of the duodenum, jejunum, and ileum, and into the large intestine, made up of the colon and rectum. Several organs and glands are connected to the gut to help digestion.

Teeth soften food by chewing it

Saliva helps to dissolve starch

Food is swallowed as a bolus

Waves of muscular action push food down esophagus into stomach

Liver

Stomach

Digestive enzymes in duodenum break down food into semifluid called chyme

Ileum absorbs digested minerals and nutrients into bloodstream

Indigestible solids pass on into colon, where water is absorbed

Muscular rectum expels waste through anus

Intestine   *Food*

Food slides forwards   *Muscle contracts behind food*

Contractions push food along

PERISTALSIS
The walls of the digestive tract contain strong muscle fibers that produce wave-like contractions to propel food along. This process is called peristalsis.

STOMACH ACTION
The stomach is a bag-like chamber that stores food. As the stomach fills with food, its walls stretch. Powerful muscles churn up the food, and gastric juices break it down so it can be digested. The food passes from the stomach into the intestines.

Undigested food enters the stomach

Gastric juices digest the food

Broken down food is pushed into the duodenum

VILLI
The lining of the small intestine has millions of microscopic fingerlike villi that absorb nutrients.

Each villus measures 0.04 in (1 mm).

Capillaries

Mucus layer

Muscles

LIVER
The liver has many functions. It stores vitamins, turns digested food into blood proteins, and makes bile, which helps break fat into tiny globules.

Esophagus

Liver

Stomach

Bile duct secretes bile into intestine

Gallbladder stores bile

Pancreas supplies digestive chemicals

DIGESTION FACTS

• Food stays in the stomach for up to five hours, and spends up to 20 hours in the colon.

• So that the stomach does not digest itself, its walls are lined with protective mucus.

• The digestive process begins as soon as you take a bite of food.

DIGESTION

135

URINARY SYSTEM

THE URINARY SYSTEM

AS BLOOD FLOWS through the kidneys, they filter out waste and drain off excess water. This is expelled from the body as urine, via the ureter, bladder, and urethra. In this way the urinary system clears the blood of toxins and regulates its water content.

Cortex

Adrenal gland

Any remaining water and waste drains into the collecting duct as urine

Medulla

Renal arte brings in blo for filteri

Renal vein takes away filtered blood

In the tubules most of the water and valuable amino acids, glucose, and salt are retrieved and returned to the blood

Urine drains from the kidneys via the ureter

KIDNEYS

The kidneys filter the blood in over a million filtering units called nephrons. In each nephron, water and tiny molecules are drawn off and channeled through little tubes called tubules. Inside these, valuable molecules and most of the water are retrieved and returned to the blood, leaving only a little water and waste to drain off as urine.

KIDNEY AND URINE FACTS

• The kidneys clean 2.7 pints (1.3 liters) of blood a minute.

• Urine is 95 percent water. The rest is toxic waste such as urea, which is produced in the liver.

HORMONES

ENDOCRINE glands secrete chemical messengers called hormones into the blood. These stimulate, regulate, and coordinate a whole range of body processes.

TESTOSTERONE

In men, the testes produce the hormone testosterone to control the development of sexual characteristics.

Testis

HORMONE FACTS

• Too much growth hormone can cause gigantism (excess growth); too little can cause slow growth.

• The hormone epinephrine can give short bursts of superhuman strength.

Pituitary gland sends out hormones that regulate other endocrine glands

Thyroid gland secretes thyroxine, which controls growth

Parathyroid glands secrete hormone that raises blood calcium levels

Adrenal glands secrete cortisone, which boosts metabolism, and epinephrine, which primes body for action

Pancreas secretes glucagon and insulin, which regulate blood sugar levels

Stomach and intestines secrete hormones that aid digestion

Ovaries in women make female sex hormones, estrogen and progesterone

REPRODUCTION

FROM PUBERTY ONWARD, the reproductive system in males and females is sufficiently developed for them to have sexual intercourse and potentially create new human beings. Pregnancy occurs when a woman's egg cell is fertilized by a man's sperm cell.

THE MALE REPRODUCTIVE SYSTEM

MALE REPRODUCTIVE SYSTEM
Male sex cells, or sperm, are made inside the testicles in tubes called seminiferous tubules. Sperm mature in tubes called the epididymides. When the penis is stimulated, muscles pump sperm from the epididymis along the vas deferens, where they mix with seminal fluid to make semen.

SINGLE SPERM

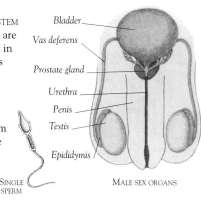

Bladder
Vas deferens
Prostate gland
Urethra
Penis
Testis
Epididymis

MALE SEX ORGANS

THE FEMALE REPRODUCTIVE SYSTEM

FEMALE REPRODUCTIVE SYSTEM
Female sex cells, or ova, are stored in the ovaries. Every 28 days or so, one ovum, or egg, is released during ovulation. The egg passes down one of two fallopian tubes to the uterus, or womb. If the ovum is fertilized, it is embedded in the womb lining. If not, both the ovum and lining are shed during menstruation.

SINGLE OVUM

Fallopian tube
Ova (eggs) stored in ovary
Uterus (womb)
Neck of womb called the cervix
Vagina

FEMALE SEX ORGANS

enis inside vagina

Umbilical cord consists of three intertwined blood vessels

etus turns head own during last w weeks of regnancy

Sexual Intercourse

During sexual intercourse, the man's penis fills with blood, becoming hard and erect. It fits into the woman's vagina, where semen is released (ejaculated). If one of the 300 million sperm reaches the egg, it may fertilize it.

Amniotic sac contains amniotic fluid

The placenta is a spongy organ on uterine lining

Oral contraceptive pills

Diaphragm

Condom

Contraceptives

Condoms and other contraceptives are used to stop conception during intercourse. They prevent sperm fertilizing the egg.

Pregnancy

Once the egg is fertilized, it becomes an embryo, which grows rapidly in the womb (uterus). Within eight weeks, it is a fetus, with recognizable features and all its internal organs. Fed through the umbilical cord with food and oxygen from the placenta, the fetus continues development. After 40 weeks, it is ready to be born.

GENES AND HEREDITY

STORED IN a cell's nucleus are packages called chromosomes, made up of long spirals of the molecule DNA. Each DNA molecule consists of genes, which are responsible for characteristics such as eye color.

A chromosome has two identical arms called chromatid

Cell

GENES
Each DNA molecule consists of millions of genes. Each gene provides instructions to make a single protein, used to build a new cell or to control a cell's activities. Genes are passed on to the next generation during sexual reproduction.

Nucleus

Each cell has 46 chromosomes, except for sex cells, which have 23

Chromosome unwinds

MITOSIS
As the body grows, or when worn-out cells need replacing, the cells divide into two by a process called mitosis. The normal number of chromosomes in each cell is 46. When the cells divide, each new cell has the same number of chromosomes – 46.

Cell copies chromosomes before it divides

MITOSIS

Each new cell has 46 chromosomes

Genes are reshuffled in original cell

MEIOSIS

MEIOSIS
Sex cells are produced during the cell division called meiosis. The original cell's genes are mixed and recombined so that the new cells produced are genetically unique.

Each pair of chromosomes splits in half and the two new cells receive half each

Chromatid

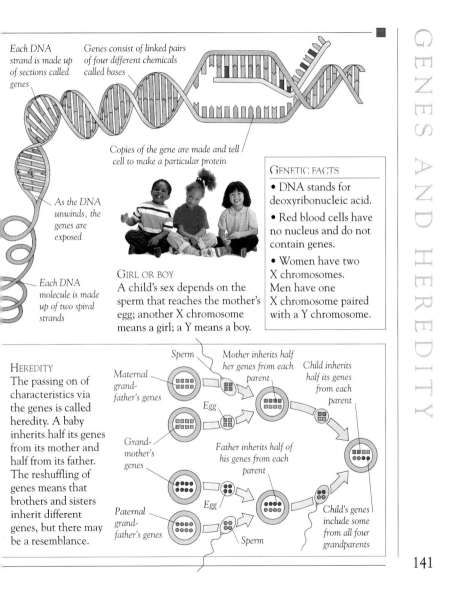

Each DNA strand is made up of sections called genes

Genes consist of linked pairs of four different chemicals called bases

Copies of the gene are made and tell cell to make a particular protein

As the DNA unwinds, the genes are exposed

Each DNA molecule is made up of two spiral strands

GIRL OR BOY

A child's sex depends on the sperm that reaches the mother's egg; another X chromosome means a girl; a Y means a boy.

GENETIC FACTS

• DNA stands for deoxyribonucleic acid.

• Red blood cells have no nucleus and do not contain genes.

• Women have two X chromosomes. Men have one X chromosome paired with a Y chromosome.

HEREDITY

The passing on of characteristics via the genes is called heredity. A baby inherits half its genes from its mother and half from its father. The reshuffling of genes means that brothers and sisters inherit different genes, but there may be a resemblance.

Maternal grand-father's genes

Sperm

Mother inherits half her genes from each parent

Egg

Child inherits half its genes from each parent

Grand-mother's genes

Egg

Father inherits half of his genes from each parent

Paternal grand-father's genes

Sperm

Child's genes include some from all four grandparents

FIGHTING INFECTION

IF BACTERIA or viruses enter the body and multiply, you can become ill. To fight infection, the body has a defense mechanism called the immune system.

Adenoid glands

Tonsils

Tonsils and adenoids produce antibodies to fight infection.

A single macrophage can ingest 100 bacteria

MACROPHAGE (BLUE)
ENGULFING A YEAST
CELL (YELLOW)

Spleen stores special white blood cells called lymphocytes

Small intestine contains lymph tissues that help fight infection

Bone marrow produces lymphocytes

Lymph capillaries drain tissue fluids into lymphatic system

SCAVENGER CELLS

Lymphocytes called phagocytes, and larger ones called macrocytes, roam through the blood, engulfing unwanted matter, such as the dirt in a cut.

IMMUNE FACTS

- A fever is caused when white blood cells release proteins called pyrogens, raising the body's temperature.

- Swollen glands are a sign of infection.

LYMPHATIC SYSTEM

Lymph fluid drains waste from the body's tissues into the ducts of the lymphatic system. Germs that enter the lymphatic system are swept towards lymph nodes, where there is a cluster of lymphocytes waiting to fight them.

THE
LYMPHATIC
SYSTEM

Virus

Antigen

Antibodies lock on to antigens

Antibody

Immune Response

Certain bacteria and viruses possess substances called antigens, which trigger the immune system into action. When the immune system first meets an antigen, it produces antibodies to fight it. Lymphocytes called B-cells make these antibodies, and each one targets a specific antigen.

Medicine

The body's immune system is remarkably effective at dealing with infection, but sometimes it breaks down or takes a long time to work. Modern drugs and traditional forms of medicine such as herbalism can help the body to combat illness.

Drugs

The drugs we use to treat illness and disease are made from plant extracts or from chemicals produced in a laboratory. They are commonly taken in the form of tablets, capsules, or liquid.

Immunization

Active or passive immunization by injection provides the body with protection from certain diseases.

ACTIVE IMMUNIZATION   PASSIVE IMMUNIZATION

Harmless extracts that cannot cause disease are injected into the body.

People donate blood that contains antibodies.

Vaccine causes B-cells to produce antibodies.

Antibodies to a disease are injected into patient.

Immune system will respond more quickly.

If disease attacks, the antibodies will fight it.

SCIENCE AND TECHNOLOGY

MATTER

FROM THE TINIEST speck of dust to giant stars, everything that exists in the universe is made up of matter. Most matter consists of minute particles called atoms. On Earth, matter usually occurs in one of three forms, or "states," called solid, liquid, or gas.

Electrode

Plasma streaks

PLASMA
A rare fourth state of matter called plasma forms when a gas becomes so hot electrons (see p.148) break away from atoms.

GAS
A gas has no fixed volume or shape. Gas particles are widely spaced and loosely bound, with the ability to move freely in all directions. A gas will expand to fill any container it is put in.

Gas dispersing from a chemical reaction

LIQUID
A liquid has a definite volume but no fixed shape. Liquid particles are more loosely bound than solid particles and can move over small distances. A liquid will flow and take the shape of its container.

Every liquid takes the shape of its container

Coins have a rigid shape

SOLID
A solid has a fixed shape and volume. Solid particles are tightly packed in regular patterns. Strong bonds allow the particles to vibrate, but keep them from moving.

CHANGING STATE

The particles of a substance are held together by bonds that weaken when heated and strengthen when cooled. Heat changes solids to liquids, and liquids to gases. When cooled sufficiently, gases condense to liquids, and liquids freeze to solids.

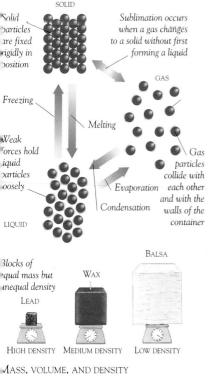

SOLID

Solid particles are fixed rigidly in position

Sublimation occurs when a gas changes to a solid without first forming a liquid

GAS

Freezing

Melting

Weak forces hold liquid particles loosely

Gas particles collide with each other and with the walls of the container

Evaporation

Condensation

LIQUID

Blocks of equal mass but unequal density

WAX

BALSA

LEAD

HIGH DENSITY   MEDIUM DENSITY   LOW DENSITY

MASS, VOLUME, AND DENSITY

The amount of matter in an object is its mass. Volume is the space it occupies. The object's density is its mass divided by its volume.

GAS LAWS

Pressure

Gas molecules

BOYLE'S LAW

At constant temperature (T), the volume of a gas (V) is inversely proportional to the pressure (P) (the gas contracts as the pressure rises): PV=constant.

PRESSURE LAW

At constant volume, the pressure of a gas is proportional to the temperature (increasing the temperature raises the gas's pressure): P/T=constant.

Temperature

CHARLES' LAW

At constant pressure, the gas's volume is proportional to the temperature (the gas expands if temperature rises): V/T=constant.

ATOMS

MATTER IS MADE UP of tiny particles called atoms. Atoms form the building blocks for everything in the universe. There are just over a hundred types of atoms, which are themselves made up of even smaller "subatomic" particles. Atoms and subatomic particles are not solid – they are clouds of energy.

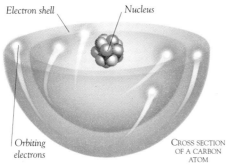

Electron shell

Nucleus

Orbiting electrons

CROSS SECTION OF A CARBON ATOM

INSIDE THE ATOM
The center, or nucleus, of all but the hydrogen atom contains protons (positively charged) and neutrons (with no charge). Negatively charged particles called electrons orbit the nucleus at very high speeds, forming layers or "shells."

NUCLEON NUMBER
The total number of protons and neutrons contained in the nucleus of an atom is called the nucleon number. The most common form of carbon is referred to as carbon–12, since it contains 6 protons and 6 neutrons.

CARBON–12 ATOM

Proton

Neutron

Nucleus contain 6 protons and 6 neutron.

CARBON–14 ATOM

Nucleus contains 6 protons and 8 neutrons

ISOTOPES
All atoms of a particular element have the same number of protons, but some forms of the element may have different numbers of neutrons. These variations are called isotopes The isotope carbon–14, for example, has two more neutrons than the isotope carbon–12.

PATHS OF PARTICLES CREATED
AFTER SUBATOMIC COLLISION

PARTICLE COLLISIONS
Scientists have discovered many new particles by smashing together subatomic particles at high speed. Most new particles exist for only a fraction of a second after the collision, but their movements can be recorded by computers.

ATOM FACTS

• Protons and neutrons are 1,836 times heavier than electrons.

• Scientists have discovered more than 200 different subatomic particles.

• Specks of dust contain a trillion atoms.

QUARKS

Particles such as neutrons and protons are called hadrons. A hadron is made up of three smaller particles called quarks, which are stuck together by tiny particles called gluons. Quarks occur in two types: "down" quarks have one-third of a unit of negative electric charge, while "up" quarks have two-thirds of a unit of positive charge.

QUARKS IN A NEUTRON

A neutron has 1 up quark and 2 down quarks, giving an overall neutral charge

QUARKS IN A PROTON

A proton has 2 up quarks and 1 down quark, giving an overall positive charge

Gluon particles hold quarks together

Down quark

Up quark

NEUTRON

Electron

Nucleus

Neutron

BINDING FORCES

Atoms are held together by four fundamental forces, or interactions. Electrons are attracted to protons by electromagnetic force, while "strong" and "weak" nuclear forces bind together particles inside the nucleus. These basic forces, plus the pull of gravity, hold the entire universe together.

149

ELEMENTS

AN ELEMENT is a substance
made from only one type of atom.
The known elements are set out in a
chart called the periodic table. This chart
arranges elements into "groups"
(columns) and "periods" (rows).

*Veins of
pure gold*

QUARTZ

NAME, NUMBER, AND SYMBOL
Each box carries basic details about
an element. The atomic number is
the number of protons in the nucleus
of one of the element's atoms.

*Atomic
number*

*Chemical
symbol*

Name of element

15
P
Phosphorus

1								
1 **H** Hydrogen	**2**							
3 **Li** Lithium	**4** **Be** Beryllium							
11 **Na** Sodium	**12** **Mg** Magnesium	**3**	**4**	**5**	**6**	**7**	**8**	**9**
19 **K** Potassium	**20** **Ca** Calcium	**21** **Sc** Scandium	**22** **Ti** Titanium	**23** **V** Vanadium	**24** **Cr** Chromium	**25** **Mn** Manganese	**26** **Fe** Iron	**27** **Co** Cobalt
37 **Rb** Rubidium	**38** **Sr** Strontium	**39** **Y** Yttrium	**40** **Zr** Zirconium	**41** **Nb** Niobium	**42** **Mo** Molybdenum	**43** **Tc** Technetium	**44** **Ru** Ruthenium	**45** **Rh** Rhodium
55 **Cs** Cesium	**56** **Ba** Barium	**57-71** Lanthanides	**72** **Hf** Hafnium	**73** **Ta** Tantalum	**74** **W** Tungsten	**75** **Re** Rhenium	**76** **Os** Osmium	**77** **Ir** Iridium
87 **Fr** Francium	**88** **Ra** Radium	**89-103** Actinides	**104** **Unq** Unnil-quadium	**105** **Unp** Unnil-pentium	**106** **Unh** Unnil-hexium	**107** **Uns** Unnil-septium	**108** **Uno** Unnil-octium	**109** **Une** Unnil-ennium

GROUP I   GROUP II

*The number of electron
shells circling the nuclei of
an element's atoms increases
down each group. Elements
in the same group have
similar chemical properties.*

57 **La** Lanthanum	58 **Ce** Cerium	59 **Pr** Praseo-dymium	60 **Nd** Neodymium	61 **Pm** Promethium	62 **Sm** Samarium
89 **Ac** Actinium	90 **Th** Thorium	91 **Pa** Protactinium	92 **U** Uranium	93 **Np** Neptunium	94 **Pu** Plutonium

TYPES OF ELEMENTS KEY

- ALKALI METALS
- ALKALINE-EARTH METALS
- TRANSITION METALS
- LANTHANIDES
- ACTINIDES
- POOR METALS
- SEMIMETALS
- NONMETALS
- NOBLE GASES

GROUPS AND PERIODS

Each period starts on the left with a highly reactive alkali metal with an outer shell of one electron. It ends on the right with a stable noble gas in group 18 (0) with eight electrons in its outer shell. Elements in the same group have the same number of electrons in their outer shells.

As the atomic number increases by one along each period, the chemical properties of the element gradually change

An element's atomic number corresponds to the total number of electrons orbiting the nucleus of one of its atoms.

Two alternative number systems are used to group the elements

Lanthanides and actinides are set apart from the main table to make it easier to understand

MOLECULES AND BONDS

A GROUP OF ATOMS that are linked together is called a molecule. A molecule may be made up of a few or very many atoms. Molecules are formed when the electrical forces created by electron movement "bond" atoms together. Electron transfer between atoms occurs because some atoms require extra electrons to fill their outer shell.

WATER MOLECULE

CHEMICAL FORMULA
A chemical formula use letters and numbers to show how elements combine in a compound. The formul for a water molecule is H_2O as it is made up of two atom of hydrogen linked to single atom of oxygen

SODIUM ATOM

Electron transfers

CHLORINE ATOM

POSITIVELY CHARGED SODIUM ION

Both ions now have eight electrons in their outer shells

Ionic bond

IONIC BONDS
In ionic bonding, excess electrons transfer from the full outer shell of one atom to the outer shell of another that requires extra electrons to fill it. The transfer leaves both atoms as charged particles called ions. The atom losing the electron becomes a positively charged ion, or cation, and the atom gaining the electron becomes a negative ion, or anion. The force of attraction between the opposite charges binds the ions together.

NEGATIVELY CHARGED CHLORIDE ION

GIANT IONIC STRUCTURE

A crystal of salt (sodium chloride) contains sodium and chloride ions arranged in a regular, connected network that extends throughout the crystal. This network is called a giant ionic lattice.

Positive sodium ion (Na⁺)

Negative chloride ion (Cl⁻)

SODIUM CHLORIDE

Nitrogen atom bonds with three hydrogen atoms

Nitrogen atom

Hydrogen atom

Shared electrons form single bond between nitrogen and hydrogen atoms

Nitrogen nucleus

Hydrogen nucleus

AMMONIA MOLECULE (NH_3)

COVALENT BONDS

Ionic bonds are formed between metals and nonmetals. In covalent bonds, nonmetals bind together by sharing electrons. Two atoms each "donate" an electron, and the electrons form a pair that orbits both nuclei, holding the atoms together as a molecule. In a double bond, each atom donates two electrons.

ORGANIC CHEMISTRY

Carbon compounds are extremely common because carbon atoms link up easily with atoms of most other elements, and have the ability to form very stable bonds with other carbon atoms. All living things contain some compounds of carbon. The study of substances containing carbon is known as organic chemistry.

MATERIALS CONTAINING CARBON COMPOUNDS

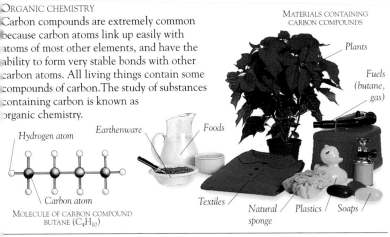

Plants

Fuels (butane, gas)

Earthenware

Foods

Hydrogen atom

Carbon atom

MOLECULE OF CARBON COMPOUND
BUTANE (C_4H_{10})

Textiles

Natural sponge

Plastics

Soaps

CHEMICAL REACTIONS

WHEN A CHEMICAL reaction occurs, new substances (called products) form from the original chemicals taking place in the reaction (called reactants). The atoms of the reactants rearrange themselves to form products.

Electron

EXOTHERMIC REACTIONS

A reaction that gives out more heat than it takes in, such as burning, is called an exothermic reaction. Oxidation and reduction are both types of exothermic reaction. Oxidation occurs when a substance combines with oxygen. Reduction takes place when a substance loses oxygen.

Heat is produced, warming surrounding air

Log burns, combining with oxygen in an oxidation reaction

ACIDS

An acid is a compound that forms hydrogen ions when it dissolves in water. The greater the concentration of ions, the stronger the acid. Strong acids are corrosive and can burn skin and dissolve metals. The pH scale measures acidity; pH 1 is the strongest acid, pH 7 is neutral.

ELECTRON TRANSFER

During the oxidation process atoms lose electrons and are "oxidized." During reduction atoms gain electrons and are "reduced."

Heat is absorbed during cooking

ENDOTHERMIC REACTIONS

Reactions that take in more heat than they give out, such as those during cooking, are endothermic

UNIVERSAL INDICATOR COLOR/pH CHART OF ACIDS

DIGESTIVE JUICES	CAR BATTERY	LEMON JUICE	VINEGAR	ACID RAIN	TAP WATER	PURE WATER

Mixtures and compounds

Most substances are made of two or more elements, either mingled loosely as mixtures or, after chemical reactions, combined strongly as compounds.

CHLORINE (GAS)

+

SODIUM (METAL)

=

SODIUM CHLORIDE OR COMMON SALT

COMPOUNDS
A compound is a substance in which the atoms of two or more elements are combined together. Common salt (sodium chloride), for example, is a compound of sodium and chlorine atoms.

Potassium permanganate forms a solution in water

COLLOIDS
In a colloid, tiny particles of one substance are dispersed evenly throughout another. Hair gel is a colloid of solid fat particles suspended in water.

HAIR GEL

SOLUTIONS
A solution is a mixture of one substance (the solute) dissolved in another (the solvent). Many compounds dissolve in water, forming weak bonds with water molecules.

BASES AND ALKALIS
A base is a compound that neutralizes acidity. Alkalis are bases that dissolve in water. The pH scale for bases ranges from neutral pure water (pH 7) to strongest alkali (pH 14).

UNIVERSAL INDICATOR COLOR/pH CHART OF BASES

PURE WATER	SOAP	BICARBONATE OF SODA	DISINFECTANT	HOUSEHOLD CLEANER	CALCIUM HYDROXIDE	OVEN CLEANER	SODIUM HYDROXIDE

FORCE AND MOTION

ALL MOVEMENT, or motion, is caused by forces. A force is invisible, but its effects are observable. Forces push or pull, causing objects to start or stop moving, change speed or direction, bend, twist, or change shape.

ATHLETES ACCELERATING UNDER FORCE FROM MUSCLES

Cue strikes white ball, transmitting momentum that overcomes ball's inertia

Ball accelerates away

White ball strikes red ball, transferring some of its momentum

Transferred momentum accelerates red ball away

INERTIA AND MOMENTUM

The tendency of all objects to resist effort to change their state or motion, whether they are actually moving or at rest, is called inertia. Momentum is the transferable force possessed by an object moving in a line, circle, or back and forth. It is calculated by multiplying the object's mass by its velocity.

VELOCITY AND ACCELERATION

The speed of an object in a particular direction is called its velocity. A cornering motorcycle, for example, keeps a constant speed but changes velocity as the direction of motion shifts. An increase in the velocity of an object is called acceleration. As its velocity decreases, the object undergoes deceleration.

NEWTON'S LAWS OF MOTION

• **First Law**: An object will remain at rest or continue traveling at a uniform velocity unless a force acts on it.

• **Second Law:** An object's acceleration is equal to the force acting on it, divided by the object's mass.

• **Third Law:** When two objects act on each other, they experience equal forces in opposite directions.

Athlete pulls on hammer, producing centipetal force

Centripetal force pulls hammer inward

Hammer's direction changes constantly

Hammer's inertia pulls it outward

Hammer flies off when released

CIRCULAR MOTION

A whirling object, such as an athlete's hammer, tries to fly off in a straight line, but circular motion, or centripetal force, pulls it toward the center of the circle. This force constantly changes the object's direction, keeping it moving in a circle.

Gravity

A force of attraction between all objects is called gravity. The greater the object's mass, the stronger the pull. The large mass of Earth generates a strong gravitational pull, keeping us on the ground.

Equal mass but different weight

ON THE MOON   ON EARTH

WEIGHT AND MASS

The force exerted on an object by gravity is called weight. Mass is the amount of matter an object contains.

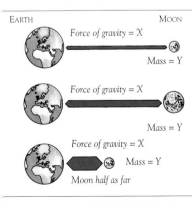

EARTH   MOON

Force of gravity = X

Mass = Y

Force of gravity = X

Mass = Y

Force of gravity = X

Mass = Y

Moon half as far

NEWTON'S LAW OF GRAVITATION

According to Newton's law, the force of gravity between two objects is calculated by multiplying their masses and dividing the result by the square of the distance between them. For example, if the Moon was half its actual distance from Earth, the force of gravity between them would be four times as strong. If the Moon had twice as much mass, the gravity between Earth and the Moon would be twice as great.

157

SIMPLE MACHINES

MACHINES can make tasks easier by changing the size or direction of a force. Many machines magnify effort, which is the level of force needed to overcome a resisting force, or load.

Axle turns with greater force

Effo applied wheel ri magnifi by ax

WHEEL AND AXL
Effort applied to th wheel rim is magnified b the axle, which turns wit greater distance. Applyin effort to an axle turns th wheel rim with less forc over a greater distance

INCLINED PLANE
An inclined plane is an angled surface, or slope, that reduces the effort required to move an object. Moving a car by pulling it up a ramp, for example, is easier than lifting it vertically. The car must travel further, but less effort is needed to move it.

Force of tension in rope pulls car up slope

Car has to travel farther than if lifted vertically

Weight of car pulls it downward

Winc magnifi force applie to a hand

A winch is form of whee and axl

Ramp (inclined plane)

Force used to wield axe magnified and transferred into log, pushing it apart

WEDGE
A wedge is a moving inclined plane that pushes an object with more force than the effort needed to move the wedge. Cutting blades, such as axes, make use of the wedge.

Screw head

Screw thread

SCREW
A screw's spiral groove, or thread, is a type of inclined plane wrapped around a shaft. When the screw head is turned, the thread moves the whole screw forward with more force than the turning effort.

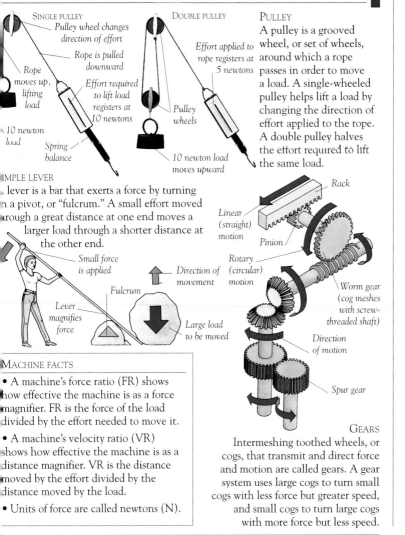

SINGLE PULLEY

Pulley wheel changes direction of effort

Rope is pulled downward

Rope moves up, lifting load

Effort required to lift load registers at 10 newtons

10 newton load

Spring balance

DOUBLE PULLEY

Effort applied to rope registers at 5 newtons

Pulley wheels

10 newton load moves upward

PULLEY

A pulley is a grooved wheel, or set of wheels, around which a rope passes in order to move a load. A single-wheeled pulley helps lift a load by changing the direction of effort applied to the rope. A double pulley halves the effort required to lift the same load.

SIMPLE LEVER

A lever is a bar that exerts a force by turning on a pivot, or "fulcrum." A small effort moved through a great distance at one end moves a larger load through a shorter distance at the other end.

Small force is applied

Direction of movement

Fulcrum

Lever magnifies force

Large load to be moved

Rack

Linear (straight) motion

Pinion

Rotary (circular) motion

Worm gear (cog meshes with screw-threaded shaft)

Direction of motion

Spur gear

GEARS

Intermeshing toothed wheels, or cogs, that transmit and direct force and motion are called gears. A gear system uses large cogs to turn small cogs with less force but greater speed, and small cogs to turn large cogs with more force but less speed.

MACHINE FACTS

• A machine's force ratio (FR) shows how effective the machine is as a force magnifier. FR is the force of the load divided by the effort needed to move it.

• A machine's velocity ratio (VR) shows how effective the machine is as a distance magnifier. VR is the distance moved by the effort divided by the distance moved by the load.

• Units of force are called newtons (N).

ENERGY AND HEAT

THE ABILITY to cause an action is
called energy. Light, sound, heat,
and electricity are forms of energy.
Human energy comes from the
chemical energy in food. Movement
energy is also called kinetic energy.

*Jack h
kinetic ener*

*Spring in
box has
potential
energy*

POTENTIAL ENER(
Stored energy
called potential energ
Squeezing or stretchin
an object makes it ga
potential energy, whic
is stored until the obje
is released. Dropping
raised object converts i
potential to fall to Ear
into kinetic energ

200 N

200 N

*Total
weight is
400 N*

*Raised
weights have
gravitational
potential energy*

*Bar carries
two sets of
200 N
weights*

WORK AND POWER
Work is done
when a force
moves something.
Energy provides
the ability to do
work. When work
is done, energy
converts from one
form to another.
The rate at which
work is done, or
energy changed
from one form to
another, is
called power.

*Weights are
raised about
4.9 ft (1.5 m)*

*Weight lifter
raises weights
in two seconds*

WEIGHT LIFTER
RAISING
WEIGHTS

WORK FACTS

• The **joule** (J) is the
SI unit of energy and
work: 1 J of energy is
used when a force
of 1 newton moves
through a distance of
1 meter. A kilojoule
(kJ) is 1,000 joules.

• The **watt** (W) is the
SI unit of power: 1 W
is the conversion of
1 joule of energy from
one form to another in
1 second. A kilowatt
(kW) is 1,000 watts.

Heat and temperature

The more energy an object's particles have, the hotter the object is. Heat is the total kinetic energy of an object's moving particles.

MEASURING TEMPERATURE

Temperature is a measure of the average kinetic energy of an object's moving particles. Most liquid and electronic thermometers measure temperature on the Celsius and Fahrenheit scales.

LIQUID THERMOMETER

Temperature

Liquid-crystal display

ELECTRONIC THERMOMETER

olumn of mercury alcohol expands temperature rises

Heat- senstive tip

eat m feet conducts into stone, wing feet feeling cold

CONDUCTION

Heat energy always passes from hot objects to cooler ones. Heat travels through solids by conduction. Particles in the heated part of the solid vibrate and excite neighboring particles.

CONVECTION AND RADIATION

Heat travels through liquids and gases by convection. Hot fluids are less dense than cold ones and float upward, sinking again as they cool. Matter can also ose or gain heat energy by radiation.

Swirling color trails show how heat spreads through liquid

Hot, colored water floats to top of jar

Bottle contains hot, colored water

SCALE OF TEMPERATURE
Temperatures are measured in degrees on the Celsius (C) and Fahrenheit (F) scales, and in Kelvins (K).

482°F, 250°C, 523K
Burning point of wood

424°F, 218°C, 491K
Explosion point of nitroglycerine

284°F, 140°C, 413K
Sauna bath

212°F, 100°C, 373K
Boiling point of water

134°F, 56.7°C, 329.7K
Midday heat in Death Valley, California

98.6°F, 37°C, 310K
Human body temperature

71.6°F, 22°C, 295K
Body temperature of spiny anteater

32°F, 0°C, 273K
Freezing point of pure water

–38°F, –39°C, 234K
Freezing point of mercury

–459°F, –273°C, 0K
Absolute zero

161

ELECTRICITY

THE MOVEMENT OF electrons between atoms creates a form of energy called electricity. A flow of electrons is called a current. Electric currents and certain materials generate a force called magnetism.

BALLOON CHARGED BY RUBBING (FRICTION)

ELECTROSTATIC INDUCTION

Electricity that does not flow in a current is called static electricity. A static charge can be produced by rubbing a balloon against an object such as a sweater. Friction causes electrons to transfer from the sweater's atoms to the balloon's atoms; the balloon gains a negative electric charge and the sweater a positive one. The charged balloon can also induce a static charge in other objects.

Negatively charged balloon repels electrons in pieces of paper, giving paper a positive static charge

Positively charged paper attracted to negatively charged balloon

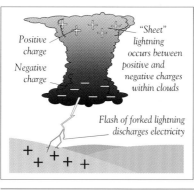

Positive charge

Negative charge

"Sheet" lightning occurs between positive and negative charges within clouds

Flash of forked lightning discharges electricity

LIGHTNING

Inside a thundercloud, positive and negative charges separate between the top and bottom of the cloud. The negative charge at the bottom of the cloud induces a positive charge to build up in the ground below. "Forked" lightning occurs when a strong pulse of electric current suddenly flows between the two opposite charges, discharging from the cloud's base to the ground and back again.

BATTERY

A battery is a device that produces and stores electric current. Many batteries produce current by using carbon and zinc conductors called electrodes and a chemical paste called an electrolyte. In a circuit, the current flows from the negative electrode (cathode) to the positive (anode). An electric current can be used to power anything from a light-bulb to a computer.

Electric current lights bulb

Carbon anode (positive electrode)

Zinc casing is cathode (negative electrode)

Electron flow

Electrical contacts

Battery

Current flows through wires

ELECTRIC MOTOR

current flows through a wire coil between e poles of a magnet. The current creates magnetic field around the coil that teracts with the field produced by the agnet, forcing the coil to turn.

Opposing magnetic fields cause coil to rotate

Rotating coil can be attached to a driveshaft or flywheel

Compass needles align with magnetic field

Iron filings show lines of magnetic force

Magnet

MAGNETISM

A magnet exerts an invisible field of magnetic force that attracts objects made of iron, and a few other metals. Every magnet has two ends, called its north and south poles, where the forces it exerts are strongest. An electromagnet is a piece of iron that exerts magnetic force when a current is passed through it.

Unlike, or opposite, magnetic poles (a north pole and a south pole) attract each other. Like poles (two north or two south poles) repel each other. Iron filings scattered near the magnets show the lines of attraction and repulsion.

South pole

ATTRACTION \ North pole

Two South poles \ REPULSION

163

LIGHT AND COLOR

THE FASTEST-MOVING form of energy is light.
It travels in waves that are part of a range
of radiation called the electromagnetic
spectrum. Visible "white light" is a mixture
of many different colors of light, each with its
own frequency and wavelength.

*Waves at right angl
to each other and
the direction of trav*

THE SUN

*As an atom gains
energy, its electrons
jump to higher orbits,
or "energy levels"*

*Electron gives out photon
as it falls back to
original orbit*

*Electric
field*

Wavelength

*Higher
orbit*

*Directio
of travel*

*Original
orbit*

*Magnetic
field*

LIGHT SOURCES
Most of the light
that reaches Earth
comes from the
Sun. The emission of
light by a hot object,
such as the Sun, is
called incandescence.
Luminescence is the
emission of light
without using heat.

PHOTONS
A photon is a particle of
electromagnetic radiation
that makes up light rays,
X rays, and radio waves.

WAVES
Electromagnetic
radiation travels as
waves of oscillating
(fluctuating) electric
and magnetic fields.

RADIO

TELEVISION

MICROWAVE OVEN

INFRARED STOVE

ELECTROMAGNETIC
SPECTRUM

Radio waves

Microwaves

*Infrared
(IR) rays*

| 10^5 | 10^4 | 10^3 | 10^2 | 10 | 1 | 10^{-1} | 10^{-2} | 10^{-3} | 10^{-4} | 10^{-5} | 1C |

SCIENCE

164

SPLITTING LIGHT

Passing a beam of white light through a prism separates out the various wavelengths of the light beam. This reveals the range of colors, or visible spectrum, that makes up white light.

YELLOW

THE SUBTRACTIVE PROCESS

The three secondary colors of yellow, magenta, and cyan are also called primary subtractive colors, since each absorbs some light wavelengths from white light but reflects others. Mixing the three colors in varying proportions subtracts, or removes, different light wavelengths to produce new colors.

RED LIGHT

CYAN

All colors absorbed, giving black

Red and blue give magenta

Green absorbed, red and blue reflected

MAGENTA

THE ADDITIVE PROCESS

Red, green, and blue are called primary additive colors, since mixing red, blue, and green light together produces white light. When two primary additive colors are mixed, the brain sees the mixture as a single, "secondary" color.

BLUE LIGHT

Blue and green give cyan

GREEN LIGHT

Red and green give yellow

Mixing red, blue, and green light gives white light

UV SUNBED
Ultraviolet (UV) rays

X RAY MACHINE
X rays

NUCLEAR EXPLOSION
Gamma rays

Waves at this end of the spectrum have more energy

WAVELENGTH (IN METERS)

| 10^{-9} | 10^{-10} | 10^{-11} | 10^{-12} | 10^{-13} | 10^{-14} | 10^{-15} | 10^{-16} | 10^{-17} |

165

SOUND

A SOUND source generates vibrations that pass though a material in waves. Our ears pick up sound waves traveling in the air around us. Sound waves can travel through solids, liquids, and gases, but not through a vacuum, since there are no particles of matter to carry vibrations.

Tuning fork vibrates, causing pressure variations in surrounding air

High pressure (compression)

Low pressure (rarefaction)

Sound wave

SOUND WAVES

A sound source produces vibrations that squeeze and stretch surrounding air. Squeezing air molecules together creates high pressure, or "compression." Stretching air creates an area of low pressure, or "rarefaction." Alternating compressions and rarefactions travel through air as sound waves.

PITCH

Pitch of a sound is how high or low a sound wave is. Pitch depends on frequency vibrations a second, measured in hertz (Hz).

NUCLEAR EXPLOSION MAKES: 0.01 Hz

DECIBELS	
140	EAR DAMAGE Rocket lifting o
120	PAIN THRESHO Jet plane taking
100	ROCK CONCER
80	BUSY TRAFFIC
60	NORMAL CONVERSATIO
	PEOPLE WHISPER 18 FT (5 M) AW
30	
10	LEAVES FALLIN 3.3 FT (1 M) AW
	THRESHOLD C HUMAN HEARIN
0	(SOUND JUST AUDIBLE)

LOUDNESS

The greater the pressure changes between a sound wave's highest and lowest points (amplitude), the louder the sound. Loudnes is measured in decibels (dB). A 10-dB increase means the sound is ten times as loud.

HUMAN HEARS: 20–20,000 Hz MAKES: 85–1,100 Hz

ELEPHAN HEARS: 1–20,0 MAKES: 12 F

RECORDING SOUND

COMPACT DISC

SOUND SYSTEMS

All sound recording systems store sound by making copies of sound waves, as spiral grooves on a vinyl record, magnetic patterns on tape, or tiny, laser-scanned pits on a compact disc.

Record groove

VINYL RECORD

Stylus picks up sound stored as electrical signals in groove

Pits pressed into CD surface store sound as a sequence of binary numbers

Magnetic field aligns particles on tape to reproduce sound

CASSETTE TAPE

MICROPHONE

In a moving-coil microphone, sound waves cause a wire coil to vibrate, or move, within a magnetic field. This makes an electric current flow through the coil. The current fluctuates in strength as the sound waves change, producing electrical signals that mirror the sound waves.

Permanent magnet

Wire coil forms an electromagnet

Diaphragm of thin plastic or metal foil

Electromagnet

Diaphragm

Permanent magnet

LOUDSPEAKER

Feeding electric signals to a loudspeaker generates a varying magnetic field around an electromagnet. The varying field causes a diaphragm to vibrate, producing sound waves.

DOG
HEARS: 15–50,000 Hz
MAKES: 450–1,080 Hz

BAT
HEARS: 1,000–120,000 Hz
MAKES: 10,000–120,000 Hz

ULTRASOUND SCANNER MAKES AND RECEIVES: 3,500,000–7,500,000 Hz

PORPOISE
HEARS: 150–150,000 Hz
MAKES: 7,000–120,000 Hz

SOUND

167

ELECTRONICS

Three layer "sandwich" of n- and p-type silicon

THE SCIENCE OF electronics is concerned with controlling and directing the movement of electrons. The complex operation of machines such as computers and jet aircraft is dependent on electronic technology.

TRANSISTOR

A transistor is a semiconducting component that boosts or switches current. In computers, transistors switch on and off many times each second, enabling rapid information processing.

SEMICONDUCTORS

A semiconductor is a material found in most electronic components that can vary its ability to conduct electricity. Adding impurities alters its electrical properties. Boron atoms in p-type silicon take up electrons from the outer shells of silicon atoms, leaving moving "holes" that carry current. In n-type silicon, extra electrons donated by added arsenic atoms carry current.

Hole in outer shell of silicon atom moves, carrying current

Extra electron moves, carrying current

P-TYPE SILICON (SEMICONDUCTOR) *Boron atom*

N-TYPE SILICON (SEMICONDUCTOR) *Arsenic atom*

INTERNATIONAL ELECTRICAL COMPONENT SYMBOLS

CAPACITOR
Stores charge

DIODE
Permits current to flow in one direction only; can also be used to convert ac signals to dc signals (a rectifier)

LIGHT-EMITTING DIODE
Emits light when current flows through it

MICROPHONE
Converts sound waves into ac signals (and vice versa)

LOUDSPEAKER
Converts ac signals into sound waves

n-p-n TRANSISTOR
Amplifies electric current, and turns it on and off

p-n-p TRANSISTOR
Amplifies electric current, and turns it on and off

INTEGRATED CIRCUITS

An integrated circuit, or "microchip," a tiny piece, or "wafer," of silicon that contains a complete circuit of thousands of electronic components. Layers of n- and p-type semi-conductors and other materials are built up on the silicon wafer and linked by fine conducting wires.

MAGNIFIED OVERLAY OF AN INTEGRATED CIRCUIT

Circuits are "printed" onto wafer photographically through transparent overlay

Detailed overlay plans are made for each layer of the chip

Each plan is a different color

BINARY CODE

Microchips store data as on/off electrical pulses called binary code. All information is broken down into sequences of ones (on) and zeros (off). The decimal number 13, for example, is 1101 in binary form.

ON　　　ON　　　OFF　　　ON

2^3　　　2^2　　　2　　　1

$(1 \times 8) + (1 \times 4) + (0 \times 2) + (1 \times 1) = 13$

Microchips, or "chips," are encased in a tough plastic or ceramic capsule

ENCASED INTEGRATED CIRCUIT

Conducting pins can be soldered or plugged into a circuit board

ENCASED CHIP

A microchip is housed in a protective casing that dwarfs the tiny chip itself. An encased chip stores data as electrical signals in binary code, and uses logic gates (see right) to process that data. A microprocessor is a chip that can store instructions in an electronic memory.

LOGIC GATES

Microchips use patterns of transistors called logic gates to process binary code. Different types of gates switch on (open) or off (close) depending on the type of input received.

OUTPUT

AND GATE
Gives an output signal when a signal is applied to one input AND to the other input.

A　B

OUTPUT

OR GATE
Gives an output signal when a signal is applied to one input OR to the other input, OR to both.

A　B

OUTPUT

NOT GATE
Gives an output signal when a signal does NOT arrive at its input.

INPUT

169

COMPUTERS

A COMPUTER IS an electronic machine that can perform a wide variety of complex tasks very quickly. Each task is reduced to a series of simple calculations, which enables rapid processing of data.

PERSONAL COMPUTER
The most familiar type of computer is the personal computer (PC), which can only be used by one person at a time. The machinery that makes up a PC, such as the keyboard and mouse, disk drive, and monitor, is called "hardware."

Monitor displays data

Disk drive uses magnetic "floppy" disks to store and run software

COMPUTER PROGRAM
A program is a set of instructions that tells computer to carry out specific task. This set of instructions may be written as long sets of numbers called "machine code," or in a computer language such as BASIC or FORTRAN. Computer programs are called "software."

Keyboard and mouse for inputting data

CENTRAL PROCESSING UNIT
A computer is controlled by a central processing unit (CPU), a single microchip containing a large number of circuits. The CPU processes data from the keyboard, ROM, and RAM. It also sends information to the RAM, outputs data to the printer, and displays software on the monitor.

ROM (read-only memory) is permanent and contains the operating system, a set of instructions that tells the computer how to work

Keyboard

RAM (random-access memory) temporarily stores programs that are currently being run

Ouput to monitor or printer

Input

CPU

SUPERCOMPUTER

Computers designed to perform complex tasks at the highest possible speeds are called supercomputers. The world's fastest computers use parallel processing. While conventional computers handle tasks one after another (in a series), parallel computers perform groups of operations at the same time. Their processing speed is also increased by cooling their components, which aids conductivity

This computer is used in the study of particle physics

CRAY X-MP/48
SUPERCOMPUTER

COMPUTER-AIDED DESIGN
Designers and architects test new ideas by using computer-aided design (CAD) to create 3-D graphic models on screen.

COMPUTER FACTS

• Neural networks are computers designed to imitate the workings of the human brain.

• The world's largest computer manufacturer is American company IBM, employing up to 225,000 people.

CD-ROM

A form of compact disc adapted for use in computers, a CD for a CD-ROM can store 450 times more information than a standard floppy disk, including pictures, text, sound, and video.

CD-ROM
*software
page*

VIRTUAL REALITY
A virtual-reality (VR) system enables the user to interact with a computer-generated "virtual" world. A headset supplies the user with 3-D images, while a "data glove" lets you "touch" what you see.

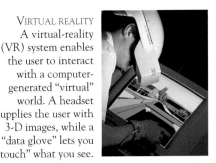

171

PRINTING TECHNOLOGY

THE PROCESS of reproducing words (text) and pictures (images) using ink is called printing. Printing presses enable numerous copies of text and images to be made very quickly. Modern print production uses computers at many stages in the printing process.

Paper fed through press

Colors are added one by one as paper comes into contact with the color plates

Adding yellow ink

Adding cyan ink

Adding magenta ink

Adding black ink

Each roller is equipped with a plate coated with a different colored ink

PRINTING PRESS
A color press uses printing plates to print text and images. Light shines through the text film and color-separated image films photographically records their details onto the light-sensitive coating of the plates. After being attached to rollers, ink is then applied to the plates. Paper is pressed against the plates, printing the text and images.

Full-color printed sheets emerge

PRINTING PRESS

PRINTED FULL-COLOR IMAGE

YELLOW

MAGENTA

CYAN

BLACK

COLOR PRINTING
Only four colors are used in color printing yellow, magenta, cyan, and black. The image to be printed is scanned electronically, producing a separate piece of film for each color. The details of these "separations" are transferred onto color plates in the printing press. The separations are then printed on top of one another, reproducing the full-color image.

TELECOMMUNICATIONS

THE SCIENCE OF broadcasting sound and pictures over long distances is called telecommunications.

WAVE MODULATION
Radio and television programs are broadcast by radio waves, which must first be modulated (coded) so that they can carry sound and picture signals. A steady radio wave is modulated by a sound signal in one of two ways. Its amplitude (strength) may be modulated (AM) or its frequency may change (FM).

AM RADIO WAVE

FM RADIO WAVE

Wave strength modulated

Wave frequency modulated

HOW A TELEVISION WORKS
The antenna of a TV receives a modulated carrier wave (carrying sound and picture signals), which is then "demodulated" into electrical signals and sent to a cathode-ray tube. The tube contains three "electron guns" that fire beams of electrons at the phosphor-coated TV screen. Magnetic fields cause the beams to scan the screen. The picture builds as the electrons make the phosphors glow.

Red, green, and blue electron guns

Electro-magnets

Circuits amplify signal

Electron beams

Input from TV antenna

TELEVISION SET

LONG-RANGE COMMUNICATIONS
Low-frequency radio waves can be sent long distances by bouncing them between the ionosphere (an ion-rich region of the atmosphere) and the ground. High-frequency waves are transmitted through the ionosphere to orbiting communication satellites, which relay the radio waves to receiving stations on Earth.

Phosphors glow red, blue, or green when hit by electron beams

High-frequency signals are sent via satellite

Short waves reflect off top of ionosphere

Some radio waves do not need to be reflected

Low-frequency waves bounce between ionosphere and ground

TRANSMITTING RADIO WAVES

MATHEMATICS

THE STUDY OF numbers and shapes is called mathematics. The different branches of mathematics enable us to create sophisticated machines, build structures, and run businesses. Algebra, for example, uses abstract symbols in place of numbers, while geometry deals with shapes and lines.

MATHEMATICAL SYMBOLS

= EQUAL TO

— SUBTRACTION

÷ DIVISION

+ ADDITION

× MULTIPLICATION

TYPES OF NUMBERS

A written number consists of digits, or numerals; the number 313, for example, has 3 digits. A positive number is any number greater than zero, such as 6. A negative number is less than zero, such as –6. A prime number can only be divided by itself and 1.

ROTATION AND ANGLES

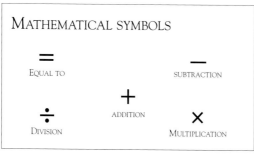

Obtuse angle
90°
130°
Reflex angle
45°
Acute angle
360° 0°
Right angle
Round angle
240°

CIRCLES AND CURVES

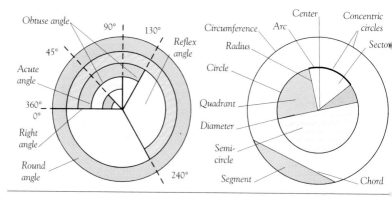

Center
Concentric circles
Circumference
Arc
Radius
Sector
Circle
Quadrant
Diameter
Semi-circle
Segment
Chord

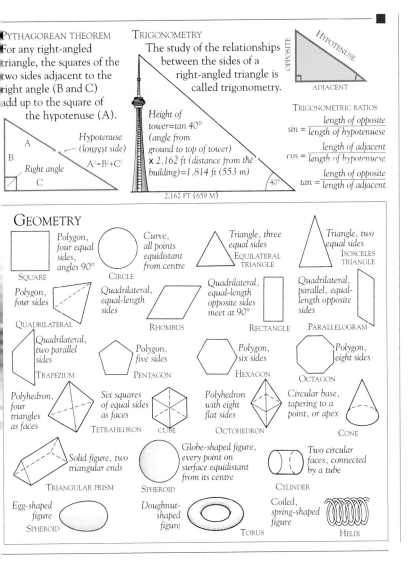

PYTHAGOREAN THEOREM

For any right-angled triangle, the squares of the two sides adjacent to the right angle (B and C) add up to the square of the hypotenuse (A).

Hypotenuse (longest side)

A

B

Right angle

C

$A^2 = B^2 + C^2$

TRIGONOMETRY

The study of the relationships between the sides of a right-angled triangle is called trigonometry.

OPPOSITE

HYPOTENUSE

ADJACENT

Height of tower=tan 40° (angle from ground to top of tower) x 2,162 ft (distance from the building)=1,814 ft (553 m)

40°

2,162 FT (659 M)

TRIGONOMETRIC RATIOS

$sin = \dfrac{length\ of\ opposite}{length\ of\ hypotenuese}$

$cos = \dfrac{length\ of\ adjacent}{length\ of\ hypotenuese}$

$tan = \dfrac{length\ of\ opposite}{length\ of\ adjacent}$

GEOMETRY

Polygon, four equal sides, angles 90°
SQUARE

Curve, all points equidistant from centre
CIRCLE

Triangle, three equal sides
EQUILATERAL TRIANGLE

Triangle, two equal sides
ISOSCELES TRIANGLE

Polygon, four sides
QUADRILATERAL

Quadrilateral, equal-length sides
RHOMBUS

Quadrilateral, equal-length opposite sides meet at 90°
RECTANGLE

Quadrilateral, parallel, equal-length opposite sides
PARALLELOGRAM

Quadrilateral, two parallel sides
TRAPEZIUM

Polygon, five sides
PENTAGON

Polygon, six sides
HEXAGON

Polygon, eight sides
OCTAGON

Polyhedron, four triangles as faces
TETRAHEDRON

Six squares of equal sides as faces
CUBE

Polyhedron with eight flat sides
OCTOHEDRON

Circular base, tapering to a point, or apex
CONE

Solid figure, two triangular ends
TRIANGULAR PRISM

Globe-shaped figure, every point on surface equidistant from its centre
SPHEROID

Two circular faces, connected by a tube
CYLINDER

Egg-shaped figure
SPHEROID

Doughnut-shaped figure
TORUS

Coiled, spring-shaped figure
HELIX

MATHEMATICS

TRANSPORTATION

ENGINES

AN ENGINE harnesses one form of
energy and converts it into motive
force, or kinetic energy. Engines
range in complexity from simple
windmills to sophisticated turbofans.

WINDMILL
The sails of a windmill
convert wind force into
rotary motion, driving a
central shaft that powers
the milling machinery

INTERNAL COMBUSTION
An internal combustion
engine provides motive
force by harnessing
the energy
released when
a mix of fuel
and air is
burned
(combusted)
inside its cylinders.
The stages of the
combustion
cycle are
called strokes.

Distributor

*Spring snaps
valve shut*

*Camshaft controls
opening and closing
of valves*

*Rocker arm
pushes valve open*

*Channels for
cooling water*

Valve

Piston

Cylinder

Flywheel

*Clutch
disconnects
engine while
driver
changes gear*

*Crankshaft drives
wheels via gearbox
and clutch*

*Oilpan contains
reservoir of oil for
lubricating engine parts*

*Crankshaft bearing
where crankshaft runs
through engine block*

*Fan belt
drives
cooling fan*

*Dipstick for
checking level of
lubricating oil*

FOUR-CYLINDER
GAS ENGINE

FOUR-STROKE ENGINE CYCLE

Inlet valve opens

Cylinder

Piston slides down cylinder, sucking in mix of fuel and air (charge)

INDUCTION STROKE

Inlet valve shuts

Piston rises, compressing charge into small space

COMPRESSION STROKE

Spark plug ignites compressed charge

Expanding gases force piston down

Piston spins crankshaft

POWER STROKE

Exhaust valve opens

Rising piston pushes out hot gases

Cycle restarts

EXHAUST STROKE

Blades rotate and compress incoming air

Fan blade

Bypass air provides main thrust

Outer drive-shaft

Bypass air duct

Inner driveshaft

Fuel inlet

Fuel (kerosene) and air ignited

Turbine spins outer shaft, driving compressor

TURBOFAN

TURBOFAN JET ENGINE

A turbofan jet engine sucks in and compresses air, which is then mixed with fuel and ignited. The hot gases produced create forward thrust and drive air-circulating turbines that cool the engine.

Casing of rocket

Most liquid-fuel rockets use liquid hydrogen and liquid oxygen

Liquid hydrogen and liquid oxygen mixture ignited in combustion chamber

Escaping gases provide thrust for rocket

ROCKET ENGINE

A rocket engine burns solid or liquid fuel in an open-ended combustion chamber. The escaping hot gases thrust the rocket upward.

ENGINE FACTS

• The smallest internal combustion engine is the 0.1 cc model aircraft.

• Temperatures inside an internal combustion engine can reach 3,100°F (1,700°C).

179

TRAINS

PEOPLE AND GOODS are transported along railroads in long trains of trucks and carriages. These trains are pulled by powerful engine units called locomotives.

STEAM TRAVEL

Water in a steam locomotive's boiler is heated by a coal fire in the firebox, making steam. Pressure from the steam moves a piston back and forth; a connecting rod and crank linked to the piston makes the wheels turn. Steam locomotives were used to pull the earliest trains, eventually being replaced by electric and diesel locomotives in the 1960s.

The tracks rests on concrete or wooden beams known as ties or sleepers

Ra..

When a switch takes place, short sections of rail swing across to guide the train on to the new track

Switc
(point

TRACKS AND SWITCHES

Rails are often welded into one continuous track as they are laid, allowing trains to run smoothly. Trains change tracks at pivoting sections called switches, or points

Water tank Coal space Boiler Crank

Coal burned in firebox Coupling rod Connecting rod drives wheels Pistoni linked t connecting ro

1804 BRITISH ENGINEER RICHARD TREVITHICK BUILDS THE FIRST STEAM LOCOMOTIVE

1829 ROBERT STEPHENSON'S ROCKET HERALDS THE AGE OF THE PASSENGER TRAIN

1890 WORLD'S FIRST ELECTRIC UNDERGROUND RAILROAD OPENS IN UK

MONORAIL
Some trains run on or hang underneath a single (mono) electric rail. Monorails are fast and clean, and do not interfere with ground traffic.

Air-conditioned carriage

Electric motors drive wheels of power cars and leading carriage

Pantograph picks up electric current from overhead cables

Power cars at each end of TGV drive train

Radio keeps driver in touch with signaling center and other trains

Computer in driver's cab checks for faults on train

Leading carriage

Streamlined shape reduces air resistance, enabling TGV to travel at high speed

PARTS OF A TRAIN
The high-speed French *Train à Grand Vitesse* (TGV) runs on specially built tracks with gentle curves and slopes. First introduced in 1981, the TGV has a top speed of 186 mph (300 km/h).

Trucks of four or more wheels enable train to go around curves

1938 MALLARD SETS WORLD SPEED RECORD FOR A STEAM LOCOMOTIVE AT 126 MPH (203 KM/H)

1934 PIONEER ZEPHYR DIESEL-ELECTRIC TRAIN INTRODUCED IN US

1990S FRENCH TGV SETS WORLD SPEED RECORD FOR AN ELECTRIC LOCOMOTIVE

CARS

MODERN CARS use a variety of mechanical and
electrical systems to provide the transportation we
take for granted. Car manufacturers are always
looking for new ways to make cars
safer and more efficient.

*Gearshift changes gears,
which enable the engine to run
at efficient speeds while the
car slows down or speeds up*

ENGINE LAYOUTS

FRONT ENGINE,
REAR-WHEEL DRIVE

REAR ENGINE,
REAR-WHEEL DRIVE

FRONT ENGINE,
FRONT-WHEEL DRIVE

MIDENGINE,
REAR-WHEEL DRIVE

Design features
Compromise
between traction
(roadgrip),
handling, and
internal space
requirements.

Provides
maximum
traction, but
reduces amount
of internal space.

Maximizes
internal space,
and provides
good traction.
Used by most
family cars.

Good handling
and traction, but
little internal
space. Fast sports
cars use this
engine layout.

Fuel tank

Sunroof

*Rear drive
wheel*

*Hand brake
and ratchet*

*Driveshaft transmits
the movements of the
engine to the wheels*

THE ANATOMY OF A CAR
Most cars have four wheels, an
engine at the front, and room for at
least two passengers. This illustration
shows the main features of a rear-
wheel drive hatchback.

TYPES OF BRAKES

Modern disk brakes use hydraulic pressure to squeeze a steel disk attached to the wheel between two brake pads, slowing the car. In older drum brakes, curved brake "shoes" push against the inside of a metal drum attached to the wheel.

Disk

Brake shoe

Drum

Callipor holding brake pads

DISK BRAKE

DRUM BRAKE

SUSPENSION SYSTEMS

Ball joint

V-shaped "wishbone" arms

Lower arm

Spring/damper strut

FRONT SUSPENSION

Spring

Damper unit

Lower arm

Ball joint

MACPHERSON STRUT

Suspension isolates the wheels from the rest of the car, providing a smoother ride.
Front suspension uses hinged, swiveling V-shaped arms that enable the steered wheels to go up and down as well as swivel. A MacPherson Strut is a swiveling coil and damper unit that gives lighter suspension for front or rear wheels.

Rear-view mirror

Windshield

Steering wheel connected to rod that swivels the front wheels

Air filter cleans air before it is mixed with fuel

Battery

Headlights

Front bumper

Radiator cools water flowing around the engine

Distributor ensures that spark plugs fire in sequence

Generator produces electricity when the engine is running; this electricity is stored in the battery

Fan helps cool water in the radiator

183

Types of cars

Since 1901, when the Oldsmobile became the first mass-produced motor vehicle, car design has changed drastically. Today, there are many different designs to suit a wide variety of purposes, from driving to work, to racing.

1898 BENZ VELO

1898 BENZ VELO
German engineer Karl Benz produced the first car to be sold to the public in 1885. The Benz Velo, introduced in 1894, was the first car to sell in significant numbers.

1903 DE DION BOUTON MODEL Q
Produced by the French De Dion Bouton company, the 698 cc Model Q is typical of the light, reliable cars popular in the early years of the 20th century.

1903 DE DION BOUTON MODEL Q

Coach-type leaf-spring suspension

Wooden spoked wheels inherited from the horse cart

Solid rubber tire

Propeller shaft carrying drive from gearbox to final-drive

Folding hood

Folding windshield for rear-seat passenger

1909 ROLLS-ROYCE SILVER GHOST
Demand for more luxurious cars led to the manufacture of quality vehicles such as the Rolls-Royce Silver Ghost.

"Spirit of Ecstasy" mascot added in 1911

1909 ROLLS-ROYCE SILVER GHOST

Air-filled "pneumatic" tires

1957 MERCEDES-BENZ 300SL GULL WING
The futuristic design of the 300SL sports car features upward-swinging doors that resemble the wings of a seagull.

"Gull wing" doors

CAR FACTS

• The Aston Martin Lagonda was the first car with all-electronic instruments.

• The jet-engined car Thrust 2 holds the Land Speed Record, reaching 633.5 mph (1019.2 km/h) in 1983.

SYN126F

Rear wing forces wheels onto ground

Ferrari Boxer 312 12-cylinder engine

Light fiberglass body shell

Driver's cockpit

1979 FERRARI 312T4
Powerful engines and road-gripping wide tires allow Formula One racing cars to travel at over 190 mph (300 km/h).

CONTEMPORARY CARS
Modern cars are designed to cater to specific driving requirements.

FOUR-WHEEL DRIVE OFF-ROAD VEHICLE, SUZUKI VITARA

MULTI-PURPOSE VEHICLE (MPV), FIAT ULYSSES

COMPACT CITY CAR, RENAULT TWINGO

FOUR-WHEEL DRIVE, LUXURY SEDAN, AUDI A8

BICYCLES

APART FROM WALKING there is no simpler and cheaper way to travel than on a bicycle. Bicycles were invented in Europe little more than 200 years ago, but today they are popular worldwide for both transportation and leisure.

MODERN RACING BIKE
Air-filled tires, an efficient gearing system, and a cushioned saddle make modern bicycles more comfortable and easier to ride than their predecessors.

TYPES OF BICYCLES

RACING BIKE FOR ROAD RACES

BMX FOR ROUGH TERRAIN

MOUNTAIN BIKE

TANDEM FOR TWO PEOPLE

Crossbar

Saddle

Spoke

Brake block

Tire

Front derailleur

Rim

Chainrings

Rear derailleur (gear changer)

Sprockets or cogs

1790 THE COMTE DE SIVRAC BUILDS THE *CELERIFERE*

1813 CARL VON DRAIS BUILDS THE *DRAISIENNE*

1839 "BONESHAKER" IS FIRST BIKE WITH PEDAL-DRIVEN BACK WHEEL

1861 FIRST BIKE WITH PEDAL-DRIVEN FRONT WHEEL

TOUR DE FRANCE
Cycle races range from track sprints held over 1,094 yd (1,000 m) to multistage events lasting several weeks. One of the most famous road races is he 24-day Tour de France.

BICYCLE FACTS
• The longest bicycle, ridden by four people for a short distance in 1988, is 72.97 ft (22.24 m) long.

• There are 800 million bicycles in the world. They outnumber cars two to one.

Brake cable

Handlebar

Brake lever

Stem

Gearshift

Pedal

Fork blade

Large cogs used for climbing uphill

Small cogs allow fast travel downhill or on flat ground

Chain

Pedal

Hub axle or spindle

Valve

GEAR SYSTEMS
Many bicycles have gear systems that enable the cyclist to travel quickly or slowly while pedaling at a comfortable rate. By moving the gearshift, the cyclist lifts the chain from one cog to another.

C.1870 THE "PENNY FARTHING" FIRST APPEARS

1839 THE "BICYCLETTE" IS THE FIRST COMMERCIAL BICYCLE

1959 THE "MOULTON" IS FIRST NEW BIKE DESIGN FOR 50 YEARS

1990s "HPV" HUMAN-POWERED VEHICLE

MOTORCYCLES

THE SMALLEST and lightest form of motorized
transportation, motorcycles range from small-engined
commuter mopeds to racers that can reach speeds
of more than 300 mph (500 km/h).

TYPES OF MOTORCYCLES

TRAIL BIKE
FOR ROUGH
TERRAIN

PERSONALLY
ADAPTED
"CUSTOM"
MOTORCYCLE

LOW-POWER
50 CC MOPED

SMALL-
WHEELED
MOTOR
SCOOTER

PARTS OF A MOTORCYCLE
A motorcycle is essentially a bicycle powered by an
engine. Motorcycle engine sizes range from 50 cc
(cubic capacity) to more than 1,000 cc.

Saddle

Exhaust

Brake disk

Drive chain

Four-cylinder
1,002 cc engine

1885 MAYBACH AND
DAIMLER'S WOODEN
MOTORCYCLE

1892 FIRST
COMMERCIALLY
PRODUCED MOTORCYCLE

1901 WERNER COMPANY
PRODUCES ONE OF FIRST
PRACTICAL MOTORCYCLES

1904 FIRST HARLEY-DAVIDSON
MOTORCYCLE, THE SILENT
GRAY FELLOW, PRODUCED

CORNERING
Motorcyclists lean over on curves to prevent the motorcycle's momentum from overturning the bike.

Brake levers

Mirror

Fuel tank

Windshield

1992 YAMAHA FZR 1000 EXUP

Fairing (front enclosure)

Throttle connected to handlebar grip

Telescopic suspension forks

ide fairing emoved to how engine

Three-spoke wheels

Radiator

MOTORCYCLE FACTS

• The fastest motorcycle built for general sale is the Bimota YB81E Furano, which has a top speed of 180 mph (290 km/h).

Exhaust port

TWO-STROKE ENGINE
Smaller motorcycles often use valveless two-stroke engines. Fuel enters and exhaust is ejected through cylinder openings called ports. The moving piston opens and closes the ports.

1910 FIRST POPULAR MOTORCYCLE SIDECARS

1959 TRIUMPH COMPANY INTRODUCES THE HIGH PERFORMANCE *BONNEVILLE*

1978 MOTORCYCLE SPEED RECORD OF 318 MPH (512 KM/H) SET BY DONALD VESCO

1990s BMW COMPANY LAUNCHES COMPUTERIZED R1100

189

SHIPS AND BOATS

BOATS AND SHIPS have been used to transport people and goods across rivers, lakes, and oceans for thousands of years. From the first dugout canoes to ocean liners, boats have played a major role in world trade.

Lugsail made from reed

Bipod or "double" mast

TITICACA RAF
The elegar
rafts made b
the people c
Lake Titicac
in the Ande
mountair
are bui
from reec
that grow i
the lake

ALGONQUIN TRANSPORTATION
Birch bark canoes were used by the native Canadian Algonquins to traverse the St. Lawrence River, in what is now called Ontario. The boats ranged in length from 10 ft (3 m) vessels to 35 ft (10.5 m) war canoes.

Cross-strut strengthens canoe

Birch bark hull

Yard *Mast*

Batten keep s straige

Fou sided s

OCEAN LINER
From the early 1900s to the 1950s, huge, luxurious liners carried many passengers across the oceans. Cheap, fast air travel caused their popularity to decline.

CHINESE JUNK
Traditional Chinese vessels, or "junks," have four-sided sails that hang from a yard that crosses the mast at an angle.

CUNARD LINE
MAURETANIA

Bridge

Funnels expel exhaust fumes from boiler rooms

Dec cap

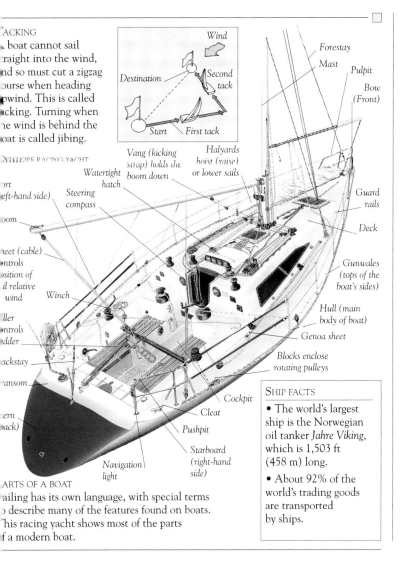

TACKING

A boat cannot sail straight into the wind, and so must cut a zigzag course when heading upwind. This is called tacking. Turning when the wind is behind the boat is called jibing.

Wind

Destination

Second tack

Start

First tack

OFFSHORE RACING YACHT

Forestay

Mast

Pulpit

Bow (Front)

Vang (kicking strap) holds the boom down

Halyards hoist (raise) or lower sails

Watertight hatch

Guard rails

Port (left-hand side)

Steering compass

Deck

Boom

Sheet (cable) controls position of sail relative to wind

Winch

Gunwales (tops of the boat's sides)

Hull (main body of boat)

Tiller controls rudder

Genoa sheet

Backstay

Blocks enclose rotating pulleys

Transom

Stern (back)

Cockpit

Cleat

Pushpit

Navigation light

Starboard (right-hand side)

SHIP FACTS

• The world's largest ship is the Norwegian oil tanker *Jahre Viking*, which is 1,503 ft (458 m) long.

• About 92% of the world's trading goods are transported by ships.

PARTS OF A BOAT

Sailing has its own language, with special terms to describe many of the features found on boats. This racing yacht shows most of the parts of a modern boat.

WARSHIPS AND SUBMARINES

THERE ARE MANY types of fighting vessel, from light, speedy destroyers, to huge aircraft carriers and nuclear submarines.

1700S "MAN-OF-WAR"
By the 18th century, sailing ships had become floating fortresses. Rival northern European powers built heavily armed fighting ships called "men-of-war."

Mizzen topgallant sail
Main topgallant sail
Fore mast topgallant sail
Fore ma...
topsc...
Fore topsc...
Jib s...
Mizzen topsail
Spr...
topsc...
1700S 74-GUN SHIP
Main topsail
Gun ports

TYPES OF WARSHIPS

AIRCRAFT CARRIER
The largest warship, a carrier houses 100 aircraft and a crew of over 2,000.

DESTROYER
Armed with guided missiles, the destroyer's role is to defend the fleet.

CRUISER
The cruiser is designed for speed and endurance at sea.

MINESWEEPER
This small vessel carries special equipment for locating and destroying mines.

BATTLESHIP
Most heavily armed battleships have been replaced by carriers.

PARTS OF A WARSHIP

Modern warships are armed with guns and guided missiles for attack and defense. Most vessels are also equipped with advanced electronic equipment for tracking and hitting targets.

Surveillance radar

Lynx helicopter

Seacat missile launcher

Funnel

Mast

Sonar torpedo decoy

Exocet missile launcher

Gun turret

F174

Rudder | Variable pitch propeller | Antisubmarine torpedo tube | Liferaft cylinder | Rocket launcher | Pennant number | Sonar bulge | 4.4 in (11 cm) gun

MODERN WARSHIP

MILITARY SUBMARINES

There are two main types of underwater warships. Patrol submarines seek and destroy other vessels, while missile-carrying submarines are equipped with nuclear warheads aimed at enemy cities and military targets.

Periscope

Senior enlisted man's mess

Stabilized fin

Aft hydroplane

Main turbine

Control room

Conning tower

Galley

Officers' mess

Propeller | Lower rudder | Diesel motor compartment | Nuclear reactor | Junior enlisted man's mess | Torpedo compartment | Torpedo tube

NUCLEAR-POWERED SUBMARINE

AIRCRAFT

THE FIRST PLANE flew
in only 1903, yet today
millions of people fly
each year. Airplanes are
heavier-than-air aircraft
with fixed wings, usually
powered by propellers
or jet turbines.

Lift (upward force)

Drag (backward force)

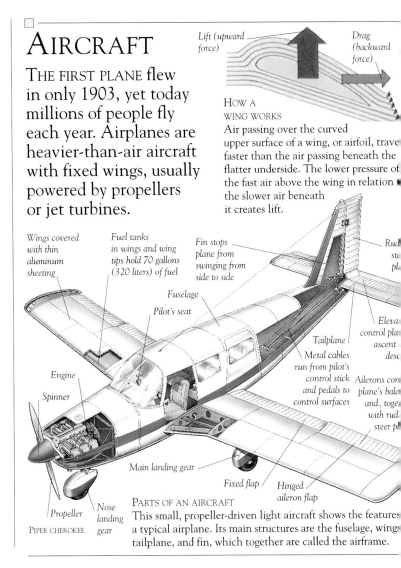

HOW A
WING WORKS

Air passing over the curved
upper surface of a wing, or airfoil, trave
faster than the air passing beneath the
flatter underside. The lower pressure of
the fast air above the wing in relation
the slower air beneath
it creates lift.

Wings covered
with thin
aluminum
sheeting

Fuel tanks
in wings and wing
tips hold 70 gallons
(320 liters) of fuel

Fin stops
plane from
swinging from
side to side

Rud
ste
pl

Fuselage

Pilot's seat

Eleva
control pla
ascent
desc

Tailplane

Metal cables
run from pilot's
control stick
and pedals to
control surfaces

Engine

Ailerons con
plane's bala
and, toge
with rud
steer pl

Spinner

Main landing gear

Fixed flap

Hinged
aileron flap

Propeller   Nose
landing
PIPER CHEROKEE   gear

PARTS OF AN AIRCRAFT
This small, propeller-driven light aircraft shows the features
a typical airplane. Its main structures are the fuselage, wings
tailplane, and fin, which together are called the airframe.

FUSELAGE OF AN AIRLINER

The airframe of a jet airliner has to be capable of withstanding the stresses of high-speed flight and pressurization and depressurization of the passenger cabin. Airliners are built from light, strong materials such as aluminum alloys, titanium, and carbon fiber.

Brackets for overhead luggage lockers

Sound-proofing insulation

Luggage hold

Aluminum alloy skin

Stringers give fuselage extra strength

Hydraulic control pipes

Electric control wires

Floor panels

FUSELAGE SECTION

CONTROLLING THE PLANE

The wings and tail of an airplane are equipped with hinged flaps, or control surfaces, that allow it to pitch up or down, roll from side to side, or yaw left and right. To turn, the plane is banked, rolling and yawing at the same time.

Nose comes up

Elevators raised, pushing down the tail

Wing meets air at a sharper angle, increasing lift

PITCHING UP

To pitch up and climb, pilot pulls control column backward

Left aileron rises, reducing lift on left wing

Right aileron lowers, increasing lift on right wing

ROLLING LEFT

Pilot pushes control column to left

Rudder swings left, causing plane to yaw (swerve) to the left

Aircraft banks into left turn, rolling and yawing at same time

Left aileron rises

Right aileron lowers

TURNING LEFT

Pilot pushes control column to left while pushing rudder pedal with left foot

Types of aircraft

An aircraft is essentially any machine that enables people to fly.
Powered airplanes and helicopters, hot-air balloons, gas-filled
airships, and unpowered gliders are all different types of aircraft.
There are many different types of aircraft for different uses,
including transportation, warfare, and recreation.

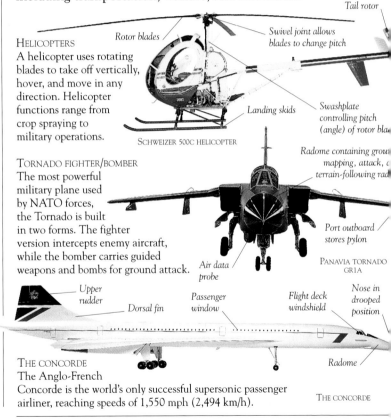

Tail rotor

Rotor blades

Swivel joint allows
blades to change pitch

HELICOPTERS
A helicopter uses rotating
blades to take off vertically,
hover, and move in any
direction. Helicopter
functions range from
crop spraying to
military operations.

Landing skids

Swashplate
controlling pitch
(angle) of rotor bla

SCHWEIZER 500C HELICOPTER

Radome containing grou
mapping, attack, a
terrain-following rad

TORNADO FIGHTER/BOMBER
The most powerful
military plane used
by NATO forces,
the Tornado is built
in two forms. The fighter
version intercepts enemy aircraft,
while the bomber carries guided
weapons and bombs for ground attack.

Air data
probe

Port outboard
stores pylon

PANAVIA TORNADO
GR1A

Upper
rudder

Dorsal fin

Passenger
window

Flight deck
windshield

Nose in
drooped
position

THE CONCORDE
The Anglo-French
Concorde is the world's only successful supersonic passenger
airliner, reaching speeds of 1,550 mph (2,494 km/h).

Radome

THE CONCORDE

196

Strengthened glass
fiber nose cone

Elevator flaps to help
climbing or diving

...as-filled
...velope

Crew and
passenger cabin,
or "gondola"

Propellers

Rudder
for steering

SKYSHIP 500HL AIRSHIP

Envelope
fills with
hot air

Nylon load
tapes attach
cables to
envelope

Stainless-
steel cables

Twin gas
burners
provide
hot air

Burner
frame

...LLOONS AND AIRSHIPS

...eated air rises, and when trapped in an envelope,
... balloon, it provides lift. Hot-air balloons were the
...rliest aircraft, first appearing in the late 1700s.
...as-filled airships, powered by propellers, were a
...pular form of passenger air travel in the early 20th
...ntury, but are now used mainly for advertising.

HOT-AIR BALLOON
AND BASKET

Basket

Tow rope
attachment

Streamlined
cockpit

Aileron

Slim, tapering
fuselage

T-shaped
tail improves
aerodynamics

EVW

Rudder

SCHELICHER K25 GLIDER

Fabric wings
allow hang
glider to ride
thermals

...IDERS AND HANG GLIDERS

... glider is an unpowered plane with a
...de wingspan that uses currents of hot,
...ng air (thermals) to stay aloft.
...iders are tugged into the air by a winch
... towing vehicle. Hang gliders are made of
...terial stretched across a simple frame, forming
...ngs, and are launched from a hilltop or cliff.

Pilot hangs
from harness

HANG GLIDER

197

THE WORLD

How to use this section

These pages show you how to use the World section of the encyclopedia. The maps are organized by continent: North America, Central and South America, Europe, Africa, North and West Asia, South and East Asia, and Australasia. Information-packed country fact pages separate the maps.

Key to icons
All the icons used on the maps are listed below.

The Arts

Climate

Communications

Environment

Flora and Fauna

History

Industry

Natural Features

People

Heading

Locator map

Introduction

Scale and compass

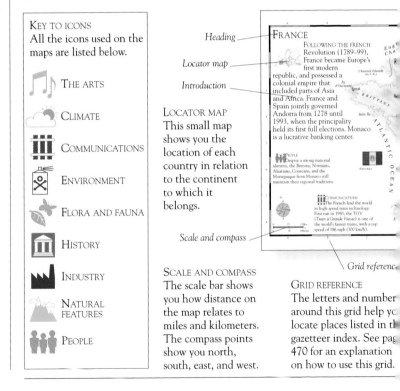

Locator map
This small map shows you the location of each country in relation to the continent to which it belongs.

Scale and compass
The scale bar shows you how distance on the map relates to miles and kilometers. The compass points show you north, south, east, and west.

Grid reference

Grid reference
The letters and number around this grid help yo locate places listed in th gazetteer index. See pag 470 for an explanation on how to use this grid.

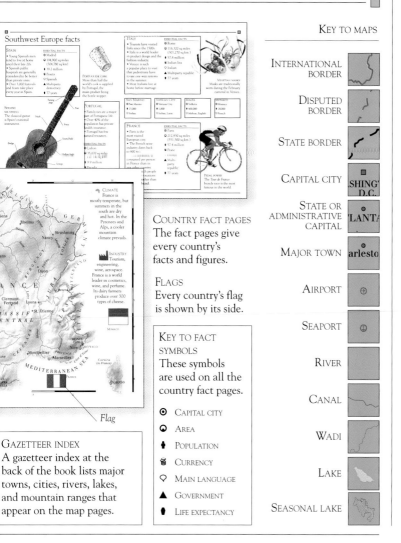

Southwest Europe facts

SPAIN

ESSENTIAL FACTS
- Young Spanish men tend to live at home until their late 20s.
- Spanish public hospitals are generally considered to be better than private ones.
- Over 3,000 festivals and feasts take place every year in Spain.

⊙ Madrid
○ 194,900 sq miles (504,782 sq km)
♦ 39.2 million
🐚 Peseta
♀ Spanish
▲ Multiparty democracy
● 77 years

SPANISH GUITAR
The classical guitar is Spain's national instrument.

PORTUGAL

PORT OR THE CORK
More than half the world's cork is supplied by Portugal, the main product being the bottle stopper.

- Family ties are a major part of Portuguese life.
- Over 40% of the population has private health insurance.
- Portugal has few natural resources.

ESSENTIAL FACTS
⊙ Lisbon
○ 35,672 sq miles (92,389 sq km)
♦ 9.9 million
♀ Family

ITALY

- Tourists have visited Italy since the 1500s.
- Italy is a world leader in product design and the fashion industry.
- Venice is such a popular place to visit that pedestrians have to use one-way systems in the summer.
- Most Italians live at home before marriage.

ESSENTIAL FACTS
⊙ Rome
○ 116,322 sq miles (301,252 sq km)
♦ 57.8 million
🐚 Italian lira
♀ Italian
▲ Multiparty republic
● 77 years

VENETIAN MASKS
Masks are traditionally worn during the February carnival in Venice.

SAN MARINO
⊙ San Marino
♦ 23,000
♀ Italian

VATICAN CITY
⊙ Vatican City
♦ 1,000
♀ Italian, Latin

MALTA
⊙ Valletta
♦ 400,000
♀ Maltese, English

MONACO
⊙ Monaco
♦ 28,000
♀ French

FRANCE

- Paris is the most visited European city.
- The French wine industry dates back to 600 BC.
- ... consumed per person in France than in any other country.

ESSENTIAL FACTS
⊙ Paris
○ 212,930 sq miles (551,500 sq km)
♦ 57.4 million
🐚 Franc
♀ French
▲ Multiparty republic
● 77 years

PEDAL POWER
The Tour de France bicycle race is the most famous in the world.

CLIMATE
France is mostly temperate, but summers in the south are dry and hot. In the Pyrenees and Alps, a cooler mountain climate prevails.

INDUSTRY
Tourism, engineering, wine, aerospace. France is a world leader in cosmetics, wine, and perfume. Its dairy farmers produce over 300 types of cheese.

Flag

COUNTRY FACT PAGES

The fact pages give every country's facts and figures.

FLAGS

Every country's flag is shown by its side.

KEY TO FACT SYMBOLS

These symbols are used on all the country fact pages.

⊙ CAPITAL CITY
○ AREA
♦ POPULATION
🐚 CURRENCY
♀ MAIN LANGUAGE
▲ GOVERNMENT
● LIFE EXPECTANCY

GAZETTEER INDEX

A gazetteer index at the back of the book lists major towns, cities, rivers, lakes, and mountain ranges that appear on the map pages.

KEY TO MAPS

INTERNATIONAL BORDER	
DISPUTED BORDER	
STATE BORDER	
CAPITAL CITY	SHING' D.C.
STATE OR ADMINISTRATIVE CAPITAL	LANTA
MAJOR TOWN	arlesto
AIRPORT	⊕
SEAPORT	⊕
RIVER	
CANAL	
WADI	
LAKE	
SEASONAL LAKE	

GUIDE TO MAP PAGES

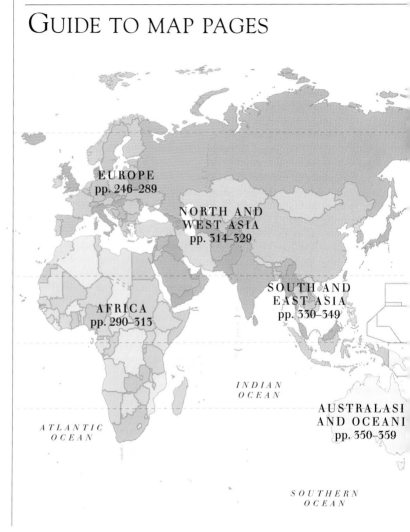

EUROPE
pp. 246–289

NORTH AND
WEST ASIA
pp. 314–329

SOUTH AND
EAST ASIA
pp. 330–349

AFRICA
pp. 290–313

*INDIAN
OCEAN*

AUSTRALASI
AND OCEANI
pp. 350–359

*ATLANTIC
OCEAN*

*SOUTHERN
OCEAN*

ARCTIC
OCEAN

Arctic Circle

ATLANTIC
OCEAN

NORTH AMERICA
pp. 204–227

PACIFIC
OCEAN

Tropic of Cancer

Equator

CENTRAL AND
SOUTH AMERICA
pp. 228–245

PACIFIC
OCEAN

Tropic of Capricorn

ATLANTIC
OCEAN

NORTH AMERICA

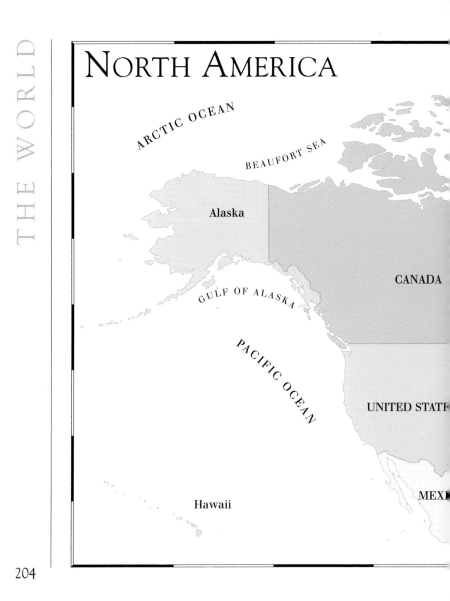

ARCTIC OCEAN

BEAUFORT SEA

Alaska

CANADA

GULF OF ALASKA

PACIFIC OCEAN

UNITED STATES

Hawaii

MEXICO

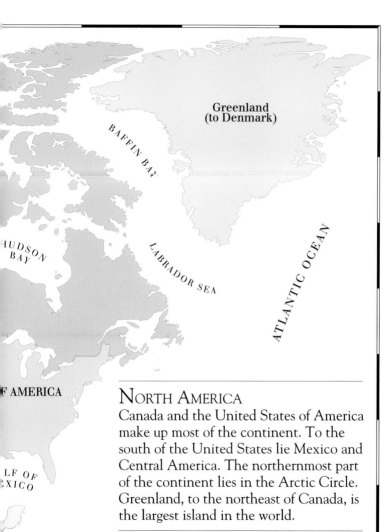

Greenland
(to Denmark)

BAFFIN BAY

HUDSON BAY

LABRADOR SEA

ATLANTIC OCEAN

F AMERICA

LF OF XICO

NORTH AMERICA

Canada and the United States of America
make up most of the continent. To the
south of the United States lie Mexico and
Central America. The northernmost part
of the continent lies in the Arctic Circle.
Greenland, to the northeast of Canada, is
the largest island in the world.

ALASKA AND
WESTERN CANADA

AT THE END OF the last ice age, people traveled from Asia into North America over the Bering land bridge, which connected the continents at present-day Alaska.

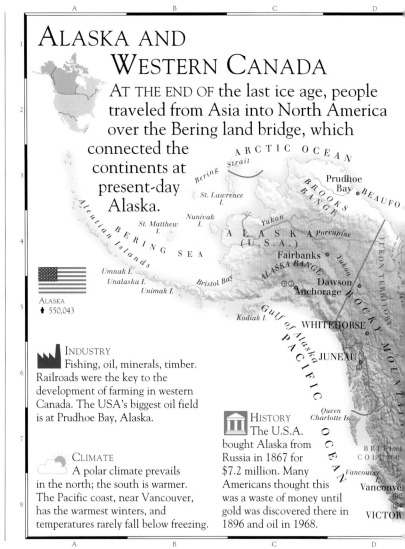

ARCTIC OCEAN

Bering Strait

Prudhoe Bay

BROOKS RANGE

BEAUFO

St. Lawrence I.

Nunivak I.

St. Matthew I.

Yukon

ALASKA (U.S.A.)

Porcupine

Umnak I.

Aleutian Islands

BERING SEA

Unalaska I.

Unimak I.

Bristol Bay

Fairbanks

ALASKA RANGE

Yukon

YUKON TERRITORY

Dawson

Anchorage

ROCKY

Kodiak I.

Gulf of Alaska

WHITEHORSE

PACIFIC

JUNEAU

MOUNTAINS

OCEAN

Queen Charlotte Is.

BRITISH COLUMBIA

Vancouver I.

Vancouver

VICTOR

ALASKA
✦ 550,043

INDUSTRY
Fishing, oil, minerals, timber. Railroads were the key to the development of farming in western Canada. The USA's biggest oil field is at Prudhoe Bay, Alaska.

CLIMATE
A polar climate prevails in the north; the south is warmer. The Pacific coast, near Vancouver, has the warmest winters, and temperatures rarely fall below freezing.

HISTORY
The U.S.A. bought Alaska from Russia in 1867 for $7.2 million. Many Americans thought this was a waste of money until gold was discovered there in 1896 and oil in 1968.

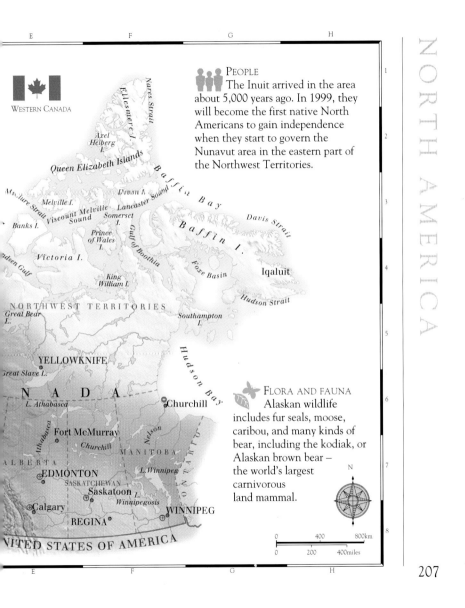

WESTERN CANADA

Nares Strait

Ellesmere I.

Axel Heiberg I.

Queen Elizabeth Islands

$B \, a \, f \, f \, i \, n$

Devon I.

$B \, a \, y$

M'Clure Strait

Melville I.

Viscount Melville Sound

Lancaster Sound

Somerset I.

Banks I.

Prince of Wales I.

Gulf of Boothia

Davis Strait

$B \, a \, f \, f \, i \, n \, I.$

Victoria I.

Amundsen Gulf

King William I.

Foxe Basin

Iqaluit

NORTHWEST TERRITORIES

Great Bear L.

Southampton I.

Hudson Strait

YELLOWKNIFE

Great Slave L.

$H \, u \, d \, s \, o \, n$

$B \, a \, y$

C A N A D A

L. Athabasca

Churchill

Athabasca

Fort McMurray

Churchill

Nelson

MANITOBA

ALBERTA

EDMONTON

L. Winnipeg

SASKATCHEWAN

Saskatoon

L. Winnipegosis

Calgary

WINNIPEG

REGINA

UNITED STATES OF AMERICA

PEOPLE

The Inuit arrived in the area about 5,000 years ago. In 1999, they will become the first native North Americans to gain independence when they start to govern the Nunavut area in the eastern part of the Northwest Territories.

FLORA AND FAUNA

Alaskan wildlife includes fur seals, moose, caribou, and many kinds of bear, including the kodiak, or Alaskan brown bear – the world's largest carnivorous land mammal.

N

0	400	800km

0	200	400miles

EASTERN CANADA

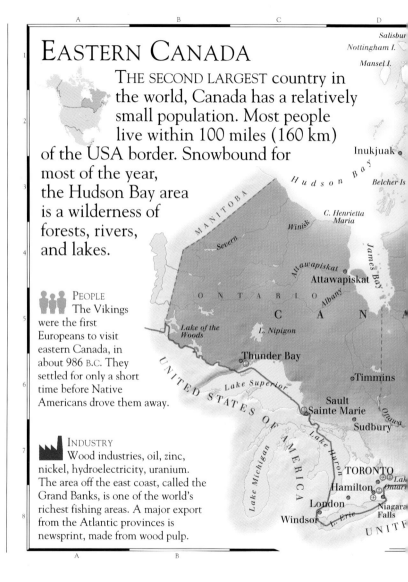

THE SECOND LARGEST country in the world, Canada has a relatively small population. Most people live within 100 miles (160 km) of the USA border. Snowbound for most of the year, the Hudson Bay area is a wilderness of forests, rivers, and lakes.

PEOPLE
The Vikings were the first Europeans to visit eastern Canada, in about 986 B.C. They settled for only a short time before Native Americans drove them away.

INDUSTRY
Wood industries, oil, zinc, nickel, hydroelectricity, uranium. The area off the east coast, called the Grand Banks, is one of the world's richest fishing areas. A major export from the Atlantic provinces is newsprint, made from wood pulp.

Salisbur
Nottingham I.
Mansel I.
Inukjuak
Hudson Bay
Belcher Is
MANITOBA
C. Henrietta Maria
Winisk
Severn
Attawapiskat
James Bay
Attawapiskat
ONTARIO
Albany
CAN
Lake of the Woods
L. Nipigon
Thunder Bay
Timmins
UNITED STATES OF
Lake Superior
Sault Sainte Marie
Sudbury
Ottawa
Lake Michigan
Lake Huron
TORONTO
AMERICA
Hamilton
Lak Ontari
London
Niagara Falls
Windsor
L. Erie
UNITE

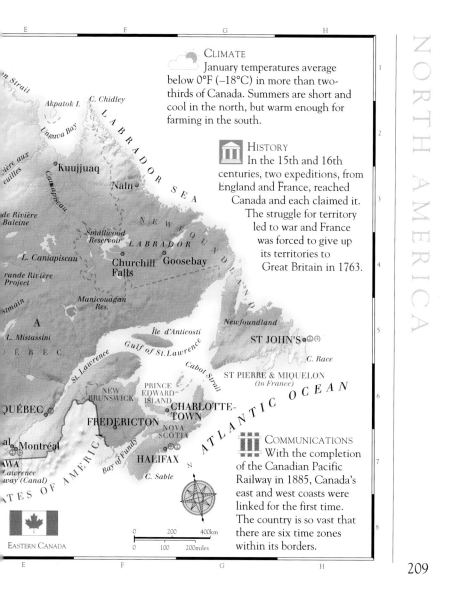

CLIMATE

January temperatures average below 0°F (−18°C) in more than two-thirds of Canada. Summers are short and cool in the north, but warm enough for farming in the south.

HISTORY

In the 15th and 16th centuries, two expeditions, from England and France, reached Canada and each claimed it. The struggle for territory led to war and France was forced to give up its territories to Great Britain in 1763.

COMMUNICATIONS

With the completion of the Canadian Pacific Railway in 1885, Canada's east and west coasts were linked for the first time. The country is so vast that there are six time zones within its borders.

**Map labels:**

Akpatok I. · C. Chidley · LABRADOR SEA · Kuujjuaq · Nain · Smallwood Reservoir · LABRADOR · Churchill Falls · Goosebay · L. Caniapiscau · Manicouagan Res. · L. Mistassini · QUÉBEC · Île d'Anticosti · NEWFOUNDLAND · Newfoundland · ST JOHN'S · C. Race · Gulf of St.Lawrence · Cabot Strait · ST PIERRE & MIQUELON (to France) · ATLANTIC OCEAN · St. Lawrence · NEW BRUNSWICK · PRINCE EDWARD ISLAND · CHARLOTTE-TOWN · FREDERICTON · NOVA SCOTIA · Montréal · HALIFAX · Bay of Fundy · C. Sable · Ungava Bay · rande Rivière Project · de Rivière Baleine · ière aux uilles · n Strait

EASTERN CANADA

| 0 | 200 | 400km |
| 0 | 100 | 200miles |

209

NORTHEASTERN STATES

WITH ITS RICH MINERAL resources and safe harbors, the Northeast was the first area on the continent to be colonized by Europeans. In 1620, English pilgrims sailed on the *Mayflower* to settle in a region that is still called New England. During the mid-19th century, European immigrants settled in New York City and in other East Coast cities. Today, this region is the most densely populated and heavily industrialized area of the USA.

CLIMATE
This area of the U.S.A has a temperate climate, with warm and humid summers. However, the northeastern region, in particular, can experience very heavy snowfall from November to April.

NORTHEASTERN STATES
♦ 51.5 million

PEOPLE
Northeastern Native American tribes, such as the Wampanoag, the Algonquin, and the tribes of the Iroquois League, were the first to come into contact with European settlers and explorers.

INDUSTRY
Oil, iron, steel, chemicals, maple sugar, blueberries, cranberries, fishing, tourism. Vermont is the main producer of maple syrup in the USA. The stock exchange on Wall Street, New York City, is the largest in the world.

Lake Erie Bu

Erie

PENNSYLV

Pittsburg

WEST VIRGINIA

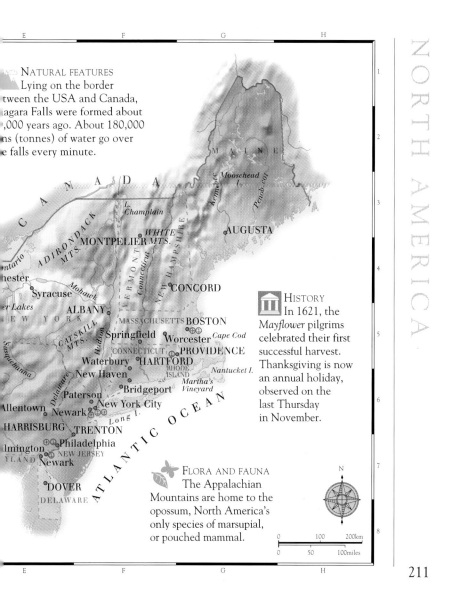

NATURAL FEATURES
Lying on the border
tween the USA and Canada,
agara Falls were formed about
,000 years ago. About 180,000
ns (tonnes) of water go over
e falls every minute.

HISTORY
In 1621, the
Mayflower pilgrims
celebrated their first
successful harvest.
Thanksgiving is now
an annual holiday,
observed on the
last Thursday
in November.

FLORA AND FAUNA
The Appalachian
Mountains are home to the
opossum, North America's
only species of marsupial,
or pouched mammal.

N

0   100   200km
0   50   100miles

SOUTHERN STATES

BY THE 19TH CENTURY, the wealth of the South was based on crops like tobacco, indigo, rice, and especially cotton, which was grown on large plantations by African slaves. The area is known today for New Orleans' jazz, Florida's Disney World, and the Kentucky Derby. The city of Washington, in the District of Columbia, was made the US capital in 1800.

MISSOURI
OKLAHOMA
BOSTON MTS.
LITTLE ROCK
ARKANSAS
Memphis
Ouachita
Arkansas
Mississippi
Shreveport
Yazoo
MISSISSI
Red R.
JACKSO
TEXAS
Mississippi
LOUISIANA
BATON ROUGE
Pontchartrain
Mobil
New Orleans

Mississippi Delta

CLIMATE
Summers are long and hot; winters are mild, but temperatures are generally warmer on the coast than inland. Southern Florida is tropical.

INDUSTRY
Soybeans, coal, peanuts, cotton, citrus fruits, tobacco, oil, tourism. Georgia grows half of the USA's peanuts – most are used to make peanut butter.

THE ARTS
The French brought Mardi Gras to America in the early 1700 Celebrated in many of the souther states, the most famous festival is held in New Orleans, where parad last for a week before Mardi Gras Day, the day before Lent starts.

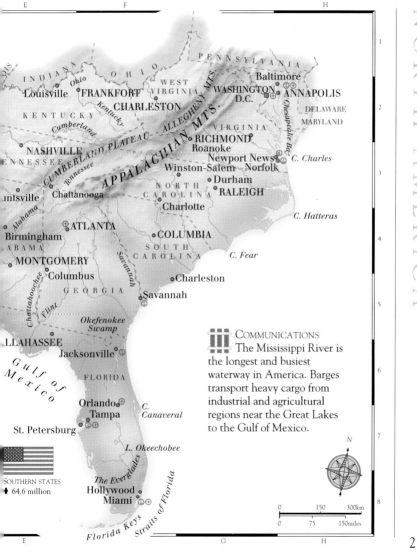

E   F   H

1

2

3

4

5

6

7

8

INDIANA   *Ohio*   OHIO

Louisville   FRANKFORT   WEST   WASHINGTON   ANNAPOLIS
VIRGINIA   D.C.

KENTUCKY   CHARLESTON   Baltimore

DELAWARE

MARYLAND

Kentucky

Cumberland   ALLEGHENY MTS.   *Chesapeake Bay*

NASHVILLE   VIRGINIA

TENNESSEE   CUMBERLAND PLATEAU   RICHMOND

Tennessee   APPALACHIAN   Roanoke

Newport News   C. Charles

Winston-Salem   Norfolk

...ntsville   Chattanooga   NORTH   Durham
CAROLINA   RALEIGH

Alabama   Charlotte

C. Hatteras

Birmingham   ATLANTA   COLUMBIA

...ABAMA   SOUTH
CAROLINA

MONTGOMERY   *Savannah*   C. Fear

Chattahoochee   Columbus

Flint   GEORGIA   Charleston

Savannah

*Okefenokee
Swamp*

...LLAHASSEE

Jacksonville

*Gulf
of
Mexico*   FLORIDA

Orlando
Tampa   *C.
Canaveral*

St. Petersburg

L. Okeechobee

The Everglades

Hollywood
Miami

Florida Keys   *Straits of Florida*

🏛 COMMUNICATIONS
The Mississippi River is
the longest and busiest
waterway in America. Barges
transport heavy cargo from
industrial and agricultural
regions near the Great Lakes
to the Gulf of Mexico.

N

SOUTHERN STATES
♦ 64.6 million

0   150   300km
0   75   150miles

E   G   H

THE GREAT LAKES

THE STATES OF Indiana, Illinois, Michigan, Ohio, Wisconsin, and Minnesota, all of which border on one or more of the five Great Lakes, are often called the industrial and agricultural heartland of the United States. The region is rich in natural resources, with large areas of fertile farmland on flat plains called prairies.

CLIMATE

The region around the Great Lakes has warm summers but quite severe winters, and parts of the lakes can freeze over. Minnesota, in particular, suffers from heavy snowstorms.

GREAT LAKES STATES
46.4 million

ENVIRONMENT

The Great Lakes – Ontario, Huron, Superior, Michigan, and Erie – together form the largest area of freshwater in the world. Heavy industry has caused severe water pollution, and in some areas it is dangerous to eat the fish or swim.

INDUSTRY

Vehicles, coal, iron, grains, cherries. Nearly half of the world's corn crop and a third of the cherry crop are grown in the Great Lakes region. Detroit is known as "motor city" because it is the center of the US car industry.

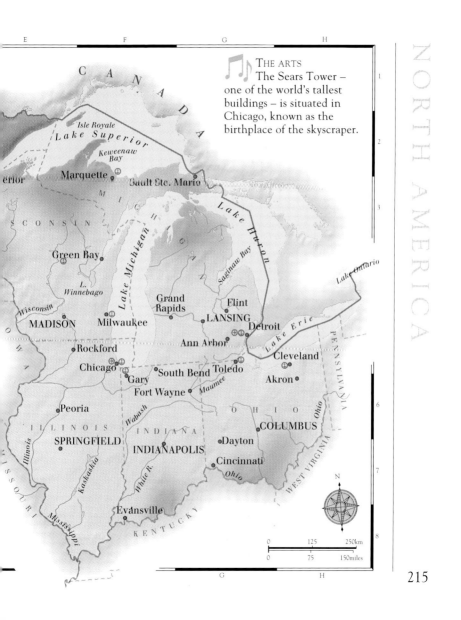

THE ARTS
The Sears Tower –
one of the world's tallest
buildings – is situated in
Chicago, known as the
birthplace of the skyscraper.

1

2

3

C A N A D A

Isle Royale
Lake Superior
Keweenaw
Bay

erior
Marquette
Sault Ste. Marie

M I C H I G A N

S C O N S I N

Lake Michigan

Lake Huron

Green Bay

L.
Winnebago

Saginaw Bay

Wisconsin

Grand
Rapids

Flint

MADISON
Milwaukee

LANSING
Detroit

Lake Erie

I O W A

Rockford

Ann Arbor

Chicago
Gary
South Bend
Toledo

Cleveland

Akron

P E N N S Y L V A N I A

Lake Ontario

Fort Wayne
Maumee

Peoria

6

I L L I N O I S

Wabash

I N D I A N A

O H I O

Ohio

COLUMBUS

Illinois

SPRINGFIELD

INDIANAPOLIS

Dayton

W E S T V I R G I N I A

7

M I S S O U R I

Kaskaskia

White R.

Cincinnati

Ohio

N

Evansville

Mississippi

K E N T U C K Y

0   125   250km

0   75   150miles

8

G H

215

CENTRAL AND MOUNTAIN STATES

THE GREAT Plains, the Rocky Mountains, and the Mississippi lowlands dominate the landscape of the Midwest. Once home to Native Americans and herds of bison, the Great Plains were settled in the 19th century by Europeans, who forced the Native Americans onto reservations and slaughtered the bison to near-extinction.

HISTORY
Pioneers traveling to the West had to cross the Great Plains, which were known as the "Great American Desert." The last region to be settled, it is now a wealthy agricultural region.

CLIMATE
Summers are cooler and winters warmer than they are east of the Rockies. The Great Plains have an extreme climate, which can change quite suddenly and violently – blizzards, hail, thunderstorms, and tornadoes may occur.

CENTRAL AND MOUNTAIN STATES
♦ 18.7 million

NATURAL FEATURES
The Rocky Mountains exte[r] through Canada and the USA for more than 3,000 miles (4,800 km). Dividing North America, they separate the rivers flowing west to the Pacific from those flowing east to the Atlantic.

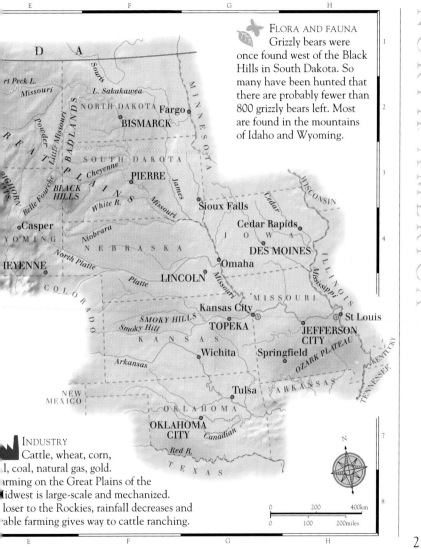

FLORA AND FAUNA
Grizzly bears were once found west of the Black Hills in South Dakota. So many have been hunted that there are probably fewer than 800 grizzly bears left. Most are found in the mountains of Idaho and Wyoming.

D A

rt Peck L.
Missouri
Souris
L. *Sakakawea*

NORTH DAKOTA • Fargo
• BISMARCK

MINNESOTA

SOUTH DAKOTA

Cheyenne
• PIERRE
James

WISCONSIN

BLACK HILLS
Belle Fourche   *White R.*   *Missouri*
• Sioux Falls
Cedar

• Casper
Niobrara
NEBRASKA
IOWA
• Cedar Rapids
• DES MOINES

YOMING

HEYENNE
North Platte

COLORADO
Platte
• LINCOLN
• Omaha
Missouri

ILLINOIS
Mississippi

SMOKY HILLS
Smoky Hill
• Kansas City
• TOPEKA
MISSOURI
• St Louis

KANSAS
• Wichita
• Springfield
JEFFERSON CITY

Arkansas
OZARK PLATEAU
KENTUCKY

NEW MEXICO
• Tulsa
ARKANSAS
TENNESSEE

OKLAHOMA
• OKLAHOMA CITY
Canadian

N

Red R.

TEXAS

INDUSTRY
Cattle, wheat, corn, l, coal, natural gas, gold. rming on the Great Plains of the idwest is large-scale and mechanized. loser to the Rockies, rainfall decreases and able farming gives way to cattle ranching.

| 0 | 200 | 400km |
| 0 | 100 | 200miles |

SOUTHWESTERN STATES

THE FIRST Europeans in the Southwest were the Spanish, who traveled north from Mexico. This resulted in a mingling of Spanish and Native American cultures in this region. Gold and silver mining and cattle-ranching attracted other settlers in the mid 19th century, when this area became part of the USA after the Mexican War.

Map labels: OREGON, IDAHO, BLACK ROCK DESERT, GREAT, Pyramid L., Humboldt, BASIN, Reno, L. Tahoe, CARSON CITY, Great Salt Lake Desert, GREAT SALT LAKE DESERT, NEVADA, Sevier, Bryce Canyon, Las Vegas, L. Mead, Grand Canyon, COLORADO PLATEAU, Colorado, ARIZONA, PHOENIX, SONORAN, Mesa, DESERT, Tucson

NATURAL FEATURES

The Colorado plateau has some unusual landforms, including natural bridges and arches of solid rock. Over the last million years, the Colorado River has cut away the plateau, forming the world's largest river gorge – the Grand Canyon.

HISTORY

At the end of the Mexican War (1846–48), the USA acquired Utah, Nevada, California, and parts of Arizona, New Mexico, Colorado, and Wyoming. One of the causes of the war was a border dispute between Texas and Mexico.

SOUTHWESTERN STATES
♦ 28.4 million

PEOPLE

Some of the earliest Native Americans lived in the Nevada area. Bones and ashes discovered near Las Vegas indicate that they may have lived there more than 20,000 years ago. Today, the region has the largest concentration of Native Americans in the country.

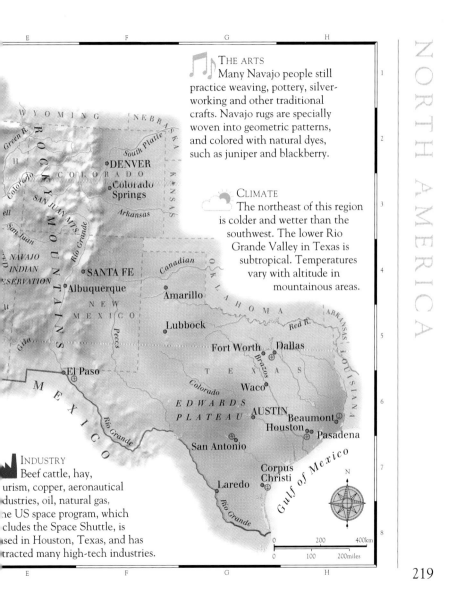

E   F   G   H

1

2

THE ARTS
Many Navajo people still practice weaving, pottery, silver-working and other traditional crafts. Navajo rugs are specially woven into geometric patterns, and colored with natural dyes, such as juniper and blackberry.

CLIMATE
The northeast of this region is colder and wetter than the southwest. The lower Rio Grande Valley in Texas is subtropical. Temperatures vary with altitude in mountainous areas.

3

4

W Y O M I N G   N E B R A S K A

Green R.

R O C K Y   M O U N T A I N S

Colorado

San Juan

●DENVER

South Platte

C O L O R A D O

●Colorado Springs

K A N S A S

Arkansas

SAN JUAN MTS.

NAVAJO INDIAN RESERVATION

Rio Grande

●SANTA FE

Canadian

●Albuquerque

Amarillo

O K L A H O M A

N E W   M E X I C O

Pecos

Lubbock

Red R.

ARKANSAS

Gila

●El Paso

● Fort Worth   Dallas

LOUISIANA

M E X I C O

T E X A S

Brazos

Colorado

Waco●

E D W A R D S
P L A T E A U

AUSTIN●

Beaumont●

Houston●   ● Pasadena

San Antonio

Rio Grande

Corpus Christi

Gulf of Mexico

Laredo

N

Rio Grande

5

6

7

8

INDUSTRY
Beef cattle, hay, tourism, copper, aeronautical industries, oil, natural gas. The US space program, which includes the Space Shuttle, is based in Houston, Texas, and has attracted many high-tech industries.

0   200   400km

0   100   200miles

E   F   G   H

219

PACIFIC STATES

ALL THREE STATES on the West Coast are major agricultural producers – Washington and Oregon supply one-third of the softwood timber for the USA, and California produces half of the country's fruit and vegetables. Situated where two of the Earth's plates meet, the area suffers from earthquakes and volcanic activity. Mount St. Helens, dormant since 1857, erupted in 1980, losing some 1,300 ft (400 m) off its height.

NATURAL FEATURES

The lowest point in the western hemisphere is in Death Valley, 282 ft (86 m) below sea level. One of the driest, hottest places on Earth, the highest temperature, 135°F (57°C), was recorded there in 1913, and its average rainfall is only 1.5 in (38 mm) per year.

CANADA

Strait of Juan de Fuca

San Juan Is.

Everett
Bellevue
Seattle
Tacoma
OLYMPIA

WASHINGTON

CASCADE RANGE

Columbia
Banks L.
Franklyn D. Roosevelt L.
Spokane

Yakima
Columbia

Snake

Walla Walla

BLUE MOUNTAINS

Baker City

IDAHO

Portland

SALEM
Newport
Eugene

OREGON

OCEAN

CLIMATE
Climate varies from the moderate coast to the snow-capped Sierra Nevada mountains. Much of California is arid desert.

INDUSTRY
Timber, aerospace industries, wine. The Santa Clara Valley, or Silicon Valley, specializes in high-tech industry. Hollywood is considered the center of the US film industry, although many major studios are no longer located there.

FLORA AND FAUNA
Redwoods are believed to be the tallest and oldest trees in the world. They are found along the West Coast from central California to southern Oregon and rarely occur more than 50 miles (80 km) inland.

PACIFIC STATES
♦ 37.5 million

221

MEXICO

THE ANCIENT empires of the Maya and Aztec flourished for centuries before the Spanish invaded Mexico in 1519, lured there by legends of hoards of gold and silver. Mexico gained its independence in 1810, after 300 years of Spanish rule. Today, most Mexicans are *mestizo*, a mix of Spanish and Native American. Although Spanish is the official language, Native American languages such as Maya, Nahuatl, and Zapotec are also widely spoken.

Tijuana Mexicali

UNITED STATE

Nogale

Ángel de la Guarda I.

Cedros I.   Tiburón I.   Hermosillo

Gulf of California

Culiac

La Paz

CLIMATE
The Mexican plateau and mountains are warm for most of the year. The Pacific coast has a tropical climate.

MEXICO

FLORA AND FAUNA
The Mexican beaded lizard and the gila monster are the only two poisonous lizards known. The largest of all cacti is the giant saguaro, which grows in the Sonora Desert to a height of more than 60 ft (18 m).

NATURAL FEATURES
The plateau of Mexico is enclosed to the west and east by the Sierra Madre mountain ranges, which occupy 75 percent of the total land area. Mexico is so mountainous and arid in parts that only 12 percent of the land is arable.

ENVIRONMENT
Poor air quality is a problem in Mexico City because it is surrounded by mountains, which stop fumes released by cars and factories from escaping.

HISTORY
The remains of Mayan and Aztec cities are found all over Mexico and Central America. Mexico City is built on the ruins of the Aztec capital, Tenochtitlán.

INDUSTRY
Oil, natural gas, tourism, minerals, brewing, agriculture. Tourism employs nine percent of the workforce. Mexico is one of the largest oil producers and supplies one-fifth of the world's silver.

idad
árez

AMERICA

Bravo del Norte

hihuahua

SIERRA MADRE ORIENTAL

chos

MEXICO

Rio Grande

ODENTAL

Monterrey

San Luis Potosí
Río Grande de
Santiago
Aguascalientes
Ciudad Madero
León
Guadalajara
Poza Rica
L. Chapala
MEXICO CITY
L. Texcoco
Puebla
Balsas
SIERRA MADRE DEL SUR
Acapulco

CIFIC

N

OCEAN

Gulf of Mexico

Bay of Campeche

Mérida

Campeche
Cozumel I.

YUCATÁN PENINSULA

Villahermosa

Coatzacoalcos

Oaxaca

Tuxtla Gutiérrez

BELIZE

Gulf of Tehuantepec

Tapachula

GUATEMALA

200 400km
100 200miles

North America facts

UNITED STATES OF AMERICA

• The US economy is the largest in the world.
• The nation is made up of 50 states plus the District of Columbia.
• The world's leading computer software is produced in the US.

ESSENTIAL FACTS

⊙ Washington, DC
◐ 3,618,760 sq miles (9,372,610 sq km)
♦ 257.8 million
💲 American dollar
♡ English
▲ Multiparty republic
♦ 76 years

BEAUTIFUL BIRD
The American national symbol is the bald eagle.

WYOMING LANDSCAPE
The varied American scenery ranges from arid desert in Arizona through to areas of mountainous lakes in Wyoming.

SOUTHWESTERN STATES

ARIZONA
⊙ Phoenix
♦ 3.6 million

COLORADO
⊙ Denver
♦ 3.3 million

NEVADA
⊙ Carson City
♦ 1.1 million

NEW MEXICO
⊙ Santa Fe
♦ 1.5 million

TEXAS
⊙ Austin
♦ 17 million

UTAH
⊙ Salt Lake City
♦ 1.7 million

COWBOYS
Cattle ranching is still big business in Texas today.

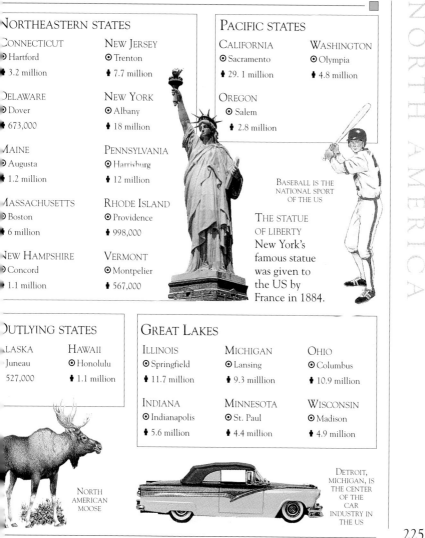

NORTHEASTERN STATES

CONNECTICUT
⊙ Hartford
♦ 3.2 million

DELAWARE
⊙ Dover
♦ 673,000

MAINE
⊙ Augusta
♦ 1.2 million

MASSACHUSETTS
⊙ Boston
♦ 6 million

NEW HAMPSHIRE
⊙ Concord
♦ 1.1 million

NEW JERSEY
⊙ Trenton
♦ 7.7 million

NEW YORK
⊙ Albany
♦ 18 million

PENNSYLVANIA
⊙ Harrisburg
♦ 12 million

RHODE ISLAND
⊙ Providence
♦ 998,000

VERMONT
⊙ Montpelier
♦ 567,000

PACIFIC STATES

CALIFORNIA
⊙ Sacramento
♦ 29. 1 million

OREGON
⊙ Salem
♦ 2.8 million

WASHINGTON
⊙ Olympia
♦ 4.8 million

BASEBALL IS THE
NATIONAL SPORT
OF THE US

THE STATUE
OF LIBERTY
New York's
famous statue
was given to
the US by
France in 1884.

OUTLYING STATES

ALASKA
Juneau
527,000

HAWAII
⊙ Honolulu
♦ 1.1 million

GREAT LAKES

ILLINOIS
⊙ Springfield
♦ 11.7 million

INDIANA
⊙ Indianapolis
♦ 5.6 million

MICHIGAN
⊙ Lansing
♦ 9.3 milllion

MINNESOTA
⊙ St. Paul
♦ 4.4 million

OHIO
⊙ Columbus
♦ 10.9 million

WISCONSIN
⊙ Madison
♦ 4.9 million

NORTH
AMERICAN
MOOSE

DETROIT,
MICHIGAN, IS
THE CENTER
OF THE
CAR
INDUSTRY IN
THE US

CENTRAL AND MOUNTAIN STATES

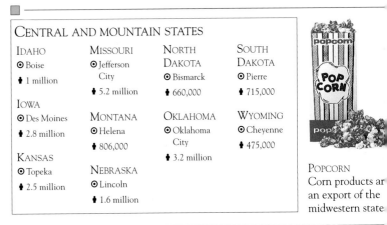

IDAHO
⊙ Boise
✚ 1 million

IOWA
⊙ Des Moines
✚ 2.8 million

KANSAS
⊙ Topeka
✚ 2.5 million

MISSOURI
⊙ Jefferson City
✚ 5.2 million

MONTANA
⊙ Helena
✚ 806,000

NEBRASKA
⊙ Lincoln
✚ 1.6 million

NORTH DAKOTA
⊙ Bismarck
✚ 660,000

OKLAHOMA
⊙ Oklahoma City
✚ 3.2 million

SOUTH DAKOTA
⊙ Pierre
✚ 715,000

WYOMING
⊙ Cheyenne
✚ 475,000

POPCORN
Corn products ar
an export of the
midwestern state

SOUTHERN STATES

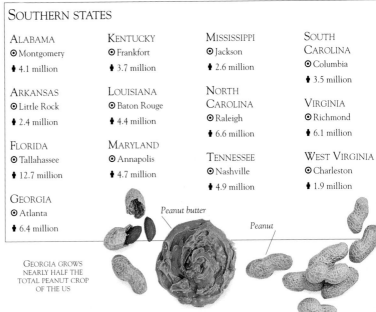

ALABAMA
⊙ Montgomery
✚ 4.1 million

ARKANSAS
⊙ Little Rock
✚ 2.4 million

FLORIDA
⊙ Tallahassee
✚ 12.7 million

GEORGIA
⊙ Atlanta
✚ 6.4 million

KENTUCKY
⊙ Frankfort
✚ 3.7 million

LOUISIANA
⊙ Baton Rouge
✚ 4.4 million

MARYLAND
⊙ Annapolis
✚ 4.7 million

MISSISSIPPI
⊙ Jackson
✚ 2.6 million

NORTH CAROLINA
⊙ Raleigh
✚ 6.6 million

TENNESSEE
⊙ Nashville
✚ 4.9 million

SOUTH CAROLINA
⊙ Columbia
✚ 3.5 million

VIRGINIA
⊙ Richmond
✚ 6.1 million

WEST VIRGINIA
⊙ Charleston
✚ 1.9 million

Peanut butter

Peanut

GEORGIA GROWS
NEARLY HALF THE
TOTAL PEANUT CROP
OF THE US

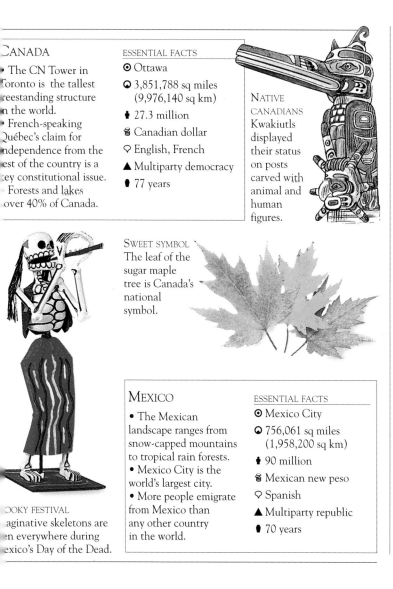

CANADA

- The CN Tower in Toronto is the tallest freestanding structure in the world.
- French-speaking Québec's claim for independence from the rest of the country is a key constitutional issue.
- Forests and lakes over 40% of Canada.

ESSENTIAL FACTS

⊙ Ottawa

◔ 3,851,788 sq miles (9,976,140 sq km)

✦ 27.3 million

💲 Canadian dollar

♥ English, French

▲ Multiparty democracy

♦ 77 years

NATIVE CANADIANS Kwakiutls displayed their status on posts carved with animal and human figures.

SWEET SYMBOL The leaf of the sugar maple tree is Canada's national symbol.

SPOOKY FESTIVAL Imaginative skeletons are seen everywhere during Mexico's Day of the Dead.

MEXICO

- The Mexican landscape ranges from snow-capped mountains to tropical rain forests.
- Mexico City is the world's largest city.
- More people emigrate from Mexico than any other country in the world.

ESSENTIAL FACTS

⊙ Mexico City

◔ 756,061 sq miles (1,958,200 sq km)

✦ 90 million

💲 Mexican new peso

♥ Spanish

▲ Multiparty republic

♦ 70 years

227

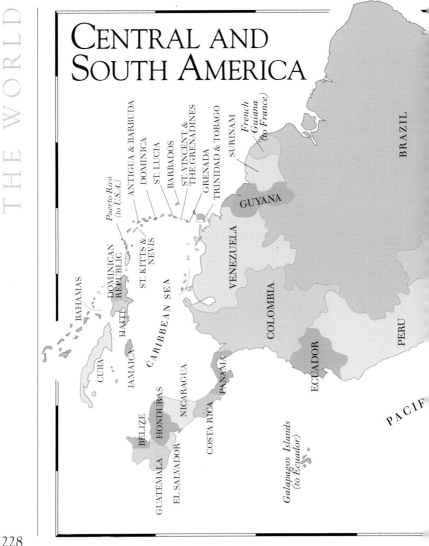

CENTRAL AND SOUTH AMERICA

BRAZIL

French Guiana (to France)

SURINAM

GUYANA

ANTIGUA & BARBUDA
DOMINICA
ST. LUCIA
BARBADOS
ST. VINCENT & THE GRENADINES
GRENADA
TRINIDAD & TOBAGO

Puerto Rico (to U.S.A.)

VENEZUELA

DOMINICAN REPUBLIC
ST. KITTS & NEVIS
HAITI

BAHAMAS

COLOMBIA

CARIBBEAN SEA

CUBA
JAMAICA

PERU

ECUADOR

NICARAGUA
PANAMA

BELIZE
HONDURAS

COSTA RICA

PACIFIC

GUATEMALA
EL SALVADOR

Galapagos Islands (to Ecuador)

ATLANTIC OCEAN

PARAGUAY

URUGUAY

ARGENTINA

CHILE

Falkland Islands
(to U.K.)

EAN

CENTRAL AND SOUTH AMERICA

Until three million years ago, South America was an island with its own unique flora and fauna. The narrow Isthmus of Panama is the continent's only link to North America. South America's southernmost tip, Cape Horn, is only 600 miles (970 km) from Antarctica.

CENTRAL AMERICA AND THE CARIBBEAN

CENTRAL AMERICA FORMS a narrow land bridge joining North and South America. To the east lie the Caribbean islands, many of which are uninhabited.

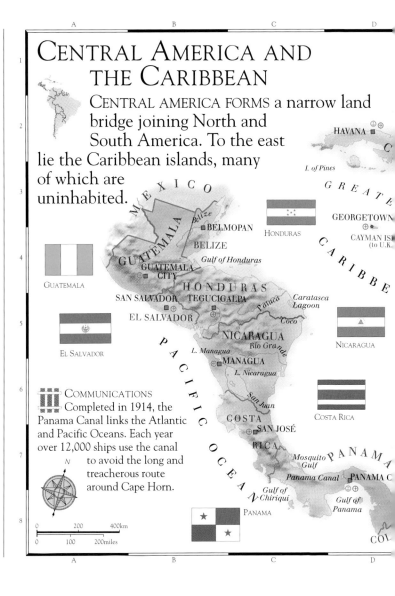

HAVANA

I. of Pines

GREATE

GEORGETOWN

CAYMAN IS
(to U.K.)

HONDURAS

BELMOPAN

BELIZE

Gulf of Honduras

GUATEMALA
CITY

GUATEMALA

HONDURAS

SAN SALVADOR   TEGUCIGALPA

Patuca

Caratasca Lagoon

EL SALVADOR

Coco

CARIBBE

NICARAGUA

Río Grande

L. Managua

MANAGUA

L. Nicaragua

NICARAGUA

COMMUNICATIONS
Completed in 1914, the Panama Canal links the Atlantic and Pacific Oceans. Each year over 12,000 ships use the canal to avoid the long and treacherous route around Cape Horn.

San Juan

COSTA

SAN JOSÉ

RICA

COSTA RICA

Mosquito Gulf

PANAMA

Panama Canal   PANAMA C

Gulf of Chiriquí

Gulf of Panama

PANAMA

PACIFIC OCEAN

N

0	200	400km
0	100	200miles

COL

GUATEMALA

EL SALVADOR

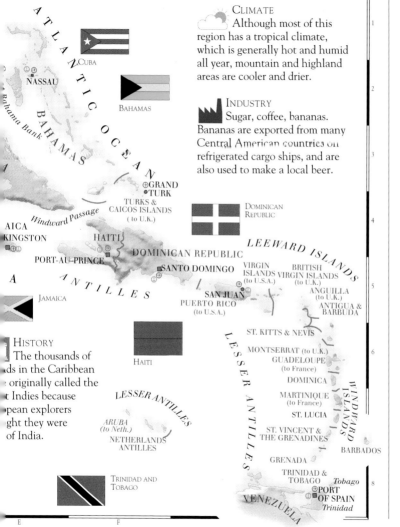

E   F   G   H

ATLANTIC

CUBA

NASSAU

BAHAMAS

Bahama Bank

OCEAN

BAHAMAS

CLIMATE

Although most of this region has a tropical climate, which is generally hot and humid all year, mountain and highland areas are cooler and drier.

INDUSTRY

Sugar, coffee, bananas. Bananas are exported from many Central American countries on refrigerated cargo ships, and are also used to make a local beer.

⊕GRAND
•TURK

TURKS &
CAICOS ISLANDS
(to U.K.)

DOMINICAN
REPUBLIC

Windward Passage

AICA

KINGSTON

PORT-AU-PRINCE

HAITI

DOMINICAN REPUBLIC

LEEWARD ISLANDS

A

ANTILLES

JAMAICA

SANTO DOMINGO

SAN JUAN
PUERTO RICO
(to U.S.A.)

VIRGIN
ISLANDS
(to U.S.A.)

BRITISH
VIRGIN ISLANDS
(to U.K.)

ANGUILLA
(to U.K.)

ANTIGUA &
BARBUDA

ST. KITTS & NEVIS

HISTORY

The thousands of
ds in the Caribbean
originally called the
t Indies because
pean explorers
ght they were
of India.

HAITI

LESSER ANTILLES

ARUBA
(to Neth.)

NETHERLANDS
ANTILLES

LESSER ANTILLES

MONTSERRAT (to U.K.)

GUADELOUPE
(to France)

DOMINICA

MARTINIQUE
(to France)

ST. LUCIA

ST. VINCENT &
THE GRENADINES

GRENADA

WINDWARD ISLANDS

BARBADOS

TRINIDAD AND
TOBAGO

TRINIDAD &
TOBAGO   Tobago

⊕PORT
OF SPAIN
Trinidad

VENEZUELA

E   F

Central America facts

NICARAGUA

- Lake Nicaragua is the only freshwater lake in the world to contain ocean animals.

ESSENTIAL FACTS

- ⊙ Managua
- ◐ 50,193 sq miles (130, 000 sq km)
- ♦ 4.1 million
- ☺ New córdoba
- ♀ Spanish

HONDURAS

- The swampy Caribbean shoreline of Honduras is known as the Mosquito Coast.

ESSENTIAL FACTS

- ⊙ Tegucigalpa
- ◐ 43,278 sq miles (112,090 sq km)
- ♦ 5.6 million
- ☺ Lempira
- ♀ Spanish

QUETZAL
Inca headdresses were decorated with the colorful tail feathers of the quetzal bird.

COTTON
The export of cotton is a major Nicaraguan industry.

BANANAS
Honduras has huge banana plantations. The work is hard and the pay is low.

GUATEMALA

- The ruined remains of temples and pyramids built by the ancient Mayans can still be seen in the forests of Guatemala.

ESSENTIAL FACTS

- ⊙ Guatemala City
- ◐ 42,043 sq miles (108,890 sq km)
- ♦ 10 million
- ☺ Quetzal
- ♀ Spanish

EL SALVADOR

- Coffee accounts for 90% of the country's exported goods.
- El Salvador means "the saviour," referring to Christ.

ESSENTIAL FACTS

- ⊙ San Salvador
- ◐ 28,124 sq miles (1,040 sq km)
- ♦ 5.4 million
- ☺ Salvadorean colón
- ♀ Spanish

COSTA RICA

• The constitution of Costa Rica is the only one in the world to ban National Armies.
• The name Costa Rica means "rich coast" in Spanish.

ESSENTIAL FACTS
⊙ San José
◑ 19,730 sq miles (51,100 sq km)
♦ 3.3 million
🖀 Costa Rican colón
♡ Spanish

MAHOGANY
Costa Rica's forests have been devastated by excessive felling of trees, such as mahogany and cedar, for timber. Today, much forested land is protected.

CUBAN BEE HUMMINGBIRD

PANAMA

• Many rare bird and animal species are threatened by the wholesale destruction of Panama's rain forests.

ESSENTIAL FACTS
⊙ Panama City
◑ 29,761 sq miles (77,080 sq km)
♦ 2.6 million
🖀 Balboa
♡ Spanish

CUBA

• As a result of fuel shortages, the bicycle is the main form of public transportation.
• Cuba is the only communist country in the Americas.

ESSENTIAL FACTS
⊙ Havana
◑ 42,803 sq miles (110,860 sq km)
♦ 10.9 million
🖀 Cuban peso
♡ Spanish

EXPORTS
Belize exports grapefruit. Sugar is made from cane, which grows in Panama.

BELIZE

• The Belizean barrier reef is the second largest in the world.
• Belize was formerly known as British Honduras, gaining independence in 1981.

ESSENTIAL FACTS
⊙ Belmopan
◑ 8,865 sq miles (22,960 sq km)
♦ 200,000
🖀 Belizean dollar
♡ English

Caribbean facts

DOMINICAN REPUBLIC

• Founded in 1496 by Christopher Columbus's brother, Santo Domingo is the oldest American city.

ESSENTIAL FACTS

⊙ Santo Domingo

◒ 18,815 sq miles (48,730 sq km)

♦ 7.6 million

✇ Dominican Republic peso

♡ Spanish

HAITI

• Many Haitians still practice the folk religion of voodoo.
• Haiti became the first independent black republic in 1804.

ESSENTIAL FACTS

⊙ Port-au-Prince

◒ 10,714 sq miles (27,750 sq km)

♦ 6.9 million

✇ Gourde

♡ French, Creole

Molasses

Rum, m[...] from c[...] ju[...]

Sugar cane

CANE PRODUCTS
Sugar cane thrives in the tropical Caribbean

JAMAICA

• Reggae music originated in Jamaica.
• The Rastafarians of Jamaica worship Haile Selassie, the late emperor of Ethiopia.
• Large areas of Kingston are ruled by gang leaders, or *Dons*.

ESSENTIAL FACTS

⊙ Kingston

◒ 4,243 sq miles (10,990 sq km)

♦ 2.5 million

✇ Jamaican dollar

♡ English

Steel drum, made from an oil drum

Guiora, percussion instrument

Wooden maracas

ISLAND SOUNDS
Caribbean music, such as calypso and reggae, shows a strong African influence.

GRENADA
- ⊙ St. George's
- ♦ 91,000
- ♡ English, Creole

ST. LUCIA
- ⊙ Castries
- ♦ 156, 000
- ♡ English, French

THE BAHAMAS
- ⊙ Nassau
- ♦ 300,000
- ♡ English, Creole

DOMINICA
- ⊙ Roseau
- ♦ 72,000
- ♡ English, French

ISLE OF SPICES
Many varieties of spice are grown on the island of Grenada.

Mace

Cloves

Bay leaf

Saffron

Cinnamon stick

Ground cinnamon

ST. KITTS & NEVIS
- ⊙ Basseterre
- ♦ 44,000
- ♡ English, Creole

ST. VINCENT & THE GRENADINES
- ⊙ Kingstown
- ♦ 109,000
- ♡ English, Creole

BARBADOS
- ⊙ Bridgetown
- ♦ 260,000
- ♡ English, Creole

TRINIDAD & TOBAGO
- ⊙ Port-of-Spain
- ♦ 1.3 million
- ♡ English

ANTIGUA & BARBUDA
- ⊙ St. John's
- ♦ 200,000
- ♡ English, Creole

STORMY WEATHER
The Caribbean islands are often subject to extreme weather, such as hurricanes and typhoons.

235

NORTHERN SOUTH AMERICA

THE INCAS RULED MUCH of this area in the 15th century, and today large numbers of their descendants live in Peru, Ecuador, and Bolivia. In 1533, the last Incan emperor was executed by the Spanish, who colonized this region. Countries east of Venezuela were later settled by the French, Dutch, and British, although all but French Guiana are now independent.

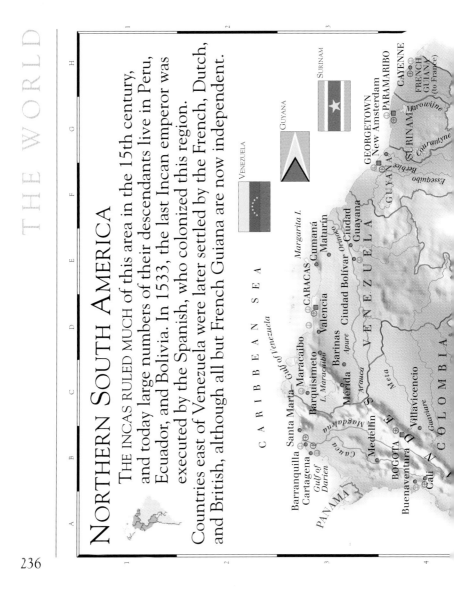

VENEZUELA

GUYANA

SURINAM

CARIBBEAN SEA

Gulf of Venezuela

Margarita I.

Maracaibo
L. Maracaibo
Barquisimeto
Valencia
CARACAS
Cumaná
Maturín
Ciudad Bolívar
Orinoco
Ciudad Guayana

Santa Marta
Barranquilla
Cartagena
Gulf of Darien

Barinas
Apure
Mérida
Arauca
Magdalena

VENEZUELA

Meta
Medellín
Villavicencio
Guaviare
BOGOTÁ
Buenaventura
Cali

COLOMBIA

Cauca

PANAMA

GUYANA
SURINAM
FRENCH GUIANA (to France)

GEORGETOWN
New Amsterdam
PARAMARIBO
CAYENNE

Essequibo
Berbice
Courantyne
Maroweijne

CLIMATE
Coastal areas are hot and humid. The Andes are divided into three climatic zones – cold highlands, which have springlike weather all year round, temperate uplands, and hot lowlands.

INDUSTRY
Oil, bauxite, rice, coal, coffee, bananas, gold, silver, tin. Colombia and Bolivia are the largest exporters of the illegal drug cocaine, made from the leaves of the coca bush.

NATURAL FEATURES
Lake Titicaca, the world's highest navigable lake, lies in the Andes at 12,497 ft (3,809 m) above sea level. Wood is scarce, so native South Americans make boats from reeds that grow around the lake.

COLOMBIA

ECUADOR

BOLIVIA

PERU

N

0   150   300
0   300   600km
0   150   300miles

NORTHERN SOUTH AMERICA

237

Northern South America facts

SURINAM

- Jaguars, pumas, ocelots, and iguanas live wild in Surinam.

ESSENTIAL FACTS

- Paramaribo
- 63,039 sq miles (163,270 sq km)
- 400,000
- Surinam guilder
- Dutch

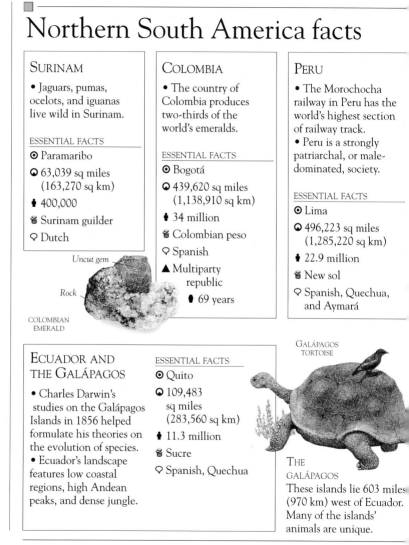

Uncut gem

Rock

COLOMBIAN EMERALD

COLOMBIA

- The country of Colombia produces two-thirds of the world's emeralds.

ESSENTIAL FACTS

- Bogotá
- 439,620 sq miles (1,138,910 sq km)
- 34 million
- Colombian peso
- Spanish
- ▲ Multiparty republic
  - 69 years

PERU

- The Morochocha railway in Peru has the world's highest section of railway track.
- Peru is a strongly patriarchal, or male-dominated, society.

ESSENTIAL FACTS

- Lima
- 496,223 sq miles (1,285,220 sq km)
- 22.9 million
- New sol
- Spanish, Quechua, and Aymará

ECUADOR AND THE GALÁPAGOS

- Charles Darwin's studies on the Galápagos Islands in 1856 helped formulate his theories on the evolution of species.
- Ecuador's landscape features low coastal regions, high Andean peaks, and dense jungle.

ESSENTIAL FACTS

- Quito
- 109,483 sq miles (283,560 sq km)
- 11.3 million
- Sucre
- Spanish, Quechua

GALÁPAGOS TORTOISE

THE GALÁPAGOS

These islands lie 603 miles (970 km) west of Ecuador. Many of the islands' animals are unique.

ANDEAN CONDOR
The heaviest bird of prey in the world, the condor lives in the highest parts of the Andes.

Wing span of more than 10 ft (3m)

BOLIVIA

• La Paz is the highest capital city in the world.
• Many Bolivian farmers are very poor, growing just enough food for their families to live on.
• Bolivia has the world's highest golf course and ski run.

ESSENTIAL FACTS

⊙ La Paz
◑ 424,162 sq miles (1,098,580 sq km)
✚ 7.8 million
☙ Boliviano
♀ Spanish, Quechua, and Aymará

VENEZUELA

• Many Venezuelan people live in poverty.
• Venezuela is the most urbanized country in South America.
• Angel Falls, the highest waterfall in the world, lies in southern Venezuela.

ESSENTIAL FACTS

⊙ Caracas
◑ 352,143 sq miles (912,050 sq km)
✚ 20.6 million
☙ Bolivár
♀ Spanish

CAYENNE PEPPER
Crushed South American chilies are used to make cayenne pepper.

GUYANA

• The Guyanese nation is the only English-speaking country in South America.
• Guyana means "land of many waters."

ESSENTIAL FACTS

⊙ Georgetown
◑ 83,000 sq miles (214,970 sq km)
✚ 800,000
☙ Guyana dollar
♀ English, Creole

FRENCH GUIANA

• The European Space Agency conducts its rocket launches from French Guiana.
• The territory of French Guiana is the last remaining colony in South America.

ESSENTIAL FACTS

⊙ Cayenne
◑ 35,135 sq miles (90,996 sq km)
✚ 114,800
☙ French franc
♀ French

BRAZIL

OCCUPYING NEARLY HALF of South America, Brazil has the largest river basin in the world. Many Brazilians are descendants of Portuguese, who colonized Brazil in the 16th century and Africans, who were brought to work on sugar plantations. Brazil's Native American tribes have little contact with the outside world. In 1992, the United Nations held its first Earth Summit in Rio, partly to highlight the destruction of the Amazon rainforest, the largest rainforest in the world.

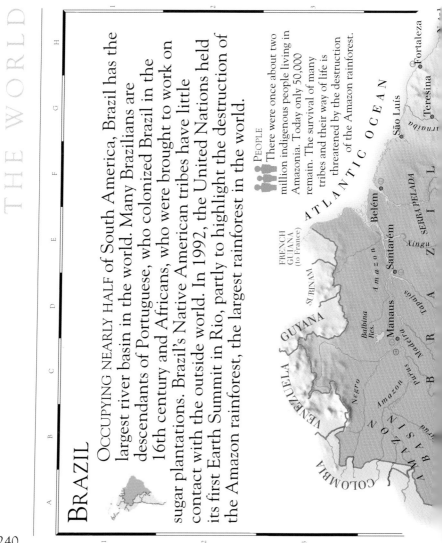

PEOPLE

There were once about two million indigenous people living in Amazonia. Today only 50,000 remain. The survival of many tribes and their way of life is threatened by the destruction of the Amazon rainforest.

FRENCH GUIANA (to France)

SURINAM

GUYANA

VENEZUELA

COLOMBIA

AMAZON BASIN

ATLANTIC OCEAN

BRAZIL

Negro

Amazon

Purus

Madeira

Balbina Res.

Manaus

Japurá

Amazon

Santarém

Tapajós

Xingu

SERRA PELADA

Belém

São Luís

Teresina

Fortaleza

Parnaíba

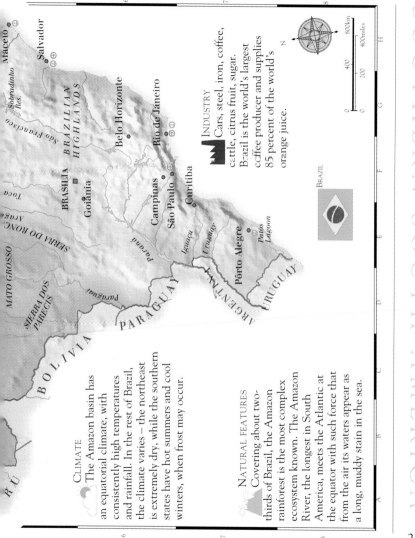

CLIMATE

The Amazon basin has an equatorial climate, with consistently high temperatures and rainfall. In the rest of Brazil, the climate varies – the northeast is extremely dry, while the southern states have hot summers and cool winters, when frost may occur.

NATURAL FEATURES

Covering about two-thirds of Brazil, the Amazon rainforest is the most complex ecosystem known. The Amazon River, the longest in South America, meets the Atlantic at the equator with such force that from the air its waters appear as a long, muddy stain in the sea.

INDUSTRY

Cars, steel, iron, coffee, cattle, citrus fruit, sugar. Brazil is the world's largest coffee producer and supplies 85 percent of the world's orange juice.

BRAZIL

| 0 | 200 | 400 | | 800km |
| 0 | | 200 | 400miles |

N

Salvador

Maceió

Sobradinho
Res.

São Francisco

BRAZILIAN HIGHLANDS

Belo Horizonte

Rio de Janeiro

BRASILIA

Goiânia

Toca

Ara...

SERRA DO RONC...

Campinas

São Paulo

Curitiba

Iguaçu

Paraná

Uruguay

Pôrto Alegre

Patos
Lagoon

URUGUAY

PARAGUAY

ARGENTINA

Paraguay

MATO GROSSO

SIERRA DOS PARECIS

BOLIVIA

...RU

SOUTHERN SOUTH AMERICA

SOUTHERN SOUTH AMERICA

THE LANDSCAPE OF this region of South America varies from snow-capped volcanoes in the Andes to the wastelands of Patagonia. In the heart of Argentina lie the Pampas, fertile grasslands where vast herds of cattle graze. In parts, grasses grow up to 10 ft (3 m) high. Chile is separated from the rest of the region by the Andes, which run the length of the continent.

PARAGUAY

CLIMATE

Paraguay is subtropical, farther south is temperate. The Andes have snow year-round, while parts of the Atacama desert in Chile have had no rain for 400 years.

URUGUAY

SOUTHERN SOUTH AMERICA

INDUSTRY
Copper, wool, beef, wheat. Chile is the world's largest copper producer, and Uruguay is the second-largest wool exporter.

ARGENTINA

HISTORY
Before the discovery of Cape Horn at the tip of the continent in 1616, ships used the dangerous Straits of Magellan to travel between the Atlantic and the Pacific Oceans. Today, ships use the Panama Canal.

NATURAL FEATURES
The longest chain of mountains in the world, the Andes are 4,500 miles (7,240 km) in length. They are the most recently formed mountains on Earth, and the area suffers from earthquakes and volcanic activity. Glaciers, fjords, lakes, and deep-sea channels are features of the southern Andes.

CHILE

Southern South America Facts

CHILE

• Democracy was restored in Chile in 1989 after 12 years of military rule under General Pinochet.
• The Atacama Desert in northern Chile is the driest place on Earth.

ESSENTIAL FACTS

⊙ Santiago
◑ 292,258 sq miles (756,950 sq km)
♦ 13.8 million
🐚 Chilean peso
♥ Spanish
▲ Multiparty republic
● 72 years

TREE OF MYSTERY
The Chile pine, also known as the monkey puzzle tree, is native to the Andes, the world's longest mountain range.

URUGUAY

• The country of Uruguay is the smallest in South America.
• Almost half of the population lives in Montevideo.
• Hydroelectric power generates 86% of the country's electricity.
• Uruguay is tolerant of all forms of religion.

ESSENTIAL FACTS

⊙ Montevideo
◑ 68,498 sq miles (177,410 sq km)
♦ 3.1 million
🐚 Uruguayan peso
♥ Spanish

WOOLEN SCARF

TEXTILES
Uruguay is a major exporter of handmade wool products.

PARAGUAY

• The majority of Paraguayans are *mestizo* – a mixture of native Guaraní Indian and Spanish blood.
• Half the work force is employed in agriculture.

ESSENTIAL FACTS

⊙ Asunción
◑ 157,046 sq miles (406,750 sq km)
♦ 4.5 million
🐚 Guaraní
♥ Spanish, Guaraní

GAUCHO
Argentinian cowboys
are known as gauchos.

ARGENTINA

- Crop production and cattle and sheep rearing produce three-quarters of the nation's income.
- The Argentinian daily drink is a tea called *maté*.
- The tango, a dance, originated in Buenos Aires in the late 19th century.

ESSENTIAL FACTS

- ◉ Buenos Aires
- ◔ 1,068,296 sq miles (2,766,890 sq km)
- ♦ 33.5 million
- ⬛ Argentinian peso
- ♀ Spanish
- ▲ Multiparty republic
- ♦ 71 years

PUDU
Southern Argentina's
Patagonia region is
home to the pudu, the
world's smallest deer.

BRAZILIAN SOCCER
Soccer is Brazil's favorite
sport, with more than
0,000 teams.

BRAZIL

- São Paulo is the world's second largest city, with 17 million inhabitants.
- Rio de Janeiro's *Mardi Gras* carnival is a major tourist attraction.
- Brazil has rich gold and diamond reserves.
- Many Brazilians live in poverty, despite the country's resources.

ESSENTIAL FACTS

- ◉ Brasília
- ◔ 3,286,472 sq miles (8,511,970 sq km)
- ♦ 156.6 million
- ⬛ Reál
- ♀ Portuguese
- ▲ Multiparty republic
- ♦ 66 years

EUROPE

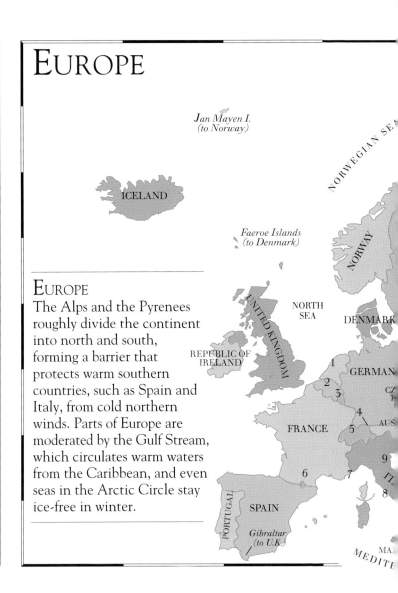

Jan Mayen I.
(to Norway)

NORWEGIAN SEA

ICELAND

Faeroe Islands
(to Denmark)

NORWAY

EUROPE

The Alps and the Pyrenees roughly divide the continent into north and south, forming a barrier that protects warm southern countries, such as Spain and Italy, from cold northern winds. Parts of Europe are moderated by the Gulf Stream, which circulates warm waters from the Caribbean, and even seas in the Arctic Circle stay ice-free in winter.

NORTH SEA

DENMARK

UNITED KINGDOM

REPUBLIC OF IRELAND

GERMANY

CZ

FRANCE

AUS

PORTUGAL

SPAIN

Gibraltar
(to U.K.)

MEDITE

MA

1
2
3
4
5
6
7
8
9

BARENTS SEA

FINLAND

IC SEA

ESTONIA

LATVIA

LITHUANIA

RUSSIAN
FEDERATION

BELARUS

AND

AKIA

ARY   16

UKRAINE

ROMANIA

13

14

BULGARIA

BLACK SEA

GEORGIA

AZERBAIJAN

ARMENIA

5

GREECE

EAN SEA

1 NETHERLANDS
2 BELGIUM
3 LUXEMBOURG
4 LIECHTENSTEIN
5 SWITZERLAND
6 ANDORRA
7 MONACO
8 VATICAN CITY
9 SAN MARINO
10 SLOVENIA
11 CROATIA
12 BOSNIA/HERZEGOVINA
13 YUGOSLAVIA
14 MACEDONIA
15 ALBANIA
16 MOLDOVA

SCANDINAVIA AND FINLAND

DURING PAST ICE AGES, much of Scandinavia and Finland were covered in glaciers that carved out the land, leaving steep-sided valleys, fjords, and lakes. The Finns, originally from the east via Russia, differ from Scandinavians in culture and language.

CLIMATE
Norway's west coast is warmed by the Gulf Stream. Northern temperatures fall to −22°F (−30°C) during the six-month winter; the south is milder.

INDUSTRY
Fishing, timber, wood-pulp, paper, oil, gas, car manufacture. Norway is western Europe's largest producer of oil.

FINLAND

NORWAY

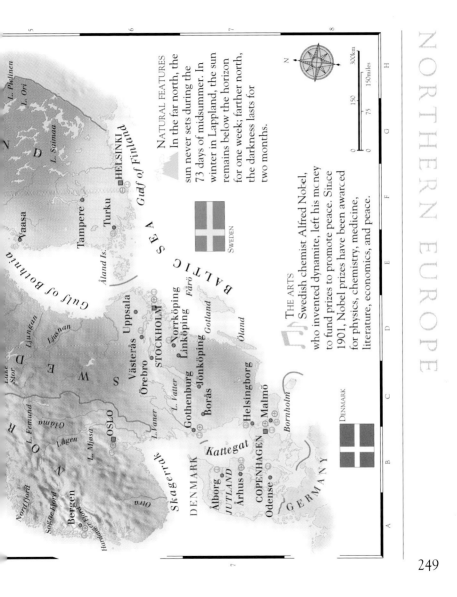

NATURAL FEATURES
In the far north, the sun never sets during the 73 days of midsummer. In winter in Lappland, the sun remains below the horizon for one week; farther north, the darkness lasts for two months.

THE ARTS
Swedish chemist Alfred Nobel, who invented dynamite, left his money to fund prizes to promote peace. Since 1901, Nobel prizes have been awarded for physics, chemistry, medicine, literature, economics, and peace.

SWEDEN

DENMARK

N

0 — 150 — 300km
0 — 75 — 150miles

L. Päijänne
L. Ori
L. Saimaa
N
D
■HELSINKI
Gulf of Finland
Vaasa
Tampere
Turku
Åland Is.
Gulf of Bothnia
Ljungan
Ljusnan
Uppsala
Västerås
Örebro
STOCKHOLM
Norrköping
Linköping
Fårö
Jönköping
Gotland
Borås
Öland
Gothenburg
L. Vänern
L. Vätter
S
W
E
D
E
OSLO
Glama
Lågen
L. Femund
L. Mjøsa
Nordfjord
Sogne fjord
Bergen
Hardanger fjord
Otra
R
O
N
Skagerrak
BALTIC SEA
Kattegat
DENMARK
Ålborg
JUTLAND
Århus
COPENHAGEN
Odense
Helsingborg
Malmö
Bornholm
GERMANY

Northern Europe facts

ICELAND

- The remote interior of Iceland can only be reached by special vehicle, pony, or small plane.
- Iceland has the lowest population in Europe.
- Heating is provided by geothermal power.

ESSENTIAL FACTS

- ⊙ Reykjavik
- ◔ 139,770 sq miles (103,000 sq km)
- ⚲ 300,000
- 🏛 New Icelandic krona
- ♥ Icelandic
- ▲ Multiparty republic
- ◗ 78 years

ICELANDIC COD
More than a third of the world's cod-liver oil is produced in Iceland.

NORWAY

- According to Norway's constitution, the government's duty is to create conditions enabling every person to find work.

ESSENTIAL FACTS

- ⊙ Oslo
- ◔ 125,060 sq miles (323,900 sq km)
- ⚲ 4.2 million
- 🏛 Norwegian krone
- ♥ Norwegian
- ▲ Multiparty democracy
- ◗ 77 years

GRASS ROOFS
Some Norwegian vacation homes have turf-covered roofs.

LAND OF LEGO
Lego building blocks, known by children worldwide, were invented in Denmark.

DENMARK

- Single parents and cohabiting couples raise 40% of Danish children.
- Denmark is Europe's oldest monarchy, dating back to the 1100s.

ESSENTIAL FACTS

- ⊙ Copenhagen
- ◔ 16,629 sq miles (43,069 sq km)
- ⚲ 5.2 million
- 🏛 Danish krone
- ♥ Danish
- ▲ Multiparty democracy
- ◗ 75 years

SWEDEN

- Over 50% of Swedish women go out to work.
- Sweden has maintained a position of armed neutrality since 1815.
- Swedish law requires cars to travel with their headlights on at all times.
- Many Swedes invest in overseas property.

ESSENTIAL FACTS

- ⊙ Stockholm
- ◔ 173,730 sq miles (449,960 sq km)
- ♦ 8.7 million
- ⊛ Swedish krona
- ♡ Swedish
- ▲ Multiparty democracy
- ♦ 78 years

SMÖRGÅSBORD
A Swedish smörgåsbord, meaning "sandwich table," is a spread of local delicacies served cold.

FINNISH TIMBER
Most of Finland's wealth is provided by its timber exports.

GREENLAND

Dependency of Denmark
(*Atlantic Ocean*, pp.360–361)

- ⊙ Nuuk
- ♦ 55,385
- ♡ Inuit, Danish

Ladle

Sauna bucket

STEAM CLEANING
The Finns invented the steam bath, or sauna, over 1,000 years ago.

FINLAND

- Over half of Finland's population lives in the five districts around Helsinki.
- Finland was the first country to allow women to run for parliament.
- Finland's inland waterway system is the largest in Europe.

ESSENTIAL FACTS

- ⊙ Helsinki
- ◔ 130,552 sq miles (338,130 sq km)
- ♦ 5 million
- ⊛ Markka
- ♡ Finnish, Swedish
- ▲ Multiparty republic
- ♦ 75 years

THE BRITISH ISLES

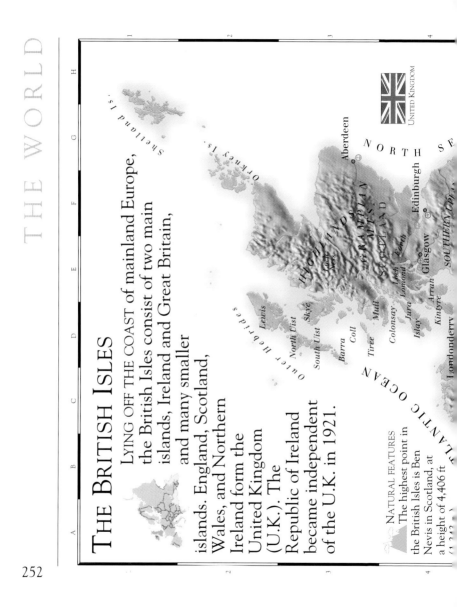

LYING OFF THE COAST of mainland Europe, the British Isles consist of two main islands, Ireland and Great Britain, and many smaller islands. England, Scotland, Wales, and Northern Ireland form the United Kingdom (U.K.). The Republic of Ireland became independent of the U.K. in 1921.

NATURAL FEATURES
The highest point in the British Isles is Ben Nevis in Scotland, at a height of 4,406 ft

UNITED KINGDOM

Shetland Is.

Orkney Is.

Outer Hebrides

Lewis

North Uist

South Uist

Barra

Skye

Coll

Tiree

Mull

Colonsay

Jura

Islay

Arran

Kintyre

HIGHLANDS

GRAMPIAN MTS.

SCOTLAND

Loch Ness

Loch Lomond

Aberdeen

NORTH SEA

Edinburgh

Glasgow

SOUTHERN UPL

Londonderry

ATLANTIC OCEAN

252

NORTHWEST EUROPE

CLIMATE
Warmed by the Gulf Stream, the climate is mild but changeable. Rainfall is well distributed throughout the year.

INDUSTRY
Pharmaceuticals, aerospace industry, oil, natural gas, dairy products, computer parts, livestock. Ireland has one of Europe's fastest growing economies.

IRELAND

THE LOW COUNTRIES

BELGIUM, THE NETHERLANDS, and Luxembourg are known as the "Low Countries" because they are flat and low-lying. Much of the Netherlands lies below sea level and has been reclaimed from the sea. The Low Countries, also called "Benelux," are Europe's most densely populated countries.

CLIMATE
The region is mostly temperate. Coastal areas are mildest, warmed by the Gulf Stream. Luxembourg's winters are cold

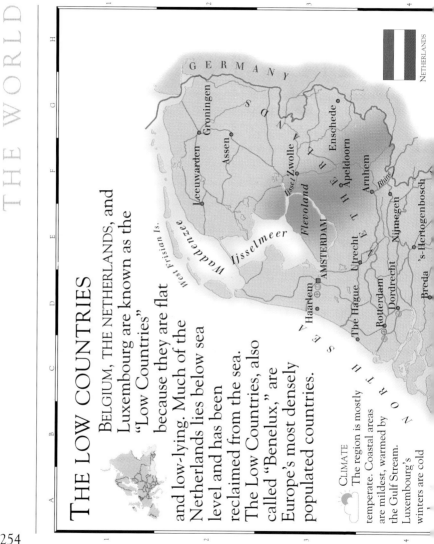

GERMANY

Groningen

Leeuwarden

Assen

West Frisian Is.

Waddenzee

Ijsselmeer

Flevoland

Zwolle

Ijssel

Enschede

Apeldoorn

Arnhem

Rhine

Nijmegen

's-Hertogenbosch

Breda

Haarlem

AMSTERDAM

Utrecht

The Hague

Rotterdam

Dordrecht

NORTH SEA

NETHERLANDS

NORTHWEST EUROPE

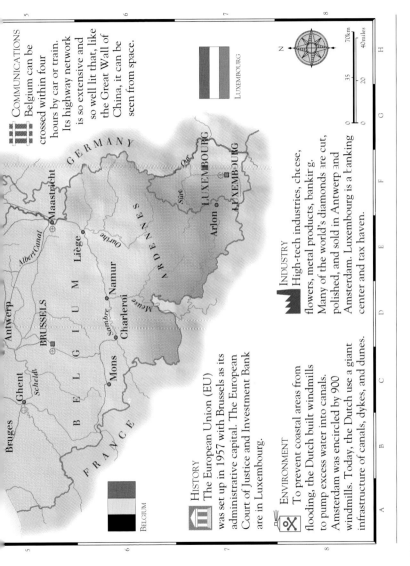

COMMUNICATIONS
Belgium can be crossed within four hours by car or train. Its highway network is so extensive and so well lit that, like the Great Wall of China, it can be seen from space.

LUXEMBOURG

HISTORY
The European Union (EU) was set up in 1957 with Brussels as its administrative capital. The European Court of Justice and Investment Bank are in Luxembourg.

ENVIRONMENT
To prevent coastal areas from flooding, the Dutch built windmills to pump excess water into canals. Amsterdam was encircled by 900 windmills. Today, the Dutch use a giant infrastructure of canals, dykes, and dunes.

INDUSTRY
High-tech industries, cheese, flowers, metal products, banking. Many of the world's diamonds are cut, polished, and sold in Antwerp and Amsterdam. Luxembourg is a banking center and tax haven.

BELGIUM

N

0   35   70km
0   20   40miles

Northwest Europe facts

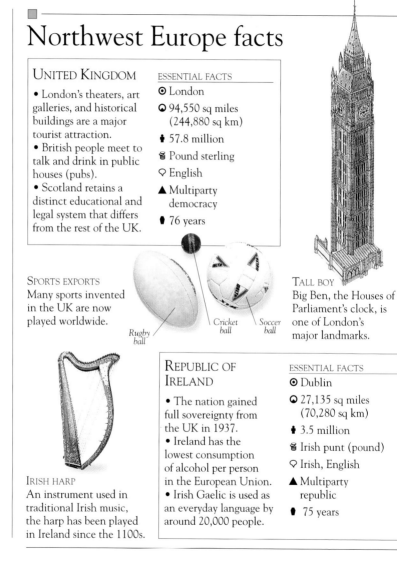

UNITED KINGDOM

- London's theaters, art galleries, and historical buildings are a major tourist attraction.
- British people meet to talk and drink in public houses (pubs).
- Scotland retains a distinct educational and legal system that differs from the rest of the UK.

ESSENTIAL FACTS

⊙ London
◔ 94,550 sq miles (244,880 sq km)
♦ 57.8 million
💲 Pound sterling
♡ English
▲ Multiparty democracy
♦ 76 years

SPORTS EXPORTS
Many sports invented in the UK are now played worldwide.

Rugby ball

Cricket ball

Soccer ball

TALL BOY
Big Ben, the Houses of Parliament's clock, is one of London's major landmarks.

IRISH HARP
An instrument used in traditional Irish music, the harp has been played in Ireland since the 1100s.

REPUBLIC OF IRELAND

- The nation gained full sovereignty from the UK in 1937.
- Ireland has the lowest consumption of alcohol per person in the European Union.
- Irish Gaelic is used as an everyday language by around 20,000 people.

ESSENTIAL FACTS

⊙ Dublin
◔ 27,135 sq miles (70,280 sq km)
♦ 3.5 million
💲 Irish punt (pound)
♡ Irish, English
▲ Multiparty republic
♦ 75 years

BELGIUM

- The cultural mix of French-speaking Walloons and Flemings forms the national identity of Belgium.
- Belgium's highway network is so extensive and well lit that it can be seen from space.
- The country is the world's third largest producer of chocolate.

ESSENTIAL FACTS

- ⊙ Brussels
- ◔ 12,780 sq miles (33,100 sq km)
- ⚲ 10 million
- 🛆 Belgian franc
- ♥ French, Dutch, Flemish
- ▲ Multiparty democracy
- ⚫ 76 years

SPACE-AGE STRUCTURE
The design of Belgium's futuristic Atomium building is based on the molecular structure of an iron crystal.

NETHERLANDS

- Dutch laws on sexuality and drugs are less strict than in other parts of Europe.
- Rotterdam is the world's largest port.

ESSENTIAL FACTS

- ⊙ Amsterdam, The Hague
- ◔ 14,410 sq miles (37,330 sq km)
- ⚲ 15.3 million
- 🛆 Guilder
- ♥ Dutch
- ▲ Multiparty democracy
- ⚫ 77 years

DUTCH TULIPS
The Netherlands is Europe's largest producer of flowers. The cultivation of bulbs such as daffodils and tulips is a specialty.

LUXEMBOURG

- ⊙ Luxembourg City
- ⚲ 400,000
- ♥ Letzeburgish

LUXEMBOURG BANKING
The nation of Luxembourg is a center of international banking and finance.

SPAIN AND PORTUGAL

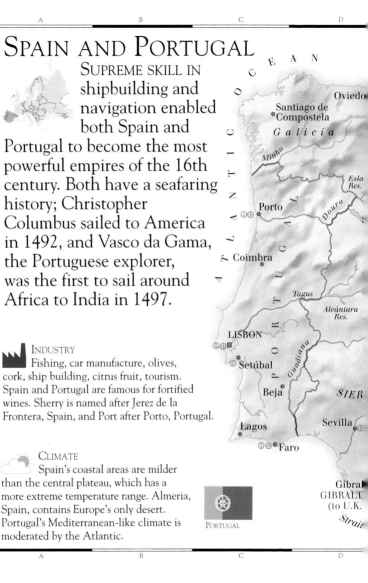

SUPREME SKILL IN shipbuilding and navigation enabled both Spain and Portugal to become the most powerful empires of the 16th century. Both have a seafaring history; Christopher Columbus sailed to America in 1492, and Vasco da Gama, the Portuguese explorer, was the first to sail around Africa to India in 1497.

INDUSTRY
Fishing, car manufacture, olives, cork, ship building, citrus fruit, tourism. Spain and Portugal are famous for fortified wines. Sherry is named after Jerez de la Frontera, Spain, and Port after Porto, Portugal.

CLIMATE
Spain's coastal areas are milder than the central plateau, which has a more extreme temperature range. Almeria, Spain, contains Europe's only desert. Portugal's Mediterranean-like climate is moderated by the Atlantic.

PORTUGAL

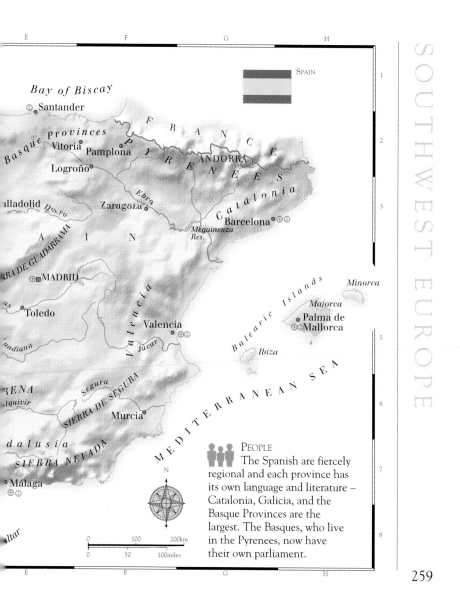

Bay of Biscay

⊕ Santander

Basque provinces

Vitoria ⊙
Pamplona ⊙
Logroño ⊙

F R A N C E

P Y R E N E E S

ANDORRA

Catalonia

lladolid

Duero

Zaragoza ⊙

Ebro

Mequinenza Res.

Barcelona ⊙⊕⊕

A I N

RA DE GUADARRAMA

⊙■ MADRID

us

Toledo

uadiana

Valencia

Valencia ⊙⊕⊕

Júcar

Balearic Islands

Minorca

Majorca

Palma de
⊙⊕ Mallorca

Ibiza

RENA

lquivir

Segura

SIERRA DE SEGURA

Murcia ⊙

M E D I T E R R A N E A N   S E A

dalusia

SIERRA NEVADA

⊕⊕ Málaga

ltar

N

0   100   200km
0   50   100miles

PEOPLE

The Spanish are fiercely regional and each province has its own language and literature – Catalonia, Galicia, and the Basque Provinces are the largest. The Basques, who live in the Pyrenees, now have their own parliament.

SPAIN

E   F   G   H

259

FRANCE

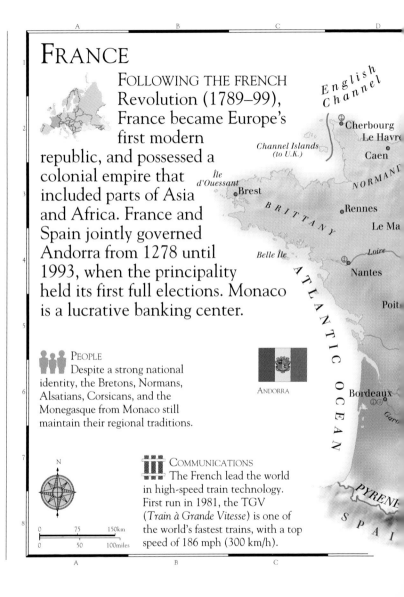

FOLLOWING THE FRENCH Revolution (1789–99), France became Europe's first modern republic, and possessed a colonial empire that included parts of Asia and Africa. France and Spain jointly governed Andorra from 1278 until 1993, when the principality held its first full elections. Monaco is a lucrative banking center.

PEOPLE
Despite a strong national identity, the Bretons, Normans, Alsatians, Corsicans, and the Monegasque from Monaco still maintain their regional traditions.

ANDORRA

COMMUNICATIONS
The French lead the world in high-speed train technology. First run in 1981, the TGV (*Train à Grande Vitesse*) is one of the world's fastest trains, with a top speed of 186 mph (300 km/h).

N

| 0 | 75 | 150km |
| 0 | 50 | 100miles |

English Channel

Cherbourg
Le Havre
Channel Islands (to U.K.)
Caen

NORMANDY

Île d'Ouessant
Brest

BRITTANY

Rennes
Le Ma

Loire

Belle Île
Nantes

Poit

ATLANTIC OCEAN

Bordeaux
Garo

PYRENE

S P A I

Strait of Dover

Calais
Lille

Somme
eppe Amiens
uen

Seine

BELGIUM

LUXEMBOURG

GERMANY

Rheims
Meuse
Marne
PARIS
Seine

Nancy
Moselle

Strasbourg

VOSGES

Orléans

BURGUNDY

Saône

Dijon

JURA

SWITZERLAND

ANCE

Loire

Geneva

Clermont-
Ferrand

Lyons

ITALY

Limoges

MASSIF

St. Étienne

ALPS

CENTRAL

ogne

CEVENNES

Rhône

Durance

MONTE
CARLO

Nice

MONACO

Toulouse

Montpellier

PROVENCE

Marseilles

Côte d'Azur

MEDITERRANEAN SEA

ANDORRA
ANDORRA
LA VELLA

FRANCE

Corsica
(to France)

Ajaccio

CLIMATE
France is mostly temperate, but summers in the south are dry and hot. In the Pyrenees and Alps, a cooler mountain climate prevails.

INDUSTRY
Tourism, engineering, wine, aerospace. France is a world leader in cosmetics, wine, and perfume. Its dairy farmers produce over 300 types of cheese.

MONACO

ITALY AND MALTA

THE BOOT-SHAPED PENINSULA of Italy stretches from the Alps to the Ionian Sea and includes Sardinia, Sicily, and other small, offshore islands. Italy also contains two independent enclaves – the Vatican City in Rome and the Republic of San Marino near Rimini. The Romans, Arabs, French, Turks, Spanish, and British have all fought for or colonized Malta, which has been independent since 1964.

PEOPLE

Venetians were a seafaring people, whose ships carried silks and spices from Asia. The Venetian trader and explorer Marco Polo is said to have brought the recipe for pasta from China.

HISTORY

Italy was once a collection of small kingdoms and city-states, which were vulnerable to internal wars. It was united in 1870, through the efforts of the soldier Guiseppe Garibaldi and the politician Count Camillo di Cavour

SLOVENIA

ADRIATI

Trieste

Gulf of Venice

Venice

Piave

Mestre

Comacchio

Padua

Lagoon

SAN

MARINO

SAN MARINO

Bologna

Po

Reno

Verona

APENN

Florence

Arno

Milan

Genoa

L. Maggiore

Gulf of Genoa

Turin

LIGURIAN SE

SAN MARINO

Bari

Taranto

Gulf of Taranto

IONIAN SEA

Gulf of Squillace

CALABRIA

Strait of Messina

Lipari Is *Stromboli*

Messina

Catania

SICILY

Salso

ITALY

Ofanto

Bradano

Agri

Naples

Sarno

Ischia

Capri

VATICAN CITY
(VATICAN CITY STATE)

ROME

Tiber

TYRRHENIAN SEA

VATICAN CITY

Ustica

Palermo

MEDITERRANEAN SEA

Egadi Is.

Pantelleria

Gozo

MALTA

VALLETTA

Pelagie Is.

MALTA

Tuscan Arch.

Strait of Bonifacio

Cagliari

SARDINIA

Tirso

Mannu

San Pietro

Sant'Antioco

C. Spartivento

N

200km

100miles

0   50   100

A   B   C   D   E   F   G   H

5   6   7   8

CLIMATE
Southern Italy and Malta have a Mediterranean climate with hot summers and mild winters. Northern Italy is cooler and wetter.

INDUSTRY
Cars, olives, wine, tourism. Italy is a leader in industrial design, textiles, and household goods and is the world's largest wine producer. Tourism is Malta's chief source of income.

263

Southwest Europe facts

SPAIN

- Young Spanish men tend to live at home until their late 20s.
- Spanish public hospitals are generally considered to be better than private ones.
- Over 3,000 festivals and feasts take place every year in Spain.

ESSENTIAL FACTS
- ⊙ Madrid
- ◔ 194,900 sq miles (504,780 sq km)
- ⚲ 39.2 million
- ⚄ Peseta
- ♀ Spanish
- ▲ Multiparty democracy
- ⚱ 77 years

SPANISH SIX-STRING
The classical guitar is Spain's national instrument.

Tuning pegs
Nut
Neck
Frets
Sound hole
Hollow body
Bridge
Strings

PORTUGUESE CORK
More than half the world's cork is supplied by Portugal, the main product being the bottle stopper.

PORTUGAL

- Family ties are a major part of Portuguese life.
- Over 40% of the population has private health insurance.
- Portugal has few natural resources.

ESSENTIAL FACTS
- ⊙ Lisbon
- ◔ 35,670 sq miles (92,390 sq km)
- ⚲ 9.9 million
- ⚄ Escudo
- ♀ Portuguese
- ▲ Multiparty republic
- ⚱ 74 years

ANDORRA
- ⊙ Andorra la Vella
- ⚲ 58,000
- ♀ Catalan

ITALY

- Tourists have visited Italy since the 1500s.
- Italy is a world leader in product design and the fashion industry.
- Venice is such a popular place to visit that pedestrians have to use one-way systems in the summer.
- Most Italians live at home before marriage.

ESSENTIAL FACTS
- ⊙ Rome
- ◔ 116,320 sq miles (301,270 sq km)
- ✚ 57.8 million
- 🖺 Italian lira
- ♥ Italian
- ▲ Multiparty republic
- ♦ 77 years

VENETIAN MASKS
Masks are traditionally worn during the February carnival in Venice.

SAN MARINO
- ⊙ San Marino
- ✚ 23,000
- ♥ Italian

VATICAN CITY
- ⊙ Vatican City
- ✚ 1,000
- ♥ Italian, Latin

MALTA
- ⊙ Valletta
- ✚ 400,000
- ♥ Maltese, English

MONACO
- ⊙ Monaco
- ✚ 28,000
- ♥ French

FRANCE

- Paris is the most visited European city.
- The French wine industry dates back to 600 B.C.
- More medicine is consumed per person in France than in any other country.
- Most French people spend their vacations in France, rather than traveling abroad.

ESSENTIAL FACTS
- ⊙ Paris
- ◔ 212,930 sq miles (551,500 sq km)
- ✚ 57.4 million
- 🖺 Franc
- ♥ French
- ▲ Multi-party republic
- ♦ 77 years

PEDAL POWER
The *Tour de France* bicycle race is the most famous in the world.

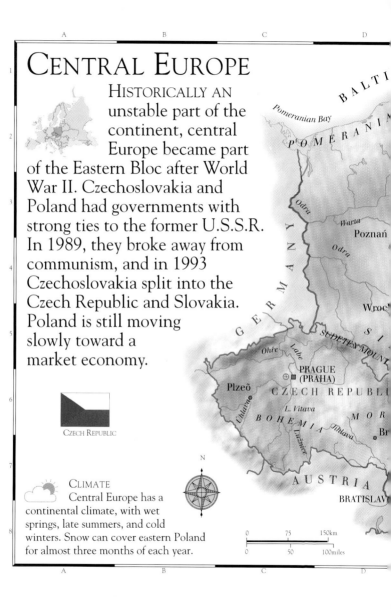

CENTRAL EUROPE

HISTORICALLY AN unstable part of the continent, central Europe became part of the Eastern Bloc after World War II. Czechoslovakia and Poland had governments with strong ties to the former U.S.S.R. In 1989, they broke away from communism, and in 1993 Czechoslovakia split into the Czech Republic and Slovakia. Poland is still moving slowly toward a market economy.

CZECH REPUBLIC

CLIMATE
Central Europe has a continental climate, with wet springs, late summers, and cold winters. Snow can cover eastern Poland for almost three months of each year.

BALTI

Pomeranian Bay

POMERANIA

Odra

Warta

Poznań

Odra

Wroc

SUDETEN MOUNT

Ohře

Labe

PRAGUE
(PRAHA)

Plzeō

CZECH REPUBLIC

L. Vltava

Vltava

BOHEMIA

Jihlava

MOR

Br

Lužnice

AUSTRIA

BRATISLAV

N

0   75   150km
0   50   100miles

POLAND

INDUSTRY

Wood industries, coal, sulphur, iron, steel, copper, fruit. Beer, made from barley grown locally, is one of the best-known products to come out of the Czech Republic. Mining and metal production has a long history in Slovakia, and Poland is a major world exporter of coal.

ENVIRONMENT

After 1945, the central European states industrialized rapidly. Today only four percent of Poland's rivers have water fit for consumption, and half of its cities have no sewage treatment facilities. In central Europe acid rain has harmed trees and eroded buildings across the region.

SLOVAKIA

GERMANY

IT WAS NOT UNTIL 1871 that many small independent states were united under Prussia to form Germany. After 1945, the country was divided again, into a democratic West Germany and a Soviet-dominated East Germany.

Reunified in 1990, Germany is, like France, a leading member of the European Union and is currently Europe's strongest economic power.

INDUSTRY
Cars, heavy and precision engineering, electronics, chemicals. Germany has a strong industrial sector and is Europe's main car producer.

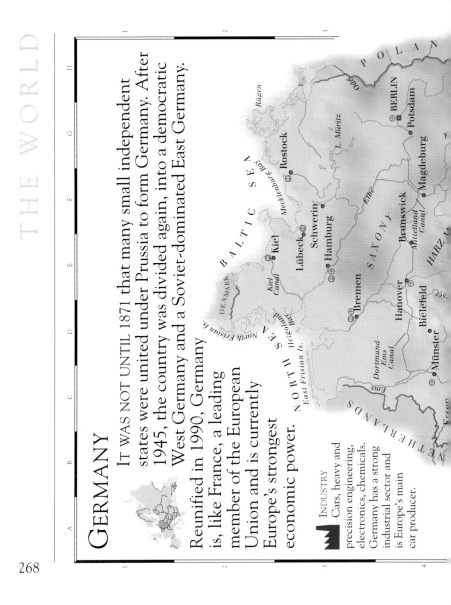

POLAND

Rügen

BALTIC SEA

Oder

BERLIN

Potsdam

L. Müritz

Rostock

Mecklenburg Bay

Magdeburg

Schwerin

Elbe

Brunswick

Kiel

Lübeck

Hamburg

DENMARK

Kiel Canal

Mittelland Canal

SAXONY

HARZ M

Bremen

Hanover

Bielefeld

North Frisian Is.

NORTH SEA

East Frisian Is.

Helgoland

Weser

Dortmund-Ems Canal

Ems

Münster

NETHERLANDS

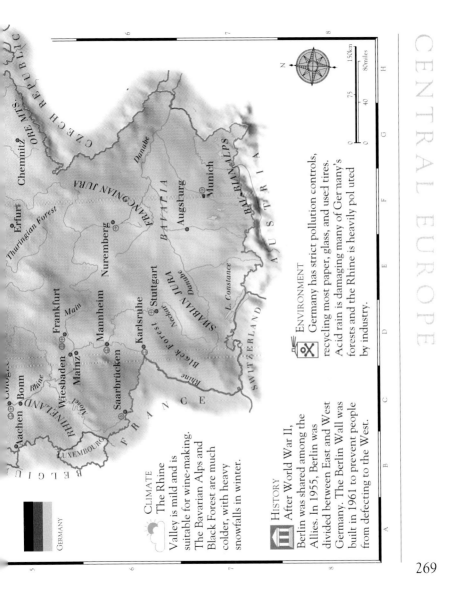

GERMANY

CLIMATE
The Rhine Valley is mild and is suitable for wine-making. The Bavarian Alps and Black Forest are much colder, with heavy snowfalls in winter.

HISTORY
After World War II, Berlin was shared among the Allies. In 1955, Berlin was divided between East and West Germany. The Berlin Wall was built in 1961 to prevent people from defecting to the West.

ENVIRONMENT
Germany has strict pollution controls, recycling most paper, glass, and used tires. Acid rain is damaging many of Germany's forests and the Rhine is heavily polluted by industry.

SWITZERLAND AND AUSTRIA

ONCE THE CENTER OF the vast Hapsburg
Empire, the Republic of Austria was
created after World War I. Switzerland
has been a neutral country since 1815,
and many international organizations such as the
Red Cross have their headquarters there.
Liechtenstein is closely allied to
Switzerland, which handles
its foreign relations.

LIECHTENSTE

SWITZERLAND

G E R M A N Y

L. Constance

Basle   Rhine   Winterthur   Bregenz

St. Gallen

Zurich   L. Zurich

LIECHTENSTE
VADUZ

L. Biel   Aare   L. Lucerne

BERN

L. Neuchâtel   L. Thun   S W I T Z E R L A N D   ALPS

A L P S   RHAETIAN ALPS

Lausanne

L. Geneva   BERNESE ALPS

Geneva   Rhône   L. Maggiore
PENNINE ALPS   L. Lugano

N

COMMUNICATIONS
The St. Gotthard road tunnel runs under
the Swiss Alps. At over 10 miles (16 km) in
length, it is the world's longest road tunnel.

0   50   100km
0   25   50miles

CLIMATE

Altitude determines climate, th alpine areas experiencing lder temperatures and ore rainfall. South of e Alps is nsiderably rmer and nnier.

*Map labels:*

CZECH REPUBLIC

SLOVAKIA

VIENNA

Linz · St. Pölten · *Danube* · L. Neusiedler

A U S T R I A · Eisenstadt

L. Atter · L. Traun · Salzburg

ERMANY · *Enns* · NIEDERE TAUERN · HUNGARY

Inn · HOHE TAUERN · Graz

nsbruck · ZILLERTAL ALPS

Klagenfurt · *Drau* · S L O V E N I A

AUSTRIA

THE ARTS

Many famous musicians, such Beethoven, Mozart, Schubert, and ahms, lived and worked in Vienna.

NATURAL FEATURES

The Alps form part of an almost ntinuous mountain-belt, stretching om the Pyrenees in France to the imalayas in Asia. They are also e source of Europe's largest rivers – e Rhine, Rhône, and Danube.

INDUSTRY

Pharmaceuticals, financial services, tourism, chemicals, electrical engineering. Liechtenstein is the center of world dental manufacture. False teeth and dental materials are exported to over 100 countries.

Central Europe facts

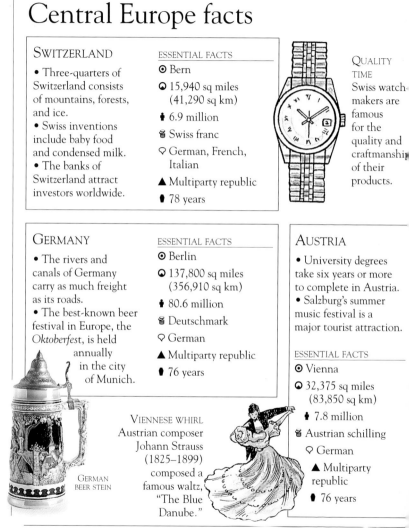

SWITZERLAND

- Three-quarters of Switzerland consists of mountains, forests, and ice.
- Swiss inventions include baby food and condensed milk.
- The banks of Switzerland attract investors worldwide.

ESSENTIAL FACTS

- ⊙ Bern
- ⊘ 15,940 sq miles (41,290 sq km)
- ♦ 6.9 million
- ⵚ Swiss franc
- ♡ German, French, Italian
- ▲ Multiparty republic
- ♦ 78 years

QUALITY TIME
Swiss watchmakers are famous for the quality and craftmanship of their products.

GERMANY

- The rivers and canals of Germany carry as much freight as its roads.
- The best-known beer festival in Europe, the *Oktoberfest*, is held annually in the city of Munich.

ESSENTIAL FACTS

- ⊙ Berlin
- ⊘ 137,800 sq miles (356,910 sq km)
- ♦ 80.6 million
- ⵚ Deutschmark
- ♡ German
- ▲ Multiparty republic
- ♦ 76 years

GERMAN BEER STEIN

AUSTRIA

- University degrees take six years or more to complete in Austria.
- Salzburg's summer music festival is a major tourist attraction.

ESSENTIAL FACTS

- ⊙ Vienna
- ⊘ 32,375 sq miles (83,850 sq km)
- ♦ 7.8 million
- ⵚ Austrian schilling
- ♡ German
- ▲ Multiparty republic
- ♦ 76 years

VIENNESE WHIRL
Austrian composer Johann Strauss (1825–1899) composed a famous waltz, "The Blue Danube."

CZECH REPUBLIC

- The Czech homeland was originally called Bohemia.
- Prague's gilded church roofs gave the city the name *zlata Praha*, or "golden Prague."
- The Czech Republic is the most polluted country in Europe.

ESSENTIAL FACTS

- ☉ Prague
- ◔ 30,260 sq miles (78,370 sq km)
- ⚥ 10.4 million
- 💶 Czech koruna
- ♡ Czech
- ▲ Multiparty republic
- �‖ 71 years

SLOVAKIA

- Separation from the Czech Republic in 1993 resulted in full independence for Slovakia for the first time in over 1,000 years.

ESSENTIAL FACTS

- ☉ Bratislava
- ◔ 19,100 sq miles (49,500 sq km)
- ⚥ 5.3 million
- 💶 Slovak koruna
- ♡ Slovak

LIECHTENSTEIN

- ☉ Vaduz
- ⚥ 29,000
- ♡ German, Alemannish

POLAND

- The largest remaining herds of European bison are found in the eastern forests of Poland.
- Poland has seven international borders.
- Polish women hold prominent policy-making posts in politics and business.

ESSENTIAL FACTS

- ☉ Warsaw
- ◔ 120,720 sq miles (312,680 sq km)
- ⚥ 38.5 million
- 💶 Zloty
- ♡ Polish
- ▲ Multiparty republic
- �‖ 72 years

PRAGUE, CZECH REPUBLIC
Dating from medieval times, the beautiful capital city of Prague is now a popular tourist destination. The city lies on both banks of the Vltava River and is connected by a series of bridges. It is often called "city of a hundred spires" because it has so many churches

273

SOUTH CENTRAL EUROPE

FOR CENTURIES the countries of this region have had strong ties with Europe. In the early 1990s Slovenia, Croatia, and Bosnia and Herzegovina declared their independence from Yugoslavia, to which they had been annexed after World War 1. This area boasts the snow-capped Alps, the sunny Adriatic Sea in the south, as well as Hungary's fertile plain.

SLOVENIA

CROATIA

CLIMATE
The climate in the region is just as varied as its geography. The interior has a continental climate, with warm summers and bitterly cold winters. Coastal areas in Croatia benefit from Mediterranean temperatures suitable for growing plums, apricots, and grapes.

AUSTRIA

ITALY

Maribor

Cakov

LJUBLJANA

Sava

SLOVENIA

ZAGREB

C R

Kupa

Prijed

C. Kamenjak

Cres

Una

Pag

Zadar

D

A

L

Split

ADRIATIC

C.Ploàa

Braà

Hvà

SEA

N

0   75   150km
0   50   100miles

E F G H

1

2

SLOVAKIA

UKRAINE

Miskolc

Tisza

Debrecen

Danube

BUDAPEST

HUNGARY

3

HUNGARIAN PLAIN

Balaton

Danube

Sersiz

Danube

Berettyö

Körüe

Tisza

ROMANIA

HUNGARY

4

Kapos

Pécs

TIA

Osijek

Danube

5

Bosna

ja Luka

Tuzla

Zenica

YUGOSLAVIA

BOSNIA &

ERZEGOVINA

6

SARAJEVO

Mostar

7

Dubrovnik

BOSNIA–HERZEGOVINA

8

INDUSTRY
Mercury ore, timber, tourism, paprika. Hungary's workforce is skilled in science and engineering. Elsewhere, industry has been affected by the conflict in Yugoslavia, but tourists are now returning to the lakes and coasts of Croatia.

PEOPLE
Historically, this region has been at the crossroads of many different empires, each influencing the language, religion, and customs of the people. Although this has created problems, the Slovenes, Croatians, and Muslims still maintain their own traditions.

SOUTHEAST EUROPE

THIS REGION IS often referred to as the Balkans, from the Turkish word for "mountain." It is made up of countries that have a long history of invasion and occupation. From its source in the Alps, the mighty Danube River flows eastward through Romania and Bulgaria, before pouring into the Black Sea.

YUGOSLAVIA

ROMANIA

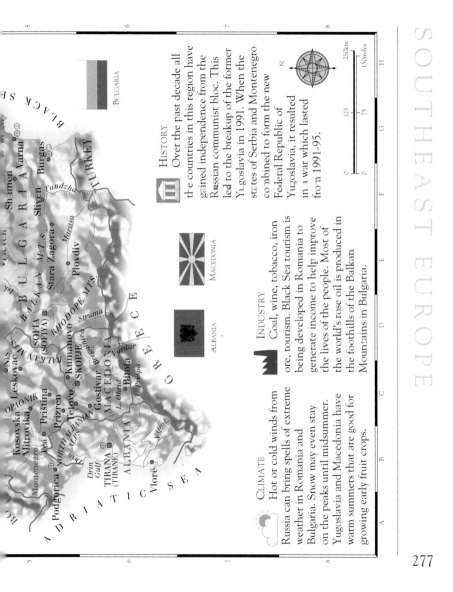

BLACK SEA

BULGARIA

MACEDONIA

ALBANIA

HISTORY

Over the past decade all the countries in this region have gained independence from the Russian communist bloc. This led to the breakup of the former Yugoslavia in 1991. When the states of Serbia and Montenegro combined to form the new Federal Republic of Yugoslavia, it resulted in a war which lasted from 1991-95.

INDUSTRY

Coal, wine, tobacco, iron ore, tourism. Black Sea tourism is being developed in Romania to generate income to help improve the lives of the people. Most of the world's rose oil is produced in the foothills of the Balkan Mountains in Bulgaria.

CLIMATE

Hot or cold winds from Russia can bring spells of extreme weather in Romania and Bulgaria. Snow may even stay on the peaks until midsummer. Yugoslavia and Macedonia have warm summers that are good for growing early fruit crops.

N

0   125   250km
0   75   150miles

BULGARIA

BALKAN MTS.

RHODOPE MTS.

Shumen
Varna
Burgas
Sliven
Stara Zagora
Plovdiv
Tundzha
Maritsa
Struma

TURKEY

GREECE

Kumanovo
SKOPJE
Tetovo
Gostivar
MACEDONIA
Bitola
L. Ohrid
L. Prespa
Vardar
Bregalnica

SOFIA (SOFIYA)

BALKAN MTS.

Leskovac
Kosovska
Mitrovica
Peć
Priština
Prizren
OPAONIK
NORTH ALBANIAN ALPS
ALBANIA
TIRANA (TIRANË)
Drin
Vlorë
Vjosa

Montenegro
Podgorica
Drin
Gulf

ADRIATIC SEA

GREECE

SURROUNDED BY THE Aegean, Ionian, and Cretan seas, no part of Greece is more than 85 miles (137 km) from the coast. Its territory includes the mainland on the Balkan peninsula, and over 1,400 islands. The country is mountainous and less than one-third of the land is cultivated. Greece gained its independence in 1830 after a long and fierce war, ending 400 years of Turkish rule.

CLIMATE
Northwestern Greece is alpine, while parts of Crete are almost subtropical. The islands and the large central plain of the mainland have a Mediterranean climate, with high summer temperatures and mild winters.

GREECE

ENVIRONMENT
Athens suffers from smog, known as *nefos*, which damages its ancient monuments. The Parthenon, on the Acropolis, has suffered more erosion in the previous two decades than in the previous two thousand years.

HISTORY
Regarded as the founders of democracy, the ancient Greeks were advanced for their time. They were the first to study medicine, geometry, and physics (on a scientific basis), and Greece was home to great thinkers such as Plato, Aristotle, and Socrates.

Map labels: MAC, L. Presp, ALBANIA, Aliakmon, Corfu, Corfu, PINDUS MTS., Levkas, IONIAN, L. Trikhonis, Kefallinia, Gulf of Patras, Pat, P, SEA, Zakinthos

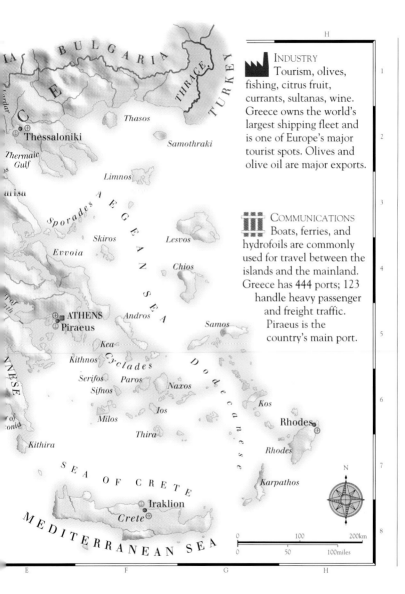

BULGARIA

THRACE

TURKEY

Thasos

Thessaloniki

Samothraki

Thermaic
Gulf

Larisa

Limnos

Sporades

AEGEAN SEA

Skiros

Lesvos

Evvoia

Chios

ATHENS
Piraeus

Andros

Samos

Kea

Kithnos

Cyclades

Dodecanese

Serifos

Paros

Sifnos

Naxos

Kos

Milos

Ios

Rhodes

Kithira

Thira

Rhodes

SEA OF CRETE

Karpathos

N

Iraklion

Crete

MEDITERRANEAN SEA

INDUSTRY
Tourism, olives, fishing, citrus fruit, currants, sultanas, wine. Greece owns the world's largest shipping fleet and is one of Europe's major tourist spots. Olives and olive oil are major exports.

COMMUNICATIONS
Boats, ferries, and hydrofoils are commonly used for travel between the islands and the mainland. Greece has 444 ports; 123 handle heavy passenger and freight traffic. Piraeus is the country's main port.

0   100   200km

0   50   100miles

Southern Europe facts

CROATIA

- One-third of Croatia is held by the Serbs.
- The Adriatic coastline of Croatia was a popular tourist destination before the recent civil war.

DALMATIANS

The Dalmatian dog is named after its first known home, the Dalmatian coastal region of Croatia.

ESSENTIAL FACTS
- ⊙ Zagreb
- ◔ 21,830 sq miles (56,540 sq km)
- ♦ 4.9 million
- ≋ Kuna
- ♡ Croatian

BOSNIA AND HERZEGOVINA

- The Bosnian civil war made over two million people homeless by the year 1995.

ESSENTIAL FACTS
- ⊙ Sarajevo
- ◔ 19,741 sq miles (51,130 sq km)
- ♦ 4.5 million
- ≋ Bosnian dinar
- ♡ Serbo-Croat

ALBANIA

- The Albanian's name for their nation is *Shqipërisë*, which means "land of the eagle."

ESSENTIAL FACTS
- ⊙ Tirana
- ◔ 11,100 sq miles (28,750 sq km)
- ♦ 3.3 million
- ≋ New lek
- ♡ Albanian

YUGOSLAVIA

- Settlers have lived on the site of present-day Belgrade for 7,000 years.

ESSENTIAL FACTS
- ⊙ Belgrade
- ◔ 9,929 sq miles (25,715 sq km)
- ♦ 10.6 million
- ≋ New Yugoslav dinar
- ♦ Serbian

SLOVENIA

- The average wage in Slovenia is the highest among the former Yugoslav republics.

ESSENTIAL FACTS
- ⊙ Ljubljana
- ◔ 7,820 sq miles (20,250 sq km)
- ♦ 2 million
- ≋ Tolar
- ♡ Slovene

SLOVENIA IS A MAJOR PRODUCER OF MERCURY, WHICH IS USED IN THERMOMETERS

ROMANIA

• The tuberculosis rate in Romania is the highest in Europe.
• The Romanian Danube delta is to be used as a site for a biosphere reserve.

ESSENTIAL FACTS
☉ Bucharest
◔ 91,700 sq miles (237,500 sq km)
⚲ 23.4 million
💷 Leu
♡ Romanian

GREECE

• People throughout the Greek Islands use the flat roofs of their houses to dry fruit in summer and collect rain in winter.

ESSENTIAL FACTS
☉ Athens
◔ 50,961 sq miles (131,990 sq km)
⚲ 10.2 million
💷 Drachma
♡ Greek
▲ Multiparty republic
♦ 77 years

GREEK MUSIC
The bouzouki is a traditional Greek stringed instrument.

MACEDONIA

• Lake Ohrid in Macedonia is the deepest lake in Europe.

MACEDONIA FACTS
☉ Skopje
◔ 9,929 sq miles (25,715 sq km)
⚲ 1.9 million
💷 Denar
♡ Macedonian

HUNGARY

• The Hungarian language has features not found in any other western language.
• The city of Budapest was originally Buda and Pest, two towns located on either side of the Danube River.

BULGARIA

• In Bulgaria there is a national museum devoted entirely to humor and satire.
• Bulgarians nod for "no" and shake their heads for "yes."
• People in Sofia travel by trolleybuses that get their power from overhead electric cables.

ESSENTIAL FACTS
☉ Sofia
◔ 42,822 sq miles (110,910 sq km)
⚲ 8.9 million
💷 Lev
♡ Bulgarian
▲ Multiparty republic
♦ 72 years

ESSENTIAL FACTS
☉ Budapest
◔ 35,919 sq miles (93,030 sq km)
⚲ 10.5 million
💷 Forint
♡ Hungarian
▲ Multiparty republic
♦ 70 years

THE BALTIC STATES AND BELARUS

LITHUANIA, ESTONIA, AND LATVIA – the three Baltic States – were the first republics to declare their independence from the Soviet Union in 1990-91. Economic reform has been slow and problems still remain. Many areas of Belarus are still affected by the 1986 Chernobyl nuclear disaster. The cleanup will take decades, and is a major drain on the nation's finances.

PEOPLE

Russians, Belorussians, and Ukrainians resettled in Latvia when it was part of the USSR. Today Latvians make up only about half of the whole population, and they are a minority in the capital.

ESTONIA

LATVIA

BELARUS

LITHUANIA

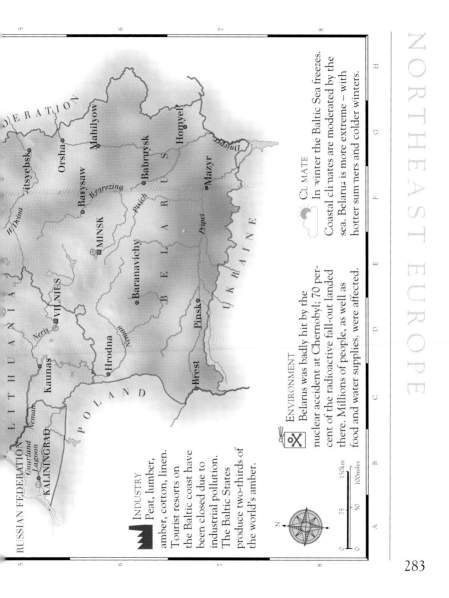

RUSSIAN FEDERATION

ODERATION

Vitsyebsk

Orsha

Mahilyow

Barysaw

MINSK

Berezina

Babruysk

Homyel

Dvina

Ptsich

Mazyr

Dnieper

LITHUANIA

VILNIUS

Neris

Nemah

Courtland Lagoon

KALININGRAD

Kaunas

B E L A R U S

Baranavichy

Hrodna

Neman

Pinsk

Tuman

Pripet

Pripet

Brest

U K R A I N E

P O L A N D

INDUSTRY
Peat, lumber, amber, cotton, linen. Tourist resorts on the Baltic coast have been closed due to industrial pollution. The Baltic States produce two-thirds of the world's amber.

ENVIRONMENT
Belarus was badly hit by the nuclear accident at Chernobyl; 70 per-cent of the radioactive fall-out landed there. Millions of people, as well as food and water supplies, were affected.

CLIMATE
In winter the Baltic Sea freezes. Coastal climates are moderated by the sea. Belarus is more extreme – with hotter summers and colder winters.

N

0   75   150km
0   50   100miles

EUROPEAN RUSSIA

SPANNING THE TWO continents of Europe and Asia, the Russian Federation is the world's largest country. In 1917 the world's first communist government took power, and in 1923 Russia became the USSR, which included many territories that were once part of the Russian Empire. Economic reforms in the 1980s led to changes that resulted in the fall of communism in 1991.

INDUSTRY
Oil, gas, gold, diamonds, hydrocarbons, precious metals. Russia has large reserves of iron, coal, and nickel. Huge factories, which have grown without environmental controls, are causing pollution problems.

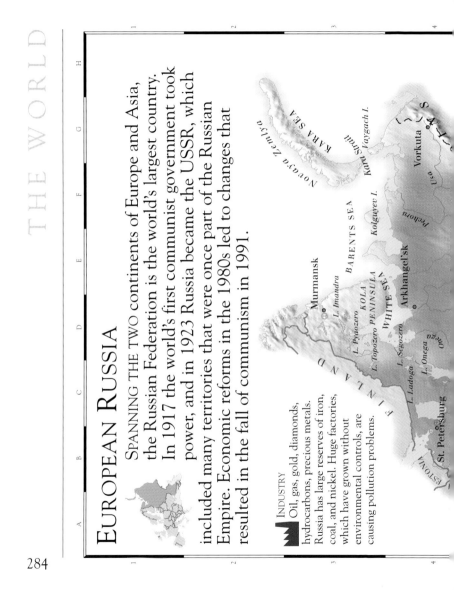

KARA SEA

Novaya Zemlya

Kara Strait

Kara Vaygach I.

BARENTS SEA

Vorkuta

Usa

Pechora

Kolguyev I.

Murmansk

L. Imandra

KOLA

L. Pyaozero PENINSULA

L. Topozero

WHITE SEA

Arkhangel'sk

L. Segozero

L. Onega

Onega

FINLAND

L. Ladoga

St. Petersburg

ESTONIA

Some believe that Russia took its name from a Viking tribe called *Varangian Russes*. The first Russian state was established at Kiev in A.D. 800.

CLIMATE
Russia has a cold continental climate, open to influence by the Arctic and Atlantic Oceans. Snow covers more than half the country for six months of the year.

COMMUNICATIONS
The Trans–Siberian Railroad, started in 1881 and completed in 1916, is the longest continuous rail line in the world. The 5,785-mile-(9,310-km) journey from Moscow to Vladivostok takes seven days.

THE ARTS
The Hermitage Musuem in St. Petersburg contains 2.5 million objects in 1,000 rooms. Its buildings include the Winter Palace, which was stormed in the 1917 Revolution by Lenin's Bolshevik forces.

EUROPEAN RUSSIA

R U S S I A N   F E D E R A T I O N

URAL

MONGOLIA

Kama
Kama
Res.
Perm'
Izhevsk
Naberezhnyye
Chelny
Ufa
Orenburg'

Vyatka
Nizhniy Novgorod
Kazan'
Simbirsk
Samara
Tol'yatti

Volga

K A Z A K H S T A N

MOSCOW
Tula
Ryazan'
Penza
Saratov
Voronezh

Don

Rostov-na-
Donu
Volgograd

Volga
Tsimlyansk
Res.

CASPIAN SEA

Astrakhan
Kuma

Krasnodar
Kuban

CAUCASUS MTS.
GEORGIA
AZERBAIJAN

Sea of Azov

BLACK SEA

UKRAINE

BELARUS

N

600km
300miles
300
150
0   0

285

UKRAINE AND THE CAUCASUS

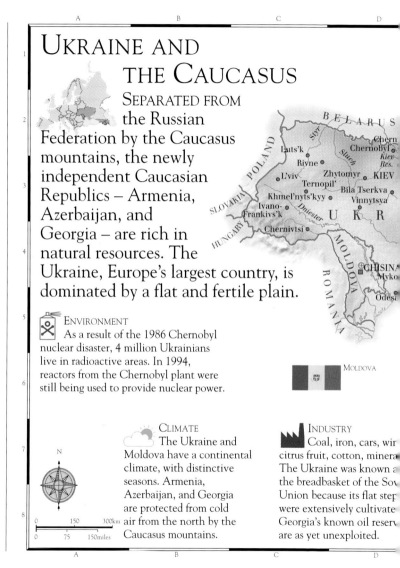

SEPARATED FROM the Russian Federation by the Caucasus mountains, the newly independent Caucasian Republics – Armenia, Azerbaijan, and Georgia – are rich in natural resources. The Ukraine, Europe's largest country, is dominated by a flat and fertile plain.

ENVIRONMENT

As a result of the 1986 Chernobyl nuclear disaster, 4 million Ukrainians live in radioactive areas. In 1994, reactors from the Chernobyl plant were still being used to provide nuclear power.

MOLDOVA

CLIMATE

The Ukraine and Moldova have a continental climate, with distinctive seasons. Armenia, Azerbaijan, and Georgia are protected from cold air from the north by the Caucasus mountains.

N

| 0 | 150 | 300km |
| 0 | 75 | 150miles |

INDUSTRY

Coal, iron, cars, wir citrus fruit, cotton, minera The Ukraine was known a the breadbasket of the Sov Union because its flat step were extensively cultivate Georgia's known oil reserv are as yet unexploited.

E   F   G   H

UKRAINE

PEOPLE
There are about 40 languages and 150 dialects spoken in the Caucasian republics. No relationship has yet been established between languages spoken within the Caucasus and those outside it.

NATURAL FEATURES
The Caucasus mountains extend for 750 miles (1,200 km). They form a natural boundary between Europe and Asia, and separate temperate climate zones from warmer areas.

FLORA AND FAUNA
The Russian sturgeon grows up to 23 ft (7m) long. Its eggs, called caviar, are a delicacy, but numbers of sturgeon are falling owing to polluted water.

GEORGIA

AZERBAIJAN

RUSSIAN FEDERATION

my.

Kharkiv
enchuk
FEDERATION

Kramators'k
ropetrovs'k   DONBASS
Horlivka   Luhans'k
Rih   Donets'k   Makiyivka
eper   Zaporizhzhya
Kakhovka Res.
Mariupol
n

SEA OF AZOV

Kerch
Strait

Simferopol'
astopol'

BLACK SEA

RUSSIAN FEDERATION

CAUCASUS

GEORGIA MTS.

K'ut'aisi   TBILISI   Mingäçevir
Res. AZERBAIJAN
Gyumri   Vanadzor   BAKU
TURKEY   ARMENIA   Gäncä   Kura
YEREVAN
AZERBAIJAN
IRAN

CASPIAN SEA

HISTORY
With its strategic tion, the Crimean insula has had a bled history. It was of Greece until 100 , Turkey from 1475, Russia from 1783, was the scene of the nean War in 1853-56.

ARMENIA

E   F   G   H

■

Northeast Europe facts

EUROPEAN RUSSIA

(See **Russian Federation**
ESSENTIAL FACTS, p.329)

• Many Russians now have satellite dishes and tune in to Western TV channels for news and entertainment.

• Hospital food is normally provided by patients' families due to lack of funds.

ST. BASIL'S CATHEDRAL
This 16th century Russian building, with its nine great domes, is situated within Moscow's Kremlin fortress.

LATVIA

• The national flag is said to represent a sheet stained with the blood of a 13th-century Latvian hero.

• Latvia is the most built-up Baltic State.

ESSENTIAL FACTS

⊙ Riga

◑ 24,938 sq miles (64,589 sq km)

🀆 2.7 million

🖱 Lats

♀ Latvian

ESTONIA

• The standard of living in Estonia is higher than in any former Soviet republic.

ESSENTIAL FACTS

⊙ Tallinn

◑ 17,423 sq miles (45,125 sq km)

🀆 1.6 million

🖱 Kroon

♀ Estonian

LITHUANIA

• Most of the Baltic States' amber is found on Lithuania's Amber Coast.

ESSENTIAL FACTS

⊙ Vilnius

◑ 25,174 sq miles (65,200 sq km)

🀆 3.8 million

🖱 Litas

♀ Lithuanian

BELORUS

• Cancer cases have increased dramatically since the Chernobyl nuclear disaster in 1986.

ESSENTIAL FACTS

⊙ Minsk

◑ 80,154 sq miles (207,600 sq km)

🀆 10.3 million

🖱 Belorussian rouble

♀ Belorussian

GEORGIA

- Most Georgians live in poverty.
- In Greek mythology, the legendary Golden Fleece was found in western Georgia.

ESSENTIAL FACTS

- ⊙ Tbilisi
- ◓ 26,911 sq miles (69,700 sq km)
- ⬧ 5.5 million
- 🗢 Coupon
- ♀ Georgian

ARMENIA

- In the fourth century, Armenia became the first country in the world to adopt Christianity as its state religion.

ESSENTIAL FACTS

- ⊙ Yerevan
- ◓ 11,505 sq miles (29,000 sq km)
- ⬧ 3.6 million
- 🗢 Armenian dram
- ♀ Armenian

AZERBAIJAN

- The nation of Azerbaijan became the first of the former Soviet republics to declare independence from Moscow in 1991.

ESSENTIAL FACTS

- ⊙ Baku
- ◓ 33,436 sq miles (86,600 sq km)
- ⬧ 7.3 million
- 🗢 Manat
- ♀ Azerbaijani

UKRAINE

- Western Ukrainians oppose their eastern counterparts' proposed closer ties with Russia.
- The name Ukraine means "frontier."

ESSENTIAL FACTS

- ⊙ Kiev
- ◓ 233,090 sq miles (603,700 sq km)
- ⬧ 52.2 million
- 🗢 Karbovanets (coupons)
- ♀ Ukrainian
- ▲ Multiparty republic
- ⬧ 70 years

Sour cream

orscht

Pierogi (dumplings)

BORSCHT

Russia's famous beet soup, *borscht*, comes from the Ukraine.

MOLDOVA

- The underground wine vaults of Moldova contain entire "streets" of bottles built into rock quarries.
- Moldova was part of Romania until Soviet incorporation in 1940.

ESSENTIAL FACTS

- ⊙ Kishinev
- ◓ 13,000 sq miles (33,700 sq km)
- ⬧ 4.4 million
- 🗢 Moldovan leu
- ♀ Romanian

289

AFRICA

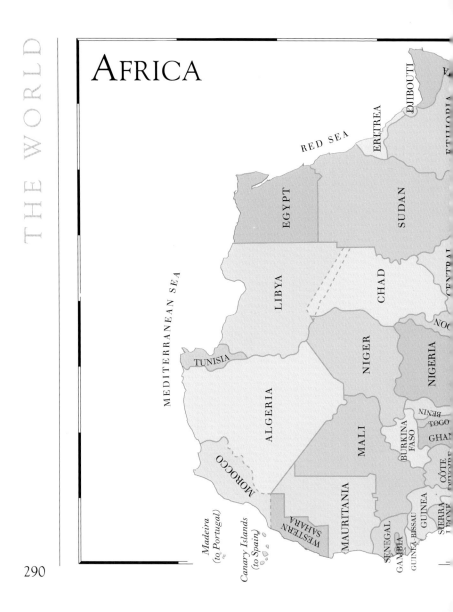

MEDITERRANEAN SEA

RED SEA

TUNISIA

EGYPT

ERITREA

DJIBOUTI

ETHIOPIA

ALGERIA

LIBYA

SUDAN

CHAD

NIGER

CENTRAL

MOROCCO

MALI

NIGERIA

NOG

BURKINA FASO

BENIN

TOGO

GHAN

CÔTE

WESTERN SAHARA

MAURITANIA

SENEGAL

GAMBIA

GUINEA-BISSAU

GUINEA

SIERRA LEONE

Madeira (to Portugal)

Canary Islands (to Spain)

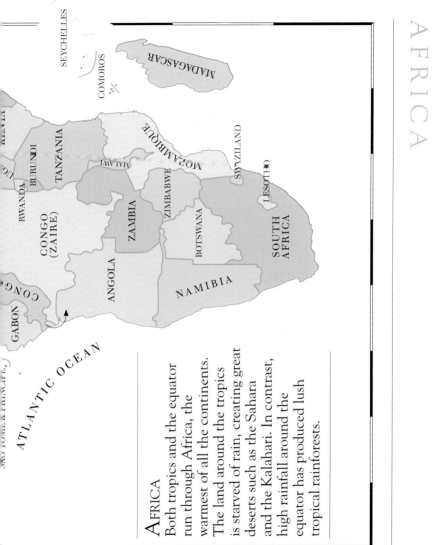

AFRICA

Both tropics and the equator run through Africa, the warmest of all the continents. The land around the tropics is starved of rain, creating great deserts such as the Sahara and the Kalahari. In contrast, high rainfall around the equator has produced lush tropical rainforests.

WEST AFRICA

BY 1914, MANY European countries, such as France, Britain, and Portugal, had divided up almost all of Africa between them. Despite independence, foreign companies still own many of the coffee and cocoa plantations in the region.

GAMBIA

INDUSTRY
Bauxite, oil, gypsum, cocoa, phosphates, peanuts, fishing. This region produces nearly half of the world's supply of cocoa beans. The world's largest deposits of gypsum are found in Mauritania.

CLIMATE
Coastal areas have a tropical climate, with high temperatures and one or two rainy seasons. The hot and dry Sahel is marked by the dusty *harmattan* wind.

GUINEA

GUINEA-BISSAU

SIERRA LEONE

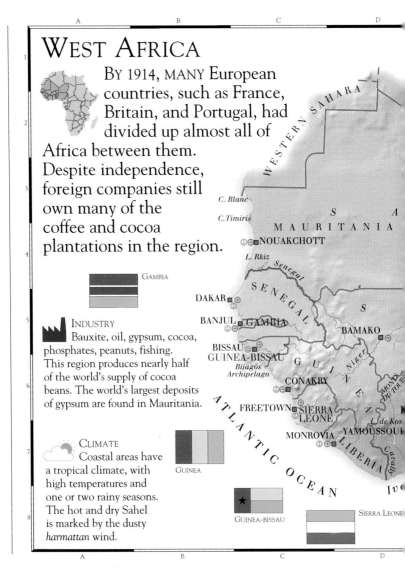

SAHARA

WESTERN

C. Blanc
C. Timiris
MAURITANIA
S A
⊕⊕■NOUAKCHOTT
L. Rkiz
Senegal
S E N E G A L
DAKAR■⊕
BANJUL■GAMBIA
BISSAU⊕■
GUINEA-BISSAU
Bijagós
Archipelago
CONAKRY
⊕⊕■
FREETOWN■SIERRA
LEONE
MONROVIA
⊕⊕■
S
BAMAKO
■⊕
Niger
G U I N E
MONTS
DU TOU
L. de Kos
YAMOUSSOU
LIBERIA
ATLANTIC OCEAN
1v

NEGAL

MAURITANIA

MALI

BURKINA FASO

NIGER

NIGERIA

A L G E R I A

L I B Y A

PLATEAU DE MANGUENI

CH

T A L A K

T E N E R E

A I R

A L I

N I G E R

Timbuktu

aguibine

L. Niangay

Niger

E L

BURKINA FASO

NIAMEY

OUAGADOUGOU

o-Dioulasso

Black Volta

White Volta

BENIN

Sokoto

L. Chad

Kano

N I G E R I A

C A M E R O O N

JOS PLATEAU

Ouémé

Niger

Benue

BENIN

TOGO

GHANA

L. Volta

LOME

Abeokuta

Ilorin

Ogbomosho

Oshogbo

Ibadan

ABUJA

Kumasi

ACCRA

Lagos

PORTO-NOVO

Onitsha

TOGO

ljan

Port Harcourt

st

Bight of Benin

Niger Delta

LIBERIA

COTE D'IVOIRE

GHANA

N

0   250   500km

0   150   300miles

NORTHWEST AFRICA

SPANNING THE continent of Africa from the Atlantic to the Red Sea, the Sahara is the world's largest desert, covering 3.5 million sq miles (9 million sq km). Drought and the overuse of land for farming are causing the Sahara to spread into the Sahel (semiarid grasslands). Italy, the UK, Spain, and France have had colonies in this region.

Strait of Gibraltar

Ceuta *(to Spain)*   Meli
Tangier   *(to Spa*

RABAT
Casablanca   Fe

M O R O C C
Marrakesh

Agadir   M
A T L A S   Béc

EL AAIUN

Dakhla

M A U R I T A N I A

M

Morocco occupied the whole of Western Sahara in 1979.

INDUSTRY

Oil, gas, phosphates, tourism, olives, dates, fruit. Morocco and Tunisia attract millions of tourists every year and are also leading phosphate producers. Algeria and Libya have significant oil reserves.

MOROCCO

CLIMATE

Coastal areas have a temperate climate with hot, dry summers and wet winters. Mountain areas are cooler. Most areas are affected by the many different kinds of Sahara wind, such as the *sirocco*, the *chergui*, and the *chili*.

NATURAL FEATURES

The Atlas Mountains exten over 1,500 miles (2,410 km) from the Canary Islands in the Atlantic to Tunisia. Like the Alps, the Atl Mountains were formed when the continental plates of Europe and Africa pushed together.

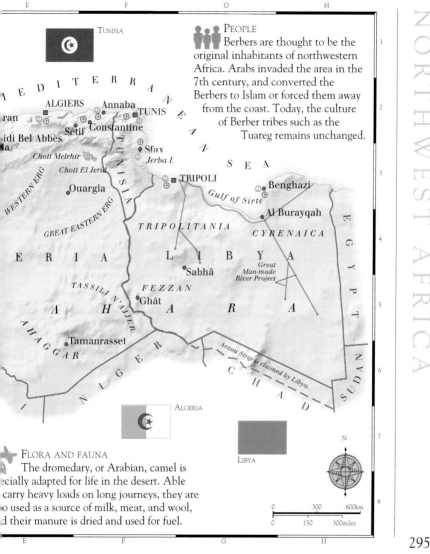

TUNISIA

PEOPLE

Berbers are thought to be the original inhabitants of northwestern Africa. Arabs invaded the area in the 7th century, and converted the Berbers to Islam or forced them away from the coast. Today, the culture of Berber tribes such as the Tuareg remains unchanged.

MEDITERRANEAN

ALGIERS   Annaba
ran   TUNIS
idi Bel Abbès   Sétif   Constantine
Ia
Chott Melrhir   Sfax
Chott El Jerid   Jerba I.

S E A

Ouargla   TRIPOLI   Benghazi
                Gulf of Sirte
                    Al Burayqah

WESTERN ERG

GREAT EASTERN ERG   TRIPOLITANIA   CYRENAICA

E   R   I   A   L   I   B   Y   A

Sabhā   Great
Man-made
River Project

TASSILI N'AJJER   FEZZAN

Ghāt   A   R   A

A   H

AHAGGAR   Tamanrasset

N   I   G   E   R

Aozou Strip is claimed by Libya.

C   H   A   D   SUDAN

EGYPT

ALGERIA

LIBYA

N

FLORA AND FAUNA

The dromedary, or Arabian, camel is
ecially adapted for life in the desert. Able
carry heavy loads on long journeys, they are
o used as a source of milk, meat, and wool,
d their manure is dried and used for fuel.

0   300   600km
0   150   300miles

West Africa facts

IVORY COAST

- Yamoussoukro's giant Christian basilica is the second largest church in the world.
- The Ivory Coast is home to 66 different West African tribes.
- Most people live on the sandy coastal strip.

ESSENTIAL FACTS

- ⊙ Yamoussoukro
- ◷ 124,503 sq miles (322,463 sq km)
- ⚲ 13.4 million
- ⛁ CFA franc
- ♥ French, Akran

Peanut p ripe unde grou

GROUNDNUT PLANT
Peanuts, or groundnuts, are a major crop in West Africa.

LIBERIA

- The country of Liberia was founded in 1847 as a home for freed slaves from the US.
- Human rights have have frequently been abused in Liberia, with citizens being massacred or forced to flee to neighboring states.

ESSENTIAL FACTS

- ⊙ Monrovia
- ◷ 43,000 sq miles (111,370 sq km)
- ⚲ 2.8 million
- ⛁ Liberian dollar
- ♥ English

Animal skin

Leather thongs

Squeezing the "waist" changes the drum's sound

WEST AFRICAN KALUNGU, OR "TALKING DRUM"

WESTERN SAHARA

- ⊙ No capital
- ⚲ 200,000
- ♥ Varied Arab dialects

SENEGAL

- The name Senegal comes from the Islamic Zenegar Berbers, who invaded the region in the 1300s.
- Senegal produced the first satirical journal in Africa with the founding of the publication *Le Politicien* in 1978.

ESSENTIAL FACTS

- ⊙ Dakar
- ◷ 75,950 sq miles (196,720 sq km)
- ⚲ 7.9 million
- ⛁ CFA franc
- ♥ French

GHANA

• Mining has polluted the environment and destroyed areas of land.
• Ghana was the first British colony in Africa to gain independence.

ESSENTIAL FACTS

⊙ Accra
◔ 92,100 sq miles (238,540 sq km)
✚ 16.4 million
💲 Cedi
♡ English

SIERRA LEONE

• The citizens of Freetown are largely descended from slaves freed from Britain and the US.
• Sierra Leone is one of the world's poorest nations.

ESSENTIAL FACTS

⊙ Freetown
◔ 27,699 sq miles (71,740 sq km)
✚ 4.5 million
💲 Leone
♡ English

BENIN

• Positions of power in Benin's retail trade are often held by women.

ESSENTIAL FACTS

⊙ Porto-Novo
◔ 43,480 sq miles (112,620 sq km)
✚ 5.1 million
💲 CFA franc
♡ French

MAURITANIA

• Slavery, although officially illegal, still persists in Mauritania.

ESSENTIAL FACTS

⊙ Nouakchott
◔ 395,953 sq miles (1,025,520 sq km)
✚ 2.2 million
💲 Ouguiya
♡ French

COCOA
West Africa grows half the world's cocoa.

BURKINA

• Droughts and poor soils in Burkina force many men to migrate seasonally to Ghana and the Ivory Coast for work.

ESSENTIAL FACTS

⊙ Ouagadougou
◔ 105,870 sq miles (274,200 sq km)
✚ 9.8 million
💲 CFA franc
♡ French

MALI

• The Malian town of Timbuktu was the center of the huge Malinke empire in the 14th century.
• Malians strongly disapprove of flaunted wealth.

ESSENTIAL FACTS

⊙ Bamako
◔ 478,837 sq miles (1,240,190 sq km)
✚ 10.1 million
💲 CFA franc
♡ French

West Africa facts

NIGER

• The threat of drought and desertification is Niger's primary concern.

ESSENTIAL FACTS
- ⊙ Niamey
- ◔ 489,188 sq miles (1,267,000 sq km)
- ♦ 8.5 million
- ⌑ CFA franc
- ♡ French

CAPE VERDE
(*Atlantic Ocean,* pp.360–361)
- ⊙ Praia
- ♦ 400,000
- ♡ Portuguese, Creole

GAMBIA
- ⊙ Banjul
- ♦ 900,000
- ♡ English

GUINEA

• The three bright colors of Guinea's flag represent the national motto of "work, justice, solidarity."

ESSENTIAL FACTS
- ⊙ Conakry
- ◔ 94,926 sq miles (245,860 sq km)
- ♦ 6.3 million
- ⌑ Guinea franc
- ♡ French

TOGO

• The retail trade in Togo is dominated by the "Nana Benz," or market women, of Lomé.

ESSENTIAL FACTS
- ⊙ Lomé
- ◔ 21,927 sq miles (56,290 sq km)
- ♦ 3.9 million
- ⌑ CFA franc
- ♡ French, Kabye, Ewe

GUINEA-BISSAU
- ⊙ Bissau
- ♦ 1 million
- ♡ Portuguese

NIGERIA

• Modern medicine is not available in rural Nigeria; the health service is concentrated in urban areas.
• Nigeria is the most heavily populated country in Africa.

ESSENTIAL FACTS
- ⊙ Abuja
- ◔ 356,668 sq miles (923,770 sq km)
- ♦ 119 million
- ⌑ Naira
- ♡ English
- ▲ Military regime
- ♦ 52 years

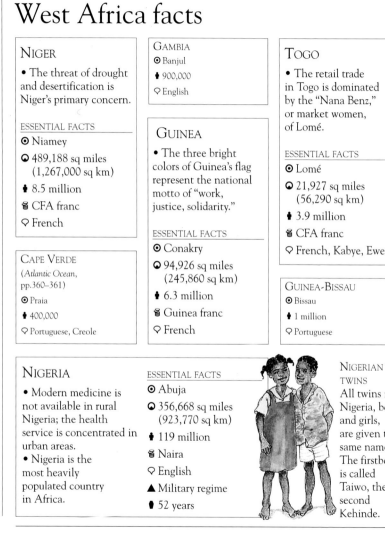

NIGERIAN TWINS
All twins in Nigeria, boy and girls, are given th same names The firstbor is called Taiwo, the second Kehinde.

Northwest Africa facts

TUNISIA

- The Berber village of Matmata was a location for the planet Tatooine in the 1977 film *Star Wars*.
- Esparto grass grown on the plains of Tunisia is used to make quality paper.
- Tunisians use falcons to hunt partridge, quail, and hare in the summer.

ESSENTIAL FACTS

- ⊙ Tunis
- ⊙ 63,170 sq miles (163,610 sq km)
- ⬥ 8.6 million
- ⬥ Tunisian dinar
- ⬥ Arabic

ALGERIA

- The Algerian population is mainly Arab, under 30 years of age, and urban.
- The highest sand dunes in the world are found in east central Algeria.
- More than 80% of Algeria lies within the Sahara desert.

ESSENTIAL FACTS

- ⊙ Algiers
- ⊙ 919,590 sq miles (2,381,740 sq km)
- ⬥ 27.1 million
- ⬥ Dinar
- ⬥ Arabic

PATTERNED
LEATHER BAG

LEATHER GOODS
Morocco and Tunisia produce quality leather goods for tourists to buy.

MOROCCO

- The Karuecin University at Fès, which was founded in A.D. 859, is the world's oldest existing educational institution.

ESSENTIAL FACTS

- ⊙ Rabat
- ⊙ 6269,757 sq miles (98,670 sq km)
- ⬥ 27 million
- ⬥ Moroccan dirham
- ⬥ Arabic

LIBYA

- The West has ignored Libya due to its past links with terrorist groups.
- Libyan oil contains no sulfur, resulting in little pollution when it is burned.

ESSENTIAL FACTS

- ⊙ Tripoli
- ⊙ 679,358 sq miles (1,759,540 sq km)
- ⬥ 5.5 million
- ⬥ Libyan dinar
- ⬥ Arabic

NORTHEAST AFRICA

THE NILE, THE LONGEST river in the world, carries rich mud from the highlands of Sudan into Egypt, creating some of the most fertile land in the world. About 99 percent of Egypt's population live on the river's banks. Ethiopia, Somalia, and Sudan have been beset by drought, famine, and war, so about half of Africa's 4.5 million refugees come from this area.

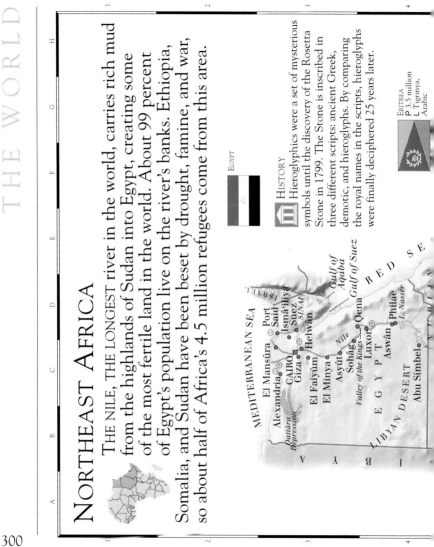

EGYPT

HISTORY

Hieroglyphics were a set of mysterious symbols until the discovery of the Rosetta Stone in 1799. The Stone is inscribed in three different scripts: ancient Greek, demotic, and hieroglyphs. By comparing the royal names in the scripts, hieroglyphs were finally deciphered 25 years later.

ERITREA
P 3.5 million
L Tigrinya,
Arabic

(map labels)
MEDITERRANEAN SEA
El Mansûra
Alexandria
Port Said
Ismâ'ilîya
Suez
Qattâra Depression
CAIRO
Giza
Helwân
SINAI
ISRAEL
Gulf of Aqaba
Gulf of Suez
El Faiyûm
El Minya
Asyût
Sohâg
Nile
Valley of the Kings
Luxor
Qena
RED SEA
E G Y P T
Aswân
Philae
L. Nasser
LIBYAN DESERT
Abu Simbel

NORTHEAST AFRICA

SOMALIA

ETHIOPIA

SUDAN

COMMUNICATIONS
Opened in 1869, the Suez Canal
connects the Mediterranean and the
Red Seas, shortening the route from
Europe to the Far East. More than
17,000 ships use it each year.

INDIAN OCEAN

Gulf of Aden

HORN OF AFRICA

DJIBOUTI
DJIBOUTI
Berbera
Hargeysa

Dahlak Archipelago

ERITREA
ASMARA

Khartoum North
Omdurman
KHARTOUM
Wad Medani
El Obeid

Atbara

Blue Nile

White Nile

Gonder
L. Tana

ETHIOPIAN
HIGHLANDS

ADDIS ABABA

Awash

Dire
Dawa

Shebeli

Genale

Omo

L. Abaya

L. Turkana

KENYA

Jubo

MOGADISHU

Kismaayo

S O M A L I A

SUDD

SUDAN

CHAD

CENTRAL AFRICAN
REPUBLIC

ZAIRE

UGANDA

Southeast Sudan
is administered
by Kenya

500km
300miles
0   250
0   150

N

301

CENTRAL AFRICA

MUCH OF THIS region is covered in dense tropical rainforest, drained by the Congo (Zaire) River, which flows in a huge arc on its way to the Atlantic. In the 16th century Portugal and Spain set up trading posts on the west coast as part of the slave trade. Millions of Africans from this region were sent as slaves to the New World. Many people in coastal areas still speak Spanish and Portuguese.

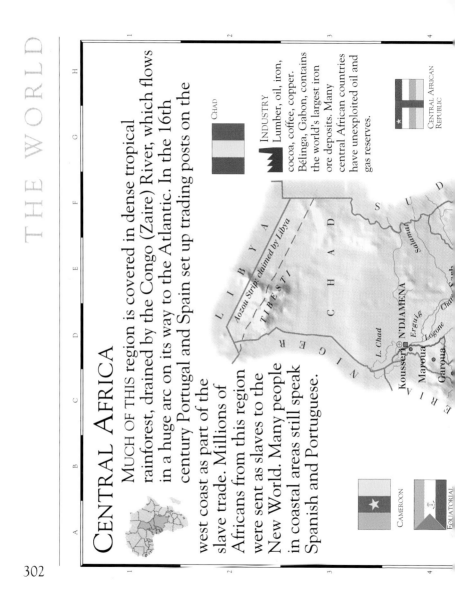

CHAD

INDUSTRY
Lumber, oil, iron, cocoa, coffee, copper. Bélinga, Gabon, contains the world's largest iron ore deposits. Many central African countries have unexploited oil and gas reserves.

CENTRAL AFRICAN REPUBLIC

CAMEROON

EQUATORIAL

CENTRAL AFRICA

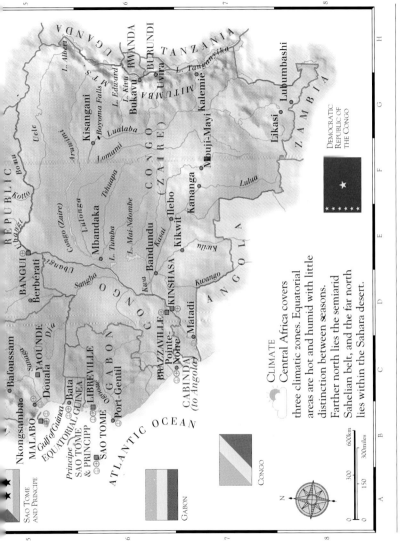

CLIMATE
Central Africa covers three climatic zones. Equatorial areas are hot and humid with little distinction between seasons. Farther north lies the semiarid Sahelian belt, and the far north lies within the Sahara desert.

DEMOCRATIC REPUBLIC OF THE CONGO

GABON

CONGO

SAO TOME AND PRINCIPE

303

CENTRAL EAST AFRICA

LARGE AREAS OF savanna, or grassland, in central Africa provide grazing for domestic and wild animals alike. Industry is poorly developed in the region – Zambia, Rwanda, Burundi, and Uganda suffer from having no seaports. Lake Victoria is the largest lake in Africa, and a source of the Nile River.

FLORA AND FAUNA

Poaching remains a major problem in this area. To combat this, all the countries in this region have set up wildlife parks to protect animals such as elephants and zebra.

INDUSTRY

Tobacco, coffee, tea, tourism, cloves, copper. Zambia is the world's fifth-largest producer of copper. Wildlife parks in this region

UGANDAh

RWANDA

KENYA

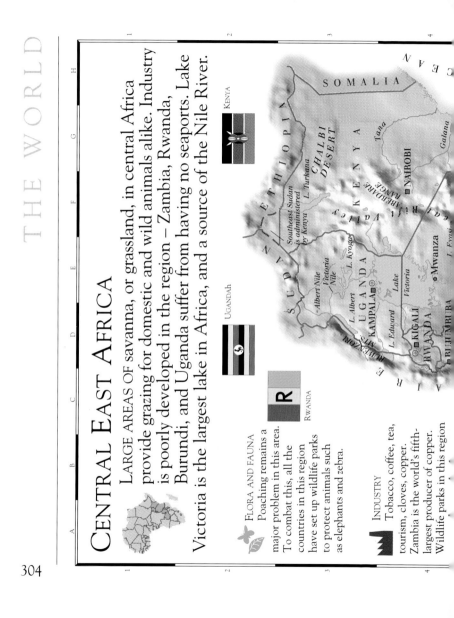

SOMALIA

ETHIOPIA

Southeast Sudan
is administered
by Kenya

L. Turkana

CHALBI
DESERT

KENYA

Tana

ABERDARE
RANGE

NAIROBI

Galana

SUDAN

Albert Nile

Victoria
Nile

L. Kyoga

Lake
Victoria

UGANDA

KAMPALA

L. Edward

L. Albert

RUWENZORI
MTS

KIGALI

RWANDA

BUJUMBURA

Mwanza

I N D I A

Zanzibar

Zazibar

Dar es Salaam

Mafia I.

TANZANIA

DODOMA

T A N Z A N I A

Rufiji

Great Ruaha

L. Rukwa

Mbeya

Ruvuma

MOZAMBIQUE

Rusus

MALAWI

LILONGWE

Blantyre

M O Z A M B I Q U E

Great Rift Valley

L. Tanganyika

L. Mweru

L. Bangweulu

MUCHINGA MTS

Luangwa

Lower Zambezi

Mtulira

Ndola

Chingola

Kitwe

Luanshya

Kabwe

Z A M B I A

LUSAKA

KAFUE FLATS

Kafue

L. Kariba

Victoria Falls

Zambezi

Z I M B A B W E

NAMIBIA

BOTSWANA

A N G O L A

Z A I R E

BURUNDI

ZAMBIA

TANZANIA

MALAWI

NATURAL FEATURES
The Great Rift Valley is part
of a fault system that extends for
6,000 miles (9,600 km) from Turkey
to Mozambique. In Kenya, the walls
of the valley rise almost straight up
for 4,000 ft (1,250 m).

CLIMATE
The south of this region is
tropical, while the central plateau in
Tanzania is semiarid. Lake Victoria
moderates the climate around it.

N

0   250   500km
0   150   300miles

305

Northeast Africa facts

EGYPT

- Overpopulation is a major problem in Eygpt, where it is estimated a baby is born every 24 seconds.
- The ancient pyramids were built to house the mummified bodies of Egyptian kings.

ESSENTIAL FACTS

- ⊙ Cairo
- ◑ 386,660 sq miles (1,001,450 sq km)
- ♦ 56.1 million
- 🖺 Egyptian pound
- ♥ Arabic
- ▲ Multiparty republic

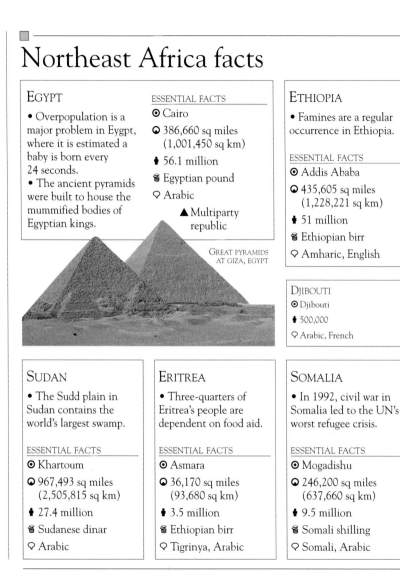

GREAT PYRAMIDS AT GIZA, EGYPT

ETHIOPIA

- Famines are a regular occurrence in Ethiopia.

ESSENTIAL FACTS

- ⊙ Addis Ababa
- ◑ 435,605 sq miles (1,228,221 sq km)
- ♦ 51 million
- 🖺 Ethiopian birr
- ♥ Amharic, English

DJIBOUTI

- ⊙ Djibouti
- ♦ 500,000
- ♥ Arabic, French

SUDAN

- The Sudd plain in Sudan contains the world's largest swamp.

ESSENTIAL FACTS

- ⊙ Khartoum
- ◑ 967,493 sq miles (2,505,815 sq km)
- ♦ 27.4 million
- 🖺 Sudanese dinar
- ♥ Arabic

ERITREA

- Three-quarters of Eritrea's people are dependent on food aid.

ESSENTIAL FACTS

- ⊙ Asmara
- ◑ 36,170 sq miles (93,680 sq km)
- ♦ 3.5 million
- 🖺 Ethiopian birr
- ♥ Tigrinya, Arabic

SOMALIA

- In 1992, civil war in Somalia led to the UN's worst refugee crisis.

ESSENTIAL FACTS

- ⊙ Mogadishu
- ◑ 246,200 sq miles (637,660 sq km)
- ♦ 9.5 million
- 🖺 Somali shilling
- ♥ Somali, Arabic

Central East Africa facts

KENYA

- Ethnic violence is the main political issue.
- Kenya has over 40 national parks and game reserves, and two marine parks in the Indian ocean.

ESSENTIAL FACTS
- ☉ Nairobi
- ✺ 224, 081 sq miles (580,370 sq km)
- ♦ 26.1 million
- 💰 Kenya shilling
- ♡ Swahili

RWANDA
- ☉ Kigali
- ♦ 7.5 million
- ♡ Kinyarwanda, French

MASAI WARRIORS
The Masai are a tribe of nomadic herders who live on the borders of Kenya and Tanzania.

GORILLAS OF RWANDA
Rwanda is one of the last remaining sanctuaries of the mountain gorilla.

BURUNDI
- ☉ Bujumbura
- ♦ 5.8 million
- ♡ Kirundi, French

UGANDA

- The rugged Ruwenzori mountains of Uganda arealso known as the "Mountains of the Moon."

ESSENTIAL FACTS
- ☉ Kampala
- ✺ 91,073 sq miles (235,880 sq km)
- ♦ 19.2 million
- 💰 New Uganda shilling
- ♡ English

TANZANIA

- One-third of Tanzania is national park or game reserve.
- The use of Swahili as a universal language has reduced ethnic rivalries.

ESSENTIAL FACTS
- ☉ Dodoma
- ✺ 364,900 sq miles (945,090 sq km)
- ♦ 28.8 million
- 💰 Tanzanian shilling
- ♡ English, Swahili

307

Central Africa facts

ZAMBIA

• Victoria Falls in Zambia is called *Musi-o-Tunyi* by African people; this means "the smoke that thunders."

ESSENTIAL FACTS

◉ Lusaka

◔ 290,563 sq miles (752,610 sq km)

♦ 8.9 million

☙ Zambian kwacha

♥ English, Bemba, Tonga

CHAD

• The tropical, cotton-producing south is Chad's most heavily populated region.
• The Tibesti plateau is a site of prehistoric rock painting.

ESSENTIAL FACTS

◉ N'Djamena

◔ 495,752 sq miles (1,284,000 sq km)

♦ 6 million

☙ CFA franc

♥ French, Sara, Maba

FISH FOOD
Lake Chad's fish, such as this tilapia, are a major source of food for people who live in the region.

EQUATORIAL GUINEA

◉ Malabo

♦ 400,000

♥ Spanish, Fang

Alluvial diamond

LITTLE GEMS
Congo (Zaire) is the world's largest producer of diamonds used in industry.

CONGO (ZAIRE)

• The rain forests of Congo (Zaire) comprise almost 50% of Africa's remaining woodlands.

ESSENTIAL FACTS

◉ Kinshasa

◔ 905,563 sq miles (2,345,410 sq km)

♦ 41.2 million

☙ New zaire

♥ French

CENTRAL AFRICAN REPUBLIC

• Hunting of elephants in the CAR was finally banned in 1985.

ESSENTIAL FACTS

◉ Bangui

◔ 240,530 sq miles (622,980 sq km)

♦ 3.3 million

☙ CFA franc

♥ French

CONGO

• In 1970, Congo became the first declared communist state in Africa.
• Congo has been used in the past as a dump for Western toxic waste.

ESSENTIAL FACTS

☪ Brazzaville
☉ 132,040 sq miles (342,000 sq km)
♦ 2.4 million
☷ CFA franc
♥ French

CAMEROON

• The Portuguese explorers who colonized Cameroon fished for shrimp called *camaroes*, from which the country derived its name.

ESSENTIAL FACTS

☪ Yaoundé
☉ 183,570 sq miles (475,440 sq km)
♦ 12.5 million
☷ CFA franc
♥ English, French

RESPECT FOR THE DEAD
This wooden figure from Cameroon was made to honor an ancestor.

SÃO TOMÉ & PRÍNCIPE

☉ São Tomé
♦ 121,000
♥ Portuguese

SPIRITED FIGURE
Central African folk religions believe fetish figures like this are inhabited by spirits.

GABON

• Libreville was founded as a settlement for freed French slaves in 1849.
• Menial jobs in Gabon are done by immigrant workers.

ESSENTIAL FACTS

☉ Libreville
☉ 103,347 sq miles (267,670 sq km)
♦ 1.3 million
☷ CFA franc
♥ French

MALAWI

• Lake Malawi contains at least 500 species of fish.
• Malawi's name means "the land where the sun is reflected in the water like fire."

ESSENTIAL FACTS

☉ Lilongwe
☉ 45,745 sq miles (118,480 sq km)
♦ 10.7 million
☷ Kwacha
♥ English, Chewa

SOUTHERN AFRICA

THE RICHEST DEPOSITS of valuable minerals in Africa, such as gold and diamonds, are found in its southern region. Many countries surrounding South Africa rely on it for work and trade. Racial segregation under apartheid operated from 1948 until South Africa's first multiracial elections were held in 1994. Namibia won its independence from South Africa in 1990, but neighboring Angola has been in a state of civil war since 1975.

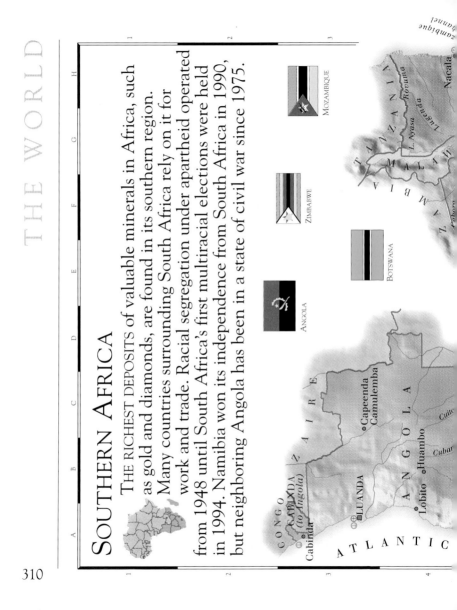

ANGOLA

BOTSWANA

ZIMBABWE

MOZAMBIQUE

Zambique
tunnel

Nacala

Rovuma

Lugenda

T A N Z A N I A

L. Nyasa

M A L A W I

Z A M B I A

Chora

C O N G O

Z A I R E

CABINDA
(to Angola)

Cabinda

■ LUANDA

A N G O L A

Lobito

Huambo

Capeenda
Camulemba

Cuito

Cubar

Lobito

A T L A N T I C

SWAZILAND

LESOTHO

CLIMATE
This region varies in climate from tropical in northern areas to temperate in the south. Parts of some countries are prone to drought.

INDUSTRY
Oil, diamonds, uranium, gold. Namibia has the world's largest uranium mine. Gold from South Africa is often sold as special coins called *Krugerrands*.

FLORA AND FAUNA
The unique Namibian desert elephant, of which only 34 remain, and the black rhino are threatened both by illegal poaching and the disease anthrax.

NAMIBIA

SOUTH AFRICA

N

0   300   600km
0   150   300miles

311

Southern Africa facts

ZIMBABWE

- Most people in Zimbabwe belong to the Shona or Ndebele tribes.
- Zimbabwe was formerly known as Southern Rhodesia.

ESSENTIAL FACTS
- ⊙ Harare
- ◐ 150,800 sq miles (390,580 sq km)
- ♦ 10.9 million
- 🕮 Zimbabwe dollar
- ♥ English

COLORFUL DECOR
Ndebele women decorate their homes with bright geometric patterns.

MOZAMBIQUE

- Over 90% of the citizens of Mozambique live in poverty.
- Polygamous marriages are common among those wealthy enough to take second wives.

ESSENTIAL FACTS
- ⊙ Maputo
- ◐ 309,493 sq miles (801,590 sq km)
- ♦ 15.3 million
- 🕮 Metical
- ♥ Portuguese

BOTSWANA

- The people of Botswana place such value on rain as a resource that their currency, the pula, is named in its honor.

ESSENTIAL FACTS
- ⊙ Gaborone
- ◐ 224,600 sq miles (581,730 sq km)
- ♦ 1.4 million
- 🕮 Pula
- ♥ English

SWAZILAND
- ⊙ Mbabane
- ♦ 800,000
- ♥ Siswati, English

ANGOLA

- Injuries caused by exploding mines have led to the nation of Angola having the highest number of amputees in the world.

ESSENTIAL FACTS
- ⊙ Luanda
- ◐ 481,351 sq miles (1,246,700 sq km)
- ♦ 10.3 million
- 🕮 New kwanza
- ♥ Portuguese

SPRINGBOKS
These small antelopes live in the grasslands of South Africa.

Characteristic leap is known as "pronking"

MADAGASCAR
Indian Ocean,
pp.362–363)

• This country is the world's largest producer of vanilla.
• Madagascar is a unique environment; 80% of its plants and animal species are found nowhere else.

ESSENTIAL FACTS
⊙ Antananarivo
◷ 226,660 sq miles (587,040 sq km)
♦ 13.3 million
💰 Malagasy franc
♀ Malagasy, French

LESOTHO
⊙ Maseru
♦ 1.9 million
♀ English, Sesotho

LARGEST LEMUR
Madagascar is home to the indri, the largest of the world's lemurs.

COMOROS
⊙ Moroni
♦ 600,000
♀ Arabic, French

NAMIBIA

• The Namib is Earth's oldest, and one of its driest, deserts.

ESSENTIAL FACTS
⊙ Windhoek
◷ 318,260 sq miles (824,290 sq km)
♦ 1.6 million
💰 South African rand
♀ English

SOUTH AFRICA

• President Nelson Mandela and former president F. W. De Klerk were awarded the Nobel Peace Prize in 1994 for their work dismantling apartheid.
• Tourists are increasingly attracted to South Africa's beaches, stunning scenery, and prize-winning vineyards.

ESSENTIAL FACTS
⊙ Pretoria, Cape Town, Bloemfontein
◷ 471,443 sq miles (1,221,040 sq km)
♦ 37.4 million
💰 Rand
♀ Afrikaans, English, 9 African languages
▲ Multiparty republic
♦ 62 years

BURIED TREASURE
South Africa has the world's deepest goldmine, descending 12,392 ft (3,777 m) underground.

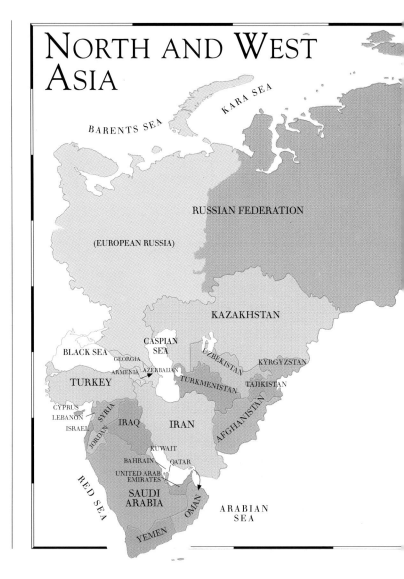

NORTH AND WEST ASIA

BARENTS SEA

KARA SEA

RUSSIAN FEDERATION

(EUROPEAN RUSSIA)

KAZAKHSTAN

CASPIAN SEA

BLACK SEA

GEORGIA

ARMENIA AZERBAIJAN

UZBEKISTAN

KYRGYZSTAN

TURKEY

TURKMENISTAN

TAJIKISTAN

CYPRUS

LEBANON

ISRAEL

SYRIA

JORDAN

IRAQ

IRAN

AFGHANISTAN

KUWAIT

BAHRAIN

QATAR

UNITED ARAB EMIRATES

RED SEA

SAUDI ARABIA

OMAN

ARABIAN SEA

YEMEN

NORTH AND WEST ASIA

Asia is the largest continent in the world,
occupying nearly one-third of the world's total
land area. In the south, the Arabian Peninsula
is mostly hot, dry desert. In the north lie cold
deserts, treeless plains called steppes and the
largest needleleaf forest in the world, which
stretches from Siberia to northern Europe.

315

THE NEAR EAST

AT THE JUNCTION of Africa, Asia, and Europe, the Near East is a mosaic of deserts, mountains, and fertile valleys. After centuries of conflict, there are now hopes for peace in the region. Lebanon is beginning to emerge from a civil war that began in 1975 and the disputes over territories in Israel, such as the West Bank and the Gaza Strip, are starting to be resolved.

LEBANON

INDUSTRY
Oil, potash, cotton, fruit. Water is in short supply in this region and special irrigation techniques are used in order to avoid waste. Syria's main cash crop is cotton.

ISRAEL

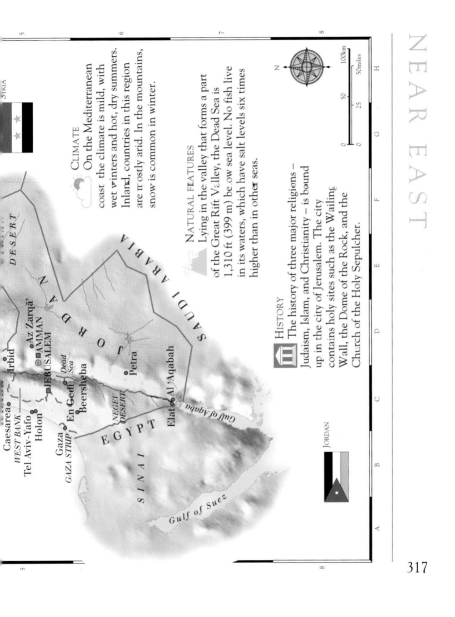

CLIMATE

On the Mediterranean coast the climate is mild, with wet winters and hot, dry summers. Inland, countries in this region are mostly arid. In the mountains, snow is common in winter.

NATURAL FEATURES

Lying in the valley that forms a part of the Great Rift Valley, the Dead Sea is 1,310 ft (399 m) below sea level. No fish live in its waters, which have salt levels six times higher than in other seas.

HISTORY

The history of three major religions – Judaism, Islam, and Christianity – is bound up in the city of Jerusalem. The city contains holy sites such as the Wailing Wall, the Dome of the Rock, and the Church of the Holy Sepulcher.

SYRIA

DESERT

WEST BANK

Caesarea
Tel Aviv-Yafo
Holon
Gaza
GAZA STRIP
Beersheba
En Gedi
Dead Sea
JERUSALEM
Irbid
Az Zarqā'
AMMAN
JORDAN
Petra
Al 'Aqabah
Elat
Gulf of Aqaba
NEGEV DESERT
SINAI
EGYPT
SAUDI ARABIA
Gulf of Suez

JORDAN

N

0   50   100km
0   25   50miles

TURKEY AND CYPRUS

BRIDGING THE CONTINENTS of Europe and Asia, Turkey was once the center of the Ottoman Empire, which at one time controlled one-quarter of Europe. Independent of the UK in 1960, Cyprus was invaded by Turkey in 1974. Southern Cyprus is Greek; Northern Cyprus is still occupied by Turkey.

TURKEY

Map labels: BULGARIA, GREECE, Bosporus, Zongul, Istanbul, Sea of Marmara, Izmit, Dardanelles, Gallipoli, Adapa, Bursa, Sak, Balikesir, Eskişehir, Kütahya, T, U, AEGEAN SEA, Manisa, Izmir, L. Egridir, Ephesus, Pamukkale, Isparta, Kuşadasi, Denizli, L. Beyşel, Antalya, MEDITERRANE

INDUSTRY

Wheat, corn, sugar beets, nuts, fruit, cotton, tobacco, tourism. Carpet-weaving is a tradition dating back centuries. Figs and peaches are grown on the coast of the Mediterranean.

ENVIRONMENT

Turkey's dam-building projects on the Tigris and Euphrates Rivers have met with disapproval from Syria and Iraq, whose own rivers will have reduced flow as a result.

PEOPLE

The Kurds are Turkey's main minority group and one of the largest groups of stateless people in the world. Their homeland, Kurdistan, straddles three countries: Turkey, Iraq, and Iran. Kurds are fighting for recognition of their rights within Turkey.

NATURAL FEATURES

Turkey lies within the
pine-Himalayan mountain belt.
e Arabian, African, Eurasian,
gean, and Turkish plates all
verge within its borders,
ulting in severe seismic activity.

CLIMATE

Coastal regions of Turkey and
Cyprus have a Mediterranean climate.
The Turkish interior has cold, snowy
winters and hot, dry summers.

BLACK SEA

PONTIC MOUNTAINS

GEORGIA

ARMENIA

IRAN

IRAQ

SYRIA

AZ MTS.

Kızılırmak

NKARA

Samsun

Trabzon

Erzurum

Sivas

MUNZUR MTS.

Kızılırmak

KEY

CAPPADOCIA

Göreme

Kayseri

Elazığ

Malatya

Murat

Tigris

L. Van

Van

Seyhan

ya

Ceyhan

Kahramanmaraş

Diyarbakir

Gaziantep

Şanliurfa

RUS MTS.

Adana

Euphrates

Mersin

Antakya

CYPRUS

NICOSIA

Famagusta

Larnaca

imassol

CYPRUS

HISTORY

Greeks colonized the Aegean
coast in 700 B.C. The Temple of
Artemis in the city of Ephesus
is one of the seven wonders
of the ancient world.

N

0   150   300km
0   100   150miles

MIDDLE EAST

ISLAM WAS FOUNDED in A.D. 570 in Mecca, Saudi Arabia, and spread throughout the Middle East, where today it is the main religion. Oil has brought wealth to the region, but in 1991 the area was financially devastated by the Gulf War.

IRAQ

INDUSTRY
Oil, natural gas, fishing, carpet-weaving, offshore banking. Saudi Arabia has the world's largest oil reserves. Over 60 percent of the world's desalination plants are used in this region to make seawater drinkable.

CLIMATE
Most of the countries in this region are semiarid, with low rainfall. Inland, summer temperatures can reach 119°F (48°C) with winter temperatures falling to freezing.

HISTORY
Ancient civilizations developed about 5,500 years ago in Mesopotamia, between the Tigris and Euphrates Rivers. The Sumerian civilization had advanced methods of irrigation, sophisticated architecture, and a complex form of writing called cuneiform.

SAUDI ARABIA
KUWAIT
BAHRAIN
QATAR
UNITED ARAB EMIRATES
YEMEN

EGYPT
Gulf of Aqaba
H E J
RED SEA
Mecca
Jedda
Hode
Al Mu
Bab el Me

IRAN

TURKEY

L. Urmia
Ardabīl
Rasht
CASPIAN SEA
TURKMENISTAN

Mosul
Irbil
Kirkūk
Zanjān
As Sulaymānīyah
Sanandaj
ELBURZ MTS.
Sarī
Semnān

I R A Q
TEHRAN
Bakhtarān
Qom
Mashhad

BAGHDAD
Karbala
Al-Hillah
Īlām
Arāk
DASHT-E KAVIR

An-Najaf
Dezfūl
Esfahān

SYRIA

Euphrates

Tigris

An Nāṣirīyah
Al 'Amārah
Ahvāz
Yazd

Al-Basrah
Ābādān
DASHT-E LUT

KUWAIT CITY
Yāsūj
Kermān
Zāhedān

KUWAIT
Shīrāz

Persian
Gulf
ZAGROS MTS.

uraydah

Ad
Dammām
Bandar-e Abbās
Jaz Mūrīan
Salt Lake

MANAMA
BAHRAIN
Strait of
Hormuz
Khasab
(to Oman)

RIYADH
Al Hufūf
DOHA
QATAR

ABU DHABI
Dubai

S A U D I
UNITED ARAB
EMIRATES

R A B I A
AD DAHNA
AD DAFRAH
Gulf of Oman
MUSCAT

RUB' AL KHALI
O M A N
OMAN

ILAT AS SAB'ATAYN
Masīrah I.
Gulf of Masīrah
N

Y E M E N
HADHRAMAUT

A R A B I A N   S E A

0		300		600km
0	150		300miles	

Near East facts

ISRAEL

• The average age in Israel is only 25.6 years.
• Israeli citizenship is the right of all Jews.

ESSENTIAL FACTS

⊙ Jerusalem
◑ 7,992 sq miles (20,700 sq km)
⚥ 5.4 million
💰 New shekel
♡ Hebrew, Arabic
▲ Multiparty republic
❦ 76 years

WAILING WALL, JERUSALEM

CYPRUS
⊙ Nicosia
⚥ 700,000
♡ Greek, Turkish

LEBANON

• The press has greater freedom in Lebanon than in any other Arab country.

ESSENTIAL FACTS

⊙ Beirut
◑ 4,015 sq miles (10,400 sq km)
⚥ 2.9 million
💰 Lebanese pound
♡ Arabic

SYRIA

• The world's first alphabet was found in the ancient Syrian city of Ugarit.

ESSENTIAL FACTS

⊙ Damascus
◑ 71,498 sq miles (185,180 sq km)
⚥ 13.8 million
💰 Syrian pound
♡ Arabic

JORDAN

• King Hussein, the longest-reigning Arab ruler, has led Jordan since 1952.

ESSENTIAL FACTS

⊙ Amman
◑ 34,440 sq miles (89,210 sq km)
⚥ 4.4 million
💰 Jordanian dinar
♡ Arabic

TURKEY

• Grapes, one of the world's oldest crops, were first grown in Anatolia, Turkey.

ESSENTIAL FACTS

⊙ Ankara
◑ 300,950 sq miles (779,450 sq km)
⚥ 59.6 million
💰 Turkish lira
♡ Turkish
▲ Multiparty republic
❦ 67 years

Middle East facts

IRAN

ESSENTIAL FACTS
- ◉ Tehran
- ◔ 636,293 sq miles (1,648,000 sq km)
- ✦ 63.2 million
- ✎ Iranian rial
- ♥ Farsi
- ▲ Islamic republic
- ● 67 years

SAUDI ARABIA

ESSENTIAL FACTS
- ◉ Riyadh
- ◔ 829,995 sq miles (2,149,690 sq km)
- ✦ 16.5 million
- ✎ Saudi riyal
- ♥ Arabic
- ▲ Absolute monarchy
- ● 69 years

QATAR
- ◉ Doha
- ✦ 500,000
- ♥ Arabic

BAHRAIN
- ◉ Manama
- ✦ 500,000
- ♥ Arabic

IRAQ

ESSENTIAL FACTS
- ◉ Baghdad
- ◔ 169,235 sq miles (438,320 sq km)
- ✦ 19.9 million
- ✎ Iraqi dinar
- ♥ Arabic
- ▲ Single-party republic
- ● 66 years

ARAB HEADDRESSES
Men and women wear headcloths to protect them from the sun.

UNITED ARAB EMIRATES

ESSENTIAL FACTS
- ◉ Abu Dhabi
- ◔ 32,278 sq miles (83,600 sq km)
- ✦ 1.7 million
- ✎ UAE dirham
- ♥ Arabic

KUWAIT

ESSENTIAL FACTS
- ◉ Kuwait City
- ◔ 6,880 sq miles (17,820 sq km)
- ✦ 1.8 million
- ✎ Kuwaiti dinar
- ♥ Arabic

OMAN

ESSENTIAL FACTS
- ◉ Muscat
- ◔ 82,030 sq miles (212,460 sq km)
- ✦ 1.7 million
- ✎ Omani rial
- ♥ Arabic

YEMEN

ESSENTIAL FACTS
- ◉ Sana
- ◔ 203,849 sq miles (527,970 sq km)
- ✦ 13 million
- ✎ Yemen riyal
- ♥ Arabic

CENTRAL ASIA

FOR CENTURIES, many people in central Asia lived in mountains as nomads, or in cities that sprang up along the Silk Road. When the region came under Soviet rule, industry was developed and irrigation schemes made farming possible.

INDUSTRY
Cotton, gold, gas, sulfur, mercury, opium, hydroelectricity. Uzbekistan has the largest single gold mine in the world. Tajikistan has 14 percent of the world's known uranium resources.

HISTORY
In the early 1900s, most of this region, except for Afghanistan, came under Soviet rule, which restricted the use of local languages and Islam. Today, these newly independent countries are resuming the religions, languages, and traditions of their past.

TURKMENISTAN

ENVIRONMENT
Crop irrigation draws water from the Amu Darya River, reducing the amount of water flowing into the Aral Sea. By the year 2000 the Sea will have shrunk to a third of its original size.

USTYURT PLATEAU
ARAL SEA
TURAN LOWLAND
L. Sarykamysh
Nukus
UZ
Zaliv Kara-Bogaz-Gol
Tashauz
Urgench
CASPIAN SEA
Krasnovodsk
Nebit Dag
TURKMENISTAN
ASHKABAD
Tedzhen
Kara
I R A N
H
A

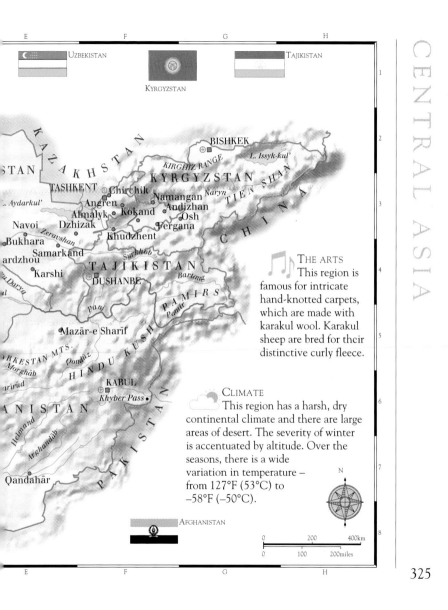

UZBEKISTAN

KYRGYZSTAN

TAJIKISTAN

K A Z A K H S T A N

STAN

TASHKENT   Chirchik
L. Aydarkul'   Angren   Namangan   Naryn
Almalyk   Kokand   Andizhan
Navoi   Dzhizak   Osh
Zeravshan   Fergana
Bukhara   Khudzhent
ardzhou   Samarkand   Surkhob
Karshi   T A J I K I S T A N
DUSHANBE   Bartang
u Darya   Panj   P A M I R S
al   Pamir

Mazār-e Sharīf

RKESTAN MTS.   Qonduz
Morghāb   H I N D U   K U S H
arirud   KABUL
N I S T A N   Khyber Pass
Helmand   P
Arghandāb   A
Qandahār   K
I
S
T
A
N

BISHKEK
KIRGHIZ RANGE   L. Issyk-kul'
K Y R G Y Z S T A N   SHAN
T I E N
C H I N A

THE ARTS
This region is famous for intricate hand-knotted carpets, which are made with karakul wool. Karakul sheep are bred for their distinctive curly fleece.

CLIMATE
This region has a harsh, dry continental climate and there are large areas of desert. The severity of winter is accentuated by altitude. Over the seasons, there is a wide variation in temperature – from 127°F (53°C) to –58°F (–50°C).

N

AFGHANISTAN

0   200   400km
0   100   200miles

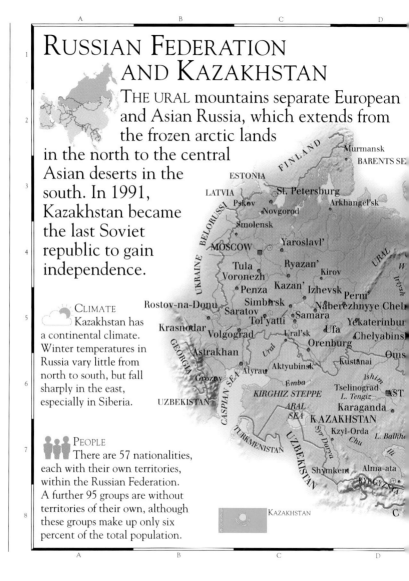

RUSSIAN FEDERATION AND KAZAKHSTAN

THE URAL mountains separate European and Asian Russia, which extends from the frozen arctic lands in the north to the central Asian deserts in the south. In 1991, Kazakhstan became the last Soviet republic to gain independence.

CLIMATE
Kazakhstan has a continental climate. Winter temperatures in Russia vary little from north to south, but fall sharply in the east, especially in Siberia.

PEOPLE
There are 57 nationalities, each with their own territories, within the Russian Federation. A further 95 groups are without territories of their own, although these groups make up only six percent of the total population.

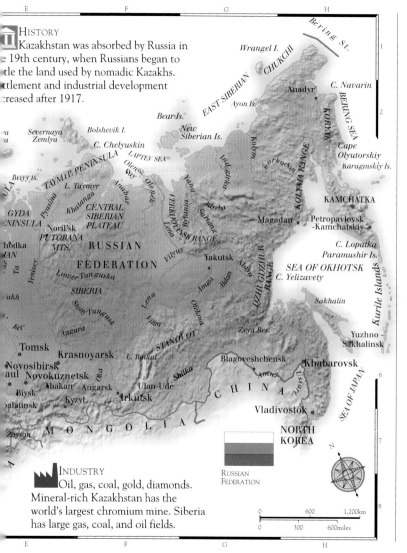

HISTORY

Kazakhstan was absorbed by Russia in
e 19th century, when Russians began to
tle the land used by nomadic Kazakhs.
ttlement and industrial development
creased after 1917.

INDUSTRY

Oil, gas, coal, gold, diamonds.
Mineral-rich Kazakhstan has the
world's largest chromium mine. Siberia
has large gas, coal, and oil fields.

Bering St.

Wrangel I.

EAST SIBERIAN
CHUKCHI

Ayon Is.

Anadyr'

C. Navarin

BERING SEA

KORYAK

Cape
Olyutorskiy

Karaginskiy Is.

Bear Is.

New
Siberian Is.

Kolyma

Chorkaasin

KOLYMA RANGE

KAMCHATKA

Severnaya
Zemlya

Bolshevik I.

C. Chelyuskin

LAPTEV SEA

Olenek

Indigirka

Magadan

Petropavlovsk
-Kamchatskiy

Beiyy Is.

TAYMIR PENINSULA

L. Taymyr

Anabar

Olenek

VERKHOYANSK RANGE

Yana

Omoloy

Alazeya

Adyeha

C. Lopatka

Paramushir Is.

GYDA
ENINSULA

Khatanga

Pyasina

CENTRAL
SIBERIAN
PLATEAU

Noril'sk

Lena

Aldan

SEA OF OKHOTSK

C. Yelizavety

hodka

AN

PUTORANA
MTS.

RUSSIAN

Vilyuy

Yakutsk

Aldan

DZHUGDZHUR RANGE

Ta

Yenisey

FEDERATION

Lower Tunguska

Amga

Olekma

Sakhalin

vakh

SIBERIA

Lena

Stony Tunguska

Lim

Zeya Res.

Kurile Islands

Ket'

Angara

STANOVOY

Olekma

Tomsk

Krasnoyarsk

L. Baikal

Blagoveshchensk

Khabarovsk

Yuzhno -
Sakhalinsk

Novosibirsk
aul Novokuznetsk

Abakan

Oka

Angarsk

Ulan-Ude

Shilka

Amur

SEA OF JAPAN

Biysk

palatinsk

Kyzyl

Irkutsk

C H I N A

Ussuri

Zaysan

M O N G O L I A

Vladivostok

NORTH
KOREA

N

RUSSIAN
FEDERATION

0		600	1,200km
0	300	600miles	

Central Asia facts

UZBEKISTAN

• Many young Uzbeks are sent to Turkey to study business practice.
• Arranged marriages are still the custom in rural areas.

ESSENTIAL FACTS
⊙ Tashkent
◔ 439,733 sq miles (1,138,910 sq km)
⸙ 21.1 million
⸙ Som
♡ Uzbek

UZBEK HEADWEAR
Velvet hats like this one are commonly worn in Uzbekistan.

TURKMENISTAN

• Ashgabat is a breeding center for the Akhal-Teke, a breed of racehorse able to maintain its speed in desert conditions.
• Most Turkmen live around desert oases.

ESSENTIAL FACTS
⊙ Ashgabat
◔ 188,455 sq miles (488,100 sq km)
⸙ 4 million
⸙ Manat
♡ Turkmen

TAJIKISTAN

• The traditions and language of Tajikistan are similar to those of Iran.
• Violence perpetrated by armed gangs is a major problem in all but the most remote areas.

ESSENTIAL FACTS
⊙ Dushanbe
◔ 55,251 sq miles (143,100 sq km)
⸙ 5.7 million
⸙ Ruble
♡ Tajik

KYRGYZSTAN

• The nation of Kyrgyzstan is the most rural ex-Soviet republic.

ESSENTIAL FACTS
⊙ Bishkek
◔ 76,640 sq miles (198,500 sq km)
⸙ 4.6 million
⸙ Som
♡ Kyrgyz

AFGHANISTAN

• Most Afghans live in extreme poverty.

ESSENTIAL FACTS
⊙ Kabul
◔ 251,770 sq miles (652,090 sq km)
⸙ 20.5 million
⸙ Afghani
♡ Persian, Pashtu

CARROTS WERE FIRST GROWN FOR FOOD IN AFGHANISTAN

Russian Federation and Kazakhstan facts

RUSSIAN FEDERATION

• Moscow and St. Petersburg are the most popular tourist destinations in the Commonwealth of Independent States (CIS).
• Russia still maintains a military presence in most of the former USSR.
• Organized crime bosses are Russia's wealthiest group.

ESSENTIAL FACTS

⊙ Moscow

◍ 6,592,800 sq miles (17,075,400 sq km)

⚲ 149.2 million

💲 Ruble

♀ Russian

▲ Multiparty republic

⚬ 70 years

(See also **European Russia**, p.288)

EAR OF WHEAT
Kazakhstan's steppes, or grasslands, were plowed up to grow grain crops in the 1950s.

KAZAKHSTAN

• Many foreign businesspeople now live in Alma-Ata.
• Kazakhstan joined the International Monetary Fund (IMF) in 1992.
• The Kazakhs remain committed to Islam and loyal to the three clan federations, or Hordes.

ESSENTIAL FACTS

⊙ Astana

◍ 1,049,150 sq miles (2,717,300 sq km)

⚲ 17.2 million

💲 Tenge

♀ Kazakh

▲ Multiparty republic

⚬ 69 years

KAZAKHSTAN SPACE CENTER
The Russian space program is based at Baykonour in Kazakhstan.

The "Buran" unmanned Russian space shuttle

SIBERIAN HUSKIES
The husky is used for pulling sleds and hunting.

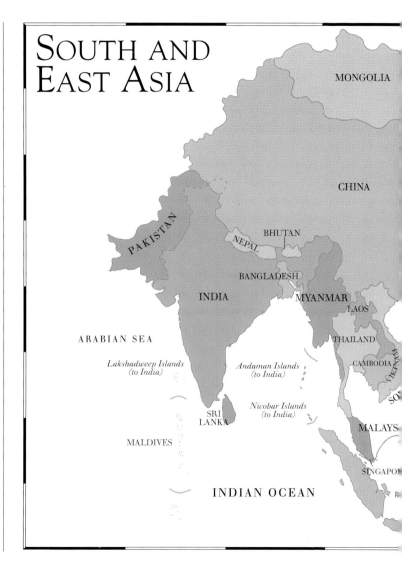

SOUTH AND EAST ASIA

MONGOLIA

CHINA

PAKISTAN

NEPAL

BHUTAN

BANGLADESH

INDIA

MYANMAR

LAOS

ARABIAN SEA

THAILAND

Lakshadweep Islands
(to India)

Andaman Islands
(to India)

CAMBODIA

VIETNAM

SRI
LANKA

Nicobar Islands
(to India)

MALAYS

MALDIVES

SINGAPO

INDIAN OCEAN

SO

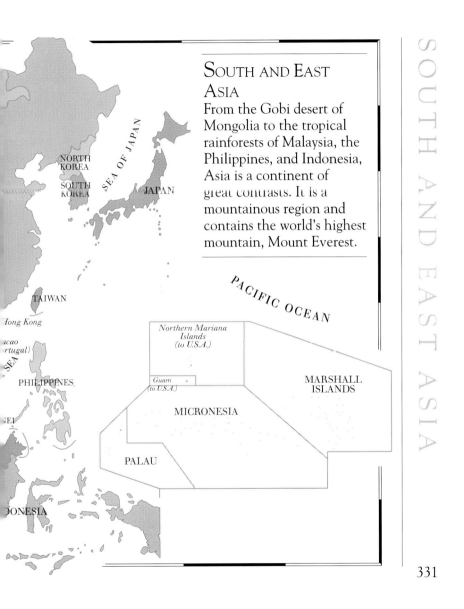

SOUTH AND EAST ASIA

From the Gobi desert of Mongolia to the tropical rainforests of Malaysia, the Philippines, and Indonesia, Asia is a continent of great contrasts. It is a mountainous region and contains the world's highest mountain, Mount Everest.

NORTH KOREA

SEA OF JAPAN

SOUTH KOREA

JAPAN

TAIWAN

Hong Kong

acao
rtugal)

SEA

PHILIPPINES

EI

ONESIA

PACIFIC OCEAN

Northern Mariana Islands
(to U.S.A.)

Guam
(to U.S.A.)

MICRONESIA

MARSHALL ISLANDS

PALAU

THE INDIAN SUBCONTINENT

SEPARATED FROM THE rest of Asia by the Himalayas, India is the second most populated country after China. It is estimated that India's population will overtake that of China by 2030. To the north, Nepal and Bhutan lie nestled in the Himalayas between China and India, and to the south lies Sri Lanka, once known as Ceylon.

AFGHANISTAN

TOBAK-EKAR RANGE

CHAGAI HILLS

IRAN

PAKISTAN

MAKRAN

Indus

TH

Hyderaba

Karachi

ARABIAN

Gulf of Kutch

SEA

Rajko

Gulf o

Khamb

INDIA

INDUSTRY
Tea, jute, iron, cut diamonds, cotton, rice, sugarcane, textiles. Bangladesh exports 80 percent of the world's jute fiber. Sri Lanka is the largest tea exporter in the world. Pakistan is a major exporter of rice.

HISTORY
In 1947, when India gained independence, religious differences led to the creation of two countries – Hindu India and Muslim Pakistan. In 1971, a short civil war broke out between East and West Pakistan and East Pakistan became Bangladesh.

NATURAL FEATURES
The Himalayas were formed as a result of a violent crumpling of the Earth's crust. Frequent earthquakes indicate that the process is continuing. The highest peaks in the world, including Mount Everest, are in this mountain system.

N

| 0 | 350 | 700 |
| 0 | 200 | 400mi |

PAKISTAN

NEPAL

BHUTAN

awar
ISLAMABAD
Srinagar
alpindi
Gujranwala
hore Amritsar
alabad Jalandhar
tan Ludhiana Chandigarh
Meerut
NEW
DELHI Bareilly
Jaipur Agra KATHMANDU THIMPHU
Gwalior Lucknow BHUTAN Brahmaputra
hpur Kota Kanpur Varanasi Guwahati
Gandi Res. Allahabad Patna Imphal
madabad Bhopal Jabalpur Dhanbad DACCA Agartala
Indore Narmada Ranchi Calcutta Khulna
dodara Nagpur Chittagong
rat Tapti
Nasik Mahanadi
Thane
ombay DECCAN Godavari
Pune Sholapur Vishakhapatnam
Hyderabad
aji PLATEAU Vijayawada
Dharwad

KASHMIR
HIMALAYA
CHINA
INDIA
NEPAL
BHUTAN
MYANMAR
BANGLADESH
Rajshahi
EASTERN GHATS
COROMANDEL COAST
B a y o f B e n g a l
DECCAN

Mangalore
Bangalore Madras
Coimbatore
Cochin
Madurai Jaffna
rivandrum
SRI LANKA
COLOMBO
Galle

BANGLADESH

SRI LANKA

CLIMATE

Sri Lanka and southern India are tropical, with little seasonal variation in temperature. The north has a cold alpine climate. Cyclones regularly build up in the Bay of Bengal. Bangladesh is often flooded during the monsoon.

Indian Subcontinent facts

INDIA

- The Bombay film industry is the world's biggest producer of feature films.
- Nearly half of India's adults are illiterate.
- Cultural and religious pressures in India encourage people to have large families.

ESSENTIAL FACTS

- ⊙ New Delhi
- ◔ 1,289,338 sq miles (3,287,590 sq km)
- ♦ 896.6 million
- 🪙 Rupee
- ♡ Hindi, English
- ▲ Multiparty republic
- ♦ 60 years

REGAL BEAST
The national symbol of India is the Royal Bengal tiger, which is a protected species.

THE SPICE OF LIFE
Indian cooking uses intense, zesty seasonings and subtle combinations of spices to flavor each dish.

Cilantro

Coriander

Cardamom pods

Ground turmeric

Fresh ginger

SRI LANKA

- In 1960, Sri Lanka became the first country in the world to elect a woman prime minister.
- Ethnic tension between the minority Tamils and majority Sinhalese led to civil war in 1983.

ESSENTIAL FACTS

- ⊙ Columbo
- ◔ 25,332 sq miles (65,610 sq km)
- ♦ 17.9 million
- 🪙 Sri Lanka rupee
- ♡ Sinhalese, Tamil

BANGLADESH

- Most transportation in Bangladesh is via rivers and waterways.
- Destruction of crops by cyclones and flooding is a frequent problem.

ESSENTIAL FACTS

- ⊙ Dhaka
- ◔ 55,598 sq miles (143,998 sq km)
- ♦ 122.2 million
- 🪙 Taka
- ♡ Bengali, Urdu

PAKISTAN

• The first woman ever to lead a Muslim country was Benazir Bhutto, elected prime minister of Pakistan in 1988.
• The Punjabi majority controls Pakistan's army and bureaucracy.

ESSENTIAL FACTS

⊙ Islamabad

◒ 307,374 sq miles (796,100 sq km)

✚ 128.1 million

🐚 Pakistani rupee

♡ Urdu, Punjabi

▲ Multiparty republic

● 58 years

TOP TEAM
The nation of Pakistan has one of the world's best cricket teams.

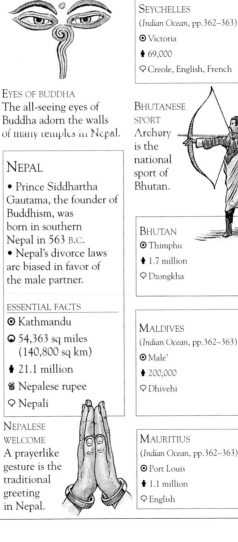

EYES OF BUDDHA
The all-seeing eyes of Buddha adorn the walls of many temples in Nepal.

NEPAL

• Prince Siddhartha Gautama, the founder of Buddhism, was born in southern Nepal in 563 B.C.
• Nepal's divorce laws are biased in favor of the male partner.

ESSENTIAL FACTS

⊙ Kathmandu

◒ 54,363 sq miles (140,800 sq km)

✚ 21.1 million

🐚 Nepalese rupee

♡ Nepali

NEPALESE WELCOME
A prayerlike gesture is the traditional greeting in Nepal.

SEYCHELLES
(*Indian Ocean*, pp.362–363)

⊙ Victoria

✚ 69,000

♡ Creole, English, French

BHUTANESE SPORT
Archery is the national sport of Bhutan.

BHUTAN

⊙ Thimphu

✚ 1.7 million

♡ Dzongkha

MALDIVES
(*Indian Ocean*, pp.362–363)

⊙ Male'

✚ 200,000

♡ Dhivehi

MAURITIUS
(*Indian Ocean*, pp.362–363)

⊙ Port Louis

✚ 1.1 million

♡ English

CHINA AND MONGOLIA

ISOLATED FROM THE western world for centuries, the Chinese were the first to develop the compass, paper, gunpowder, porcelain, and silk. Three autonomous regions lie within western China – Inner Mongolia, Xinjiang, and Tibet. The Gobi desert, in vast Mongolia, is the world's most northern desert.

PEOPLE
Han Chinese make up 93 percent of China's population. China has relaxed its 1979 one-child policy for minority groups, such as the Mongolians, Tibetans, and Muslim Uygurs, after some groups faced near extinction.

HISTORY
Tibet was invaded by China in 1950. The Chinese have destroyed Tibet's traditional agricultural society and Buddhist monasteries. In 1959 there were more than 6,000 monasteries – by 1980, only 179 remained.

L. Uvs
Har Us L.
ALTAI MTS
KAZAKHSTAN
XINJIANG UIGHUR
Ürümqi
AUTONOMOUS
TIEN MTS.
Tarim
L. Bosten
REGION
Tarim Basin
Lop Nur
TAKLA MAKAN
DESERT
ALTUN MTS. H
KUNLUN MTS.
BAY
TIBETAN
Aksai
Chin
(Controlled by
China, claimed
by India)
Demchok AUTONOMOUS
(Claimed by both
TANGGULA MTS
China and India)
REGION
GANGDISE RANGE
Brahmaputra (Yarlung Zangbo)
Lhasa
AFGHANISTAN
PAKISTAN
KYRGYZSTAN
TAJIKISTAN
KARAKORAM MTS.

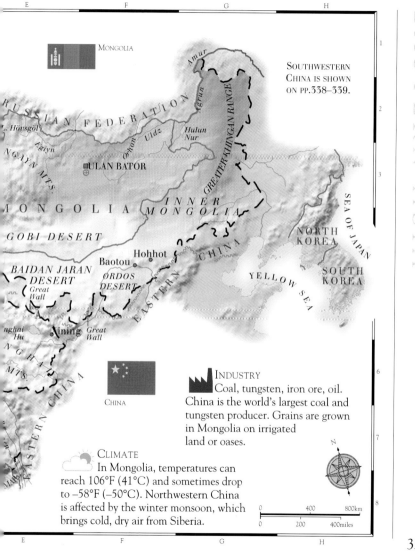

MONGOLIA

SOUTHWESTERN
CHINA IS SHOWN
ON PP. 338–339.

Amur

Argun

R U S S I A N   F E D E R A T I O N

Höysgöl

Egiyn

NOAYN MTS.

Onon *Uldz* *Hulun Nur*

GREATER KHINGAN RANGE

■ULAN BATOR

M O N G O L I A

I N N E R
M O N G O L I A

SEA OF JAPAN

G O B I   D E S E R T

NORTH
KOREA

BAIDAN JARAN
DESERT

Baotou

Hohhot

CHINA

ORDOS
DESERT

Great Wall

YELLOW SEA

SOUTH
KOREA

EASTERN CHINA

nghai Hu

ining

Great Wall

N   MTS.

MA

CHINA

INDUSTRY
Coal, tungsten, iron ore, oil.
China is the world's largest coal and
tungsten producer. Grains are grown
in Mongolia on irrigated
land or oases.

CLIMATE
In Mongolia, temperatures can
reach 106°F (41°C) and sometimes drop
to –58°F (–50°C). Northwestern China
is affected by the winter monsoon, which
brings cold, dry air from Siberia.

N

0   400   800km
0   200   400miles

CHINA AND KOREA

ONE-FIFTH OF the world's population lives in China – mostly in the eastern part of the country. Annexed to Japan in 1910, Korea was divided between the USA and Communist Russia after World War II. North and South Korea were formed in 1948.

NORTHWESTERN CHINA IS SHOWN ON PP.118–119.

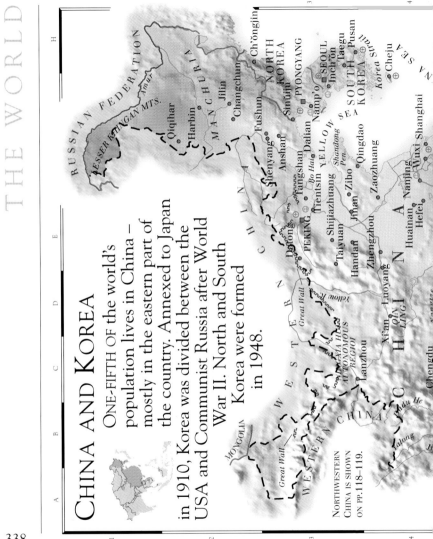

RUSSIAN FEDERATION

LESSER KHINGAN MTS.

Amur

MANCHURIA

Qiqihar

Harbin

Changchun

Jilin

Ch'ŏngjin

NORTH KOREA

PYONGYANG

Sinŭiju

Fushun

Shenyang

Anshan

Dalian

Tangshan

Bo Hai

Trentsin

Nam'p'o

Inch'ŏn

SEOUL

Taegu

Pusan

SOUTH KOREA

Cheju

EA

Korea Strait

YELLOW SEA

Shandong Pen.

Qingdao

Zaozhuang

MONGOLIA

Great Wall

Great Wall

Yellow River

Datong

PEKING

Taiyuan

Shijiazhuang

Handan

Zhengzhou

Luoyang

Xi'an

QIN LING

Zibo

Jinan

Huainan

Hefei

Nanjing

Wuxi

Shanghai

Lanzhou

AUTONOMOUS REGION

WESTERN CHINA

Chengdu

Yalong

CHINA

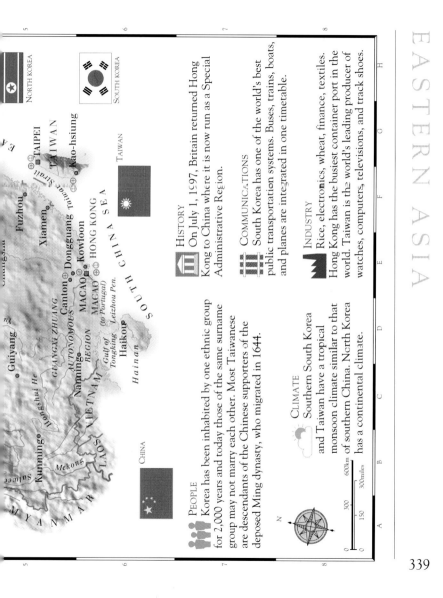

EASTERN ASIA

NORTH KOREA

SOUTH KOREA

TAIWAN

TAIPEI
Kao-hsiung

Taiwan Strait

Fuzhou

Xiamen

Canton Dongguang
Kowloon
MACAO HONG KONG
MACAO
(to Portugal)
Leizhou Pen.
Gulf of
Tongking
Haikou

SOUTH CHINA SEA

Hainan

Chongqing

Guiyang

GUANGXI ZHUANG
AUTONOMOUS
Nanning REGION

Guilin

Hongshui He

VIETNAM

LAOS

Kunming

Mekong

Saigon

MYANMAR

CHINA

PEOPLE
Korea has been inhabited by one ethnic group for 2,000 years and today those of the same surname group may not marry each other. Most Taiwanese are descendants of the Chinese supporters of the deposed Ming dynasty, who migrated in 1644.

CLIMATE
Southern South Korea and Taiwan have a tropical monsoon climate similar to that of southern China. North Korea has a continental climate.

HISTORY
On July 1, 1997, Britain returned Hong Kong to China where it is now run as a Special Administrative Region.

COMMUNICATIONS
South Korea has one of the world's best public transportation systems. Buses, trains, boats, and planes are integrated in one timetable.

INDUSTRY
Rice, electronics, wheat, finance, textiles. Hong Kong has the busiest container port in the world. Taiwan is the world's leading producer of watches, computers, televisions, and track shoes.

N

0   150   300
0   300miles   600km

JAPAN

CONSISTING OF FOUR main islands and 4,000 smaller ones, Japan is the world's leading industrial nation. Since two-thirds of the land is mountainous, the majority of people live on the coast. Japan has about 1,500 minor earthquakes a year, but severe earthquakes, such as the one in Kobe in 1995, occur every few years. Underwater earthquakes sometimes cause huge surge waves, or *tsunami*, along Japan's Pacific coast.

INDUSTRY

Fishing, ship building, motor vehicles, computers, televisions, high-tech electronics. Motor vehicles are Japan's biggest export, and its stock exchange ranks second in the world. Japan excels at producing

HISTORY

Japan was once ruled by warlords called *shoguns*, who discouraged contact with the outside world. In 1639, Japan cut ties with other nations and ordered all Europeans to leave, except the Dutch who were allowed one trading ship per year.

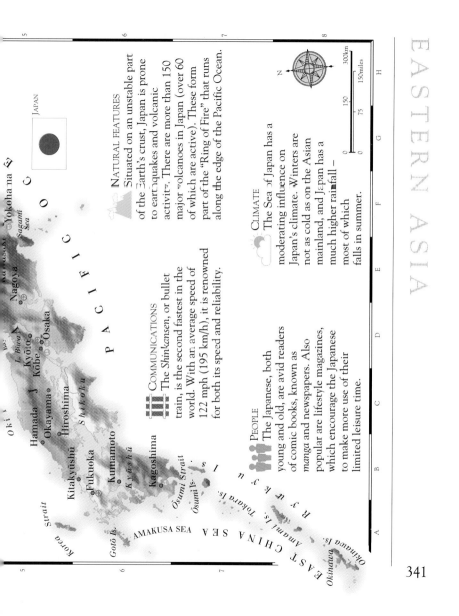

EASTERN ASIA

JAPAN

NATURAL FEATURES

Situated on an unstable part of the Earth's crust, Japan is prone to earthquakes and volcanic activity. There are more than 150 major volcanoes in Japan (over 60 of which are active). These form part of the "Ring of Fire" that runs along the edge of the Pacific Ocean.

CLIMATE

The Sea of Japan has a moderating influence on Japan's climate. Winters are not as cold as on the Asian mainland, and Japan has a much higher rainfall – most of which falls in summer.

COMMUNICATIONS

The *Shinkansen*, or bullet train, is the second fastest in the world. With an average speed of 122 mph (195 km/h), it is renowned for both its speed and reliability.

PEOPLE

The Japanese, both young and old, are avid readers of comic books, known as *manga* and newspapers. Also popular are lifestyle magazines, which encourage the Japanese to make more use of their limited leisure time.

N

0   75   150   300km
0   75   150miles

PACIFIC OCEAN

Yokohama
Sagami Sea
Nagoya
I. Biwa
Kyōto
Kobe
Osaka
Okayama
Hamada
Hiroshima
Shikoku
Kitakyūshū
Fukuoka
Kumamoto
Kyūshū
Kagoshima
Ōsumi Strait
Ōsumi Is.
Ryukyu Is.
Tokara Is.
Amami Is.
AMAKUSA SEA
EAST CHINA SEA
Gotō Is.
Korea Strait
Okinawa Is.
Okinawa

Eastern Asia facts

CHINA

- China has the world's oldest continuous civilization; recorded history began 4,000 years ago.
- Mao Tse-tung founded and dominated communist China from 1949 until his death in 1976.

ESSENTIAL FACTS
- ☉ Beijing
- ◓ 3,628,166 sq miles (9,396,960 sq km)
- ♦ 1.2 billion
- 🕮 Yuan
- ♥ Mandarin
- ▲ Single-party republic
- ♦ 71 years

WONDERWALL
The Great Wall of China is the longest man-made structure in the world.

BAMBOO LUNCH
Pandas living in the forests of China's Szechwan mountains feed on bamboo shoots.

MONGOLIA

- The Mongolian press is strongly outspoken, with no slander or libel laws.
- Most Mongolians are nomadic, but some now live on state-run farms.
- The poorest people in Mongolia cannot even afford to buy bread.

ESSENTIAL FACTS
- ☉ Ulan Bator
- ◓ 604,247 sq miles (1,565,000 sq km)
- ♦ 2.4 million
- 🕮 Tughrik
- ♥ Khalkha Mongolian

MACAO

Chinese territory under Portuguese administration until 1999.

- ☉ Macao
- ♦ 477,850
- ♥ Chinese, Portuguese

MONGOLIAN YAK
Yaks provide Mongolian herders with milk, butter, meat, wool, and leather.

HONG KONG

Territory reverted to Chinese administration in 1997.

- ☉ Victoria
- ♦ 5.8 million
- ♥ English, Cantonese

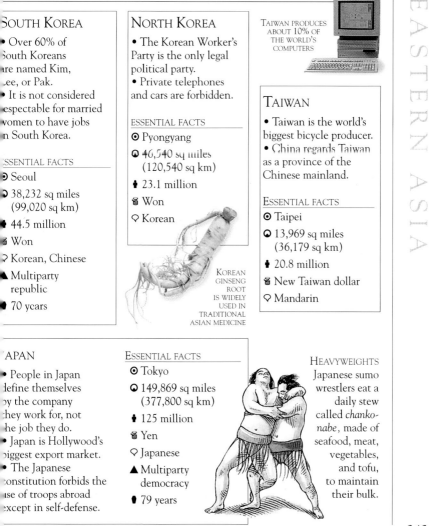

SOUTH KOREA

- Over 60% of South Koreans are named Kim, Lee, or Pak.
- It is not considered respectable for married women to have jobs in South Korea.

ESSENTIAL FACTS

- ⊙ Seoul
- ⌀ 38,232 sq miles (99,020 sq km)
- ✶ 44.5 million
- 💲 Won
- ♀ Korean, Chinese
- ▲ Multiparty republic
- ⬤ 70 years

NORTH KOREA

- The Korean Worker's Party is the only legal political party.
- Private telephones and cars are forbidden.

ESSENTIAL FACTS

- ⊙ Pyongyang
- ⌀ 46,540 sq miles (120,540 sq km)
- ✶ 23.1 million
- 💲 Won
- ♀ Korean

KOREAN GINSENG ROOT IS WIDELY USED IN TRADITIONAL ASIAN MEDICINE

TAIWAN PRODUCES ABOUT 10% OF THE WORLD'S COMPUTERS

TAIWAN

- Taiwan is the world's biggest bicycle producer.
- China regards Taiwan as a province of the Chinese mainland.

ESSENTIAL FACTS

- ⊙ Taipei
- ⌀ 13,969 sq miles (36,179 sq km)
- ✶ 20.8 million
- 💲 New Taiwan dollar
- ♀ Mandarin

JAPAN

- People in Japan define themselves by the company they work for, not the job they do.
- Japan is Hollywood's biggest export market.
- The Japanese constitution forbids the use of troops abroad except in self-defense.

ESSENTIAL FACTS

- ⊙ Tokyo
- ⌀ 149,869 sq miles (377,800 sq km)
- ✶ 125 million
- 💲 Yen
- ♀ Japanese
- ▲ Multiparty democracy
- ⬤ 79 years

HEAVYWEIGHTS Japanese sumo wrestlers eat a daily stew called *chanko-nabe*, made of seafood, meat, vegetables, and tofu, to maintain their bulk.

343

MAINLAND SOUTHEAST ASIA

FOR MOST OF its history, Thailand has been an independent kingdom. Malaysia includes 11 states on the mainland (Malaya), as well as Sabah and Sarawak in Borneo. Cambodia, Laos, and Vietnam have suffered from years of civil war. Myanmar has become more isolated from the world by its repressive government.

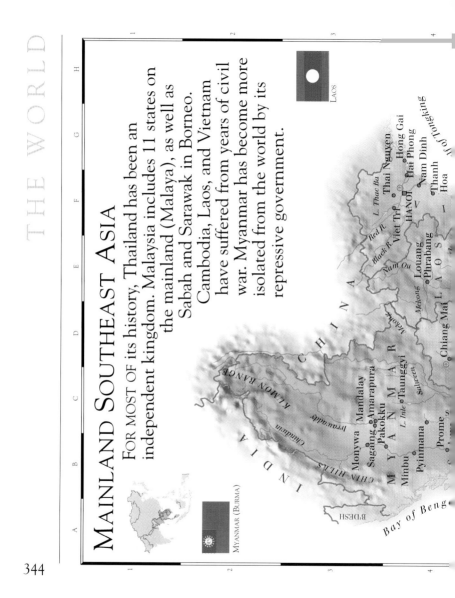

MYANMAR (BURMA)

LAOS

Bay of Bengal

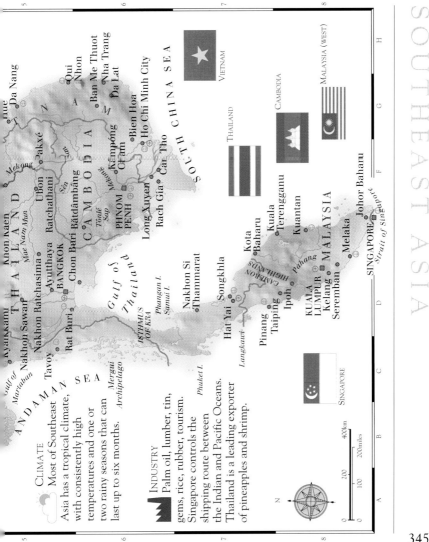

SOUTHEAST ASIA

CLIMATE
Most of Southeast Asia has a tropical climate, with consistently high temperatures and one or two rainy seasons that can last up to six months.

INDUSTRY
Palm oil, lumber, tin, gems, rice, rubber, tourism. Singapore controls the shipping route between the Indian and Pacific Oceans. Thailand is a leading exporter of pineapples and shrimp.

VIETNAM

THAILAND

CAMBODIA

MALAYSIA (WEST)

SINGAPORE

SOUTH CHINA SEA

ANDAMAN SEA

Gulf of
Thailand

Gulf of
Martaban

ISTHMUS
OF KRA

Mergui
Archipelago

Strait of Singapore

CAMERON
HIGHLANDS

VIETNAM

THAILAND

CAMBODIA

MALAYSIA

SINGAPORE

Da Nang
Qui Nhon
Ban Me Thuot
Nha Trang
Da Lat
Bien Hoa
Ho Chi Minh City
Can Tho
Kampong Cham
Rach Gia
Long Xuyen
PHNOM PENH
Bàtdâmbâng
Tonle Sap
Mekong
Sen
Ubon Ratchathani
Pakxé
Khon Kaen
Nakhon Ratchasima
Mae Nam Mun
Ayutthaya
BANGKOK
Chon Buri
Rat Buri
Nakhon Sawan
Ayuthaya
Tavoy
Nakhon Si Thammarat
Songkhla
Hat Yai
Langkawi
Pinang
Taiping
Ipoh
KUALA LUMPUR
Kelang
Seremban
Melaka
Johor Baharu
SINGAPORE
Kota Baharu
Kuala Terengganu
Kuantan
Pahang
Phuket I.
Phangan I.
Samui I.

N

400km
0   200
0   100   200miles

345

MARITIME SOUTHEAST ASIA

SCATTERED BETWEEN the Indian and Pacific Oceans are thousands of tropic mountainous islands. Once called the East Indies, Indonesia was ruled by the Dutch for 350 years. More than half of its 13,677 islands are still uninhabited. The Philippines lie on the "Ring of Fire," and are subject to earthquakes and volcanic activity. Borneo is shared among Indonesia, Malaysia, and Brunei.

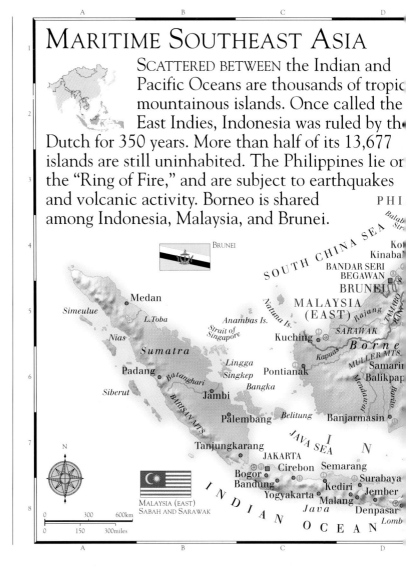

PHI

Balab
Sir

BRUNEI

SOUTH CHINA SEA

Ko
Kinaba

BANDAR SERI
BEGAWAN

BRUNEI

Natuna Is.

MALAYSIA
(EAST)

Rajang

TALABO

Medan

Simeulue

L.Toba

Anambas Is.

SARAWAK

Nias

Strait of
Singapore

Kuching

Borne

Sumatra

Lingga

Kapuas

MULLER MTS.

Padang

Batanghari

Singkep

Pontianak

Samarin

Siberut

Bangka

Balikpap

BARISAN MTS.

Jambi

Mendawai

Barito

Palembang

Belitung

Banjarmasin

JAVA SEA

I

N

Tanjungkarang

JAKARTA

Bogor
Bandung

Cirebon

Semarang

Surabaya

Yogyakarta

Kediri

Jember

Malang

Java

Denpasar

Lomb

INDIAN OCEAN

N

MALAYSIA (EAST)
SABAH AND SARAWAK

| 0 | 300 | 600km |
| 0 | 150 | 300miles |

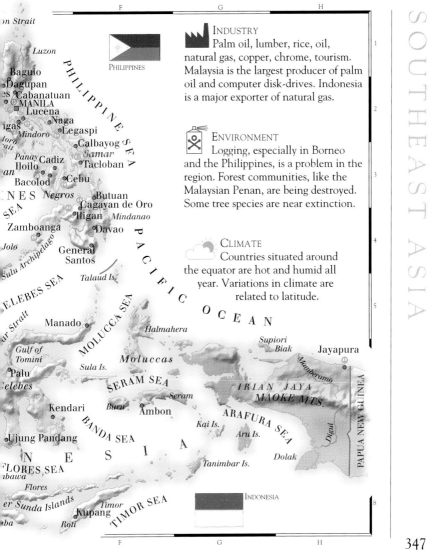

on Strait

Luzon

Baguio
Dagupan
es Cabanatuan
MANILA
Lucena
Naga
gas
Mindoro Legaspi
loro
ait
Calbayog
Panay Cadiz *Samar*
Iloilo Tacloban
an
Bacolod Cebu
N E S *Negros* Butuan
S E A Cagayan de Oro
Iligan *Mindanao*
Zamboanga Davao
Jolo
General
Santos
Sulu Archipelago
Talaud Is.
ELEBES SEA

PHILIPPINES

PHILIPPINE SEA

P A C I F I C

O C E A N

INDUSTRY
Palm oil, lumber, rice, oil,
natural gas, copper, chrome, tourism.
Malaysia is the largest producer of palm
oil and computer disk-drives. Indonesia
is a major exporter of natural gas.

ENVIRONMENT
Logging, especially in Borneo
and the Philippines, is a problem in the
region. Forest communities, like the
Malaysian Penan, are being destroyed.
Some tree species are near extinction.

CLIMATE
Countries situated around
the equator are hot and humid all
year. Variations in climate are
related to latitude.

Manado

Halmahera

Supiori
Biak Jayapura

Gulf of Tomini
MOLUCCA SEA
Sula Is.
Moluccas
Mamberamo

Palu
Celebes
SERAM SEA
Seram
I R I A N   J A Y A
MAOKE MTS.

Kendari
Buru Ambon
ARAFURA SEA
Kai Is.

BANDA SEA
Ujung Pandang
Aru Is.
Digul

I N   E   S   I   A

Dolak

FLORES SEA
abawa
Tanimbar Is.

Flores
er Sunda Islands
Timor
Kupang
TIMOR SEA
ba *Roti*

PAPUA NEW GUINEA

INDONESIA

Southeast Asia facts

MYANMAR

- This country is also called Burma.
- Myanmar exports the most teak in the world.

ESSENTIAL FACTS

⊙ Rangoon

◑ 261,200 sq miles (676,550 sq km)

⚦ 44.6 million

💰 Kyat

♀ Myanmar (Burmese)

LAOS

- In 1994, the Mekong River's "Friendship Bridge" became the first Thai–Laos road link.

LAOS FACTS

⊙ Vientiane

◑ 91,428 sq miles (236,800 sq km)

⚦ 4.6 million

💰 Kip

♀ Lao, Miao, Yao

SINGAPORE

- The nation is the world leader in new biotechnologies.
- Chewing gum is banned by law in Singapore.

SINGAPORE FACTS

⊙ Singapore City

◑ 239 sq miles (620 sq km)

⚦ 2.8 million

💰 Singapore dollar

♀ Malay, Chinese, Tamil, English

THAILAND

- Criticism of the Thai king, who is head of state, is not allowed.
- Thailand, meaning "land of the free," is the only Southeast Asian nation never to be colonized.

MOBILE SHOP
Floating markets are a common sight on the waterways of Southeast Asia.

THAILAND FACTS

⊙ Bangkok

◑ 198,116 sq miles (13,120 sq km)

⚦ 56.9 million

💰 Baht

♀ Thai

▲ Multiparty democracy

⚦ 69 years

VIETNAM

- A new species of mammal, the Vu Quang Ox, was recently discovered in the forests of northern Vietnam.
- The Vietnam war cost two million lives.

VIETNAM FACTS

⊙ Hanoi

◑ 127,243 sq miles (329,560 sq km)

⚦ 70.9 million

💰 New dong

♀ Vietnamese

KOMODO DRAGON
The "dragon" of Komodo in Indonesia is the world's largest lizard.

INDONESIA

- The world's biggest island chain, Indonesia is made up of 13,677 islands spread over 3,000 miles (4,830 km) and three time zones.
- Indonesia was formerly known as the Dutch East Indies.
- Forest survival is threatened by logging.

INDONESIA FACTS
- ⊙ Jakarta
- ⊘ 735,355 sq miles (1,904,570 sq km)
- ✦ 194.6 million
- ✸ Rupiah
- ♀ Bahasa Indonesia
- ▲ Multiparty republic
- ♦ 62 years

BRUNEI
- ⊙ Bandar Seri Begawan
- ✦ 300,000
- ♀ Malay

THE PHILIPPINES

- The Filipino nation is the only Christian country in Asia.

PHILIPPINES FACTS
- ⊙ Manila
- ⊘ 115,831 sq miles (300,000 sq km)
- ✦ 66.5 million
- ✸ Philippine peso
- ♀ Filipino, English
- ▲ Multiparty republic
- ♦ 65 years

CAMBODIA

- Over one million Cambodians died between 1975 and 1979 under Pol Pot's Marxist Khmer Rouge regime.
- Cambodians are descended from the Khmers, who arrived in Southeast Asia around 2,000 B.C.
- Aid provides 70% of government revenue.

CAMBODIA FACTS
- ⊙ Phnom Penh
- ⊘ 69,000 sq miles (181,040 sq km)
- ✦ 9 million
- ✸ Riel
- ♀ Khmer

MALAYSIA

- The nation is the world's leading producer of natural rubber.

ESSENTIAL FACTS
- ⊙ Kuala Lumpur
- ⊘ 127,317 sq miles (329,750 sq km)
- ✦ 19.2 million
- ✸ Ringgit
- ♀ Malay

MALAYSIAN RUBBER
Workers extract latex by cutting rubber trees and collecting the sap that oozes from the cut.

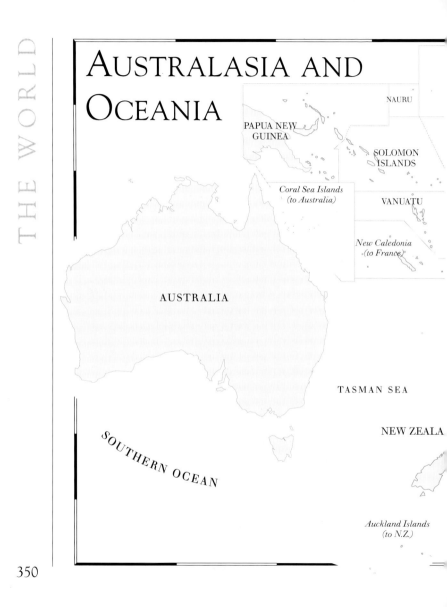

AUSTRALASIA AND OCEANIA

NAURU

PAPUA NEW GUINEA

SOLOMON ISLANDS

Coral Sea Islands
(to Australia)

VANUATU

New Caledonia
(to France)

AUSTRALIA

TASMAN SEA

NEW ZEALA

SOUTHERN OCEAN

Auckland Islands
(to N.Z.)

KIRIBATI

Tokelau
(to N.Z.)

WESTERN
SAMOA
*Futuna
e)*

*American
Samoa
(to U.S.A.)*

*Cook Islands
(to N.Z.)*

*Niue
(to N.Z.)*

TONGA

*French Polynesia
(to France)*

*Pitcairn
Islands
(to U.K.)*

*Chatham Island
(to N.Z.)*

AUSTRALASIA AND OCEANIA

Millions of years ago, the continent of
Australia and the islands of New Guinea
and New Zealand split away from the
other southern continents. These island
countries have many unique plants and
animals, such as Australia's marsupials,
or pouched mammals. The thousands of
islands scattered in the Pacific are either
volcanic islands or coral atolls.

PACIFIC OCEAN

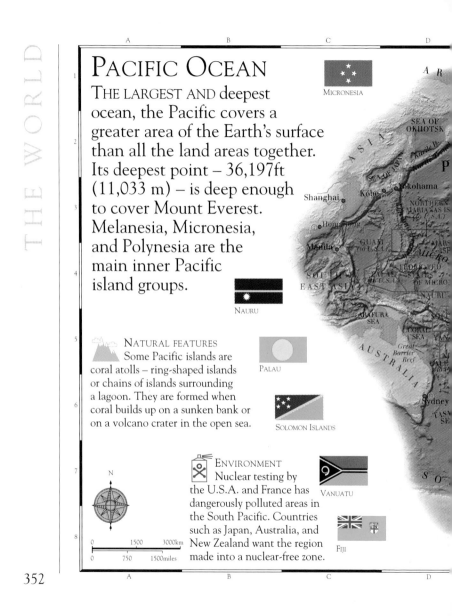

PACIFIC OCEAN

THE LARGEST AND deepest ocean, the Pacific covers a greater area of the Earth's surface than all the land areas together. Its deepest point – 36,197ft (11,033 m) – is deep enough to cover Mount Everest. Melanesia, Micronesia, and Polynesia are the main inner Pacific island groups.

MICRONESIA

NAURU

NATURAL FEATURES
Some Pacific islands are coral atolls – ring-shaped islands or chains of islands surrounding a lagoon. They are formed when coral builds up on a sunken bank or on a volcano crater in the open sea.

PALAU

SOLOMON ISLANDS

ENVIRONMENT
Nuclear testing by the U.S.A. and France has dangerously polluted areas in the South Pacific. Countries such as Japan, Australia, and New Zealand want the region made into a nuclear-free zone.

VANUATU

FIJI

N

0   1500   3000km
0   750   1500miles

MARSHALL ISLANDS

KIRIBATI

TONGA

WESTERN SAMOA

TUVALU

AUSTRALIA AND PAPUA NEW GUINEA

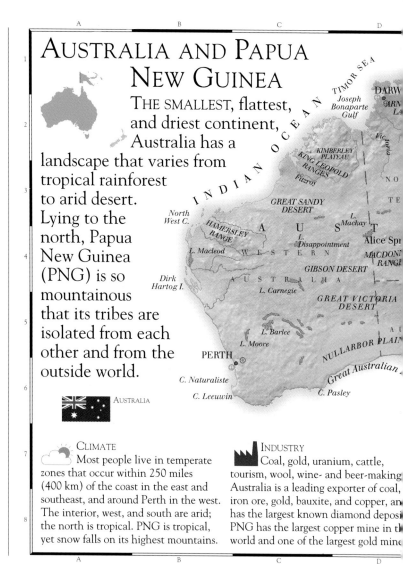

THE SMALLEST, flattest, and driest continent, Australia has a landscape that varies from tropical rainforest to arid desert. Lying to the north, Papua New Guinea (PNG) is so mountainous that its tribes are isolated from each other and from the outside world.

AUSTRALIA

TIMOR SEA

DARW

Joseph Bonaparte Gulf

INDIAN OCEAN

KIMBERLEY PLATEAU

KING LEOPOLD RANGES

Fitzroy

GREAT SANDY DESERT

North West C.

HAMERSLEY RANGE

L. Macleod

WESTERN

A U S

L. Disappointment

L. Mackay

Alice Spr

MACDONI RANGE

GIBSON DESERT

Dirk Hartog I.

AUSTRALIA

L. Carnegie

GREAT VICTORIA DESERT

L. Barlee

L. Moore

PERTH

NULLARBOR PLAIN

Great Australian

C. Naturaliste

C. Leeuwin

C. Pasley

CLIMATE
Most people live in temperate zones that occur within 250 miles (400 km) of the coast in the east and southeast, and around Perth in the west. The interior, west, and south are arid; the north is tropical. PNG is tropical, yet snow falls on its highest mountains.

INDUSTRY
Coal, gold, uranium, cattle, tourism, wool, wine- and beer-making Australia is a leading exporter of coal, iron ore, gold, bauxite, and copper, an has the largest known diamond deposi PNG has the largest copper mine in th world and one of the largest gold mine

E · F · G · H

*FURA
EA*

Torres Strait

. Arnhem

CAPE
YORK
PENINSULA

*Gulf of
arpentaria*

Mitchell

Flinders

GREAT DIVIDING RANGE

Townsville

PACIFIC

Great Barrier Reef

OCEAN

L · I · A

Diamantina

QUEENSLAND

*SON
RT*

Cooper Creek

A

*FLINDERS
RANGES*

Darling

N E W
S O U T H
W A L E S

BRISBANE
Gold
Coast

Newcastle
SYDNEY
Wollongong

Murray

Murrumbidgee

ADELAIDE · CANBERRA
AUSTRALIAN
CAPITAL
TERRITORY

garoo I.

VICTORIA

Geelong · MELBOURNE

Bass Strait *Flinders I.*

*TASMAN
SEA*

N

C. Grim

TASMANIA

HOBART
*South
East C.*

300 · 600km
150 · 300miles

Bismarck
Archipelago *New
Ireland*
BISMARCK SEA
New Guinea *New
Britain*
PAPUA NEW
GUINEA · SOLOMON SEA
PORT
MORESBY

INDONESIA

Fly

CORAL SEA

PAPUA NEW GUINEA

PEOPLE
The first people in
Australia were Aboriginals,
a nomadic people who
reached the continent
from Southeast Asia
about 50,000 years ago.

FLORA AND FAUNA
Due to its isolation,
Australia has many unique
animals such as koalas and
kangaroos. The platypus and
the echidna, which is also
found in New Guinea, are
the only egg-laying mammals.

NATURAL FEATURES
The Great Barrier Reef, a series
of coral reefs and islands, stretches
over 1,240 miles (2,000 km) just off
the Queensland coast. It is the world's
largest marine park and is composed
entirely of living coral polyps.

NEW ZEALAND

ONE OF THE LAST places on Earth to be inhabited by people, New Zealand lies about halfway between the equator and the South Pole. It is made up of the main North and South Islands, separated by the Cook Strait, and numerous smaller islands. The first settlers were Maoris, who came from the Polynesian islands about 1,200 years ago.

FLORA AND FAUNA

Many of New Zealand's animals have been introduced – two species of bat are the only native land mammals. New

NATURAL FEATURES

New Zealand lies on the "Ring of Fire," a band of volcanic activity that almost encircles the Pacific Ocean. New Zealand has about 400 earthquakes each year, although only about 100 are strong enough to be felt.

PEOPLE

In recent years, Maoris have protested the lack of observance of the Treaty of Waitangi, which protected their rights. About 10 percent of the total population are Maori.

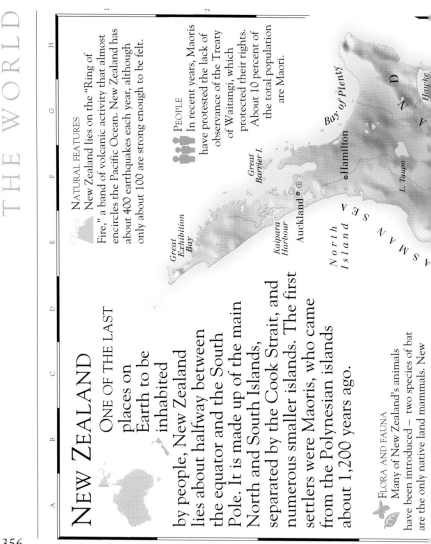

Great Exhibition Bay

Kaipara Harbour

Auckland

North Island

Great Barrier I.

Bay of Plenty

Hamilton

L. Taupo

TASMAN SEA

D

N

V

Hawke

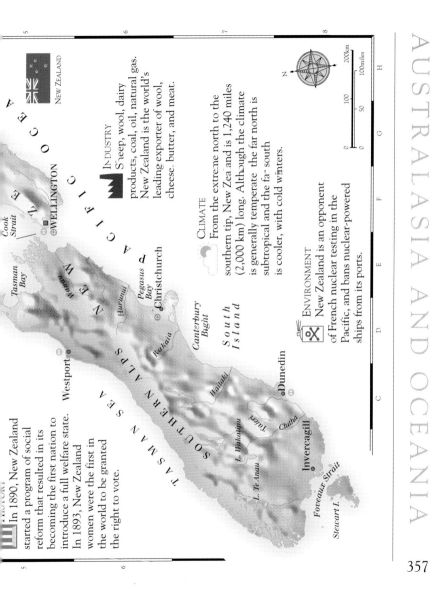

HISTORY

In 1890, New Zealand started a program of social reform that resulted in its becoming the first nation to introduce a full welfare state. In 1893, New Zealand women were the first in the world to be granted the right to vote.

INDUSTRY

Sheep, wool, dairy products, coal, oil, natural gas. New Zealand is the world's leading exporter of wool, cheese. butter, and meat.

CLIMATE

From the extreme north to the southern tip, New Zea and is 1,240 miles (2,000 km) long. Although the climate is generally temperate the far north is subtropical and the far south is cooler, with cold winters.

ENVIRONMENT

New Zealand is an opponent of French nuclear testing in the Pacific, and bans nuclear-powered ships from its ports.

NEW ZEALAND

PACIFIC OCEAN

WELLINGTON

Cook Strait

Tasman Bay

Westport

Hurunui

Rakaia

Pegasus Bay

Christchurch

Canterbury Bight

South Island

Waitaki

SOUTHERN ALPS

TASMAN SEA

L. Wakatipu

L. Te Anau

Pukaki

Clutha

Dunedin

Invercagill

Foveaux Strait

Stewart I.

N

200km

100miles

Australasia and Oceania facts

AUSTRALIA

• The suburban area of the city of Sydney is the largest in the world; it is twice as large as Beijing and six times the size of Rome.

• Aboriginal land and civil rights claims are an increasingly important item on the political agenda.

ESSENTIAL FACTS

⊙ Canberra

◔ 2,967,893 sq miles (7,686,850 sq km)

♦ 18.5 million

▩ Australian dollar

♡ English

▲ Multiparty democracy

♦ 77 years

SURF'S UP
Surfing and water sports are popular Australian leisure activities.

NEW ZEALAND

• The landscape of New Zealand is the most varied in the world relative to its size, offering mountains, fjords, lakes, glaciers, rain forests, beaches, mud pools, and geysers.

• Many of New Zealand's top jobs in business and politics are held by women.

ESSENTIAL FACTS

⊙ Wellington

◔ 103,730 sq miles (268,680 sq km)

♦ 3.5 million

▩ New Zealand dollar

♡ English

▲ Multiparty democracy

♦ 75 years

KIWI BIRD
The flightless kiwi is the most famous of New Zealand's creatures.

PAPUA NEW GUINEA

• The feathers of certain unique bird species in Papua New Guinea produce a poison that causes painful blisters on contact with human skin.

ESSENTIAL FACTS

⊙ Port Moresby

◔ 178,700 sq miles (462,840 sq km)

♦ 4.1 million

▩ Kina

♡ English

VANUATU
⊙ Port-Vila
♦ 155,000
♡ Bislama, English, French

FIJI
⊙ Suva
♦ 700,000
♡ English, Fijian

PALAU
⊙ Koror
♦ 16,000
♡ Palauan, English

KIRIBATI
⊙ Bairiki
♦ 66,000
♡ English, Kiribati

TONGA
⊙ Nuku'alofa
♦ 101,000
♡ Tongan, English

TUVALU
⊙ Fingafale
♦ 9,000
♡ Tuvaluan, Kiribati

WESTERN SAMOA
⊙ Apia
♦ 162,000
♡ Samoan, English

NAURU
⊙ No official capital
♦ 10,000
♡ Nauruan, English

MARSHALL ISLANDS
⊙ Majuro
♦ 48,000
♡ English, Marshallese

SOLOMON ISLANDS
⊙ Honiara
♦ 400,000
♡ English

MICRONESIA
⊙ Kolonia
♦ 101,000
♡ English

Thatched roof
made of palm
fronds

Simple
house

Wooden outrigger
boat with main
hull and twin
floats

Home-grown food

ISLAND LIFE
On the more remote islands of the Pacific, people
live much as their ancestors did, fishing,
keeping animals, and growing fruit and vegetables.

ATLANTIC OCEAN

BENEATH THE WATERS OF the Atlantic Ocean lies the Mid-Atlantic Ridge, one of the world's longest mountain chains. Some of its peaks are so high they form islands, such as the Azores. Apart from a wide rift-valley in the center of the ridge, the ocean consists of vast featureless plains and is 5 miles (8 km) at its deepest point.

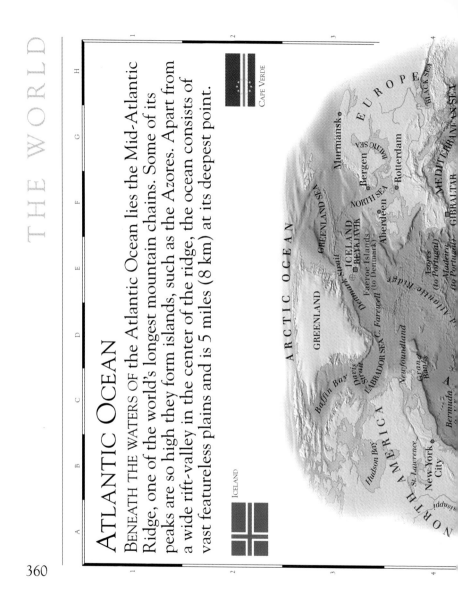

ICELAND

CAPE VERDE

ARCTIC OCEAN

EUROPE

Murmansk

BALTIC SEA

Bergen

NORTH SEA

Rotterdam

GREENLAND SEA

GREENLAND

Denmark Strait

ICELAND
REYKJAVIK

Faeroe Islands
(to Denmark)

Aberdeen

BLACK SEA

MEDITERRANEAN SEA

GIBRALTAR

Azores
(to Portugal)

Madeira
(to Portugal)

Mid-Atlantic Ridge

Baffin Bay

Davis
Strait

LABRADOR SEA C. Farewell

Newfoundland

Grand
Banks

NORTH AMERICA

Hudson Bay

St. Lawrence

New York
City

Bermuda

Mississippi

N

0	75	150	300km
0	75	150	150miles

CENTRAL CARIBBEAN SEA
AMERICA

La Guaira

PANAMA CITY

Amazon

SOUTH AMERICA

BUENOS AIRES

Río de Janeiro

Argentine Basin

Falkland Islands
(to U.K.)

South Georgia
(to U.K.)

Cape of Horn

SCOTIA SEA

South Sandwich Islands
(to U.K.)

WEDDELL SEA

ANTARCTICA

Mid-Atlantic Ridge

ATLANTIC OCEAN

Niger

Lagos

SÃO TOMÉ & PRÍNCIPE

Ascension Island
(to U.K.)

St. Helena
(to U.K.)

Tristan Da Cunha
(to U.K.)

Walvis Ridge

Congo

AFRICA

Cape Town

Cape of Good Hope

Atlantic Indian Ridge

Bouvet Island
(to Norway)

VERDE

ENVIRONMENT
The North Atlantic was once the world's richest fishing ground, but overfishing has reduced the numbers of cod and herring to low levels.

NATURAL FEATURES
Iceland lies on the rift where the North American and European continental plates are pulling apart, and has about 200 volcanoes. Domestic heating, from geothermal sources, is almost free.

INDIAN OCEAN

THE SMALLEST of the world's oceans, the Indian Ocean has some 5,000 islands scattered across its area. Beneath its surface, three great mountain ranges converge toward the ocean's center – an area of strong seismic and volcanic activity. The ocean's greatest depth, 24,400 ft (7,440 m), is in the Java Trench.

FLORA AND FAUNA
Owing to Madagascar's position off the African coast, many of its animals, such as tenrecs, lemurs, and fossas, are unique.

ENVIRONMENT
The Indian Ocean is at risk of pollution from tankers carrying oil from the Persian Gulf, which is already badly polluted.

CLIMATE
The monsoon winds blow over the Indian Ocean – from the southwest or from the northeast according to the season. The southwesterly monsoon brings heavy rains to southern Asia.

COMOROS

MALDIVES

SEYCHELLES

INDIAN OCEAN

N

0   1000   2000km
0   500   1000miles

Dar es Salaam · Aldabra Is. (to Seychelles) · Amirante Is. (to Seychelles) · INDIAN · Ridge · British Indian Ocean Territory (to UK) · Java Sea · Java · Java Trench · Ninety East Ridge · West Australian Basin · COCOS IS. (to Australia) · CHRISTMAS IS. (to Australia) · Ashmore & Cartier Is. (to Australia) · North West C. · AUSTRALIA · Fremantle

MORONI · Mayotte (to France) · COMOROS · **ANTANANARIVO** · Le Port · **PORT LOUIS** · **MAURITIUS** · Réunion (to France) · OCEAN · Broken Ridge · Amsterdam I. (to France) · St Paul I. (to France) · C. Leeuwin

Zambezi · Beira · MADAGASCAR · Madagascar Basin · Southwest Indian Ridge · Crozet Is. (to France) · Kerguelen (to France) · Heard I. & McDonald Is. (to Australia) · ANTARCTICA

Limpopo · Durban · Cape of Good Hope · Cape Town · Prince Edward Is. (to South Africa) · Atlantic-Indian Basin

MAURITIUS

MADAGASCAR

PEOPLE
Many Madagascans are descended from Indonesians who crossed the Indian Ocean. Their language, Malagasy, is Malay-Indonesian in origin.

THE ANTARCTIC

CONTAINING 80 PERCENT of the world's freshwater, the continent of Antarctica lies buried under ice more than 1.2 miles (2 km) thick. The surrounding seas are partly frozen, and icebergs barricade over 90 percent of the coastline.

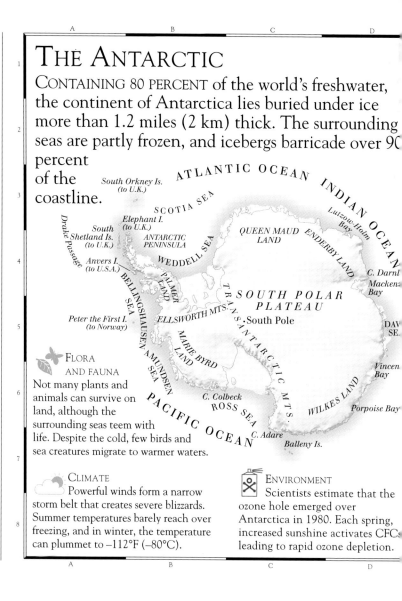

FLORA AND FAUNA

Not many plants and animals can survive on land, although the surrounding seas teem with life. Despite the cold, few birds and sea creatures migrate to warmer waters.

CLIMATE

Powerful winds form a narrow storm belt that creates severe blizzards. Summer temperatures barely reach over freezing, and in winter, the temperature can plummet to −112°F (−80°C).

ENVIRONMENT

Scientists estimate that the ozone hole emerged over Antarctica in 1980. Each spring, increased sunshine activates CFCs leading to rapid ozone depletion.

THE ARCTIC

A FROZEN OCEAN surrounded by land, the Arctic is covered by ice up to 98 ft (30 m) thick. Most of the surrounding tundra, or vast treeless plains, are permanently frozen.

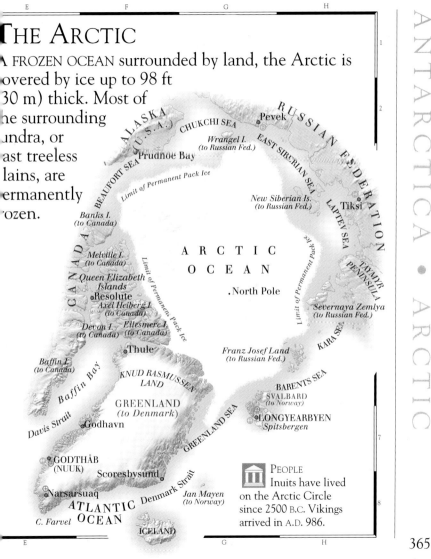

ALASKA (U.S.A.)

CHUKCHI SEA

Pevek

RUSSIAN FEDERATION

Wrangel I.
(to Russian Fed.)

EAST SIBERIAN SEA

Prudhoe Bay

BEAUFORT SEA

Limit of Permanent Pack Ice

New Siberian Is.
(to Russian Fed.)

Tiksi

LAPTEV SEA

Banks I.
(to Canada)

CANADA

Melville I.
(to Canada)

Queen Elizabeth Islands

Resolute

Axel Heiberg I.
(to Canada)

Devon I.
(to Canada)

Ellesmere I.
(to Canada)

Limit of Permanent Pack Ice

ARCTIC

OCEAN

.North Pole

TAYMYR PENINSULA

Severnaya Zemlya
(to Russian Fed.)

KARA SEA

Limit of Permanent Pack Ice

Thule

Franz Josef Land
(to Russian Fed.)

Baffin I.
(to Canada)

Baffin Bay

KNUD RASMUSSEN LAND

GREENLAND
(to Denmark)

Davis Strait

Godhavn

GREENLAND SEA

BARENTS SEA

SVALBARD
(to Norway)

LONGYEARBYEN
Spitsbergen

GODTHÅB
(NUUK)

Scoresbysund

Narsarsuaq

ATLANTIC

OCEAN

C. Farvel

Denmark Strait

Jan Mayen
(to Norway)

ICELAND

PEOPLE
Inuits have lived on the Arctic Circle since 2500 B.C. Vikings arrived in A.D. 986.

WORLD TIME ZONES

IMAGINARY LINES are drawn around the globe, either parallel to the equator (latitude) or from pole to pole (longitude, or meridians). The Earth is divided into 2~ time zones, one for each hour of the day. Greenwich i~ on 0° meridian and time advances by one hour for every 15° of longitude east of Greenwich.

TIME ZONES
The numbers on the map indicate the number of hours which must be subtracted or added to reach GMT. When it is noon at Greenwich, for example, it is 7 a.m. in New York City. Time zones are adjusted to regional administrative boundaries.

KEY TO MAP

MINUS HOURS

PLUS HOURS

GREENWICH MEAN TIME

DATE LINE

TIME ZONES

ATLANTIC
OCEAN

INDIAN
OCEAN

SOUTHE~

366

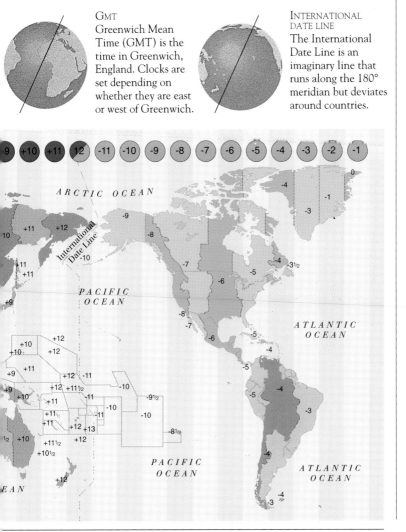

GMT
Greenwich Mean Time (GMT) is the time in Greenwich, England. Clocks are set depending on whether they are east or west of Greenwich.

INTERNATIONAL DATE LINE
The International Date Line is an imaginary line that runs along the 180° meridian but deviates around countries.

-9 +10 +11 12 -11 -10 -9 -8 -7 -6 -5 -4 -3 -2 -1

ARCTIC OCEAN

0

-4

-1

-3

-9

+11 +12

International Date Line

-8

-10

+11

-7

-4

-3½

+11

-5

+9

PACIFIC OCEAN

-6

-8

+10 +12

-7

ATLANTIC OCEAN

+10

+12

+11

-6

-5

-4

+9

+12 -11

-10

-5

+9 +10

+12 +11½

-9½

+11

-11

-10

-5

+11

+12 13

-11

-10

-3

½ +10

+11½

+12

-8½

+10½

-4

PACIFIC OCEAN

ATLANTIC OCEAN

+12

EAN

-4

-3

PEOPLE AND SOCIETY

MYTHS AND LEGENDS

ALMOST EVERY culture has stories, or myths, to explain the world around them. Legends are tales which have some basis in real events.

MYTHICAL BEASTS

Many myths are about fantastic beasts, such as the unicorn (a single-horned horse) and the phoenix (a bird that rises from its own ashes). The dragon is a winged serpent that breathes fire. It is an important symbol in cultures as far apart as Wales and China.

DRAGON'S BREATH

SACRED SITES

• Mt. Shasta in California is sacred to Native Americans.

• Uluru (Ayers Rock) in Australia is sacred to the Aboriginals.

• The Tor (mound) at Glastonbury, England, is said to be the resting place of the Holy Grail, the cup Christ drank from at the Last Supper.

KING ARTHUR

One of Britain's most famous legendary figures is the hero King Arthur, who is thought to be based on a real 5th-century Celtic chieftain. One of the many stories about King Arthur tells how he was given the magic sword Excalibur by the Lady of the Lake, as shown in the above picture.

AZTEC MYTHS

The mythical world of the Aztec people of Central Mexico was dominated by the figure of Quetzalcoatl. He was the chief god of the Aztecs, and took the form of a feathered serpent. According to myth, Quetzalcoatl created humans and gave them knowledge. Afterward, he sailed away on a raft of serpents.

This mask, made of turquoise mosaic, represents Quetzalcoatl, the chief god of the Aztecs.

Greek myths

Many stories are told about ancient Greece. Legendary tales, such as those surrounding the Trojan War, have a basis in historical fact, while myths about figures like Perseus and Medusa are more fantastic.

Theseus

Minotaur

PERSEUS AND MEDUSA

One Greek myth tells the story of Perseus, who beheaded a gorgon called Medusa. The gorgon's head had the power to turn people to stone.

Perseus

Gorgons have a head of snakes instead of hair

THESEUS AND THE MINOTAUR

The Minotaur was a mythical creature, half-man and half-bull, that lived in a labyrinth (maze) on the island of Crete. It was eventually slain by a Theban prince called Theseus.

Greek soldiers hid inside the huge wooden horse

MASK OF KING AGAMEMNON

TROJAN HORSE

According to legend, when the Greeks were fighting the Trojans, they beat them by a trick. They built a wooden horse, then hid in it, outside the gates of Troy. The Trojans dragged the wooden horse into the city to see what it was. At night, the Greek soldiers crept out and opened the city gates to let their army in.

TROJAN WARS

In *The Iliad*, which Homer wrote around 1200 B.C., the legend tells how Agamemnon, King of Mycenae, Greece, led an army against the Trojans to rescue his brother's captured wife, Helen.

RELIGIONS

MOST PEOPLE HAVE some kind of belief or faith that helps to explain life and death. Many worship either one or several gods. The four major world religions are Christianity, Islam, Hinduism, and Buddhism.

CHRISTIANITY

Christians believe that Jesus Christ is the Son of God, and when Jesus was crucified (nailed to a cross), he rose from the dead to join God in Heaven. Christianity has more followers than any other religion.

The cross is the symbol of Christianity.

ORIGIN
Christianity began in about A.D. 30 in Jerusalem, in present-day Israel.

THE BIBLE

This Christian holy book is made up of two parts called the Old and New Testaments. In the Old Testament are the sacred writings of the Jews. The New Testament tells the story of Christ's life and the origin of Christianity.

The first Bible was printed in 1455, by Johannes Gutenberg.

JESUS CHRIST

Jesus lived in the Holy Land (Israel) about 2,000 years ago. From the age of 30, he began to preach and heal the sick. He was tried and put to death for openly challenging Hebrew beliefs.

TEN COMMANDMENTS

Christians try to obey ten rules, which are adapted from the Jewish scriptures.

1 Worship one God.
2 Make no image of God.
3 Respect God's name.
4 Keep Sunday holy.
5 Honor your parents.
6 Do not kill.
7 Do not commit adultery.
8 Do not steal.
9 Do not tell lies.
10 Do not be envious.

ISLAM

A star and a crescent moon symbolize Islam.

The followers of Islam are Muslims, who believe in Allah. Islam means "submission," and Muslims believe they must obey Allah and live by the five pillars (rules) set out in their holy book, the *Koran*.

ORIGIN
Islam began in about A.D. 600 in Mecca, in present-day Saudi Arabia. It is now practiced all over the world.

THE KORAN
In Islam's holy book, Allah shows the prophet Muhammad how people should live. Muslims treat this book with great respect, and must wash before touching it.

KORAN (*Qur'an*)

MUHAMMAD
Born in Mecca, Muhammad (c. 570–632) was the last and the greatest of the 26 Islamic prophets.

• *Muhammad is Allah's messenger.*

HINDUISM

The symbol of Hinduism is the sound "Om."

Hindus worship many gods, and believe in *dharma*, the correct way to live. Like Buddhists, Hindus believe we have all lived before, as animals as well as people. By following the *dharma*, we may achieve a perfect state of *Moksha* and need never be reborn again.

ORIGIN
Hinduism began in India, around 1750 B.C. It has spread through much of Asia.

VEDAS
About 1400 B.C., Hindu beliefs were written as songs and chants in the *Vedas*.

The Rig Veda is the most important book of the Vedas.

FOUNDERS
Hinduism has no single founder. The Aryans, who invaded India nearly 4,000 years ago, brought early Hindu gods, such as Shiva.

SHIVA

BUDDHISM

The symbol of Buddhism is an eight-spoked wheel.

The Buddhist faith is based on the teachings of Buddha, who believed that we must rid ourselves of desire in order to free ourselves from suffering. Buddhists believe that life is a sequence of birth, death, and rebirth, and that by following the Eightfold path of Buddhism, we can reach a state of peace called *Nirvana*.

Extracts from the Pali Canon

THE PALI

The collected teachings of Buddha are called the *Pali Canon*. The best-known is the *Dhammapada*.

ORIGINS
Buddhism began in India in around 500 B.C. It is now the religion of around 300 million people.

BUDDHA
Prince Siddhartha Gautama (Buddha) lived about 563–483 B.C. He gave up his riches to preach and meditate.

Buddha means "enlightened one."

SIKHISM

The Khanda is the symbol of Sikhism.

This faith began in northern India. It is based on the worship of one God, the eternal Guru, and on the cycle of rebirth.

GURU GRANTH SAHIB

This book is treated with great respect

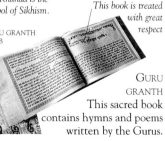

GURU GRANTH
This sacred book contains hymns and poems written by the Gurus.

ORIGINS
Sikhism began in north India and Pakistan around 1500. It has spread to North America and Britain.

Sikh men wear a turban

THE FIVE K'S

Sikhs must wear these five items: *Kesh* (uncut hair, under a turban, if a man); *Kara* (a steel bracelet); *Kangha* (a hair comb); *Kirpan* (a sword); and *Kaccha* (short pants as an undergarment).

JUDAISM

Followers of Judaism are called Jews. They believe in one God whose law is written in the *Tanach*. Judaism began about 4,000 years ago in Canaan. Today this area is mainly Israel.

The Jewish symbol is the Star of David.

ORIGINS
Judaism originated around 2000 B.C. in Canaan, "the Promised Land." Today, Judaism has spread to most parts of the world.

TANACH
The Jewish Bible, or *Tanach*, tells the history of the Jewish people. The *Torah* is the most important part, since it contains the laws that God revealed to Moses.

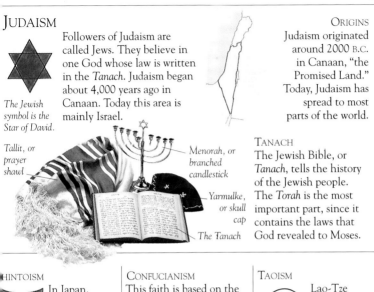

Tallit, or prayer shawl

Menorah, or branched candlestick

Yarmulke, or skull cap

The Tanach

SHINTOISM

In Japan, Shintoists worship gods of nature, and there are Shinto shrines in parks, gardens, and on mountains. Shintoists worship alone, and their symbol is the outline of a temple gate.

According to Shinto faith, Mount Fuji is a Shinto god. People come to pray at a shrine on its summit.

CONFUCIANISM

This faith is based on the teachings of K'ung-Fu tzu (551–479 B.C.), or Confucius, who was known for his wise sayings. In the *Analects*, Confucius taught the wisdom of living in harmony with nature. He said "Never do to others what you would not like them to do to you."

K'UNG-FU-TZU

TAOISM

YIN YANG

Lao-Tze founded the faith of Taoism in China 2,400 years ago. Taoists believe in many gods. Their symbol of *Yin Yang* represents the balance and harmony of opposites.

The name Lao-Tze means "Old Master."

LAO-TZE

375

GODS AND GODDESSES

MANY OF THE ANCIENT civilizations, such as those in Greece, Rome, and Egypt, worshipped several gods and goddesses.

Ancient Egypt

The gods and goddesses of ancient Egypt often had the body of a human and the head of an animal, which represented that creature's power. The chief of the gods was the Sun god Re, who had different names at different times of the day.

BASTET, THE CAT GODDESS

HORUS' EYE
The symbol of the "wadjet" eye represents the vengeful eye of Horus, torn out in the struggle for Egypt.

"WADJET" EYE

BASTET
The goddess Bastet was the daughter of Re, the Sun god. She represented the power of the sun to ripen crops, and she took the form of a cat.

OSIRIS
The god of the underworld and judge of the dead was called Osiris. People believed he ruled over a world below ground that looked like Egypt. Osiris took the form of a mummified man.

OSIRIS

ANUBIS
The son of Osiris was the god Anubis, who had the head of a jackal. Anubis was said to guide the souls of the dead to Osiris for their judgment.

ANUBIS

376

Ancient Greece

The Greeks believed that all the gods were the descendants of Gaia (the earth) and Uranos (the sky), and that they behaved in the same way as humans.

Aphrodite

HEPHAESTUS
The God of fire and the husband of Aphrodite, Hephaestus was lame.

Eros

MIRROR CASE

Pan

ZEUS
The King of the gods was Zeus, who is represented as a strong, middle-aged man. He was noble, but easily angered.

APHRODITE
The Greek goddess of love was called Aphrodite.

APOLLO
The young god of the sun and of medicine was Apollo.

Ancient Rome

The Romans adopted many Greek gods and gave them new names. Aphrodite became Venus, Zeus became Jupiter, and Ares, the god of war, became Mars.

TEMPLE OF AUGUSTUS AND LIVIA

TEMPLES
Many emperors were made gods after their death. Temples such as this were built in their honor.

JUPITER
The king of the Roman gods, Jupiter was a sky-god whose symbols were the eagle and the thunderbolt. Jupiter was much like the Greek god Zeus.

MONEY AND TRADE

THE METAL COINS and paper banknotes that we use to buy things are called money, or currency. Money also comes in the form of credit cards, checks, and the computer records of a bank account.

Cowrie shells were used as money

EARLY MONEY
Before coins were invented, people used to exchange stones, shells, beads, and furs for food and other goods.

EARLY LYDIAN COIN

THE FIRST COINS
The earliest known coins were made in the kingdom of Lydia (now Turkey) more than 2,700 years ago. These coins were weighed lumps of electrum (a mix of silver and gold), which were stamped, or "minted," to guarantee their weight.

14TH-CENTURY CHINESE PAPER MONEY

THE FIRST PAPER MONEY
In 10th-century China, people began to leave their coins with merchants, in exchange for a handwritten paper receipt. In the 11th century, the Chinese government fixed the value of these receipts. This became the first paper money.

MAKING BANKNOTES
Banknotes have to be printed in a very elaborate and secret way to reduce the chances of forgery. The four stages of making a banknote are designing, paper-making, ink-mixing, and printing. The design is engraved on a steel plate by hand. This is called "intaglio" engraving.

The design for the banknote is hand engraved back-to-front on to a steel plate

Burnisher for smoothing

Sharp "burins" for engraving the design

PRINTING PLATE

PROOF FOR
BACKGROUND

PROOF FOR MAIN DESIGN

*This design uses eight inks, printed
in reds, yellows, blues, and buffs.*

*Every note is
individually
numbered*

NUMBERING
MACHINE

*The finished
specimen
banknote is
shown to
customers all
over the world.*

FINISHED BANKNOTE

THE STOCK MARKET

People often raise money
to start a business by
selling "shares" in it.
If the business make a
profit, the shareholders
receive a dividend
(payment). The stock
market is where shares, or
stocks, are bought and sold
by "stockbrokers."

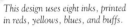

IMPORTS AND EXPORTS

BALANCE OF TRADE

Countries measure their
success at trading by their
"balance of payments,"
which is the difference
between the amount
they sell abroad
(exports) and the amount
they buy (imports).

TOKYO STOCK EXCHANGE, JAPAN

| KEY STOCK EXCHANGES | | |
Country	City	Index
Japan	Tokyo	Nikkei Average
United States	New York	Dow-Jones
United Kingdom	London	FTSE-100 *
Germany	Frankfurt	DAX **

* Financial Times Stock Exchange 100
** Deutsche Aktien Index

GOVERNMENT AND LAW

ALL COUNTRIES are run by a government. Some are harsh dictatorships, and others are liberal democracies. Every government implements policies that affect the everyday lives of the nation's people. The business of government is called politics.

DEMOCRACY
This system, in which a country is ruled by the people, or their elected representatives, began in Athens, Greece, 2,500 years ago. Many other countries are now governed in this way.

Pericles was lead of democratic Athens at the height of its powe

POLITICAL SYSTEMS
Most countries are "capitalist," and the land and businesses are owned by individuals or small groups. In "communist" countries, all businesses are state-run. "Socialists" believe that governments should grant everyone equal rights, a fair share of money, education, health, and housing.

COMMUNIST MAGAZINE

Abraha Lincoln w US preside 1861-6.

REPUBLIC
Most countries are republics, which have no king or queen. The "head of state" is a president who is elected by the people. The government is also elected by the people. A country with a king or queen is called a monarchy. Kings were once thought to rule by God's will. Their power is now usually limited by a set of rules called a constitution.

PARLIAMENT
In many countries, government policy is debated and the laws are agreed upon in an assembly called parliament. People elect members of parliament to act as their representatives.

HOUSE OF COMMONS, UK

BRANCHES OF GOVERNMENT

THE CAPITOL, HOME OF THE US CONGRESS, WASHINGTON, D.C.

LEGISLATURE
The legislature is an elected assembly, or "house," that amends and makes laws. In the US, it is called Congress.

EXECUTIVE
The executive puts laws into effect and administers the country. It is headed by a president or a prime minister who appoints heads of different departments.

JUDICIARY
The judiciary makes sure that laws are applied fairly. In the US, the highest legal body is the Supreme Court.

Law
Every country has rules, or laws, to help people live together and to keep them in order. Laws are decided by governments or religious leaders and they are enforced by the police and the courts.

CRIMINAL LAW
Criminal law covers crimes such as murder and theft.

CIVIL LAW
This kind of law deals with disputes, rather than crimes. Civil law also deals with day-to-day events such as buying a house and making a will.

COURT ROOM

Judge helps jury on points of law, and passes sentence if verdict is "guilty"

Lawyer

A person on trial is "the accused"

In Britain, a jury must consist of 12 men and women over 18 years old

TRIAL
People accused of crimes are usually taken to court to be "tried." Typically, trials are "adversarial" – one set of lawyers (the prosecution) tries to prove that the accused is guilty, while another (the defense) tries to prove that he or she is innocent. A judge or a jury (a group of ordinary men and women) decides who is right.

381

BUILDINGS

HOUSES, CHURCHES, and offices
are all buildings. The design and
construction of buildings is called
architecture.

*In Oceania, "longhouses" are built
on stilts in case of flooding*

TRADITIONAL HOMES

People around
the world build
their homes from
the materials they
have available.
From houses of
timber or stone,
to huts of mud or
woven reeds,
every country
has its own style.

*In South Africa, the dome-
shaped kraals have grass roofs.*

*Swiss chalets are built
from wooden timbers.*

*Some Asian nomads live
in canvas or felt "yurts."*

*Algerian houses are close
together to keep out the sun.*

*Japanese houses have
sliding doors.*

*North American houses
have wooden "clapboards."*

CLASSICAL ARCHITECTURE

There are three styles, or
orders, of classical Greek
architecture: Doric,
Ionic, and Corinthian.
The columns of Greek
temples often have a
decorative head, or
capital, on the top.
Across the columns is a
broad lintel called the
entablature. This
consists of an architrave,
a frieze, and a cornice.

Entablature   *Frieze*

Decorative capital

CLASSICAL GREEK TEMPLE

ORDERS

These three
orders were used
in three different
periods of history.

*Doric was used
from 700 B.C.*

*Ionic was used
from 600 B.C.*

*Corinthian was
used from 500 B.C.*

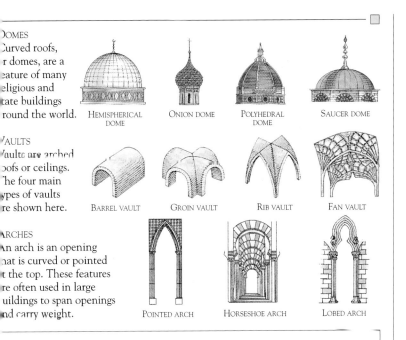

DOMES

Curved roofs, or domes, are a feature of many religious and state buildings around the world.

HEMISPHERICAL DOME

ONION DOME

POLYHEDRAL DOME

SAUCER DOME

VAULTS

Vaults are arched roofs or ceilings. The four main types of vaults are shown here.

BARREL VAULT

GROIN VAULT

RIB VAULT

FAN VAULT

ARCHES

An arch is an opening that is curved or pointed at the top. These features are often used in large buildings to span openings and carry weight.

POINTED ARCH

HORSESHOE ARCH

LOBED ARCH

SKYSCRAPERS

The invention of reinforced concrete, plate glass, and steel in the mid 1800s enabled architects to design and build extremely tall constructions, or "skyscrapers." The first skyscrapers were built in Chicago. Giant buildings are now found in most major cities. At 452 m (1,482 ft), the Petronas Tower, in Kuala Lumpur, Malaysia, is the world's tallest building.

NEW YORK SKYSCRAPERS

Many of the skyscrapers in New York City were erected in part by Iroquois and Mohawk Indians, who showed no fear of heights.

Cathedral-like spire

Art Deco crown

WOOLWORTH BUILDING 1913

GENERAL ELECTRIC BUILDING 1930s

WORLD TRADE CENTER 1971

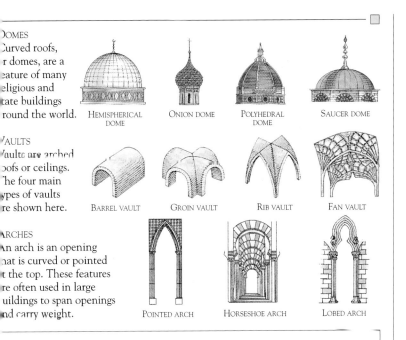

c. 6500 B.C. One the first known towns, Çatal Hüyük, is built in present-day Turkey, using rectangular mud bricks.

c. 2650–2150 B.C. Pyramids are built in the lower Nile valley, in Egypt. The Step Pyramid at Saqqara is designed by a High Priest called Imhotep, who is the first known architect.

Massive stones arranged in a huge circle

STONEHENGE, ENGLAND

c. 2200 B.C. Stonehenge is built in England, using massive stones. It was probably built as a religious monument.

c. 2112–2095 B.C. The Sumerians build stepped temples called ziggurats in Mesopotamia, using mud bricks.

c. 1700–1200 B.C. Beehive tombs, or tholos, are built by the Mycenaean civilization on the Greek mainland.

c. 1500 B.C. The Minoan Palace of Knossos is rebuilt on the Greek island of Crete.

800–200 B.C. Etruscans use arches in the construction of their buildings in what is now called Italy.

700–400 B.C. The ancient Greeks build temples of such perfect proportions that their style of building becomes known as "classical." This classical style of architecture is copied many times throughout history.

THE PARTHENON, ATHENS, GREECE

c. 300 B.C. Buddhists build stupas (mounds) in India and southeastern Asia to symbolize the dome of heaven.

c. 200 B.C.–A.D. 500 Roman architecture takes over the classical Greek style and the Etruscan arch. The Romans introduce concrete, which enables them to build huge vaults and arches.

A.D. 300–1540 Pre-Columbian civilizations in the Americas build stepped pyramids crowned with temples. One of these is the pyramid known as Giant Jaguar, at Tikal in Guatemala.

330–1453 The Byzantine style of architecture develops when the Roman Empire moves its capital to Byzantium, renaming it Constantinople (now Istanbul Turkey). The largest dome of its time, the Hagia Sophia, is built there in A.D. 537.

607–670 The oldest surviving wooden building, the Horyuji Buddhist monastery, is built at Nara, in Japan.

618–782 The earliest Chinese timber building, the Nanchan Buddhist temple, is built on a holy mountain in Shaanxi province.

690–850 Early Islamic mosques and palaces are designed around courtyards.

00–1150 The Romanesque style
architecture spreads across western
urope, featuring round-headed arches
n top of cylindrical columns.
100–1500 The Gothic style is used in
hristian churches in northern Europe.
has pointed arches and flying buttresses,
lowing very tall, light structures.
113–1150 Angkor Wat, a vast stone
ty, is built by the Khmers in what is now
ambodia.
1420 The Renaissance begins in Italy,
viving Roman and Greek building
ethods. Brunelleschi (1377–1446) and
lberti (1404–72) are key figures.

ie city is
owned
th
ires
aped
e
us buds

ANGKOR WAT,
CAMBODIA

1650 The Baroque style is developed.
rchitects are commissioned by the
atholic Church to build very grand,
nate churches and palaces.
750–1840 Neoclassical architects
turn to plain, elegant Roman and
reek styles of building.
330–1930s During a Gothic revival,
chitects build churches, public
ildings, and even train stations,
ying to recapture the style of
edieval cathedrals.

1840–90 The Industrial Revolution
provides new materials, such as plate glass,
steel, and reinforced concrete, which
transform traditional building methods.
1890 After the elevator is invented,
the first skyscrapers are built in Chicago.
1900–40s American architect Frank
Lloyd Wright (1867–1959) promotes
"organic" architecture, designing
buildings that blend in with nature.
1919–33 Walter Gropius (1883–1969)
leads a design team in Weimar,
Germany (the Bauhaus school),
creating designs based on modern
industrial technology.
1920s The Swiss architect
Le Corbusier (1887–1965) leads
the new style of International
Modernism in building design.
1970s A "hi-tech" style, with
much steel, glass, and exposed
pipes, is led by Richard Rogers
(b. 1933) and Norman
Foster (b. 1935).
Late 1970s Postmodern
design develops. New designs
blend elements from the
architectural styles of
different eras and cultures.
1980s–1990s Architects
begin to take environmental
concerns into account, such
as recycling and saving
energy. Some new buildings
feature solar power.

EMPIRE STATE BUILDING,
NEW YORK CITY

385

ARTISTS' MATERIALS

ARTISTS paint pictures and create sculptures.
The main materials that an artist needs for painting
are sketching materials (for an initial drawing or a
finished work), paint and paintbrushes, and a surface
to paint on. This surface may be paper for watercolor
painting, canvas for oils, or wood for acrylics.

SCULPTURE

A sculptor can use almost
any material for sculpting,
but bronze, marble,
and clay are the most
popular for figurative
work (based on
the human
body).

Early
sculptures, like
this figurine of a
woman, were made of clay.

MATERIAL FACTS

• The first paintbrushes
were made using hog
hairs tied to sticks.

• Thousands of years
ago in Australia, artists
mixed natural pigments
in their mouths to paint
cave walls.

DETAIL FROM CARAVAGGIO'S YOUTH WITH A RAM

A top layer of
varnish protects
painting

The oil paint
applied
laye

Size

Priming

Ground

Drawin
lay

Imprimatura

LAYERS OF A PAINTING

Traditionally, an oil painting has several layers
By analyzing each of these layers, experts are abl
to date a picture accurately, and they can also te
if it is a fake. This artwork, showing a section o
Caravaggio's Youth with a Ram, shows the layer
that were used in paintings of the 17th century

Conté crayon
Charcoal
Pencil
Graphite stick

Reed pen
and ink

DRAWING TOOLS

Most drawings are sketches (quick drawings) done as a preparation for a finished work. But a drawing can also be a finished picture in itself. Artists usually draw with dry materials such as pencils, crayons, or charcoal.

PAINTS

The three main kinds of paint are oils, which were first used in the 1400s; watercolors, popular with 18th-century landscape artists; and acrylics, popular in the 1960s.

Oil paints are a mixture of dry pigment and an oil such as linseed.

Watercolor paints are pigments bound with gum arabic. They are diluted with water.

Acrylic paints are either applied with a knife or diluted and used with a paintbrush.

PAINTBRUSHES

The two main kinds of paintbrushes are soft-hair brushes for watercolors, and bristle brushes for oil paintings and acrylics. The length and shape of the hairs on a brush may be round, flat, or "filbert."

ROUND   FLAT   FILBERT

MONA LISA

The most famous painting is Leonardo da Vinci's *Mona Lisa*, painted in 1503. It is a portrait of Lisa, the wife of a nobleman named Francesco del Gioconda. That is why the painting is sometimes called *La Gioconda*.

MONA LISA, THE LOUVRE, PARIS

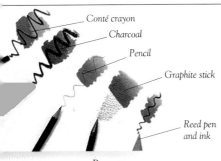

Malachite makes a green pigment.   *Lapis lazuli makes a blue pigment.*

PIGMENTS

Paint is made from powdered colors called pigments. These were originally natural colors from plants and rocks, but today most are made using chemicals.

387

2700 B.C.–A.D. 599

c. 27,000 B.C. Small clay statues of pregnant women, known as "Venus figurines" appear across Europe.

c. 15,000 B.C. Early artists use fingers, brushes and hollow reeds to paint animals on the walls of the Lascaux caves, France.

c, 4000–1000 B.C. Egyptian art includes wall and scroll paintings, gold jewelry, and painted statues sculpted from limestone.

VENUS FIGURINE, FRANCE C. 27,000 BC

2000–1100 B.C. Minoans on the island of Crete, Greece, decorate their palace walls with colored murals.

1600–1027 B.C. The Shang dynasty in China discovers how to cast bronze and create bowls and urns for food and wine.

c. 500 B.C. The Nok culture in Nigeria, West Africa, produces lifelike terra cotta figurines of humans.

c. 500–323 B.C. Greek sculptors produce statues of gods and athletes made of marble, bronze, and clay.

A.D. 100–400 Gandharan sculpture develops in the Indus valley, Pakistan. It is influenced by Greek art, and shows scenes from the life of Buddha.

100–1000 Mayan carvings are created in Central America, combining ornate figures with hieroglyphs (picture writing).

400–1110 Medieval monks in Europe create illuminated manuscripts.

600–1839

600–1185 Icons (religious portraits) are painted in Eastern Europe.

618–907 Chinese artists of the T'ang dynasty paint stunning landscapes.

1000–1200 The Romanesque style develops in the church sculptures and murals of Europe.

1000–1600 Huge stone figures are made on Easter Island, Polynesia.

1368–1644 The Ming dynasty in China is famous for its blue-glazed porcelain bowls and vases.

1400–1500 The Renaissance begins in Florence, Italy. Masaccio (1401–28) uses perspective in his paintings.

Late 1400s Islamic miniature painting flourishes in Persia.

1490–1520 The High Renaissance, exemplified in works by Leonardo da Vinci

THE ANNUNCIATION, LEONARDO DA VINCI

(1452–1519), Michelangelo (1475–1564), and Raphael (1483–1520).

1600s The golden age of Dutch painting, with pictures by Rembrandt (1606–69) and Vermeer (1632–75).

Late 1700s–mid 1800s The Romantic school, notably Turner (1775–1851) and Friedrich (1774–1840) focuses on human emotions and nature.

1840s Realism develops in France, with painters such as Courbet (1819–77) depicting people in a more lifelike way.

THE WINNOWERS, GUSTAVE COURBET 1855

1850s–70s In England, Pre-Raphaelites such as Millais (1829–96), Burne-Jones (1833–98), and Rossetti (1828–82) are influenced by artists before Raphael, but develop their own style of painting.

1860s–90s Impressionism begins in France as painters try to capture their impressions of fleeting moments, especially Monet (1840–1926) and Manet (1832–83).

1880–1905 Postimpressionist artists such as Cézanne (1839–1906), van Gogh (1853–90), and Gauguin (1848–1903) develop their own style, using strong colors and shapes.

1880s–1890s Expressionism develops in Europe as artists such as Kirchner (1880–1938) use intense color and free brush strokes to express their feelings.

1880s–90s Symbolist artists such as Moreau (1826–98) create images based on symbolic inner meanings.

1907–1920s Cubism develops in Paris with Picasso (1881–1973) and Braque (1882–1963) using bold geometric shapes.

1910–50 Artists of the Abstract movement, led by Kandinsky (1866–1944) begin to paint and sculpt ideas instead of realistic objects.

1916 The Dada movement, originally a protest against World War I, rejects traditional forms of art.

1920s Surrealist painters such as Dali (1904–89) and Ernst (1891–1976) explore their dreams and Freud's psychoanalytic ideas in their painting.

1940s Abstract Expressionism appears in New York, where artists such as Jackson Pollock (1912–56) experiment with the physical properties of paint.

1950s–60s Pop Art develops in the US and Britain as artists such as Warhol (1928–87) begin to use consumer goods and images from the media in their art.

1960s–90s Performance artists such as Gilbert (b. 1943) & George (b. 1942) combine music, theater, film, and video in their work.

1970s–90s Video artists such as Korean-born Nam Jun-Paik (b. 1932) feature video projection and computer technology in their exhibitions.

PLANTED, GILBERT AND GEORGE, 1992

MUSICAL INSTRUMENTS

THERE ARE THOUSANDS of musical instruments, each making its own distinctive sound. They are usually grouped into percussion, strings, woodwinds, brasses, and keyboards.

Strings

All stringed instruments consist of a series of stretched strings connected to a hollow box that amplifies (makes louder) the string's vibrations. The string is set in motion by being plucked, as with a harp; by the friction of a bow, as with a violin, or by being struck, as with a piano.

HARP
Harps date back at least 6,000 years. Strings stretched over a frame are finger-plucked to give a beautiful rippling sound. This harp is for traditional Irish music.

IRISH HARP

Strands of horse hair

VIOLIN AND BOW

Tuning pins are turned to change pitch of each string

Thinnest string has highest pitch

VIOLIN
The violin family was invented in around 1550 and now consists of the violin, viola, cello and bass. The strings are usually played with a bow.

All members of the violin family have an F-shaped sound hole

Screw for tightening bow

Bridge supports strings

Magnetic pick-ups convert string vibrations into electrical signals

Machine heads for tuning strings

Frets

Neck

Steel truss rod to strengthen neck

Tremolo arm

ELECTRIC GUITAR

GUITAR
The electric guitar is a key instrument in rock and pop music. On an electric guitar, plucked strings are amplified electronically.

Crash cymbal Tom-tom drums

Ride cymbal

DRUM KIT

Snare drum Bass drum

PERCUSSION

Instruments that are played by striking them are called percussion. They include drums, cymbals, xylophones, gongs, and much more. Percussion underlines the rhythm of the music.

Heavy iron frame

Hammers strike strings to make sound

Tuning pins

88-note keyboard – pressing the keys swings hammers

KEYBOARD

Keyboards, including harpsichord, piano, organ, and synthesizer, are among the most versatile of all instruments. They are played by pressing levers or keys with the fingers.

WIND INSTRUMENTS

WOODWINDS

Flutes, clarinets, oboes, and bassoons all have a reed in the mouthpiece to set up the vibrations that make the sound. They are called woodwinds even though they are often made of brass.

Mouthpiece

Pads change notes

Thumb keys   Neck

SAXOPHONE

The saxophone is neither woodwind, nor brass. It is shaped like a brass instrument but has a reed.

Bell projects sound

Blow hole

FLUTE

BRASS

Brass instruments include cornet, trumpet, horn, tuba, and trombone. The sound is made by the vibration of the player's lips against the mouthpiece.   Valve

CORNET

MUSIC

ROCK, JAZZ, AND FOLK MUSIC are often played from
memory by small groups of talented musicians.
Some types of music, such as classical music, is
written down for soloists or groups of musicians.

THE ORCHESTRA

Orchestras range from small
string orchestras to huge
symphony orchestras.
Similar instruments are
grouped together.

WOODWINDS
PERCUSSION
BRASSES
BRASSES
STRINGS
Conductor
STRINGS

*A symphony orchestra
usually has about 90 players.*

MUSICAL GROUPS

Musical groups range from duos with two
performers to symphony orchestras with
up to 120.

*A jazz quartet includes
drums and bass; a
string quartet is two
violins, viola, and cello.*

*A quintet usually
has five wind or
five brass
instruments.*

CELLO AND PIANO DUO

Violin Viola Cello

STRING TRIO

JAZZ QUARTET

MIXED QUINTET

PITCH
The pitch of each note is shown by how high it sits on the staff. Musical pitch is grouped into eight notes called an octave. The notes of each octave are named from low to high using the letters A to G, plus the A that begins the next octave.

ONE OCTAVE OF THE SCALE OF C MAJOR

C Major notes on stave correspond to white keys on piano keyboard

C D E F G A B C D E

PIANO KEYBOARD

NOTE VALUES		
Name	**Sign**	**Rest**
Whole note (4 beats)	o	—
Half note (2 beats)		
Quarter note (1 beat)		
Eighth note (½ beat)		
Sixteenth note (¼ beat)		
Thirty-second (⅛ beat)		

Key signature shows which key music is in

More than two notes played together produces a chord

Natural sign cancels sharp or flat on next note

Rest shows length of pause in music

Treble clef
The bass staff has a bass clef

Dynamic markings indicate how loud or soft to play music – mf means mezzo-forte, or moderately loud

mf

Time signature shows type and number of beats in a bar, or measure

Dot makes note half as long again

Eighths equal half a beat

Bar line marks end of bar, or time measure

sf

Sforzando means accent (emphasize) the note loudly

MUSICAL NOTATION

Composers write down music using an international code of signs and symbols that enables musicians to interpret and play a composition. The notes are written on two bands of five lines, called staves. The lower staff (bass) is for low notes; the upper staff (treble) is for higher notes. Music is divided into measures called bars, each with the same number of beats.

MUSIC

393

Before 15,000 B.C. Stone Age people play bone flutes.

c. 3000 B.C. Harps and lyres appear in Sumerian writing.

2600 B.C. Pa-Pab-Bi-gagir-gal of Ur in Mesopotamia is the first musician whose name is known.

c. 2500 B.C. Oldest known harp placed in Queen Puabi's tomb at Ur.

EGYPTIAN TOMB PAINTINGS

2200 B.C. Groups of musicians appear in Egyptian tomb paintings.

605 B.C. King Nebuchadnezzar of Babylon has an orchestra play at the dedication ceremony of an image of himself made in gold.

c. 550 B.C. The ancient Greek philosopher Pythagoras (580–500 B.C.) creates the first mathematical theory of musical harmony.

408 B.C. The oldest fragment of written music is a chorus for a play called *Orestes*, by ancient Greek dramatist Euripides (c. 484–406 B.C.).

A.D. 650 School for church music founded in Rome by Pope Gregory (c. A.D. 540–604) develops Gregorian style of singing.

700s Orchestras play *gamelan* (gongs) in Indonesia, to accompany traditional puppet shows and dance.

750 The Court of Caliph Harun al-Rashid in Persia becomes famous for its music, played by musicians like Ishaq al-Mausili (767–850).

1100s Monks add a second or third tune to the simple "plainsong" of the Gregorian chant to create the first polyphonic music.

1300s Paris becomes focus of polyphonic music, and early French composer Guillaume de Machaut (1300–77) writes ballads (songs) in this form.

1480 First printed music in Europe.

1500s Palestrina (1525–94) and Monteverdi (1567–1643) write

FIRST PRINTED MUSIC IN EUROPE

polyphonic vocal masses for church.

1500s Polyphonic music played on instruments such as viola and lutes, especially for dances such as the pavane.

1600s Opera developed by the Camerata, a group of poets and musicians in Florence, Italy.

1600–1750 Baroque-era composers write in harmony, creating melody by combining notes from the major and minor scales. Baroque pieces contrast loud and soft, fast and slow musical passages.

TIMELINE OF MUSIC

650–1700
Composers like J.S. Bach (1685–1750), Vivaldi (1678–1741), and Handel (1685–1759) write elaborate instrumental works called sonatas and concerto grossos.

J.S. BACH

750–1820
In the classical era, composers produce elegant, clearly structured instumental pieces.

Late 1700s
Classical music is brought to a peak by Mozart (1756–91) and Beethoven (1770–1827).

Early 1800s
Beethoven writes emotional, passionate pieces on a grand scale, ushering in the romantic era.

820–1900
The romantic era features composers such as Schubert (1797–1828), Berlioz (1803–69), and Wagner (1813–83), who write great piano and orchestral works.

830s–1850s
Liszt (1811–86) and Chopin (1810–49) compose dazzling, virtuoso piano music.

870s–1880s
Verdi (1813–1901) takes opera to new heights.

860s–1890s
Composers like Dvořák (1841–1904), Grieg (1843–1907), and Tchaikovsky (1840–93), are inspired by the folk music of their countries.

870s
Wagner creates a new form of music drama.

Late 1800s Blues played by black Americans.

c. 1900 Jazz music appears in New Orleans, US, combining African rhythms and Western harmony.

Early 1900s Composers, like Stravinsky (1882–1971) and Bartók (1881–1945), begin to write music in which dissonance (clashing notes) creates a thrilling sound.

1910s onward Schoenberg (1874–1951) creates "atonal" music in which the tonal center (key) shifts continually.

1930s Gershwin (1898–1937) mixes jazz and classical music in *Rhapsody in Blue*.

1950s Black Americans play rock and roll, later taken up by white singers, such as Buddy Holly and Elvis Presley.

1960s Rock and roll develops into rock, with bands such as The Who and The Rolling Stones, and pop, with groups like The Beatles and The Beach Boys.

1970s Groups such as The Bee Gees and Chic make disco music popular.

1980s Electronic dance music emerges from black American neighborhoods into mainstream music.

1990s Energetic dance beats, such as house, techno, and jungle, are popular. Emergence of guitar-based "alternative" rock.

SINGER CHUCK BERRY

DANCE TIMELINE

15,000 B.C. Stone Age rock paintings show people dancing.

TANZANIAN ROCK PAINTING

3000–1000 B.C. Ancient Egyptians use ritual dance to worship gods such as Isis.

A.D. 400 First Kagura dances are performed at Shinto shrines in Japan.

1300–1500 Mass dances in Europe cause frenzy.

Late 1400s *Ballo*, Italian dance with a story line, is the earliest form of ballet.

c. 1600 Kathakali dance emerges in India.

1830s–1840s Romantic ballet flourishes.

c. 1900 Isadora Duncan (1877–1927) develops freer forms of modern dance.

1930s Fred Astaire popularizes tap dancing.

1950s Rock-and-roll dancing.

1980s Break dancing and slam dancing are born.

FRED ASTAIRE

1990s Companies design dances for TV and stage.

DANCE

OVER THOUSANDS of years, varied styles of dance have developed all over the world.

BALLET

The three main ballet styles are romantic, classical, and modern, distinguished mainly by differences in clothing and music. All ballet dancers learn five basic positions for the arms and feet.

FIVE BASIC ARM POSITIONS

FIRST

SECOND

THIRD

FOURTH

FIFTH

FIVE BASIC FEET POSITIONS

FIRST

SECOND

THIRD

FOURTH

FIFTH

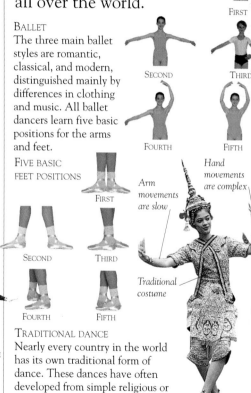
Hand movements are complex

Arm movements are slow

Traditional costume

THAI CLASSICAL DANCER

TRADITIONAL DANCE

Nearly every country in the world has its own traditional form of dance. These dances have often developed from simple religious or tribal rituals into complex dance forms with set movements.

THEATER

MODERN THEATER originated in ancient Greece, where actors wearing masks were used to tell a story or demonstrate a theme.

THEATER BUILDING

The ancient Greeks saw theater in vast open-air stadiums; modern theaters are smaller and indoors, and take many forms.

Several exits for complex plays

ENGLISH 16TH-CENTURY THEATER

Seats

Rows of tiered seats gave a good view

ANCIENT GREEK AMPHITHEATER

MODERN THEATER

SHAKESPEARE

William Shakespeare (1564–1616) was born in Stratford-upon-Avon, England. In about 1590, he moved to London, where he wrote at least 37 plays, including *Hamlet* and *Romeo and Juliet*.

KABUKI THEATER

The performers of Kabuki theater are men who wear elaborate makeup to play a particular role.

WICKED MALE

CRAB

NOBLE MALE

THEATER TIMELINE

c. 3000 B.C. Religious rituals involve music and drama.

c. 1000 B.C. Chinese and Indian dance-dramas become formalized.

c. 500 B.C. Ancient Greeks see dramas by Aeschylus (525–456 B.C.), Sophocles (496–406 B.C.), and Euripides (484–406 B.C.).

A.D. 1–100 "Pantomimus" popular in Rome.

c. 1500 Commedia dell'Arte, mimed comedy, spreads from Italy.

1603 Okuni, a young Japanese woman, creates Kabuki theater.

Early 1600s Theater flourishes in England and Spain with writers like Shakespeare and Lope de Vega (1562–1635).

COMMEDIA DELL'ARTE

c. 1800 Peking Opera begins in China.

1870s–90s New form of realistic drama created by Ibsen (1828–1906).

PEKING OPERA

3500 B.C.–A.D. 1380	1380–1840s

c. 3500 B.C. The oldest known writing, marks on clay tablets, are made at the Sumerian city of Uruk.

3300 B.C. Egyptians write in hieroglyphs (picture writing).

c. 2000 B.C. The Sumerian epic *Gilgamesh* is recorded on clay tablets.

c. 800 B.C. The Greek writer Homer writes *The Iliad*.

600 B.C. The Greek writer Aesop writes his fables, which include the story of *The Boy Who Cried Wolf* and *The Crow and Pitcher*.

AESOP'S FABLES

500 B.C. Hindu *Bhagavadgita* written.

200 B.C. Greeks invent parchment.

c. 30–19 B.C. Roman writer Virgil writes *The Aeneid*.

A.D. 105 Chinese invent paper.

868 Earliest printed book, the Chinese *Diamond Sutra*.

1007 In Japan, Murasaki Shikibu (973–1014) writes *The Tale of Genji*, the world's first novel.

1048–1123 Persian poet Omar Khayyam writes *The Rubáiyát*.

1190–1320 Icelandic saga (oral tales) written down.

1321 Dante (1265–1321) writes his *Divine Comedy* in Ravenna, Italy.

c. 1350 Boccaccio (1313–75) writes *The Decameron* in Florence.

c. 1387 Chaucer (1343–1400) writes *The Canterbury Tales* in Windsor Castle.

c. 1450 Johann Gutenberg (1390–1468) invents printing by movable type in Germany.

GUTENBERG'S BIBLE

1605 Cervantes (1547–1616) writes *Don Quixote*, a satire about an elderly Spanish knight.

1667 English poet Milton (1608–74) writes *Paradise Lost*.

1697 French author Charles Perrault (1628–1703) writes *Tales of Mother Goose*.

1719 English writer Daniel Defoe (1660–1731) writes *Robinson Crusoe*.

1808 German poet Goethe (1749–1832) writes *Faust*.

1811–1817 Jane Austen (1775–1817) writes *Pride and Prejudice, Emma,* and other novels.

1818 Mary Shelley (1797–1851) writes *Frankenstein*.

1830s French novelist Balzac (1799–1850) writes *Père Goriot*.

1841 American writer Edgar Allen Poe (1809–49) writes *Murders in the Rue Morgue*, the first detective story.

1840–70 Charles Dickens (1812–70) writes *Great Expectations, Oliver Twist,* and other novels, often in parts that were serialized in magazines of the time.

1840s Charlotte Brontë (1816–55) writes *Jane Eyre*, her sister Emily (1818–48) *Wuthering Heights*.

CHARLOTTE BRONTË

1851 American writer Herman Melville (1819–91) writes *Moby Dick*.

1852 American writer Harriet Beecher Stowe (1811–96) writes *Uncle Tom's Cabin* about the injustice of slavery.

1857 French writer Gustave Flaubert (1821–80) writes *Madame Bovary*.

1862 French writer Victor Hugo (1802–85) writes *Les Misérables*.

1864 French writer Jules Verne (1828–1905) writes *Journey to the Center of the Earth*.

1865–72 Russian writer Tolstoy (1828–1910) writes *War and Peace*.

1866 Russian writer Dostoyevsky (1821–81) writes *Crime and Punishment*.

1867 French writer Émile Zola (1840–1902) writes *Thérèse Raquin*.

1873 The first typewriter is made in the US by the Remington company.

1881 American author Henry James (1843–1916) writes *Portrait of a Lady*.

1883 Robert Louis Stevenson (1850–94) writes *Treasure Island*.

1894 Rudyard Kipling (1865–1936) writes *The Jungle Book*.

1926 A.A. Milne (1882–1956) writes *Winnie-the-Pooh*.

1870–1900 Thomas Hardy (1840–1928) writes many novels and poems.

1913 Indian poet Rabindranath Tagore (1861–1941) writes *Gitanjali*.

1913 D.H. Lawrence (1885–1930) writes *Sons and Lovers*.

1917 Czech writer Franz Kafka (1883–1924) writes *The Trial*.

1922 Publication of French writer Marcel Proust's (1871–1922) *Remembrance of Things Past*; Irish writer James Joyce's (1882–1941) *Ulysses*.

1925 American writer F. Scott Fitzgerald (1896–1940) writes *The Great Gatsby*.

1929 Ernest Hemingway (1899–1961) writes *Farewell to Arms*.

EARLY PAPERBACKS

1935 The first paperback books go on sale.

1943 Dutch Jewish girl Anne Frank (1929–1945) writes her diary.

1970s Desktop publishing arrives.

1986 The first CD-ROM book.

A CD-ROM holds text, sound, and moving images, and many books can be stored on one disk.

PHOTOGRAPHY

MILLIONS OF TIMES a day, a camera shutter clicks somewhere in the world to take a photograph, making an instant visual record of a scene, whether it is just a family snapshot or a dramatic news picture.

35MM
ROLL FILM

FILM FORMATS
Cameras are built to suit particular film formats (sizes). The most popular format is 35mm, which is used in most compacts and SLRs. Studio photographers often use a medium format for extra quality.

INSIDE AN SLR CAMERA
The type of camera most popular with serious amateurs and many professional photographers is the SLR, or Single Lens Reflex. The SLR has a prism that reflects light from the lens to the eyepiece, allowing the photographer to see directly through the camera lens. It also has interchangeable lenses.

Rear viewfinder

Shutter speed dial

Frame counter

Shutter release button

Strap attach-ment

Film

Film take-up spool

Internal lens element

Flash hot shoe

Aperture control ring

Light path through camera

Front lens element

Lens housing

Light reflects from subject and travels in rays toward the camera

Curved glass of lens refracts (bends) light rays

Converging light rays pass through an adjustable aperture (hole)

Shutter opens at different speeds to vary time film is exposed to light

When lens is focused, light rays focus on the film to create a sharp image

LIGHT INSIDE A CAMERA

A camera is essentially a lightproof box with a hole at the front holding a glass lens. The lens projects a bright, sharp picture of the world into the camera where it is recorded on film, or, in electronic cameras (such as videos), on light-sensitive cells.

PHOTOGRAPHY TIMELINE

400 B.C. Chinese scholar uses a pinhole in silk to project an image in a darkened room.

18TH-CENTURY CAMERA OBSCURA

A.D. 1020 Arab scholar Alhazen describes how a pinhole in a camera obscura (dark room) can be used to view a solar eclipse.

1558 Battista della Porta use a lens in the pinhole to sharpen the image.

1560–1860 Camera obscuras common in public buildings.

1700s Portable camera obscuras made for artists.

1727 Johann Schulze (1687–1744) shows how silver nitrate darkens when exposed to light.

c. 1800 Tom Wedgwood makes images by exposing paper coated with silver salts to the light.

1826 First photo made by Niepce (1765–1833) on a pewter plate in a camera obscura.

1839 Daguerreotype, first practical photographic process, invented by Frenchman Louis Daguerre (1789–1851).

1839 Fox Talbot (1800–77) invents Calotype process. The process produces negatives, enabling copies of photos to be made.

1851 Archer's (1813–57) Collodion allows paper prints to be made from glass negatives.

1861 Maxwell (1831–79) makes first color photo.

1888 First Kodak camera, using roll film.

1906 First practical color photo process invented by French Lumière brothers.

FIRST KODAK COLOUR FILM

1913 35mm film invented.

1924 The Leica, the first successful 35mm camera.

1935 Kodachrome color transparency (slide) film.

1947 First instant camera invented by Land (1909–91) marketed as Polaroid.

1994 First electronic still and video camera launched.

CINEMA

MOVIES ARE now a multimillion-dollar business, with people all over the world going to the movies to see feature films. Many high-budget films use complex special effects as well as "movie stars" to attract audiences.

FILM

Most movies are now recorded on 35mm film. All the pictures on the film are still, but they are run through the projector so quickly – eight frames, or pictures, a second – that we see only continuous movement on the screen. One full-length feature movie uses 1.5 miles (2.5 km) of film.

9.5-mm film introduced by French Pathé company in 1922 for amateur films

Sound track / 35MM FILM

FILM GENRES

Most feature films fall into one of several categories or "genres," including comedy (*Four Weddings and a Funeral*), romance (*Tin Cup*), science fiction (*Terminator 2*), action (*Die Hard*), or horror (*Interview with the Vampire*).

SPECIAL EFFECTS

Computer technology has dramatically increased the scope of special effects, allowing techniques such as morphing.

The points of both the hand and the spider are plotted on the computer. When the two sets of points coincide, the transformation is complete.

Morphing is used to transform one thing into another or to create animation in a live-action film.

The outline of the spider is just visible.

The midpoint of the morphing process.

The spider is almost complete.

ANIMATION

By filming drawings or models in different positions, animators can bring them to life. Computer-generated animation can produce very sophisticated animation sequences, such as those seen in *Toy Story*.

Bugs Bunny is one of the oldest cartoon characters.

Plasticine models can be moved to animate them, like this gorilla from Creature Comforts.

MOVIE TIMELINE

1879 The Zoogyroscope is developed by English photographer Eadweard Muybridge (1830–1914). It projects images of photographic sequences onto a screen in quick succession, creating an illusion of movement.

1881 Frenchman Étienne Marey (1830–1904) invents a camera that takes pictures on a revolving plate.

1894 Kinetograph (film camera) and Kinetoscope (film viewer) marketed by Americans Thomas Edison (1847–1931) and W.K. Dickson (1860–1933).

1895 French Lumière brothers show the first real movie in a movie theater in Paris.

1895 The world's first cinema opens in Atlanta, Georgia.

1913 Hollywood's first feature film, *Squaw Man*, made by Jesse Lasky (1880–1958), Cecil B. de Mille (1881–1959), and Samuel Goldwyn (1882–1974). Early films are in black and white and silent.

JAZZ SINGER POSTER

1920–1930s Picture palaces reach the peak of their popularity.

1927 *The Jazz Singer* is the first "talkie" (movie with sound).

1929 The first Oscars.

1932 Technicolor invented.

1953 Widescreen image created by Cinemascope.

1970 Steadycam allows camera operator to move while holding camera steady.

OSCAR

1990s Computer graphics used to make movies.

THE OLYMPIC GAMES

HELD EVERY FOUR YEARS, the modern Game
began in 1896 as the brainchild of French
scholar Pierre de Coubertin, who was
inspired by stories of the ancient Greek
games. Separate Winter Olympics have
been staged since 1924, and Special
Oympics for the disabled since 1960.

OLYMPIC FLAME
Following ancient
Greek tradition, the
Olympics are still
started by a torch, which
is lit on Mount Olympus
in Greece and carried by
runners in relays to the
Olympic stadium.

OLYMPIC SYMBOL
The five Olympic
rings represent the
five continents o
the world. Some 20C
nations send more than
10,000 entrants to compete
in nearly 30 different sports

OLIVE WREATH
In the ancient Greek
games, 2,000 years
ago, winners were
crowned with a
sacred olive wreath.

PARALYMPICS
Like the Olympics, the
Special Olympics for
disabled people are
held every four years.

OLYMPIC MEDALS
In the modern
Olympics, individuals
and teams compete
for gold (first), silver
(second), and
bronze (third) medals.

GOLD MEDAL FROM
THE 1984 GAMES

WINTER OLYMPICS
The Winter Games,
held two years after
the Summer Olympics
include skiing, figure
and speed skating,
and ice hockey.

CLASSIFICATION OF SPORTS

The many different types of sports can be classified into three basic groups, which can then be subdivided further.

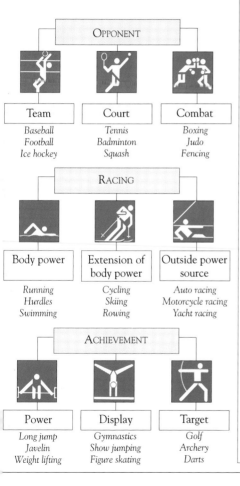

OPPONENT

Team	Court	Combat
Baseball	*Tennis*	*Boxing*
Football	*Badminton*	*Judo*
Ice hockey	*Squash*	*Fencing*

RACING

Body power	Extension of body power	Outside power source
Running	*Cycling*	*Auto racing*
Hurdles	*Skiing*	*Motorcycle racing*
Swimming	*Rowing*	*Yacht racing*

ACHIEVEMENT

Power	Display	Target
Long jump	*Gymnastics*	*Golf*
Javelin	*Show jumping*	*Archery*
Weight lifting	*Figure skating*	*Darts*

SUMMER OLYMPIC SITES

YEAR	PLACE
1896	Athens, Greece
1900	Paris, France
1904	St. Louis, US
1908	London, UK
1912	Stockholm, Sweden
1920	Antwerp, Belgium
1924	Paris, France
1928	Amsterdam, Holland
1932	Los Angeles, US
1936	Berlin, Germany
1948	London, UK
1952	Helsinki, Finland
1956	Melbourne, Australia
1960	Rome, Italy
1964	Tokyo, Japan
1968	Mexico City, Mexico
1972	Munich, Germany
1976	Montreal, Canada
1980	Moscow, USSR
1984	Los Angeles, US
1988	Seoul, South Korea
1992	Barcelona, Spain
1996	Atlanta, US
2000	Sydney, Australia

BALL GAMES

MANY TEAM GAMES are played with a large, inflated ball. Soccer, volleyball, and basketball are played with a round ball, American football and rugby with an oval ball.

FOOTBALL

Leather ball — *Helmet*

Shoulder pad

Arm pad — *Rib pad*

Leg pad

Boots

THE EQUIPMENT

THE GAME
American football is a tough game of running, passing, and body-tackling. The field is divided into strips. When a team has the ball, it tries to advance the ball strip by strip in a series of "downs."

THE SNAP
Each down starts with a snap, as the center passes the ball back to the quarterback, who sets up a play by throwing a pass or slipping the ball to a running back.

SOCCER

Team colors on shirt

SOCCER PLAYER

Round leather ball

THE GAME
Soccer is the world's most widely played game, and attracts more spectators than any other sport. A match is played between two teams of 11 players each, and the aim is to score by kicking or heading the ball into the opponent's goal.

45–90 m wide

Center circle

Halfway line

Penalty area

90-120 m long

Penalty spot

Goal area

THE FIELD
Soccer fields are almost always of grass and vary in size, but penalty areas are always the same.

VOLLEYBALL

Two teams of six players use their hands and arms to knock a ball over a net. A point is won if the ball lands in the opposition's court or if they fail to return it. The high net means players must jump high.

OVERHAND SERVE

Forearms or fingers are used to knock the ball up, ready for the spike.

UNDERHAND SERVE

PREPARING TO SPIKE (SMASH)

A team may touch the ball up to three times before returning it.

FOREARM PASS (DIG)

Rubber ball encased in leather, rubber, or synthetic material

Colorful uniform

High, padded shoes give firm support

BASKETBALL

In this fast, popular game, teams of five dribble the ball with their hands or pass and compete to throw the ball into the opponents' net.

RUGBY

Rugby Union has teams of 15 players; Rugby League has 13. Both games involve running, passing, and body-tackling. In Union, play often restarts with a scrum in which forwards interlock and try to push each other over the ball.

Scrum breaks when ball is cleared

RUGBY UNION SCRUM

AUSTRALIAN RULES

This 18-a-side game, developed in Melbourne c. 1858, is played on an oval field in four quarters of 25 minutes each. Players kick, handpass, and run with the oval ball.

Goalposts

AUSTRALIAN RULES FIELD

STICK AND BALL GAMES

MANY OF THE WORLD'S most popular games involve hitting a small ball with a stick, a bat, or a racket.

BASEBALL

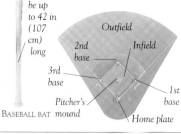

PITCH AND STRIKE
Two teams of nine take it in turns batting and fielding. The batter has three attempts to hit the ball thrown by the pitcher, then run around all the bases before the ball is fielded.

THE FIELD
The batter can only run if the ball lands within "fair territory," which consists of the infield (inside the bases) and the outfield.

Bats may be up to 42 in (107 cm) long

Outfield

2nd base

Infield

3rd base

1st base

Pitcher's mound

BASEBALL BAT

Home plate

CRICKET

BATTING
Cricket is an 11-a-side game. Two batsmen are in at any one time. The batsman stands at the crease and defends the wicket with the bat as the ball is bowled. He must try to hit the ball to score runs.

DISMISSING THE BATSMAN

BOWLED
The ball hits the wicket. If the batsman blocks a ball with his body he is "leg before wicket."

Wicket

Crease

RUN OUT
The fielders team hit a wicket before the batsmen return.

Batsman tries to hit ball

STUMPED
The batsman leaves the crease, and the fielders hit the wicket.

HOCKEY AND LACROSSE

HOCKEY
Two teams of 11 use a stick to drive the ball into their opponent's goal. Goalkeepers have to be protected from the ball, which can travel at 100 mph (160 km/h).

GOALKEEPER

HOCKEY OUTDOOR STICK

Helmet

Goal-keeper's glove

Kicker enables keeper to use his or her feet

Side shooting

Men's lacrosse teams have 10 players, women's teams have 12.

Cradling the ball

Throwing the ball

LACROSSE
Players use the net to carry and pass the ball and drive it into their opponent's goal.

RACKET GAMES

TENNIS
Players use a racket to hit a ball over a net so that the ball lands in the opposite court and cannot be returned. Matches are played in sets of games, with a maximum of five sets for men and three for women. The court may be grass or clay. A doubles court is bigger than a singles court.

TENNIS RACKET

Singles sideline

Net

Doubles sideline

TENNIS COURT

SQUASH
A squash game is played in an enclosed court. Players aim to hit the ball onto one or more walls so their opponent cannot hit it before it bounces twice on the floor. Games are played to nine points, matches to the best of three or five games.

SQUASH

COMPETITION SPORTS

ATHLETICS AND sports like gymnastics and weight lifting are based on individual prowess.

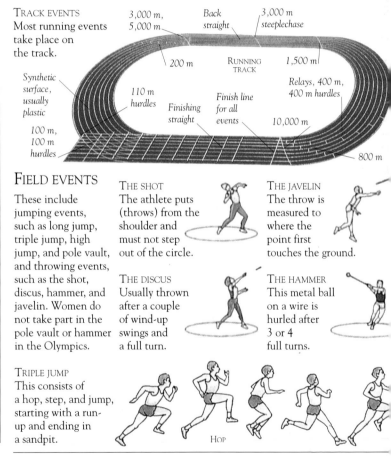

TRACK EVENTS
Most running events take place on the track.

Synthetic surface, usually plastic

100 m, 100 m hurdles

200 m

110 m hurdles

Finishing straight

3,000 m, 5,000 m

Back straight

RUNNING TRACK

Finish line for all events

3,000 m steeplechase

1,500 m

Relays, 400 m, 400 m hurdles

10,000 m

800 m

FIELD EVENTS

These include jumping events, such as long jump, triple jump, high jump, and pole vault, and throwing events, such as the shot, discus, hammer, and javelin. Women do not take part in the pole vault or hammer in the Olympics.

THE SHOT
The athlete puts (throws) from the shoulder and must not step out of the circle.

THE DISCUS
Usually thrown after a couple of wind-up swings and a full turn.

THE JAVELIN
The throw is measured to where the point first touches the ground.

THE HAMMER
This metal ball on a wire is hurled after 3 or 4 full turns.

TRIPLE JUMP
This consists of a hop, step, and jump, starting with a run-up and ending in a sandpit.

HOP

COMBINED EVENTS

First day	Second day
Decathlon (men)	
100 m race	110 m hurdle
Long jump	Discus
Shot put	Pole vault
High jump	Javelin
400 m race	1500 m race

Heptathlon (women)	
100 m hurdle	Long jump
High jump	Javelin
Shot put	800 m race
200 m race	

WEIGHT LIFTING

There are two categories: snatch, and clean and jerk.

Bar is lifted first to the shoulders, then to full arm's length overhead as the lifter stands up.

CLEAN AND JERK

SNATCH

Bar is lifted to full arm's length overhead in a single movement. The lifter then stands up.

GYMNASTICS

Gymnastics consists of exercises on the floor, beam, rings, uneven, parallel, and horizontal bars, vaulting horse, and pommel horse. Judges award marks out of ten for the gymnast's performance at the exercise. Rhythmic gymnastics for women is performed to music with ribbons, balls, ropes, clubs, or hoops.

Gymnast must change hand-holds and direction constantly

Points are given for good continuity and rhythm

UNEVEN BARS

Beam is 4 ins (10 cm) wide and 16.4 ft (5 m) long

Female gymnasts walk, run, leap, and somersault along a beam for 70–90 seconds

THE BEAM

Athlete throws arms forward, ready for landing

STEP

JUMP

WINTER SPORTS

THE SLIPPERINESS of snow and ice has inspired a range of winter sports, from the grace of figure skating to the thrill of downhill skiing.

SPEED SKATING
In long-track racing, two skaters race against the clock on an outdoor 400 m track. In short-track racing, four or six skaters race each other round a 111.12 m indoor track.

SPEED SKATER

ICE HOCKEY PLAYER

ICE HOCKEY
Ice hockey is a fast and furious six-a-side game in three 20-minute periods. The aim is to shoot the hard rubber puck into the opposition's goal.

One leg lifted behind and held parallel to ice

FIGURE SKATING
Marks out of six are given for artistic and technical merit. In spins, the skater should stay exactly on the spot. Names of jumps depend on take off and landing: axel, salchow, loop, and lutz.

CAMEL SPIN

Skater spins once or twice in the air.

LUTZ JUMP

Blocking pad

Ca gl

Leg pad

THE GOALKEEPER
Goalkeepers need a lot of extra protection from the puck, which travels at high speed.

umpers speed down a
amp and leap into the
ir for a distance of
0–90 m.

SKI JUMPER

kier adopts a
streamlined shape for
peed and distance
hrough the air

Points are
awarded for
style as well
as distance.

NORDIC SKIING
This includes
ski-jumping and
cross-country skiing,
which involves short
uphill sections.
The biathlon
involves cross-
country skiing and rifle
shooting at targets.

Narrower,
shorter ski than
Alpine skis

CROSS-COUNTRY SKIER

Skiers use
freestyle
(like a
skater) or
classical
(diagonal
stride).

Bindings allow
heel to lift off
ski

ALPINE SKIING
This type of skiing involves slalom and
downhill races, which are all run against
the clock, and freestyle, which is judged
on style and technique. In downhill
racing, each skier races once; slalom
and giant slalom are decided on the
combined time for two runs.

n downhill, skiers
urtle down a set
oute at speeds of
o to 86 mph
(140 km/h).

In slalom, skiers zigzag
between red and blue
flags without knocking
them down.

Freestyle skiers perform
acrobatics by jumping off
"moguls" (snow bumps)
and ramps.

Downhill
course

Super giant slalom, vertical
drop: 500–600 m (men);
350–500 m (women)

Giant
slalom,
vertical drop:
250–400 m
(men);
250–350 m
(women)

Slalom:
55–75 gates
(men);
40–60
gates
(women)

COURSES
AND GATES
Flags marking the course are set on
single poles for slalom gates, double
poles for giant, and super giant slalom.

WINTER SPORTS

413

WATER SPORTS

WATER SPORTS

THE POPULARITY of water sports, both indoors in pools and outdoors on rivers, lakes, and the sea, has increased greatly in recent years.

WINDSURFING
Also called board-sailing, windsurfing uses a sailboard with a swiveling sail that propels and steers the board. The windsurfer holds the boom which surrounds and supports the sail.

Mast

Sail

Window

Boom

Board

Universal joint swivels in all directions

Wet suits protect against cold

Boards are usually made of fiberglass

SURFING
Surfing is a spectacular sport in which surfers paddle out to sea on boards and ride big breakers back to shore. In competition, surfers are judged for style, grace, and timing.

YACHT TYPES

ONE-PERSON DINGHY
Simple one-person dinghys, such as the Topper class, are designed as training boats but are also raced.

TWO-PERSON BOAT WITH TRAPEZE
A two-person boat, such as the 470 class, is used in Olympic racing.

CATAMARAN
Twin-hulled, two-person catamarans , such as the Tornado class, also sail in Olympic races.

TWO-PERSON DINGHY
A two-person dinghy, such as the Flying Dutchman class, is used for training and racing.

OCEAN-GOING YACHT
An ocean-going yacht, such as the 12 m class, sail heavy seas in offshore racing.

PEOPLE AND SOCIETY

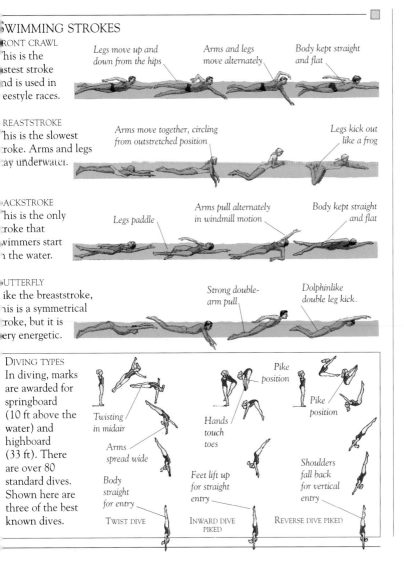

SWIMMING STROKES

FRONT CRAWL
This is the fastest stroke and is used in freestyle races.

Legs move up and down from the hips

Arms and legs move alternately

Body kept straight and flat

BREASTSTROKE
This is the slowest stroke. Arms and legs stay underwater.

Arms move together, circling from outstretched position

Legs kick out like a frog

BACKSTROKE
This is the only stroke that swimmers start in the water.

Legs paddle

Arms pull alternately in windmill motion

Body kept straight and flat

BUTTERFLY
Like the breaststroke, this is a symmetrical stroke, but it is very energetic.

Strong double-arm pull

Dolphinlike double leg kick.

DIVING TYPES
In diving, marks are awarded for springboard (10 ft above the water) and highboard (33 ft). There are over 80 standard dives. Shown here are three of the best known dives.

Twisting in midair

Arms spread wide

Body straight for entry

TWIST DIVE

Pike position

Hands touch toes

Feet lift up for straight entry

INWARD DIVE PIKED

Pike position

Shoulders fall back for vertical entry

REVERSE DIVE PIKED

415

COMBAT SPORTS

BOXING AND WRESTLING are combat sports, as are fencing, archery, and shooting, and the martial arts of East Asia.

MARTIAL ARTS

KARATE
Strikes and kicks are used in karate, which means "empty hands."

AIKIDO
Meaning "the way of all harmony," aikido uses only defensive techniques.

JU JITSU
This is the ancient Japanese fighting art from which judo and aikido developed.

KENDO
Japanese sword-fighting, or kendo, is practised in armour.

RED BELT	9TH–10TH DAN
BLACK BELT	1ST–5TH DAN
BROWN BELT	1ST KYU
BLUE BELT	2ND KYU
GREEN BELT	3RD KYU
ORANGE BELT	4TH KYU
YELLOW BELT	5TH KYU

JUDO
Competitors in the martial art of Judo, which means "the gentle way", use throw and holds to defeat their opponent. Grades or "belts range from "kyu" (student) to "dan" (advanced).

BOXING
Governed by strict protective rules, competitors wear gloves. Professional fights are up to 12 three-minute rounds. Amateurs go three rounds.

BOXING WEIGHTS	PROFESSIONAL	AMATEUR
Flyweight	108–112 lb	106–112 lb
Featherweight	122–126 lb	119–126 lb
Lightweight	130–135 lb	126–132 lb
Middleweight	154–160 lb	157–165 lb
Heavyweight	Over 190 lb	179–201 lb

ARCHERY

Archers fire "rounds" of arrows at a target. The number varies with the event. The aim is to hit the center of the target, worth ten points.

TARGET

Magnesium handle

Finger tab

Sight

Fletch

QUIVER

Glove

Stabilizer to keep bow steady

Bracer protects bow arm from string

BOW

shaft

The quiver worn on the archer's belt contains arrows with metal tips and carbon or aluminum points.

Modern bows have bowsights to help the archer adjust for wind and height.

FENCING

In fencing, two opponents compete in a bout using one of three weapons: saber, foil, or épée. A bout lasts until the agreed number of hits have been made, or until a preset time limit has been reached, e.g. five hits within a time limit of six minutes.

Weight: less than 500 g
Blade length: 88 cm

Weight; less than 500 g
Blade length: 90 cm

Weight: less than 770 g
Blade length: 90 cm

SABER

FOIL

EPEE

COMBAT SPORTS

417

EQUESTRIAN EVENTS

COMPETITIONS ON HORSEBACK are known as equestrian events. They include racing, show jumping, and eventing. In eventing, the riders' skill is tested as they take their horses through three disciplines over three days: show jumping, speed and endurance, and dressage.

THREE BASIC DRESSAGE PACES

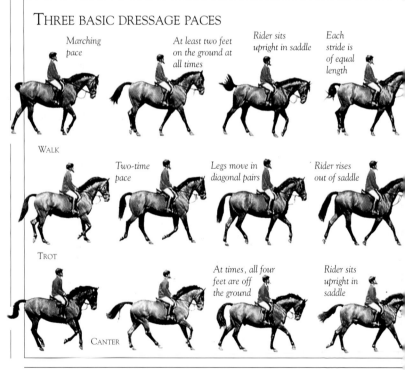

Marching pace

At least two feet on the ground at all times

Rider sits upright in saddle

Each stride is of equal length

WALK

Two-time pace

Legs move in diagonal pairs

Rider rises out of saddle

TROT

At times, all four feet are off the ground

Rider sits upright in saddle

CANTER

SHOW JUMPING

If the horse clips an obstacle, the rider incurs a fault. Riders with fewest faults compete against each other against the clock.

Landing *Flight* *Take-off*

Rider bends forwards from the hip and straightens on landing.

SHOW JUMPING COURSE

Start *Gate* *Triple bars* *Wall*

Finish

OBSTACLES
Obstacles must be jumped in a set order between start and finish.

SHOW JUMPING FAULTS

ERROR	FAULT
Fence (or part of) down	4
Foot in water	4
Refusal	3
2nd refusal	6
3rd refusal	Elimination
Fall (horse or rider)	8
Exceeding time allowance	¼ per sec
Jumps taken out of sequence	Elimination

HORSE RACING
There are two kinds of horse racing. A steeplechase, is a race over jumps, such as fences, ditches, and water; other races are over hurdles. Racehorses also race on the Flat. The horses are almost always Thoroughbreds.

JOCKEY'S HELMET
A jockey wears a crash helmet under his or her cap, and carries a whip.

THOROUGHBRED

Shirt and cap in owner's colors

Jockeys are light; some weigh under 97 lb (44.5 kg).

Thoroughbred horses are all descended from three original Arab stallions.

Whip

Pocket for lead weights to handicap horses with the best race records

Helmet covered in silk

HISTORY

A TIMELINE OF WORLD HISTORY
FROM 40,000 B.C. TO A.D. 1996

422–463

	40,000–32,501 B.C.	**32,500–25,001 B.C.**
AFRICA	**c. 34,000** Hunter-gatherers occupy areas of present-day Lesotho and Zambia.	**30,000** Disappearance of Neanderthals. **Ostrich** *Wild ostriches formed part of the ancient African diet.*
ASIA	**40,000** Cro-Magnon humans live in Palestine at Skhül and Kafzel.	**27,000–19,000** Female statuettes called "Venus" figurines, thought to have been used in worship, are made at various sites in Russia, France, and Italy.
EUROPE	**40,000** Neanderthals active in France, at La Chapelle-Aux-Saints, La Ferassie, and La Quina. Cro-Magnons start to spread to Europe. **35,000** Start of Upper Paleolithic Period. Use of flaked stone tools, and bone and horn implements.	**"Venus" figurines** *These rounded statuettes of female figures may have been symbols of fertility.*
AMERICAS	**35,000** First humans arrive in North America from Asia.	**27,000–19,000** Probable date of earliest figurative art in Dordogne, France.
OCEANIA	**40,000** Probable arrival of Aboriginals in Australia.	

Early flint tool

25,000–17,501 B.C.

20,000 The Ice Age causes the world's average temperature to drop and sea levels to lower. Humans have to adapt and work together to survive.

Mammoth hunt
Ice Age people hunted in groups and shared the kill.

17,500–10,001 B.C.

15,000 Last rainy period in northern Africa.

16,000 Coldest point in glaciation.
14,000–11,000 El-Kebarch culture in Israel builds freestanding round huts.
11,000 Natufian culture in Palestine becomes one of the first groups to form permanent settlements.
10,500 Earliest-known pottery produced, Fukui cave, Japan.

Natufian huts
The mud, reed, and timber huts of the Natufians were often used to store grain.

15,000 Wall paintings made in caves at Lascaux, France.
15,000–10,000 High point of art produced by Magdalenian culture.
12,500 Magdalenian toolmakers make the first bone and antler harpoons and fishing spears.
11,000 Cave paintings created at Altamira, Spain.

The origins of art
Early artists painted images of animals and humans on the walls of caves.

25,000 Cave dwellers present in Brazil.	**15,000** First Brazilian cave art.
24,000 Earliest-known cremation at Lake Mungo, New South Wales, Australia.	**16,000** Cave art, north coast of Australia.

423

10,000–8501 B.C.	8500–7001 B.C.

AFRICA

10,000 Hunting camps established in Sahara region after Ice Age ends.

8500 Earliest Saharan rock paintings.
8000 Pottery made in Sahara region.

ASIA

9000–8000 Wheat and barley grown in Jordan and Syria. Pottery produced at Mureybet, Syria. Goats and sheep domesticated in Iran and Jordan.

Early farming
Grain crops were first cultivated in the Middle East in 8000 B.C.

8000 Jericho, the first town, appears. Ice Age ends in Far East.
7500 Pigs domesticated in Crimea.

Domesticated pig
The modern pig evolved from the wild boar, domesticated by early farmers.

Jericho Tower
The ancient town of Jericho was strongly built to last, with a stone wall, tower, and defensive ditch.

EUROPE

10,000 Ice cap retreats.

8300 Retreat of glaciers.

AMERICAS

10,000 First people reach southern tip of South America.
9000 Clovis hunter-gatherers in the Great Plains of North America begin to hunt bison.

8500 Wild grasses and beans cultivated in Peru.
8000 Semipermanent settlements established in North America.

North American bison

OCEANIA

10,000 Tasmania separated from Australia as sea level rises.

424

7000–5501 B.C.

6500 Cattle domesticated.
7000–6000 Discovery that heating certain rocks (ores) releases pure metal that can then be shaped or molded occurs.

7000–6500 Oxen domesticated in eastern Mediterranean.
6500–5700 Important early town forms at Çatal Hüyük, Turkey. Its houses are built of mud brick and share walls.
6200 Copper smelted in Turkey.

Çatal Hüyük

6500 Britain separated from mainland as ice melts.
6500 First farming communities established in southeastern Europe.

6500 Potatoes cultivated in Peru.

6000 New Guinea separated from Australia.

5500–4001 B.C.

Early metal-workers

5000 Irrigation in Mesopotamia. Rice farming in China. Ubaid culture in Mesopotamia.
4500 Farming around Ganges River in India.
4400 Horses domesticated in Russia.

5000 Farming begins in western Europe. Gold and copper used in Balkans.
4500 First megalithic chamber tombs built in Portugal and in Brittany, France. Their remains (dolmens) show a great knowledge of engineering.

Dolmens at Carnac
Upright stones placed in a row and roofed to form a covered walk can be seen at Carnac, Brittany.

c. 5000–4000 First settlements form at Anáhuac, Mexico. Corn grown in Mexico. Pyramid temples built in Peru.

	4000–3376 B.C.	3375–2751 B.C.
AFRICA	**3750** Earliest known production of bronze alloy. The process is also developed in Sumer, southern Babylonia. **3500** First sailing vessels built in Egypt.	**3100** Pharaoh Menes the Fighter unites Upper and Lower Egypt. **3000** Hieroglyphic writing develops in Eygpt.

Egyptian mumm
Preserving the bodies o
important people was a
ancient Egyptian custom

	4000–3376 B.C.	3375–2751 B.C.
ASIA	**4000** Beginning of bronze casting in the Middle East. **3500** Earliest Chinese city at Liang-ch'eng chen. Sumerians invent the wheel and plow.	**3500** Ancient Egyptians establish one of the world's longest-lasting civilization
EUROPE	**Mesopotamian wheel**	**3250** Earliest picture-writing by Sumerians in Mesopotamia. **3000** Development of Sumerian cities. First use of the plow in China. **2850** Legendary reign of the Chinese Xia dynasty.
AMERICAS	**c. 4000** Domestication of llama and alpaca in Andes, South America. **Inca llama figurine** *The Incas of South America used llamas as pack animals and also for meat.*	**3200** Beginnings of early Cycladic civilization in Aegean islands. **3000** Spread of copper use. **2900** Danubian culture in central Europe.
OCEANIA		**3200** Corn farmed in South America. **3000** First pottery in Americas. **Corn**
		3000 Probable introduction of dogs in Australia.

2750–2126 B.C.

2686 Beginning of ancient Egyptian Old Kingdom.
2646 Pyramid of Zoser built at Saqqara.
2590 Building of Great Pyramid of Khufu at Giza begins.
2500 Sahara region begins to dry out.
2150 Decline of ancient Egyptian Old Kingdom.
2133 Rise of ancient Egyptian Middle Kingdom.

2750 The legendary King Gilgamesh reigns in Uruk, Mesopotamia.
2500 Birth of Indus Valley civilization in Pakistan. Horse domesticated in Central Asia.
2371 Semite people establish Mesopotamia's greatest empire.

Indus Valley sculpture
This sculpture of a priest or divine king was made by people in the Indus Valley city of Mohenjo-Daro.

2500 Earliest barrow burials in Britain. Beginnings of Dolmen period of Scandinavian Neolithic age.
2200 The first Stonehenge is built in England.

2500 First large settlements and building of temple mounds in Andes area.

2125–1501 B.C.

1786 Egyptian Middle Kingdom ends.
1652 War between Egypt and Asian Hyksos people.
1550 Rise of Egyptian New Kingdom.

2000 Hittites begin invasions of Anatolia.
1900 Fall of Indus civilization.
1800 Beginnings of Assyrian Empire.
1792 Birth of Hammurabi, founder of Babylonian Empire.

Lotus-design tile
This tile dates from the reign of King Akhenaten in the Egyptian New Kingdom.

2000 Rise of the prosperous Minoan sea-trading civilization in Crete.
1600 Origins of Mycenean civilization.
1500 Linear B script in use on Crete.

Minoan wall painting
The wealthy Minoan people decorated the walls of their palaces with colorful murals.

2000 Earliest Peruvian metalworking. Inuits reach northern Greenland.

2000 Beginnings of settlement of Melanesia in the South Pacific.

	1500–1276 B.C.	1275–1051 B.C.
AFRICA	**1300** Temple of Abu Simbel built in Nubia for Rameses II.	**1218** Egypt invaded by Sea Peoples from the Aegean. **1182** Second invasion of Egypt by Aegean Sea Peoples.
ASIA	**1500** Phrygia established by people moving from Thrace in the Balkans to Asia Minor. Composition of hymns of Rig Veda. **1400** Chinese capital moved to Anyang, in present-day South Korea.	**c. 1375** First alphabet script devised by Phoenicians. **1294** Egyptians fight Hittites at Qadesh for control of Palestine. **1200** Collapse of Hittite Empire. Jews settle in Palestine. **1100** Phoenician traders begin to spread out from eastern Mediterranean.
EUROPE	**1500** Beginning of Bronze Age in Scandinavia. **1450** Decline of Minoan civilization in Crete.	**1200** Decline of Mycenean culture in Greece. **c. 1120** City of Mycenae destroyed.
AMERICAS	**1300** Rise of Olmec civilization in Mexico.	
OCEANIA	**1300** Settlers from Indonesia and Philippines reach Western Polynesia (Fiji).	

Hittite soldier

Olmec stone carving
This colossal stone head of an Olmec king was carved from basalt.

Mycenean bull's head
This clay bull's head has small holes in its mouth and was used as a ritual sprinkler at religious ceremonies.

1050–826 B.C.	825–601 B.C.

1050–826 B.C.

900 Foundation of kingdom of Kushin Nubia.

1027 Zhou warriors overthrow the Shang dynasty in China.
1000 Kingdom of Israel under King David.

Shang Fang Ding
This four-legged food vessel was made in China during the Shang dynasty (c. 1600–1027 BC).

1000 Etruscans arrive in Italy and begin building a loosely connected alliance of city-states.

Etruscan warrior figurine
The Etruscans produced unique, high-quality sculpture and bronze work.

900 Height of Chavin farming civilization in Andes, South America.
800 Zapotec civilization of Central America produces first writing in Americas.

1000 Most of Polynesian Islands settled.

825–601 B.C.

814 Phoenicians found the city-state of Carthage in northern Africa.

800 Aryans from present-day Iran spread into southern India.
771 Zhou dynasty collapses in China.
721–05 Assyrian Empire at height of its powers.
660 Reign of Jimmu, legendary first Japanese emperor.
650 Chinese begin to use iron.
612 Decline of Assyrian power.
c. 604–562 Nebuchadnezzar II rules Neo-Babylonian (Chaldean) Empire. Hanging Gardens built in city of Babylon, Mesopotamia.

Sentry at the Ishtar Gate, Babylon

776 First recorded Olympic Games in Greece.
753 Foundation of Rome.
750 Greek city-states establish settlements around Mediterranean.
700 Iron Age culture of Halstatt, Austria, spreads through central and western Europe.
650 Earliest surviving Latin inscriptions.
621 The Laws of Dracon become the first written laws of Athens, Greece.

	600–451 B.C.	450–301 B.C.
AFRICA	**600** Phoenicians sail around Africa. **600** Building of Temple of the Sun at Meroë, Sudan. **500** Ironworking Nok culture begins in Nigeria.	**304** Egypt independent under Ptolemy
ASIA	**560** Lao–Tze writes his philosophical work, Tao Te Ching, in China. **550** King Cyrus II of Persia founds Persian Empire. **486** Death of Siddhartha Gautama, founder of Buddhist religion.	**403** Start of "Warring States" period in China. **334–26** Alexander the Great conquers Asia Minor, Persia, and parts of India. **323** Death of Alexander the Great and division of his empire. **322** Chandragupta founds Mauryan Empire in India. **Alexander the Great** *The Macedonian warrior-king Alexander the Great built an empire that helped spread Greek culture over western Asia.*
EUROPE	**510** Origins of Roman Republic. **505** Establishment of democracy in Athens. **500** Celtic people flourish in central Europe. **490** Greeks defeat Persians at Battle of Marathon.	**Buddhist stupa at Sanchi, India** *Mauryan emperor Asoka became a Buddhist and set up thousands of monuments (stupas) around the empire. Each is said to contain a part of the Buddha's body.*
AMERICAS	**Decorative Celtic horned helmet**	**450** Iron Age culture firmly established in central and western Europe. **431–04** Sparta defeats Athens in Peloponnesian Wars. **338** Macedonians gain control of Greece at Battle of Chaeronea.
OCEANIA	**500** Trading contacts established in South Pacific islands.	**400** Decline of Olmec civilization.

300–151 B.C.

290 Foundation of library at Alexandria, Egypt.

262 Mauryan Emperor Asoka converts to Buddhism.
240 Beginning of Parthian dynasty in northern Persia.
221 Chinese unity brought about by the first emperor, Qin Shi Huangdi.
207 Disintegration of unity in China.
202 China reunited under Han dynasty.

290 Rome gains control of central Italy.
264–41 Rome victorious against Carthage in First Punic War and wins control of Sicily.
218–01 Carthaginians, led by Hannibal, defeated in Second Punic War by Roman general Scipio.

Roman sword

300 Mound-building cultures flourish in North America. Beginning of early Mayan civilization in Central America.
200 Rise of Nazca civilization in Peru, South America.

150–1 B.C.

149–6 Rome destroys Carthage in Third Punic War and founds province of Africa.
100 Camels introduced into Sahara region.
30 Egypt becomes Roman province on death of Mark Antony and Cleopatra.

112 Opening up of "Silk Road" trade route gives the West some access to China.
64 Roman general Pompey conquers Syria.
53 Parthia halts eastward expansion of Rome.

49 Rome under Julius Caesar invades Gaul.
45 Julius Caesar becomes sole ruler of Rome after civil war.
31 Battle of Actium gives Octavian power over Rome.
27 Roman Empire replaces Republic. Octavian becomes Augustus, the first emperor.

100 Emergence of Anasazi, Hohokam, and Mogollon peoples as they begin farming in southwestern North America. Okvik hunters settle in northern Alaska.

Nazca pottery
The Nazca produced decorative textiles, metalworks, and pottery.

A.D. 1–149	A.D. 150–299
AFRICA	
c. 17–24 Tacfarinas leads Numidian people in revolt against Roman government in northern Africa. **50** Kingdom of Axum begins to expand in Ethiopia. **61–63** Roman forces move into Sudan.	**150** Berber and Mandingo barbarians start to dominate Sudan area. **250** Axum (Ethiopia) controls trade in Red Sea.

Circular Sassanian city at Firuzbad, Persia (Iraq)

ASIA

9 Overthrow of Han dynasty in China.
25 Han dynasty restored.
c. 33 Jesus Christ crucified in Jerusalem.
60 Beginning of Kushan Empire in India.
70 Romans seize control of Jerusalem in Israel and destroy Jewish temple.
105 Paper first used in China.
132 Jewish revolt against Roman rule.

200 Mishnah, the book of Jewish law, completed. Indian epics of Ramayana and Mahabharata composed. Creation of the Hindu scripture, Bhagavad Gita.

EUROPE

43 Romans invade Britain.
79 Mount Vesuvius erupts and destroys the town of Pompeii in southern Italy.
117 Height of Roman Empire.

Bust of Augustus, the first Roman emperor

AMERICAS

1 Beginning of Moche civilization in northern Peru.
50 Nazca people create vast lines and patterns in the desert.

The four tetrarchs
In A.D. 293, Emperor Diocletian divided the Roman Empire in two, appointing an emperor and deputy to rule each half. This sculpture represents the Empire's four leaders (tetrarchs).

OCEANIA

1–100 Hindu-Buddhists from Southeast Asia colonize Sumatra and Java in Indonesia.

A.D. 300–449

325 Axum destroys kingdom of Meroë.
400 Adoption of Christianity in Axum.
439 Vandals establish kingdom in northern Africa.

304 Invasion of Huns creates further division of China.
320 Chandragupta I founds Gupta Empire in northern India.

The symbol of Christianity
The teachings of the Jewish preacher Jesus Christ, who was crucified c. A.D. 33, spread around the world after his death. The faith gained widespread acceptance after the Roman emperor Constantine converted to Christianity in A.D. 313. Christ's death on the cross led to its use as a symbol of the faith.

313 Edict of Milan leads to toleration of Christianity throughout Roman Empire.
330 Emperor Constantine moves capital of Roman Empire to Constantinople, at site of present-day Istanbul, Turkey.
410 Invading Visigoths sack Rome.

300 Rise of great Monte Alban and Teotihuacán civilizations in Mexico.

300 Eastern Polynesia settled.

A.D. 450–599

533 Emperor Justinian wins back northern Africa for Rome.

480 End of Indian Gupta Empire.
520 Rise of mathematics in India with invention of decimal number system.
531 Height of Sassanian Empire in Persia.
550 Buddhism introduced into Japan.
589 Reunification of China under Sui dynasty.

Japanese carving of a sleeping Buddha

450 Angles, Jutes, and Saxons settle in Britain.
476 Overthrow of Romulus Augustulus, the last western Roman emperor.
486 Clovis people establish Frankish kingdom in present-day northern France, Belgium, and parts of western Germany.
493 Ostrogoths gain power in Italy.
552 Emperor Justinian restores Italy to Roman control.
568 Lombards take over northern Italy.

c. 450–600 Population of city of Tiahuanaco in Bolivia reaches 50,000.

A.D. 600–724

A.D. 725–849

AFRICA

c.700 Trans-Saharan trade brings prosperity to Kingdom of Ghana. Bantu Africans cross Limpopo River and take ironworking technology to the south.

751 Muslims defeat Mongols at Samarkand in central Asia.
794 Kyoto, ancient capital of Japan, established.
802 Khmers found empire in Cambodia and Laos.

ASIA

618 Reunification of China under T'ang dynasty.
622 Year One of the Islamic calendar.
637 Followers of Islam (Muslims) seize Jerusalem.

Muslim at prayer
The Arab merchant Muhammad founded the Islamic religion in A.D. 610. His teachings inspired the Arab peoples, and by A.D. 750 Muslims had gained control of land stretching from Spain to Afghanistan.

732 Defeat of Moors by Frankish leader Charles Martel halts advance of Muslims through Europe.
768 Charlemagne crowned King of the Franks.
844 Defeat of Picts unites Scotland.

EUROPE

c. 675 Nomadic Bulgar people settle in lands south of the Danube.
711 Islamic Moors invade Spain.

King Charlemagne
The Holy Roman Empire was founded by King Charlemagne of the Franks in A.D. 800 after he conquered most of the Christian lands of western Europe.

AMERICAS

600 Mayan civilization in Central America flourishes. Mayans build great pyramidal temples and develop writing and advanced mathematics.

Temple at Palenque
This Mayan temple contained the funeral chamber of the lord Pacol, who died in A.D. 683 after ruling for 68 years.

OCEANIA

A.D. 850–974

900 Hausa kingdom of Daura founded in northern Nigeria.
920 The Kingdom of Ghana in western Africa begins a prosperous golden age.

888 Chola dynasty of Tamil kings replaces the Pallavas in southern India and Sri Lanka.
935–41 Civil war in Japan.
960 Sung dynasty begins rule in China.
1007 Japanese noblewoman Murasaki Shikubu writes the first novel.

911 The Viking leader Rollo is granted land in Normandy by the King of France.
930 Córdoba becomes the seat of Arab learning in Spain.
966 Conversion of Poles to Christianity.

Viking longship
Late in the eighth century the Viking people of present-day Scandinavia went in search of treasure to plunder and new lands to settle. Their golden age of trade, exploration, and colonization lasted until A.D. 1100.

900 Beginnings of Mixtec civilization in Mexico.

950 Polynesian navigator Kupe discovers New Zealand, and Maori settlers arrive.

A.D. 975–1099

980 Arab traders settle on eastern coast of Africa.
1054 Ghana conquered by Muslim Almoravid dynasty.

Japanese literature
More than 600,000 words long, The Tale of Genji, a prince in search of love and wisdom, was the first novel.

1044 Gunpowder invented in China.

982 The Viking warrior Erik the Red settles in Greenland.
1000 Leif Eriksson, son of Erik the Red, sails down North American coast and names it "Vinland."
1066 William of Normandy defeats King Harold of England at Battle of Hastings.
1096 First Crusades begin.

980 Toltec people build their capital city at Tula in Mexico.
1000 Foundation of Chima civilization in Peru.

Maori hek tiki
This hek tiki, or neck pendant, was worn by the first Maori settlers to bring good luck or ward off evil spirits.

435

1100–1149	1150–1199

AFRICA

c. 1100 First Iron Age settlement in Zimbabwe, Southern Africa.

1169 Saladin, a Muslim warrior and commander in the Egyptian army, becomes ruler of Egypt.
1190 Lalibela rules as Emperor of Ethiopia.

ASIA

1104 Acre in Israel captured by Crusaders. Their name comes from the Latin *crux*, or cross, the symbol of Christ.

Knights of Christ
European Christians sent armed expeditions called Crusades to recapture the holy lands from Saracen Muslims.

1156 Civil war between rival clans in Japan leads to domination of the country by its Samurai warlords.
1187 Saladin captures Jerusalem from Crusaders.
1191 Zen Buddhism introduced to Japan.

EUROPE

1115 French philosopher Peter Abelard begins teaching in Paris, France. St. Bernard establishes important monastery at Clairvaux, France.
1119 Foundation of Bologna University in Italy.
1142 Alfonso Henriques becomes first King of Portugal.

Zen Buddhist monks in meditation
The practice of Zen Buddhism is unlike other faiths in its belief that the path to self-knowledge lies in personal instruction by a master rather than the study of scriptures.

AMERICAS

c. 1100 Chimu civilization flourishes in Peru on northwest coast.

1170 Murder of Thomas à Becket, Archbishop of Canterbury, England.
1174 Building of Old London Bridge in England and the "Leaning Tower" in Pisa, Italy.

"Leaning Tower" of Pisa

OCEANIA

1100s Giant statues built on Easter Island, South Pacific.

Chimu ear ornament

1170s Chichimec nomads overthrow Toltec capital city of Tula in Mexico, leading to fall of Toltec Empire.

1200–1249

1234 Sun Diata founds the Mali Empire in West Africa.

1206 Genghis Khan establishes the Mongol Empire. The Islamic faith takes root in new Kingdom of Delhi, India.

Genghis Khan
The Mongol chieftain Temujin was proclaimed Genghis Khan, or "Universal Ruler."

1229 Sixth Crusaders recapture Jerusalem.
1232 Explosive rockets used in war between Chinese and Mongols.
1237 Mongol army begins conquest of Russia.
1244 Egyptians retake Jerusalem.

1204 Constantinople sacked and looted by Fourth Crusaders.
1209 Franciscan order founded by St. Francis of Assisi, Italy.
1215 St. Dominic establishes Dominican Order in Spain. King John of England grants political rights to barons by signing the Magna Carta.
1240s Foundations laid in Germany for commercial and defensive Hanseatic League of northern European trade towns.

c.1200 Incas in Peru centered around settlement at Cuzco. First corn farmers by Mississippi River in North America.

1250–1299

1250 Mamluk rebel slave-soldiers become the rulers of Egypt.

1250 The Japanese monk Nicherin proclaims *Lotus Sutra* the supreme Buddhist scripture.
1260 Mamluks halt Mongol advance at Battle of Ain Jalut in Palestine.
1291 Saracens capture Acre, ending the Crusades.
1281 Mongol invaders' fleet driven from Japan by the Kamikaze, or "Divine Wind."
c.1294 Persians convert to Islam.

Marco Polo and fellow travelers in the Far East

1271 Aged only 16, Marco Polo begins his journeys around the Far East, traveling from Venice, Italy, to China.
1273 Rudolf Hapsburg becomes ruler of Germany and founds the powerful Hapsburg dynasty.

c. 1250 Restoration of Mayan Empire and building of a new capital at Mayapan in Mexico. Incas expand their capital at Chan-chan in northern Peru.

c. 1250 Stone platforms later used to erect religious statues built in Polynesia.

1300–1339

1340–1379

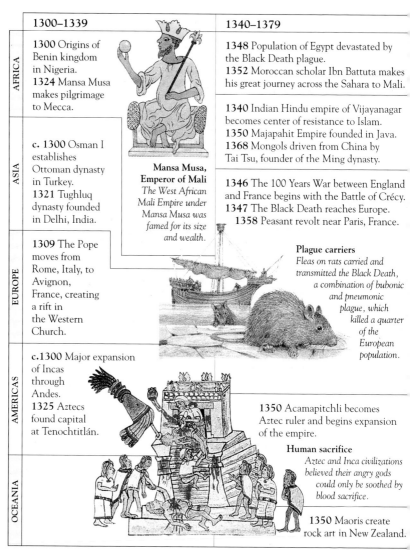

AFRICA

1300 Origins of Benin kingdom in Nigeria.
1324 Mansa Musa makes pilgrimage to Mecca.

1348 Population of Egypt devastated by the Black Death plague.
1352 Moroccan scholar Ibn Battuta makes his great journey across the Sahara to Mali.

ASIA

c. 1300 Osman I establishes Ottoman dynasty in Turkey.
1321 Tughluq dynasty founded in Delhi, India.

1340 Indian Hindu empire of Vijayanagar becomes center of resistance to Islam.
1350 Majapahit Empire founded in Java.
1368 Mongols driven from China by Tai Tsu, founder of the Ming dynasty.

Mansa Musa, Emperor of Mali
The West African Mali Empire under Mansa Musa was famed for its size and wealth.

1346 The 100 Years War between England and France begins with the Battle of Crécy.
1347 The Black Death reaches Europe.
1358 Peasant revolt near Paris, France.

EUROPE

1309 The Pope moves from Rome, Italy, to Avignon, France, creating a rift in the Western Church.

Plague carriers
Fleas on rats carried and transmitted the Black Death, a combination of bubonic and pneumonic plague, which killed a quarter of the European population.

AMERICAS

c.1300 Major expansion of Incas through Andes.
1325 Aztecs found capital at Tenochtitlán.

1350 Acamapitchli becomes Aztec ruler and begins expansion of the empire.

Human sacrifice
Aztec and Inca civilizations believed their angry gods could only be soothed by blood sacrifice.

OCEANIA

1350 Maoris create rock art in New Zealand.

1380–1419

c.1400 Kingdom of Zimbabwe thrives on gold trade.

1398 Mongol leader Tamerlane sacks Indian city of Delhi.
1404–33 Chinese navigator Chang Ho explores India and East Africa.
1405 Death of Tamerlane leads to fall of Mongol Empire.
1411 Ahmad Shah founds Ahmadabad, an important commercial city in India.

The murder of Wat Tyler
Peasant revolts in the years following the Plague were ruthlessly put down.

1381 Wat Tyler and John Ball lead Peasants' Revolt in England against high taxes and low pay. The uprising is crushed and the leaders killed.
1389 Ottoman Turks crush Christian Serbs at Kossovo, Serbia.
1415 French defeated by the English at the Battle of Agincourt in France.

c. 1400 Viracocha becomes first Inca empire builder, establishing permanent rule over conquered neighboring lands.

1420–1459

1432 Portuguese explorers reach the Azores Islands.

1448 Major reforms begin in Thailand under King Traillok.

Thai bronze Buddha
The dominant religion in 15th-century Thailand was Buddhism.

1429 Joan of Arc leads French forces and lifts the Siege of Orléans.
1450 Italian cities of Florence, Milan, and Naples form an alliance.
1450s German craftsman Johannes Gutenberg produces the first printed books in Europe.
1453 Constantinople falls to Ottoman sultan Muhammad II, ending the centuries-old Byzantine Empire.

Muhammad II
Ottoman leader Muhammad II dragged 70 ships overland to avoid a huge iron chain protecting the waterway into Byzantium when he invaded the city.

1438 Inca overlord Pachacuti greatly enlarges the Inca Empire.

	1460–1479	1480–1499
AFRICA	**1464** Sonni Ali becomes ruler of Songhai people in West Africa.	**1482** First Portuguese settlements established on Gold Coast of West Africa. **1488** Sea route from Europe to Asia opened by Portuguese navigator Bartolomeu Diaz, sailing around the Cape of Good Hope, South Africa.
ASIA	**1467** Beginning of the Onin War in Japan, which continues for more than 10 years. It leads to the end of the feudal system and the rise of large territories.	**1497–98** Portuguese explorer Vasco da Gama sails to India via Africa.

Battling warriors in the Onin civil war

Portuguese caravel
The caravel ships used by Portuguese explorers were longer, narrower, and easier to manuever than earlier craft.

EUROPE	**1463–79** Ottoman Turks and Venetians from Italy fight for control of the Mediterranean. The Turks are the eventual victors. **1479** Kingdoms of Aragon and Castille in Spain united by the marriage of King Ferdinand and Queen Isabella.	**1492** Christian conquest of Granada ends Islamic regional control in Spain and results in expulsion of Jews. **1494** Treaty of Tordesillas leads Spain and Portugal to agree to divide the unexplored world between their two nations.
AMERICAS	**1470s** Collapse of Chimu culture in Northern Peru. **1473** Aztec capital Tenochtitlán absorbs neighboring city of Tlatelolco.	**The Renaissance** *The rediscovery or "renaissance" of Greek and Roman ideas on art, literature, and science spreads through Europe from Italy during the 14-1500s.*
OCEANIA	**1450–1500** Widespread cultivation of wet taro, a starchy root vegetable, in the Hawaiian islands.	**1492** Italian explorer Christopher Columbus reaches the Caribbean islands of the Americas. **1497** John Cabot of Italy discovers Newfoundland, present-day Canada.

1500–1519

1500s Southern African Bantus trade with Europeans. Hausa states develop in West Africa.
1517 Ottomans conquer Eygpt.

1502 Safavid dynasty begins in Persia,

c. 1503 Italian artist Leonardo da Vinci begins painting the Mona Lisa.
1512 Michelangelo paints ceiling of the Sistine Chapel, Italy.
1517 European Reformation begins.

The Reformation
Protestant (protesting) churches were formed after Martin Luther called for reform of the corrupt Catholic Church in a list he nailed to his church door in 1517.

1501–02 Amerigo Vespucci of Italy explores the coast of Brazil. First African slaves taken to the West Indies.
1519 Portuguese explorer Ferdinand Magellan sails across the Pacific Ocean.
1520 Spaniard Hernando Cortés brings down the Aztec Empire.

Moctezuma's headdress
This is a replica of a headdress said to have belonged to the last Aztec ruler Moctezuma, who was murdered by Cortés of Spain in 1520.

1520–1539

1520–21 Portuguese traders reach China.
1526 Babur I becomes first Moghul Emperor of India.

Babur I of India
A descendant of Genghis Khan, Babur I was a brilliant military leader who also took an interest in art and poetry.

1529 Ottoman Turks besiege Vienna.
1533 Ivan the Terrible comes to the throne in Russia.

1532 Francisco Pizarro of Spain overthrows Incas in South America by kidnapping and murdering their Emperor, Atahualpa. The leaderless Inca Empire then crumbles.
1534 French explorer Jacques Cartier sails along the St. Lawrence River in Canada.

Inca knife

1526 Portuguese begin landings in Polynesia.

441

	1540–1564	1565–1589
AFRICA	**c. 1540s** Portuguese begin organization of the transatlantic slave trade.	**1566** Sulayman I, ruler of the Ottoman Empire, dies as his empire reaches its peak.
ASIA	**1542** Traders from Portugal reach Japan. **1546** King Tabinshweti unites Burma. **1556** Akbar the Great becomes Moghul emperor of India.	**1577** Akbar the Great completes unification of northern India, providing a structured system of government. **Akbar the Great in religious discussion** *The Islamic Moghul emperor Akbar was renowned for his tolerance of other religions.*
EUROPE	**1541** French Protestant reformer John Calvin sets up Puritan state in Geneva, Switzerland. **1545** Meeting of Catholic leaders at Council of Trent in northern Italy begins Catholic Counter-Reformation. **1564** Birth of English playwright William Shakespeare.	**1571** European alliance defeats Ottoman Turkish fleet at Battle of Lepanto, Greece. **1572** St. Bartholomew's Day Massacre of Protestants (Huguenots) in France. **1588** English navy defeats the Armada, Spain's huge invasion fleet. **St. Bartholomew's Day Massacre**
AMERICAS	**1540s** Spanish arrive in California on the west coast of North America.	**1567** Portuguese establish Rio de Janeiro in Brazil. **1579** Francis Drake claims the west coast of North America for England.
OCEANIA	**1550** Maoris sail from North Island, New Zealand, to settle on South Island. **Maori migration**	**1567** Spanish explorer Mendaña becomes first European to reach Solomon Islands.

1590–1614

1591 Moroccans and European mercenaries destroy Songhai Empire.
1600s Trading posts set up on African coast by all major European powers.

1590 Shah Abbas of Persia makes peace with Ottoman Turkey.
1592 Japan invades Korea under commander Hideyoshi.
1603 Ieyasu of Tokugawa clan becomes ruler of Japan. English East India Company established.
1602 Dutch East India Company founded.

1598 Edict of Nantes ends civil war in France, giving Catholics and Huguenots equal rights.
1604 Russians settle in Siberia.
1605 Failure of Gunpowder Plot in London, England, and arrest of ringleader Guy Fawkes.
1610 French King Henry IV assassinated.
1613 Michael Romanov becomes first Russian Romanov Tsar (king).

1607 John Smith establishes a colony in Virginia at Jamestown.
1608 Foundation of Quebec in Canada.
1609 Henry Hudson sails up the Hudson River on the east coast of North America.

1595 Mendaña lands on Marquesas Islands in the central South Pacific.
1606 Spanish explorer Luis Vaez de Torres sails between Australia and New Guinea.

1615–1639

1620s Queen Nzinga of Ndongo defeats the Portuguese in Angola.

Gatehouse of Edo Castle, Japan
The Tokugawa shogun (ruler) Ieyasu built a heavily fortified castle at the capital city of Edo, now modern Tokyo.

1620s Formation of Japanese national policy restricting contact with the outside world.

1618 Beginning of Thirty Years' War in Europe between Catholic and Protestant powers.

1620 *Mayflower* pilgrims set sail from England for North America.
1625 French begin to settle West Indies.
1626 Dutch found New Amsterdam on site of present-day New York.
1630 Dutch East India Company seizes part of Brazil for its sugar and silver.

Building Manhattan
The first brick house on the site of present-day Manhattan, New York, was built on The Strand in New Amsterdam, now Whitehall Street.

443

1640–1669

1670–1699

AFRICA

1652 Dutch found colony at Cape Town in southern Africa.
1663 Death of Queen Nzinga of Ndongo in Angola.

1670s French colonists settle in Senegal.
1690s Ashanti kingdom established on Gold Coast of West Africa.

ASIA

1644 Manchus invade China, replacing Ming dynasty.
1657 City of Edo on site of present-day Tokyo, Japan, is destroyed by fire.

Manchu lord with Chinese subjects, pigtailed to show inferiority

1683 K'ang Hsi of China conquers Formosa, now modern Taiwan.
1690 Job Caharnock of the English East India Company founds city of Calcutta.

1672 Third Anglo-Dutch trade war begins.
1677 Ottoman Empire at war with Russia.
1682 Peter the Great of Russia starts reign.
1685 Louis XIV of France abolishes Edict of Nantes' protection of the rights of Huguenot protestants. Many flee to England as a result.

EUROPE

1642 Civil War in England.
1643 Louis XIV of France begins reign.
1648 End of the Thirty Years' War in Europe.
1649 Oliver Cromwell executes Charles I of England and sets up Commonwealth.

1688 Protestant William of Orange defeats Catholic James II at the Battle of the Boyne and becomes king of England.

Louis XIV of France in classical costume

AMERICAS

1642 French explorer De Maisonneuve founds Ville-Marie (Montreal) in Canada.
1664 English forces seize New Amsterdam from Dutch and rename it New York.

1670 Colony founded in South Carolina. English Hudson's Bay Company established.
1675 War between colonists and Native Americans devastates New England.
1680 French explorer Robert Cavalier de la Salle claims Mississippi valley for France.
1692 Salem witch trials begin in New England.

OCEANIA

1642 Dutch explorer Abel Tasman becomes first European to reach Van Dieman's Land, Tasmania.

1680 The dodo becomes extinct.   **Dodo**

1700–1729

1702 French win "Asiento," or monopoly on shipping of African slaves to Spanish colonies.
1712 Rise of Futa Jalon kingdom in West Africa.

1707 Death of Moghul leader Aurangzeb leads to breakup of the empire and new opportunities for European traders.
1727 Border fixed between China and Russia.

1700 Death of Charles II of Spain, leaving a French heir, leads to War of Spanish Succession.
1703 Russian Czar Peter the Great founds St. Petersburg.
1707 Act of Union joins England and Scotland.

1709 Abraham Darby's use of coke instead of charcoal to extract metal from iron ore (smelting) starts English Industrial Revolution.

Peter the Great forced nobles to shave

1709 Mass emigration of Germans to America begins.
1710 South Sea Company increases British trade with South America.
1720–22 Spanish occupation of Texas. Collapse of English South Sea and French Mississippi Companies.

1722 Dutch navigator Roggeveen reaches Samoa and Easter Island.

1730–1759

1739 Nadir Shah of Persia defeats the Moghuls and captures city of Delhi, India.
1740s Anglo/French rivalry in India.
1750 China conquers Tibet.
1757 Bengali army defeated by the British at the Battle of Plassey.

1746 Victory of English at Battle of Culloden, Scotland, ends Scottish revolt.
1748 Maria Theresa becomes Empress of Austria.
1755 Earthquake at Lisbon in Portugal.
1756–1763 Seven Years War between Britain and France.

Captured slaves assembled for sale
Slaves transported from Africa to the Americas were often worked to death on plantations owned by European settlers.

1733 England passes the Molasses Act, forbidding trade between American and West Indian colonies. Colony of Georgia founded.
1739 Slave uprising in South Carolina.
1759 English forces defeat French on Plains of Abraham in Quebec, Canada.

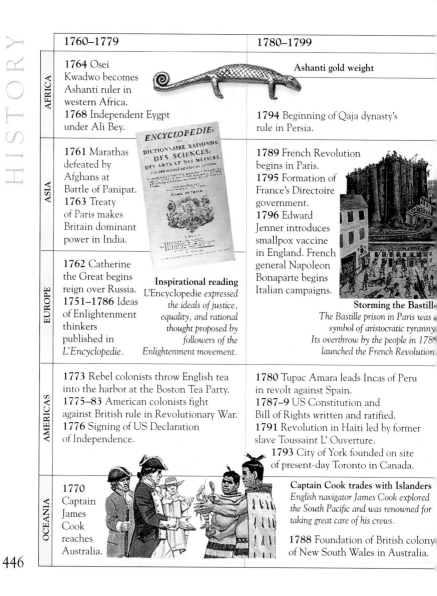

	1760–1779	1780–1799
AFRICA	**1764** Osei Kwadwo becomes Ashanti ruler in western Africa. **1768** Independent Eygpt under Ali Bey.	**Ashanti gold weight** **1794** Beginning of Qaja dynasty's rule in Persia.
ASIA	**1761** Marathas defeated by Afghans at Battle of Panipat. **1763** Treaty of Paris makes Britain dominant power in India.	**1789** French Revolution begins in Paris. **1795** Formation of France's Directoire government. **1796** Edward Jenner introduces smallpox vaccine in England. French general Napoleon Bonaparte begins Italian campaigns.
EUROPE	**1762** Catherine the Great begins reign over Russia. **1751–1786** Ideas of Enlightenment thinkers published in *L'Encyclopedie*. **Inspirational reading** L'Encyclopedie *expressed the ideals of justice, equality, and rational thought proposed by followers of the Enlightenment movement.*	**Storming the Bastille** *The Bastille prison in Paris was a symbol of aristocratic tyranny. Its overthrow by the people in 1789 launched the French Revolution.*
AMERICAS	**1773** Rebel colonists throw English tea into the harbor at the Boston Tea Party. **1775–83** American colonists fight against British rule in Revolutionary War. **1776** Signing of US Declaration of Independence.	**1780** Tupac Amara leads Incas of Peru in revolt against Spain. **1787–9** US Constitution and Bill of Rights written and ratified. **1791** Revolution in Haiti led by former slave Toussaint L' Ouverture. **1793** City of York founded on site of present-day Toronto in Canada.
OCEANIA	**1770** Captain James Cook reaches Australia.	**Captain Cook trades with Islanders** *English navigator James Cook explored the South Pacific and was renowned for taking great care of his crews.* **1788** Foundation of British colony of New South Wales in Australia.

ENCYCLOPEDIE, DICTIONNAIRE RAISONNE DES SCIENCES, DES ARTS ET DES METIERS

1800–1819

1804 British win control of Cape of Good Hope.
1816 Shaka becomes leader of the Zulu warriors.

1815 Java restored to Dutch by the British.
1819 Singapore founded by Stamford Raffles.

Zulu warrior

1805 English admiral Horatio Nelson dies victorious against the French at the Battle of Trafalgar.
1812 French rule under Emperor Napoleon Bonaparte in almost all of Europe.
1815 Napoleon finally defeated at Battle of Waterloo.

Napoleon Bonaparte

1811 Paraguay and Venezuela gain independence from Spain.
1812–1815 British Canada resists invasion from the US.

1806 First white women arrive in New Zealand.
1817 First European emigrants settle Australian grasslands.

1820–1839

1822 Liberian republic for freed slaves founded in west Africa.
1830 French invade Algeria. British and Dutch South Africans (Boers) clash in South Africa.
1836 Start of Great Trek of the Boer farmers to establish independent republics in Transvaal and the Orange Free State.

1824 Britain and Burma at war.
1839–42 China seizes opium imports from India, starting First Opium War.

1821–9 Greek War of Independence from Ottoman Turkey.
1825 First passenger railroad opens in England.
1830 French King Charles X overthrown in July Revolution.
1832 First Reform Act extends voting rights in Britain.
1837 Queen Victoria begins reign in England.

The Rocket
English engineer George Stephenson built this early steam-powered locomotive in 1829.

1821 Mexico wins independence from Spain. Mexicans rule Texas until 1836.
1822 Brazil gains independence from Portuguese.
1832 Samuel Morse invents electric telegraph in US.

S. O. S.

Morse code

1825 Charles Darwin begins a five-year voyage to the Pacific for scientific research.

447

	1840–1844	1845–1849
AFRICA	**1840** Iman Sayid Said, ruler of Oman, makes the island of Zanzibar off the east African coast his capital. **1843** British take over Boer colony in northeastern province of Natal.	**1847** Bantus defeated by British in southern Africa.
ASIA	**1842** Treaty of Nanking gives Hong Kong to Britain and opens trading links with China.	**1845–9** Anglo/Sikh war ends in defeat for Sikhs and the beginning of British rule over their homeland, the Punjab. **1848** Nasir ud-Din begins reign as Shah (ruler) of Persia.
EUROPE	**1840** The introduction of the Penny postage stamp leads to a low-cost, universally priced British postal service.	**1845–46** Failure of potato crop in Ireland leads to severe famine. **1848** Year of Revolution in Europe. **1849** Collapse of revolutionary movements.
AMERICAS	**1840** First general anesthetic used in America by C.W. Long. Upper and Lower Canada form self-governing union.	**1845** Texas and Florida become US states. **1846** US and Mexico at war over Texas. **1848** California Gold Rush leads to rapid population growth in western United States. First US women's rights convention in New York State.
OCEANIA	**1840** Treaty of Waitangi signed in New Zealand.	

Penny Black stamp

Native Americans defend their land
Increased numbers of European settlers threatened Native American territories.

British and Maoris at Waitangi
The Treaty of Waitangi gave Britain possession of New Zealand in return for recognizing ancient Maori land rights.

1850–1854

1854 Independent Orange Free State set up in South Africa.

1850–64 Taiping revolt in China.
1852–53 Second war between England and Burma.
1853–54 US Navy forces Japan to open up to Western trade.

1851 Great Exhibition celebrating the industrial age held at the Crystal Palace in London.
1853–56 Crimean War between Russia, Britain, and France.

Crystal Palace

1850 California becomes a US state.
1851 First pedal-powered sewing machine made by I.S. Singer.
1853 Completion of railroad from New York to Chicago.

1850 Australian Colonies Act enables New South Wales, Tasmania, and South Australia to have virtual self-government.
1851 Australian Gold Rush begins.

Gold miners

1855–1859

1855 Discovery of Victoria Falls by English explorer Livingstone leads to European exploration of African interior.

1856–57 Persia's seizure of Herat, Afghanistan, leads to war with Britain.

Uprising in India
The refusal of Hindu and Muslim soldiers to comply with an order on religious grounds led to a major protest against British rule in 1857.

1857 Britain governs India directly after "Indian Mutiny."
1858 Treaty of Tientsin forces China to trade with the West.

1856 Henry Bessemer invents industrial steelmaking process in England.
1859–61 Giuseppe Garibaldi leads the "red shirts" in the War of Italian Unification, capturing Sicily and southern Italy to form a new Italian state.

Garibaldi

1858 Reformer Benito Juarez becomes president of Mexico.
1856 Formation of anti-slavery Republican party in US.

1856 Major Australian colonies achieve self-government.

449

1860–1869	1870–1879

AFRICA

1860s Britain, France, Belgium, Germany, and Portugal begin to explore and colonize inner Africa.
1869 Opening of the Suez Canal in Egypt links the Mediterranean Sea with the Indian Ocean.

1879 British defeat Zulu uprising led by King Cetshwayo at Ulundi, South Africa.
1881 Boers rebel against British rule in South Africa, leading to First Boer War.

Zulu shield
The South African Zulu people fought the British and Boer settlers to protect their land

ASIA

1861 Empress Tze Hsi begins her 47-year rule of China.
1862 French occupation of Indo-China in Southeast Asia.

1870s Japan begins industrialization.
1872 Feudal control of Japan ends. Compulsory education is introduced.

EUROPE

1864–66 Prussian forces defeat Denmark and Austria.
1866 Swedish chemist Alfred Nobel invents dynamite.

Empire builder
Chief minister of the Prussian state in Germany, Otto von Bismarck united the country and founded the German Empire in 1871 with Prussian King William I as emperor.

1870s Most Western European countries start industrialization.
1871 Otto von Bismarck invades and defeats France. Britain legalizes trade unions.
1876 French build refrigerated cargo ships.

Key innovation
The late 19th century saw dramatic advances in technology with the development of new inventions like electric light and telephone.

AMERICAS

1861 US Civil War begins.
1865 Union victory in Civil War. President Abraham Lincoln assassinated.
1867 British North America Act creates Dominion of Canada.

1876 Sioux and Cheyenne tribes defeat Custer at the Battle of Little Bighorn.
1876–1911 Porfirio Diaz begins rule as President of Mexico.
1879–84 Chile defeats Peru and Bolivia in the War of the Pacific.
1883 Thomas Edison invents the lightbulb.

OCEANIA

1860–70 War between Maoris and white settlers in New Zealand.

North v. South
The split of 11 Southern states from the Union in 1861 led to civil war in the US.

1868 Last convict-settlers arrive in Australia.

1880–1889

1882 British rule of Egypt begins.
1886 Gold discovered in South Africa.

1880s Britain and France move into Burma and Vietnam.
1885 Indian National Congress Party formed.

Chinese revolt against Western power

1884 Berlin Conference decides colonial divisions in Africa. First deep underground railroad built in London.
1885 Karl Benz builds first car driven by internal combustion engine in Germany.
1888 Scottish surgeon John Dunlop patents pneumatic (air-filled) tire. Kaiser (Emperor) William II starts German reign.

Benz Motorwagen

1882 Thomas Edison designs the first hydroelectric power station.
1884 First skyscraper built in Chicago.
1889 King Pedro II deposed by army revolt and Brazil declared a republic.

1880 Tahiti becomes a French colony.
1884 Volcano erupts on Krakatoa, Indonesia.
1885-86 Opening up of gold fields in New Guinea.

1890–1899

1896 Ethiopians defeat Italian army.
1899 Second Boer War begins in South Africa.

1899-1901 Chinese government supports peasant revolt by the Society of Harmonious Fists to rid China of all foreigners. This so-called "Boxer Rebellion" is crushed by Western forces.

1896 Modern Olympic Games introduced in Greece.
1897 Greece and Turkey at war.

1890 Last massacre of Native Americans in US at Battle of Wounded Knee in Dakota. First moving picture (film) shows appear in New York.
1895 Cuban revolt against Spanish rule.
1896 Gold struck in Klondike, Canada.
1898 US wins Spanish-American War and takes over the Philippines. Cuban independence from Spain.

Sioux warrior
About 300 members of the Sioux tribe were slaughtered at the Battle of Wounded Knee.

1893 New Zealand Prime Minister Richard Seddon introduces advanced social reforms, including granting women the vote.

	1900–1904	1905–1909
AFRICA	**1902** Ovimbundu people of Angola revolt against Portuguese rule. **1904** Federation of French West Africa created.	**1905** Independent Union of former Boer republics founded in South Africa.
ASIA	**1904-5** Russo-Japanese war in Manchuria, ending in defeat for Russia and the total destruction of its fleet. **Russians fight the Japanese at the Battle of Liaio-Yang**	**1907** Discovery of oil in Persia, now modern Iran. **1909** Conflict between China and Tibet.
EUROPE	**1900** Expansion of German navy begins arms race with Britain. **1903** Votes for Women Movement formed in Britain by suffragette Emmeline Pankhurst. First Tour de France bicycle race. **1904** French and British empires agree to Entente Cordiale (friendly understanding).	**1905** Czar of Russia forced to grant democratic rights in October Manifesto. Physicist Albert Einstein formulates his Special Theory of Relativity. **1908** The AEG turbine factory in Berlin, Germany is built. It is the world's first steel and glass building.
AMERICAS	**1900** Coca-Cola first produced in US. **1901** Theodore Roosevelt becomes youngest-ever US president after assassination of President McKinley. **1902** Plastic invented in US. **1903** Orville and Wilbur Wright build the first airplane and make a successful powered flight.	**1906** US forces occupy Cuba. Major earthquake damage in San Francisco. **1907** First comic strips appear in US. **1908** Henry Ford manufactures first Model T motor car.
OCEANIA	**1901** Australia becomes a Commonwealth. New Zealand takes over the Cook Islands. **Wright Flyer**	**1907** New Zealand becomes a dominion. Minimum basic wage law set in Australia.

1910–1914	1915–1919
1911 Lamogi people of Uganda rebel against British rule. **1912** African National Congress formed to fight for black people's rights.	**1917** Ras (Prince) Tafari takes power in Ethiopia.
1910 Japan takes over Korea. **1911** Chinese revolution overthrows Manchu dynasty.	**1915** Mohandas Gandhi becomes leader of the Indian National Congress Party. **1919** British troops fire on peaceful Indian protest in Amritsar Massacre, killing 379 people.

The sinking of the *Titanic*

1910 Halley's Comet appears.
1911 Norwegian explorer Roald Amundsen reaches South Pole.
1912 The *Titanic*, the world's largest ocean liner, strikes an iceberg on her maiden voyage, sinking with the loss of 1,513 lives.
1912–13 Greece, Serbia, Bulgaria, and Montenegro unite to defeat Ottoman Turkey in the Balkan War.
1914 European alliances break down with the assassination of Archduke Ferdinand, heir to the Austro-Hungarian Empire. World War I begins.

German soldiers, World War I

1915 Bulgaria aligns with Central Powers (Germany, Austro-Hungary) and Italy joins Allies (Britain, France, Russia, Serbia) in World War I.
1916 Irish revolt against British rule in Easter Rising.
1917 Communists take over from Czar in Russian Revolution, leading to civil war. Greece joins the Allies.
1918 World War I ends with Allied victory.

Comrades in arms
Russian workers inspired by Vladimir Lenin of the Communist Bolshevik Party overthrew the tyrannical Czar Nicholas II in 1917.

1911 Mexican dictator Diaz overthrown in revolution.
1912–33 US troops occupy Nicaragua.
1914 Opening of Panama Canal.

1915–16 Unrest in Haiti and Dominican Republic put down by US troops.
1917 US enters World War I.

1914 Australia and New Zealand join the Allies in World War I.

1919 Australia acquires former German colonies in the Pacific.

453

	1920–1924	1925–1929
AFRICA	**1922** Egypt under King Faud wins conditional independence from Britain. **1923** Ethiopia joins League of Nations.	**1926** End of Berber and Arab revolt against Europeans in North Africa. **1927** Communists, led by Mao Tse-tung, attempt to overthrow Chinese government. **1929** Arabs attack Jews in Jerusalem, Palestine in a conflict over the Wailing Wall.
ASIA	**1923** Major earthquake in Tokyo, Japan. End of Ottoman Empire as Mustafa Kemal becomes president of new Republic of Turkey.	**Dictator of Italy** *Fascist leader Benito Mussolini led Italy into World War II on Germany's side in 1940. He was captured and executed in 1945.* **1925** Mussolini, Fascist leader of Italy, rules the country as a dictator. **1926** Police and army defeat general strike in Britain.
EUROPE	**1920** Communist Red Army under Leon Trotsky wins Russian Civil War. **1922** Benito Mussolini becomes prime minister of Italian government. **1923** Partial Irish independence from Britain with creation of Irish Free State. **1924** Russian leader Vladimir Lenin dies and is succeeded by Josef Stalin.	**1927** *The Jazz Singer*, starring Al Jolson, is released in the US. It is the first "talkie," or film including a synchronized speech and music soundtrack. **1929** Prices of shares on American stock exchange fall rapidly in Wall Street Crash.
AMERICAS	**1920** Prohibition (banning) of the manufacture and sale of alcohol begins in USA. **1924** US military planes make first airborne trip around the world.	**The Great Depression** *In October 1929, panicking share dealers on Wall Street, sold 13 million shares in one day. This contributed to the worldwide economic crisis called the Great Depression, in which millions of people lost their jobs, businesses, savings, and homes.*
OCEANIA	**1923** Ross area of Antarctica becomes New Zealand dependency.	**1927** Canberra becomes capital of Australia.

1930–1934

1930 Ras Tafari crowned as Haile Selassie I in Ethiopia.
1934 Lagos Youth Movement formed, demanding self-government of Nigeria.

1930s Indian leader Gandhi leads nonviolent opposition to British rule in India.
1934–35 Long March of Communists across China to find sanctuary in the Shaanxi province. Troops supporting the Nationalist leader Chiang Kai-shek pursue them daily.

Chinese Communist troops on the Long March

1933 Adolf Hitler, Führer (leader) of the Nazi Party, becomes German Chancellor.

Führer of the Nazis
Hitler's dreams of German world domination contributed to the outbreak of World War II. The war resulted in the mass murder, or holocaust, of 6 million Jews in Nazi concentration camps.

1931 British Parliament grants Canada full independence.
1933 Franklin D. Roosevelt becomes US President, ending prohibition of alcohol.

1931 First solo trans-Tasmanian flight. Airmail service between Australia and Britain introduced.

1935–1939

1935 Italian forces invade Ethiopia.

1936 Signing of alliance between Japan and Germany.
1937 Japan occupies much of Chinese coast, leading to war between the nations.

The rise of Japan
Military rule of Japan in the late 1930s led to displays of the nation's strength in warfare and empire building.

1936 Olympic Games in Berlin, Germany.
1936–39 Spanish Civil War ends in victory for Fascists and defeat for Communists.
1937 Frank Whittle invents the jet engine in Britain.
1938 Czechoslovakia taken over by German forces.
1939 Britain and France declare war on Germany after Hitler invades Poland. Beginning of World War II.

1935 US National Labor Relations Act comes into force.

1937 Formation of Royal New Zealand Air Force.
1939 Australia and New Zealand join Allied forces against Germany.

	1940–1941	1942–1943
AFRICA	**1940** British Navy sinks French fleet at Oran to prevent its capture by Germany. **1941** Allied troops overrun Italy's African colonies. German forces led by Erwin Rommel arrive in Libya to help Italy.	**1942** Allied troops land in Morocco and force Rommel's troops to retreat from El Alamein.
ASIA	**1941** French colonies in Southeast Asia taken over by Japanese. **1941–42** Japan captures the Philippines, Malaya, Hong Kong, Singapore, Burma, and Indonesia.	**1942** US Navy defeats Japan in Coral Sea of New Guinea and at Midway Island. **1943–44** Series of victories by US in Pacific islands pushes back Japanese forces.
EUROPE	**1940** Germany occupies Denmark, Norway, France, Belgium, and the Netherlands. Winston Churchill becomes Prime Minister of Britain. British air force prevents German invasion in the Battle of Britain. **1941** Hungary, Bulgaria, Greece, and parts of Yugoslavia and Russia under Germans.	**1943** Allied troops take over Sicily, then invade Italian mainland. **1943** German forces driven out of Russia.
AMERICAS	**1940** Xerox photocopying machine invented. Development of penicillin and other early antibiotics. **1941** US joins Allies in World War II after Japanese attack on US Navy at Pearl Harbor in Hawaii.	**1942** Enrico Fermi builds first US nuclear reactor. Mexico and Brazil join Allies. Nylon used for hosiery and parachutes first produced in US.
OCEANIA	**1940s** Australia prepares for the eventuality of a Japanese invasion.	**1942** Japanese bomb Darwin, Australia, and invade New Guinea and part of Papua.

Winston Churchill
The many rousing speeches given on the radio by Britain's wartime leader Winston Churchill helped inspire the Allies to victory.

Nylon stockings

Attack on Pearl Harbor
The surprise assault by Japanese forces on the US Navy fleet at Pearl Harbor, Hawaii, in 1941 sank or damaged 18 ships and destroyed 200 aircraft.

1944 Japan attacks India but is defeated at Kohima.
1945 US drops first atomic bombs on Japanese cities of Hiroshima and Nagasaki. Emperor Hirohito authorizes Japanese surrender.

Emperor Hirohito of Japan
Japanese pilots thought of Emperor Hirohito as a god and considered it an honor to die for him on "kamikaze" missions, which involved crash-diving explosive-packed planes into Allied ships.

1944 Allies invade France and drive back Germans.
1945 German forces surrender.

1945 US tests first atomic bomb in New Mexico.

Dawn of the Nuclear Age
The first atomic bomb was dropped on Hiroshima, Japan, in 1945, instantly killing about 80,000 people. A second bomb was dropped on the city of Nagasaki three days later, leading to the surrender of Japan and the end of World War II.

1944 Mass breakout of Japanese prisoners of war in Australia.
1945 Australia recovers New Guinea and Papua territory from Japan.

Gandhi and followers

1947 India gains independence from Great Britain amid riots that kill 500,000 people. Indian leader Gandhi begins a protest fast against the continuing violence.

1947 Marshall Plan offers US aid to help European countries rebuild their economies after World War II.

United Nations flag
The United Nations (UN) was established in 1945 to foster friendly relations between nations and to try to solve international disputes without war.

1947 US government promises to aid any country resisting communism.

1947 South Pacific Commission formed to discuss economic and health issues of South Pacific islands.

1940 – 1947

	1948–1950	**1951–1953**
AFRICA	**1950** Group Areas Act enforcing racial segregation (apartheid) passed in South Africa.	**1951** Libyan independence from Italy sanctioned by US. **1953** Military coup in Egypt ends anarchy and establishes a republic.

AFRICA

1950 Group Areas Act enforcing racial segregation (apartheid) passed in South Africa.

ASIA

1948 Gandhi assassinated in India. State of Israel created in Palestine. **1949** Founding of Mao Tse-tung's new Communist Republic in China.

Jewish nation
In 1948, the United Nations established the state of Israel in the ancient Jewish homeland of Palestine. The resulting conflict over territory between Israelis and Arab Palestinians has continued ever since.

EUROPE

1948 Berlin Airlift of supplies defeats USSR's blockade of West Berlin. **1949** Germany divided in two, with US, France, and Britain running the West, and USSR controlling the East. Western Europe and US form defensive NATO alliance against attack by USSR.

AMERICAS

1948 Harry Truman wins Presidential election in US. **1950** Senator Joseph McCarthy begins anti-communist "witch-hunts" in US.

OCEANIA

1951 Libyan independence from Italy sanctioned by US. **1953** Military coup in Egypt ends anarchy and establishes a republic.

1950-53 War between communist North Korea and US-occupied South Korea. **1953** Edmund Hillary and Sherpa Tenzing Norgay are first people to reach summit of Mount Everest.

Hillary and Tensing

1952 Greece and Turkey join NATO.

1950s Black Americans intensify their campaign for civil rights. **1953** Link between smoking and lung cancer first established in US.

Post-war Europe
After World War II, Europe was divided into the USSR-controlled East and the US-backed West. The uneasy peace between each side, known as the Cold War, led to an arms race between the US and USSR in which both superpowers began to stockpile nuclear weapons.

1951 Australia, New Zealand, and US sign ANZUS Pact defense alliance.

1954–1956

1954 National Liberation Front formed in Algeria to fight French rule.
1955 African National Congress (ANC) pressure group in South Africa adopts antiracist Freedom Charter.
1956 Eygptian leader Nasser captures the Suez Canal.

1954 French defeated by communist forces at Dien Bien Phu, North Vietnam. Vietnam divided into communist North and US-backed South.
1956 Israel captures Sinai peninsula from Arab forces in eight days.

Symbol of Soviet Communism

1955 Warsaw Pact defense treaty signed by communist nations, allowing Soviet (USSR) troops to be stationed in any communist Eastern European country. West Germany joins NATO and East Germany becomes part of Warsaw Pact.
1957 USSR launches Sputnik I, the world's first artificial satellite.

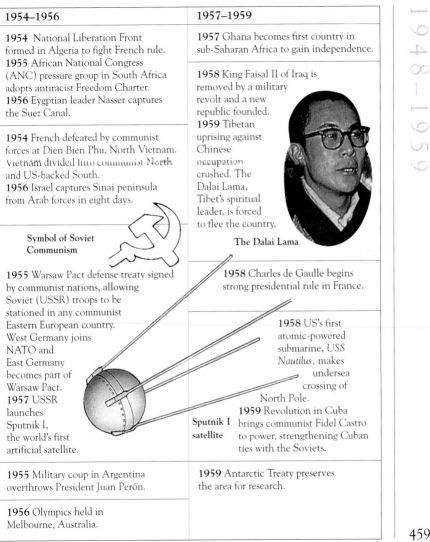

Sputnik I satellite

1955 Military coup in Argentina overthrows President Juan Perón.

1956 Olympics held in Melbourne, Australia.

1957–1959

1957 Ghana becomes first country in sub-Saharan Africa to gain independence.

1958 King Faisal II of Iraq is removed by a military revolt and a new republic founded.
1959 Tibetan uprising against Chinese occupation crushed. The Dalai Lama, Tibet's spiritual leader, is forced to flee the country.

The Dalai Lama

1958 Charles de Gaulle begins strong presidential rule in France.

1958 US's first atomic-powered submarine, *USS Nautilus*, makes undersea crossing of North Pole.
1959 Revolution in Cuba brings communist Fidel Castro to power, strengthening Cuban ties with the Soviets.

1959 Antarctic Treaty preserves the area for research.

	1960–1963	1964–1967
AFRICA	**1960** Independence gained by 17 African colonies. A peaceful demonstration in Sharpeville against white rule in South Africa ends in the death of 69 protestors and banning of the ANC.	**1964** ANC leader Nelson Mandela jailed in South Africa. **1965** White-ruled Rhodesia declares independence from Britain. **1967** Dr. Christiaan Barnard completes first heart transplant in South Africa.
ASIA	**1963** Diem, leader of South Vietnam, is assassinated in a military coup.	**Cultural revolution in China** *Mao Tse-tung's "cultural revolution" brought Chinese industry and agriculture under state control and closed schools and colleges, forcing teachers and students to work on the land. Any opposition was brutally put down by the Red Guards, the Communist Party police.*
EUROPE	**1961** Berlin Wall built. Russian cosmonaut Yuri Gagarin is first man in space. **1962** British pop group The Beatles release *Love Me Do*, their first hit record.	**1965** US troops start arriving in South Vietnam to help in the fight against communist North Vietnam. **1966** Chinese Cultural Revolution begins. **1964** Fighting between Greeks and Turks in Cyprus. **1967** Military coup in Greece.
AMERICAS	**1960** Election of John F. Kennedy, the youngest US president. **1962** Cuban Missile Crisis. **1963** President Kennedy assassinated.	**1965** Malcolm X, campaigner for black civil rights, assassinated. Riots break out in Chicago and Los Angeles.
OCEANIA	**1960** Aborigines granted the same social security benefits as the rest of Australian society.	**1965** Ferdinand E. Marcos elected President of the Philippines. **1967** Aborigines gain Australian citizenship.

Fidel Castro
In 1962, Cuban dictator Fidel Castro allowed the USSR to build missile bases on Cuban soil. The US Navy blockaded Cuba and the Russians withdrew.

Martin Luther King Jr.
During the 1960s, civil rights leaders such as Martin Luther King and Malcolm X campaigned for the rights of black Americans.

1968–1971	1972–1975

1970 Biafra region defeated by Federal Nigerian government in civil war.

1975 Portuguese colonies in Africa win independence.

1968 US soldiers kill hundreds of unarmed civilians in Vietnamese village of My Lai.
1971 East Pakistan gains independence from India, becoming Bangladesh.

Allied troops in Vietnam

1972 Ceylon becomes Republic of Sri Lanka.
1973 US, Australian, and New Zealand allied troops withdraw from Vietnam. Arab states attack Israel in October War and raise oil prices, leading to a world economic crisis.

Arabian oil
Many countries dependent on Arabian oil faced economic disaster when the Arab states raised their oil prices in 1973.

1968 Riots in Paris as students call for educational and social reform and workers demand a new minimum wage. Anti-communist uprising in Prague, former Czechoslavkia.
1969 Britain sends troops to Northern Ireland.

1968 Assassination of Martin Luther King in Memphis.
1969 US astronauts Neil Armstrong and Edwin "Buzz" Aldrin walk on the moon.

Men on the Moon
The live television broadcast of Neil Armstrong taking humankind's first steps on the lunar surface was seen by about 600 million people.

1973 Sydney Opera House opens in Australia.

1972 "Bloody Sunday" in Londonderry, Northern Ireland, as British troops fire on civil rights marchers.

1973 Elected Chilean president Allende killed in military coup led by General Pinochet.
1974 US President Richard Nixon resigns in disgrace after Watergate scandal.

1975 Australia grants Papua New Guinea independence.

HISTORY

	1976–1980	1981–1985
AFRICA	**1976** Riots in black townships across South Africa. **1979** Ugandan leader Idi Amin ousted by Tanzanian-backed rebels. **1980** Independent Zimbabwe formed under leadership of Robert Mugabe.	**1983** War and drought lead to famine in Ethiopia. **Ethiopian Famine**
ASIA	**1976** North and South Vietnam reunited as a communist country after 22 years of separation. **1979** Camp David peace treaty between Egypt and Israel. Islamic revolution in Iran.	**1982** Israeli troops invade southern Lebanon. Palestinians massacred in Beirut refugee camp. **1984** Siege at Amritsar, India, ends with Sikh extremists being forced out of Golden Temple. Indian Prime Minister Indira Gandhi assassinated by her Sikh bodyguards. **Iranian Revolution** *Ayatollah Khomeini, a fundamentalist (strict) Muslim hostile to the West, led the Islamic revolution that overthrew the Shah (King) of Iran in 1979. The exiled Shah's entry into the USA led to Iranian students taking 53 Americans hostage in the US embassy in Tehran.*
EUROPE	**1976** Adoption of Helsinki Convention on human rights. **1978** Margaret Thatcher becomes Britain's first woman Prime Minister. **1980** President Tito of Yugoslavia dies. Lech Walesa leads Solidarity trade union in Poland.	
AMERICAS	**1977** Jimmy Carter elected US President. **1979** Sandinista guerillas defeat government forces and take power in Nicaragua. **Personal computing** *The first personal desktop computer (PC) was developed by the American company IBM in 1981.*	**1981** Death of 11 Irish republican prisoners on hunger strike. **1984** French and US scientists independently identify the AIDS virus. **1980s** First personal computers developed in US. **1980** Victory for Ronald Reagan in US Presidential elections. **1982** Britain defeats Argentine forces occupying British-held Falkland islands in Falklands War. Creation of Canadian constitution independent from UK.
OCEANIA	**1978** The Solomon islands of Tuvalu and Dominica become independent nations.	**1984** New Zealand declares itself a nuclear-free zone.

462

1986–1990

1990 Dismantling of apartheid begins in South Africa as Nelson Mandela is freed after 27 years in prison. Namibia gains independence from South Africa.
1990 Civil war begins in Liberia.

1988 Ceasefire in Iran-Iraq war ends eight years of conflict.
1989 Chinese security forces kill pro-democracy protestors in Beijing's Tiananmen Square.
1990 Iraq invades Kuwait.

Protester at Tiananmen Square

1986 New Soviet leader Mikhail Gorbachev introduces the policies of *glasnost* (openess) and *perestroika* (remodeling), eventually resulting in the breakup of the Soviet Union.
1989 Communist governments overthrown in Romania, Hungary, East Germany, and Czechoslovakia.

1986 "Irangate" revelations as US President Reagan questioned on secret arms deals with Iran.
1989 George Bush becomes US President.

1986 Treaty of Rarotonga sets up South Pacific Nuclear-Free Zone.

1991–1997

1991 Collapse of government rule in Somalia.
1992 US leads UN troops into Somalia.
1993 Eritrea gains independence from Ethiopia.
1994 ANC wins South Africa's first free elections. Civil war in Rwanda.

1994 Palestinian self-rule over the Gaza Strip under 1993 peace treaty between Israel and the Palestinian Liberation Organization (PLO).

Yasser Arafat, leader of the PLO

1991 Gulf War ends with Iraq being driven from Kuwait by UN forces.
1995 Israeli Prime Minister, Yitzhak Rabin, is assassinated.

1991 Dissolution of Soviet Union into Commonwealth of Independent States.

1992–95 Civil war between countries in former Yugoslavia.
1997 Tony Blair becomes Britain's new Labour Prime Minister.

Fall of USSR

1993 Canada creates Nunavut, its largest Native territory at 850,000 sq miles (2.2 million sq km).
Bill Clinton elected as US President.

1991 John Howard becomes Australian Prime Minister.

REFERENCE SECTION

Major wars

3100 B.C. First recorded war. Pharaoh Narmer unites Upper and Lower Egypt.
c.1200 B.C. Trojan War War between Greeks and Trojans, as in Homer's *Iliad*.
264–146 B.C. Punic Wars Three wars between Rome and Hannibal's Carthage, which is destroyed.
c. A.D. 1096–1291 Crusades Series of religious wars in which European Christians try to recapture Holy Land from Muslims.
1337–1453 Hundred Years War English and French battle for control of France. The French win.
1455–1485 Wars of the Roses English war between Houses of York and Lancaster for control of English throne.
1618–1648 Thirty Years War Initially between German Catholics and Protestants but later involves all Europe.
1756–1763 Seven Years War Prussia and England fight against Austria and France for control of Germany.
1775–1783 American Revolution American colonists fight for independence from British rule. After they win, they form the USA.
1792–1815 Napoleonic Wars Fought between Napoleon's France and Austria, Britain, Russia, Prussia, and Sweden.
1821–1829 Greek War of Independence Greeks fight Turkish rule.
1825–1830 Java War Revolt of Indonesians against Dutch.
1839–1842 Opium War Trade war between Britain and China.

1846–1848 Mexican-American War Mexico and USA battle over Texas.
1853–1856 Crimean War Turkey, allied with Britain, France, and Sardinia, fights Russia in the Black Sea.
1861–1865 American Civil War Civil war between Unionists of north and Confederates of south.
1870–1871 Franco-Prussian War Prussian war against France ends with establishment of German Empire.
1894–1895 Chinese-Japanese War Japanese defeat Chinese.
1899–1902 Boer War Britain and the Commonwealth fight Boers for control of South Africa.
1914–1918 World War I Britain, France, Russia, USA and others in global war against Germany, Austria-Hungary, and Turkey.
1939–1945 World War II Global war between Axis powers of Germany, Italy, and Japan and Allied powers of Britain, USA, and USSR.
1950–1953 Korean War Communist North Korea fights against South Korea and US allies.
1965–1975 Vietnam War Communist North Vietnam fights against South Vietnam and US allies.
1967 Six Day War Egypt against Israel.
1980–88 Iran-Iraq War
1991 Gulf War Saddam Hussein's Iraq defeated by United Nations forces.
1991–1996 Bosnian war Civil war in former Yugoslavia.

Famous battles

490 B.C. Marathon (Greece) Athenians defeat Persians and save Greece.

331 B.C. Gaugamela (Persia) Alexander the Great's greatest victory, defeating the Persian King Darius II.

31 B.C. Actium (Greece) Octavian defeats Mark Antony and Cleopatra of Egypt and becomes Emperor Augustus, ending the Roman civil wars.

A.D. 378 Adrianople (Turkey) Goths (Germanic tribes) defeat Romans.

636 Yarmuk (Israel) Arabs under Khalid ibn–al Walid defeat Byzantines in desert sandstorm.

732 Tours (France) Charles Martel leads Franks to victory over Moors to halt their advance in Europe.

1066 Hastings (Britain) Normans under William the Conqueror invade England and beat the Saxons.

1429 Orléans (France) French heroine Joan of Arc lifts English siege of Orléans.

1453 Constantinople (Turkey) Turks besiege and capture Constintinople (Istanbul), ending Byzantine Empire.

1526 Panipat (India) Babur conquers Delhi and establishes Mughal empire

1571 Lepanto (Greece) End of Turkish seapower in the Mediterranean.

1588 Spanish Armada (Britain) English ships and storms defeat great Spanish invasion fleet of 130 ships.

1704 Blenheim (Germany) British-Austrian army led by Duke of Marlborough beats French, limiting French power in Europe.

1709 Poltava (Ukraine) Peter the Great of Russia defeats Swedes under Charles XII to control the Baltic Sea.

1759 Quebec (Canada) Britain gains control of Canada.

1777 Saratoga (USA) Decisive battle in American Revolution. British, led by Gen. Burgoyne, surrender to Americans.

1781 Yorktown (USA) George Washington leads Americans to final victory over British, ending American Revolution.

1805 Trafalgar (South of Spain) Nelson's British fleet destroys French and Spanish fleet.

1815 Waterloo End of Napoleonic wars. Allies under Wellington crush Napoleon.

1863 Gettysburg (USA) Decisive battle of American Civil War. Unionists defeat Confederates.

1914 Marne (France) Allies halt German advance on Paris.

1916 Somme (France) The deadliest battle of World War I. 1,265,000 men are killed in a few days.

1940 Battle of Britain Aircraft of British Royal Air Force (RAF) drive off German bombing raids.

1942 Midway (Pacific) Japanese aircraft fail to capture Midway Island from the USA.

1944 D–day (Normandy, France) Allies invade German-occupied France.

1991 Operation Desert Storm (Iraq) Airborne attack on Iraq by United Nations forces turns Gulf War.

Units of measurement

The metric system, based on the number ten, is the most common system of measurement and is used by scientists worldwide. Certain countries, such as the USA, use the older imperial system.

TEMPERATURE CONVERSIONS

To convert Fahrenheit (°F) into centigrade (°C), use the formula:
°C = (°F − 32) ÷ 1.8

To convert centigrade (°C) into Fahrenheit (°F), use the formula:
°F = (°C x 1.8) + 32

VOLUME

1 cubic in (in³)	
1 cubic ft (ft³)	144 in³
1 cubic yd (yd³)	9 ft³
1 fluid oz (fl oz)	4,840 yd³
1 pint (pt)	20 fl oz
1 gallon (gal)	
1 cubic mm (mm³)	
1 cubic cm (cm³)	100 mm³
1 cubic meter (m³)	1,000,000 cm³
1 liter (l)	1,000 cm³

LENGTH

1 inch (in)	
1 foot (ft)	12 in
1 yard (yd)	3 ft
1 mile	1,760 yd
1 millimeter (mm)	
1 centimeter (cm)	10 mm
1 meter (m)	100 cm
1 kilometer (km)	1,000 m

AREA

1 square inch (in²)	
1 sq foot (ft²)	144 in²
1 sq yard (yd²)	9 ft²
1 acre	4,840 yd²
1 sq mile	640 acres
1 sq millimeter (mm²)	
1 sq centimeter (cm²)	100 mm²
1 sq meter (m²)	10,000 cm²
1 hectare	10,000 m²
1 sq kilometer (km²)	1,000,000 m²

MASS AND WEIGHT

1 ounce (oz)	
1 pound (lb)	16 oz
1 stone	14 lb
1 hundredweight (cwt)	8 stones
1 ton	20 cwt
1 gram (g)	
1 kilogram (kg)	1,000 g
1 tonne (t)	1,000 kg

Conversions

You can convert between the metric and imperial systems of measurement by using the following conversion tables.

LENGTH

To convert	Into	X by
in	cm	2.54
ft	m	0.3048
yd	m	0.9144
miles	km	1.6093
cm	in	0.3937
m	f	3.2808
m	yd	1.0936
km	miles	0.6214

AREA

To convert	Into	X by
sq in	sq cm	6.4516
sq ft	sq m	0.0929
sq yd	sq m	0.8361
acres	hectares	0.4047
sq miles	sq km	2.59
sq cm	sq in	0.155
sq m	sq ft	10.7639
sq m	sq yd	1.1960
hectares	acres	2.4711
sq km	sq miles	0.3861

MASS AND WEIGHT

To convert	Into	X by
oz	g	28.3495
lb	kg	0.4536
stones	kg	6.3503
cwt	kg	50.802
tons	tonnes	1.0161
g	oz	0.0352
kg	lb	2.2046
kg	stones	0.1575
kg	cwt	0.0197
tonnes	tons	0.9842

VOLUME

To convert	Into	X by
in^3	cm^3 (milliliters)	16.3871
ft^3	liters	28.3169
yd^3	m^3	0.7646
fl oz	cm^3	28.4131
pints	liters	0.5683
gallons	liters	4.5461
cm^3	in^3	0.0610
cm^3	fl oz	0.0352
liters	ft^3	0.0353
m^3	yd^3	1.3080
litres	pints	1.7598
litres	gallons	0.2200

PREFIXES

kilo	=	1000	centi	=	$\frac{1}{100}$
hecto	=	100	milli	=	$\frac{1}{1,000}$
deci	=	$\frac{1}{2}$	micro	=	$\frac{1}{1,000,000}$

Index to map pages

Grid references in the Index help find places on the map. If you look up Nairobi in the Index, you will see 302 F4. The first number, 302, is the page number on which the map of Nairobi appears. Next, find the letters and numbers which border the page and trace a line across from the letter and down from the number. This will direct you to the exact grid square in which the city of Nairobi is located.

San Luis Potosí Mexico
223 F5
San Marino (Country)
262 D4
San Miguel de Tucumán
Argentina 242 C4
San Salvador El Salvador
230 B5
San Salvador de Jujuy
Paraguay 242 C3
Sanandaj Iran 321 F2
Sandoway Myanmar 344 B4
Santa Ana USA 221 D8
Santa Barbara USA 221 C8
Santa Cruz Bolivia 237 E7
Santa Fe Argentina 242 D4
Santa Fe USA 219 F4
Santa Marta Colombia
236 B3
Santander Spain 259 E2
Santarém Brazil 240 E4
Santiago Chile 243 B5
Santiago de Compostela
Spain 258 C2
Santo Domingo
Dominican Rep. 231 F5
São Francisco (R.) Brazil
241 G5
São Luís Brazil 240 G4
São Paulo Brazil 241 F6
São Tomé & Prîncipe
(Country) 361 G5/305 B6
Sapporo Japan 340 F2
Sarajevo Bosnia &
Herzegovina 275 E7
Saratov Rus. Fed. 285 C6/
326 C5
Sarawak Malaysia 346 D5
Sardinia (I.) Italy 263 B6
Sargasso Sea 360
Sarh Chad 304 E4
Sarī Iran 321 G2
Saskatchewan (Province)
Canada 207 F7

Saskatoon Canada 207 F7
Satu Mare Romania 276 D2
Saudi Arabia (Country)
321 E6
Sault Ste Marie Canada
208 C6/215 G3
Savannah USA 213 F5
Savannakhét Laos 345 F5
Saxony Germany 268 E3
Schwerin Germany 268 F3
Scilly, Isles of UK 253 C8
Scoresbysund Greenland
365 F8
Scotia Sea 364 B3/361 D7
Scotland UK 252
Seattle USA 220 B3/353 F2
Seine (R.) France 261 E2
Semarang Indonesia 346 C8
Semipalatinsk Kazakhstan
327 E6
Semnān Iran 321 G2
Sendai Japan 340 F4
Senegal (Country) 296 C4
Seoul South Korea 338 G3
Seram (I.) Indonesia 347 F6
Serbia (Republic) 276 C4
Seremban Malaysia 345 E8
Sétif Algeria 295 E2
Setúbal Portugal 258 C6
Sevastopol' Ukraine 287 E5
Severn (R.) UK 253 F7
Severnaya Zemlya (Is.)
Rus. Fed. 327 E2
Seville Spain 258 D7
Seychelles (Country)
363 D5
Sfax Tunisia 295 F3
Shanghai China 338 F4/
352 C3
Shannon (R.) Ireland
253 B5
Shaoxing China 338 F4
Sheffield UK 253 G6
Shenyang China 338 G3

's-Hertogenbosch
Netherlands 254 E4
Shetland Is. UK 252 G1
Shijiazhuang China 338 E3
Shikoku (I.) Japan 341 C6
Shírāz Iran 321 F4
Sholapur India 333 E5
Shreveport USA 212 C4
Shumen Bulgaria 277 F5
Shymkent Kazakhstan
326 D7
Šiauliai Lithuania 283 C5
Siberia Rus. Fed. 327 F5
Sibiu Romania 276 D4
Sicily (I.) Italy 263 E7
Sidi Bel Abbès Algeria
295 E2
Sierra Leone (Country)
296 C6
Sierra Madre (Mts.)
Mexico 222 D3/223
Sierra Nevada (Mts.) Spain
259 E7
Sierra Nevada USA 221 C6
Silesia Czech Republic/
Poland 266 D5
Simbirsk Rus. Fed. 285 D6/
326 C5
Simferopol' Ukraine
287 E5
Simpson Desert Australia
355 E4
Sinai (Peninsula) Egypt
300 D3
Singapore (Country)
345 E8
Sinŭiju North Korea
338 G3
Sirte, Gulf of Libya 295 G3
Sivas Turkey 319 F4
Skiros (I.) Greece 279 F4
Skopje Macedonia 277 C5
Skye (I.) UK 252 D3
Sliven Bulgaria 277 F5

Index

Acknowledgments

PAGEOne and Dorling Kindersley would like to thank:
Christiane Gunzi for editorial assistance; Sarah Watson for general assistance; Thomas Keenes for design assistance; Hilary Bird for the index; Gordon Models, Peter Griffiths, and John Holmes for model making; Ashmolean Museum; Beaulieu Motor Museum; The British Library; Capotine Museum; Ermine Street Guard Museum; Louisiana State Museum; Musée du Louvre; Museum of London; Museum of Mankind; Museum of the Moving Image; Museum of Natural History; National Railway Museum; Pitt Rivers Museum; Royal Academy of Arts; The Science Museum, London; Uffizi, Florence; University Museum of Archaeology and Anthropology, Cambridge.

Photographs by:
Geoff Brightling, Jane Burton, P. Chadwell, Peter Chadwick, Andy Crawford, Geoff Dann, Philip Dowell, Mike Dunning, Neil Fletcher, Philip Gatward, Steve Gorton, Frank Greenaway, Colin Keates, Gary Kevin, Dave King, Nick Nicholls, Andrew McRobb, Ray Moller, Stephen Oliver, Roger Phillips, Tim Ridley, Karl Shone, James Stevenson, Clive Streeter, Kim Taylor, Andreas Von Einsiedel, Matthew Ward, Jerry Young, Christian Zuber.

Illustrations by:
Evi Antoniou, Rick Blakely, Peter Bull, Mike Courtney, John Crawford Fraser, Bill Donohoe, Simone End, Eugene Fleury, Giuliano Fornari, Ann George-Marsh, Jeremy Gower, Elizabeth Gray, Andrew Green, Ray Grinaway, Nick Hewetson, Dave Hopkins, Aziz Khan, Jason Lewis, Stuart Mackay, Judith Maguire, Janos Marffy, Kevin Marks, Angus Mcbride, Sean Milne, Sergio, Colin Salmon, Michael Saunders, Rodney Shackell, Rob Shone, Clive Spong, Roger Stewart, John Temperton, Pete Visscher, Richard Ward, John Woodcock, Dan Wright.

Picture credits:
a = above, b = below, l = left, t = top
The publisher would like to thank the following for their kind permission to reproduce the photographs:

Aardman Animations 403bl; Action Plus/Glyn Kirk 412ac; AKG, London, 349acl; AKG, Berlin, 442bcr; Ancient Art and Architecture 437tc; Directed and produced by Animation City/A.C. Live 402cl; Audi 185br; Austin Brown and The Aviation Picture Library 197br; Biology Media 142cl; Bettmann Archive 443br; Bridgeman Art Library/Glraudon 389acl; Museum of Mankind 370acl; Museum of Natural History, London, 99br; The British Museum 371tr, 371ac, 376ar, 376bl, 376br, 377acl, 377acr,

377br, 378al, 378acl, 378br, 379ac, 427ar, 428br, 430tc, 439cl; Camera Press/Ian Stone 460ac; Carolco 1991, courtesy of Kobal collection 402tr; J. Allan Cash 430cr; Christie's Colour Library 313br; Bruce Coleman Ltd/Jeff Foott Productions 224cl; Christian Zuber 307tr; Colorsport © Duono; David Madlen 404bl; Comstock 432ar; James Davis 375bl; et archive 427acl, 434tr, 436al, 437cr, 439br, 452ac; Mary Evans Picture Library 69ac, 370tr, 375bc, 375br, 380tr, 397bcl; The British Library 372cl, 446acl, 446acr, 449br, 454bc; Exeter Maritime Museum 190acr, 190bcl; Fiat 185bcl, Gilbert and George, courtesy of Anthony d'Offay Gallery, London, 389br; Ronald Grant Archive 396bl, 403cr; Sonia Halliday 371br; Robert Harding Picture Library 181tr, 423bcl, 436bl, 439tr, 444bc; Michael Holford 377ar, 429acl, 432br, 434bc; Hulton-Getty Picture Collection 380cr; Robert Hunt Library 454acl; Hutchison Library, 373br, 374bl; J.G. Fuller 235bl; Image Bank/Kaz Mori 66-67; Image Select 395tcl, 399tcl, 444tcl; Ann Ronan 394cr; Simon James 377bl; David King 380cl; Kobal Collection 403bc; Magnum/ Cagnoni 460cl; Mander & Mitcheson 397cr; Museum of the Moving Image/ © Academy of Motion Picture Arts and Sciences R 3br, 403br; Nasa 5al, 32bcl, 32bcr, 36acr, 36bcr, 37cl, 37tcr, 37br, 461bc; National Maritime Museum, 190bcr, 190b, 193br, 440acr; Peter Newark Pictures 435c, 451cr; Oxford Scientific Films/Root; Okapia 111cl; Ann and Bury Peerless, 372bc, 374acr; Photostage/Donald Cooper 397br; Popperfoto 456ac, 457bc, 459acr; Press Association 380bcl; Redferns 395br;

Renault 185bl; Rex features 381tl; 461tc, 462ar; Cheryl Hatch, Sipa Press, 463acr; Coll. Privé, Sipa 457tl; Setbon, Sipa Press 462c; Royal Geographical Society/Paul Harris 288ac, jacket spine bcr; The Royal Ballet School 396bcl, 396acr; Scala 371bcl, 377tl; Biblioteca Nazionale Centrale, Florence 438bc; Science Photo Library/George Bernard 144-5; Biology Media 142cl; Chris Bjornberg 12-13; Jeremy Burgess 84tr; Cern 149tl; CNRI 79bcl; Tony Hallas 16tr; Adam Jones 38-39; James King-Holmes 171br; Thomas Ligon 198-99; Lawrence Migdale 171cr; Prof. P. Motta, Dept. of Anatomy, University Lasapienza, Rome 114-115; Professors P.M. Motta, K.R Porter & P.M Andrews 123tr; NOAO 32bc; Novostl 36cl, 329bl; Omikron 128tr; David Parker 171tr; John Sanford 32ar; David Sharfe 133cr; Simon Terrey 146tr; Sporting Pictures (UK) Ltd 156tr, 187tc, 189tc, 404bcr, 413tl, 413tr; Tony Stone Images/Tony Craddock 257tr; Sepp Dietrich 273br, Ian Murphy 396br; Hugh Sitton 306cl; Suzuki/Farquhar PR 185bcr; Warner Brothers/courtesy Kobal Collection 403cl; Werner Forman Archives 370acl, 396tl, 420-421, 428cl; Jerry Young 103br, Michael Zabé 441bc; Zefa Pictures 379bl, 464-465; Ian Bradshaw 368-369; Stockmarket 322c; Krebs 176-177; Joe Cornish 281.

Every effort has been made to trace the copyright holders and we apologise in advance for any unintentional omissions. We would be pleased to insert the appropriate acknowledgment in any subsequent edition of this publication.